INTERNET RESEARCH ANNUAL

Steve Jones
General Editor

Vol. 19

PETER LANG
New York • Washington, D.C./Baltimore • Bern
Frankfurt am Main • Berlin • Brussels • Vienna • Oxford

INTERNET RESEARCH ANNUAL

Selected Papers from the
Association of Internet
Researchers Conferences
2000–2002,
Volume 1

EDITED BY
Mia Consalvo, Nancy Baym, Jeremy Hunsinger,
Klaus Bruhn Jensen, John Logie,
Monica Murero, Leslie Regan Shade

PETER LANG
New York • Washington, D.C./Baltimore • Bern
Frankfurt am Main • Berlin • Brussels • Vienna • Oxford

Library of Congress Cataloging-in-Publication Data

Internet research annual: selected papers from the Association of Internet Researchers
Conference, 2000–2002, Volume 1 / edited by Mia Consalvo, Nancy Baym, Jeremy
Hunsinger, Klaus Bruhn Jensen, John Logie, Monica Murero, Leslie Regan Shade
p. cm. — (Digital formations; vol. 19)
Includes bibliographical references and index.
ISBN 0-8204-6840-1
ISSN 1526-3169

Bibliographic information published by **Die Deutsche Bibliothek**.
Die Deutsche Bibliothek lists this publication in the "Deutsche
Nationalbibliografie"; detailed bibliographic data is available
on the Internet at http://dnb.ddb.de/.

Cover design by Joni Holst

© 2004 Peter Lang Publishing, Inc., New York
275 Seventh Avenue, 28th Floor, New York, NY 10001
www.peterlangusa.com

All rights reserved.
Reprint or reproduction, even partially, in all forms such as microfilm,
xerography, microfiche, microcard, and offset strictly prohibited.

CONTENTS

Internet Research: There and Back Again ... 1
MIA CONSALVO

Imagining an Association ... 5
STEVE JONES

SECTION ONE: THE INTERNET AS AN AREA OF RESEARCH ... 13
KLAUS BRUHN JENSEN AND MONICA MURERO

1 Legal Consequences of the Cyberspatial Metaphor ... 17
DAN L. BURK

2 Internet Research: For and Against ... 25
PHILIP E. AGRE

3 Dangerous Futures: Artificial Intelligence and Scientific Argument ... 37
BARBARA WARNICK

4 Out of the Dot-com Bubble: A New Opportunity for Internet Research ... 46
WILLIAM H. DUTTON

5 Constructs in the Storm ... 55
SHEIZAF RAFAELI

6 Online Communication: Through the Lens of Discourse ... 65
SUSAN C. HERRING

vi Internet Research Annual

7 Cyberscience, Methodology, and Research Substance 77
MICHAEL NENTWICH

8 The Effects of New Communication and Information Technologies
on Academic Research Paradigms 86
IRENE BERKOWITZ

9 The Cathedral or the Bazaar? The AoIR Document on Internet Research
Ethics as an Exercise in Open Source Ethics 95
CHARLES ESS

SECTION TWO: PLACES, POLITICS, AND POLICIES OF THE INTERNET 107
NANCY BAYM AND JEREMY HUNSINGER

10 "IMAGINE": A Structural Analysis of the Use of the Internet
by Households in Four European Towns 109
ALAIN D'IRIBARNE

11 Musical Taste and Sociability: Evidence from Survey2000 118
JAMES WITTE AND JOHN RYAN

12 Global Reach, Local Roots: Young Danes and the Internet 129
GITTE STALD

13 Questing on the Global Stage: Brain Gain, Market Gain, and the Rhetoric
of the Internet in German and U.S. Higher Education Policy 141
DOREEN STARKE-MEYERRING

14 Learning to Use ICTs in a Gulf Arab Context 150
DAVID PALFREYMAN

15 Virtual Consumption: The Commercial Discourse of the Web 158
KAREN GUSTAFSON

16 Redlining and Redefining High-Speed Internet Access: Policy, Practice, and
Patchwork in Urban Development 166
CHRISTOPHER BODNAR

17 The Internet, Capitalism, and Policy 175
ROBIN MANSELL

18 Spiders, Spam, and Spyware: New Media and the Market for Political Information 185
PHILIP N. HOWARD AND TEMA J. MILSTEIN

SECTION THREE: NET/WORKING COMMUNITIES 195
JOHN LOGIE AND LESLIE REGAN SHADE

19 Virtual Otherness: An Example of In-Group and Out-Group Online Interaction in Yugoslavia During the NATO Bombing 197
SMILJANA ANTONIJEVIC

20 Because It's Important and Out There: From Real-Life Identity to Virtual Ethnicities 205
NILS ZURAWSKI

21 Newsgroup Interaction as Urban Life 216
STINE GOTVED

22 Community as Commodity: Empowerment and Consumerism on the Web 224
JAN FERNBACK

23 Just Do It! The Online Communication of Breast Cancer as a Practice of Empowerment 231
SHANI ORGAD

24 The Internet's "Magnifying Glass" Effect on Offline Ties in the General Social Survey 241
SORIN ADAM MATEI

25 Talking in Lists: The Consequences of Computer-Mediated Communication on Communities 250
ANDREA KAVANAUGH AND JOSEPH SCHMITZ

26 The Social Design of Virtual Worlds: Constructing the User and Community through Code 260
T. L. TAYLOR

List of Contributors 269

Related AoIR Conference Publications 277

Index 279

Mia Consalvo

INTERNET RESEARCH: THERE AND BACK AGAIN

 The original *There and Back Again* chronicles the life of a hobbit—Bilbo Baggins—as he journeys through Middle Earth. His adventures and life don't center on (or even address) technology, yet the title of his book, indicating the need for adventure as well as the grounding influence of home, might be a key metaphor for Internet researchers.

Bilbo's title is, I believe, a better way to think about the Internet than the ubiquitous Microsoft catchphrase, "Where do you want to go today?" Although Microsoft's version captures the wonder of exploring a new space, Bilbo's title more accurately describes the impact of the Internet on most of us today. Although it can be an unforgettable trip, there is always the need to return home to the everyday. Additionally, use of the Internet is becoming more than a journey "there"—it is becoming part of what we do "back" at home as well. And although Internet researchers can get caught up in their journeys and explorations—like Bilbo—they need to acknowledge how integrated the Internet is in daily life, and how it is becoming part of both "there" *and* "back again."

The work presented in this volume examines those integrations through the study of how communities and cultures are forming in and through use of the Internet, as well as how the Internet is becoming a space to research as well as a space that shapes the rest of our knowledge and research. Initially, the task of identifying and narrowing down the number of relevant pieces from three conferences for this annual seemed overwhelming, and my fellow editors bravely took on the task of doing that work and assembling a coherent group. In rereading (or reading for the first time) this body of work, often updated for this volume, the complicated connections between "there" and "back" kept appearing. So, although the "sexiness" of Internet research is perhaps on the decline, its relevance and level of sophistication are increasing.

In working with the contributors to this volume, I was awed by the breadth of knowledge and depth of research areas that have developed relating to the Internet. Although I was aware that numerous fields and disciplines were studying the Internet from their own particular angle, I had of necessity isolated myself a bit, concentrating on work done in media studies, women's studies, and digital gaming in particular. Reading a wider variety of work than that gave me new perspectives and fresh understandings about the Internet and its role in shaping our world, or, more important, our role in shaping its use and structure.

In considering how this body of work "comes together," to say larger or more generalizable things about the Internet, I'm more tentative. One thing that's easy to say is that Internet research has found a home in just about every discipline and field in the academy. As research about the Internet has infiltrated most academic areas, it has largely moved from being considered a novelty to being an integral and integrated part of larger study. We don't much believe in or study disembodied online experience anymore, looking instead at the articulations between offline and online activities. It's not enough to say that we "become someone else" online—how can that be possible when a person surfs the Web, talks on the phone, and makes dinner all at the same time? Perhaps our "multiple selves" should be reimagined as multiple life roles, of which online activities can contribute to (or detract from)—but likely not play a primary role—at least for most people.

The Internet has evolved in popular representations from a place for the weird and strange, to the dangerous, to the commercial, and now to just another part of our communication system. Yet, that communication system isn't shared by everyone, as we must continually remind ourselves. Research on the persistent digital divide, both nationally and globally, tells us that even as some gaps close, others open (such as the growing shift from dial-up to broadband or other high-speed access that is creating a new have/have not fissure). Questions also arise about the possibilities for leap-frogging past certain divides, such as with the call for wireless access for disadvantaged regions of the world, rather than relying on (non)existent phone lines. We also must keep aware that government initiatives can be defunded and folded just as quickly as they were put in place, especially in times of budget shortfalls.

As Internet research addressing issues such as these has broadened and deepened, it's become easy to fall behind in understanding how that growing body of work fits together. Even within a narrow area such as media studies, the growth of research is explosive. We are forced to become specialists within an already specialized field. Likewise, the Association of Internet Researchers (AoIR) conferences have grown in participation, so much so that there are multiple competing sessions at any one time, leading away from the cozy atmosphere of the first conference, to better mirror the larger disciplinary conferences with their separate "tracks" or "divisions." Is that the future of AoIR and Internet knowledge?

Although Steve Jones (in this volume) has written about how AoIR started as a place for people on the margins of their disciplines, when my own research career began, Internet research was not widely practiced in my school (Mass Communication), but was enthusiastically accepted as an appropriate area for research. My traditional scholarly associations all accepted "new media" research, and the sense of marginalization or exclusion felt by some earlier researchers was never my experience. I suspect that experience is growing, for many disciplines at least.

The creation of AoIR was an attempt to construct a "tent" for those working outside of the bounds of their own disciplinary homes. AoIR was a place to congregate with others who knew and understood the language of the Internet—no need to define what Usenet was here or question the value of exploring Multi-User Dungeons (MUDs) or Multi-User Dungeons that were Object Oriented (MOOs). The tent sheltering us all has grown large.

The Future of AoIR

Research about the Internet did not crash when the "Internet economy" did so, and that research will come to be increasingly vital to understanding how we as individuals, groups, and societies communicate in the 21st century. But what should or could the association be? Jones asks that question, and it bears repeating. What is so special about AoIR? Its research? Will AoIR's bubble burst?

AoIR started small, and the small-town feel of its early conferences helped us achieve a level of personal and professional intimacy that fostered quick growth. The geographic locations of each conference echoed that growth—from the small town of Lawrence, Kansas, to the Midwestern city of Minneapolis, to the international environment of Maastricht. Collaborations formed, research proliferated, and people networked. We used the Internet to study the Internet, and kept our new "social ties" strong.

Yet AoIR is growing bigger—we are approaching conferences with 500 attendees. Our discussion list has well over 1,000 members. Our conferences are developing multiple tracks, along the lines of major academic associations. Will divisions be next? Will we stay small and cozy in feel, if not in actuality? Perhaps, and perhaps not. Maybe that's not the essential quality of AoIR.

Maybe the essential or important thing about AoIR and its research is the early tent-building, which led to a multidisciplinary approach to studying the Internet. Although we all have developed areas of specialty within this field, our conferences, and this annual, are spaces to step out of our comfort zones, our normal research routines, to explore what other scholars are concerning themselves with—media studies, law, sociology, education, library sciences, political science, and so on. The conferences, distilled down into this annual, become a place to refresh ourselves, to update our knowledge.

This annual, through its yearly compilation of the best of the conferences, can play a vital role in bringing out the cutting edge in Internet research. But, rather than focusing narrowly and deeply on one particular stream of that research, it casts its net widely, bringing in work done in many areas. The annual refocuses us—giving us new ideas, new approaches, new perspectives. It's a conversation recorded about our evolving understanding of the Internet and its place in our lives.

It's a ride that takes us in different directions—directions that maybe we never thought of going in, but that ultimately will prove valuable and exciting.

Welcome to the journey. Although Bilbo saw his adventures as separate from his home life, they deeply impacted his relationships with others back home. So, too, our realization that "there" and "back" in regard to Internet use are really becoming the same thing, and so studying the Internet is really about studying our use of a communication medium in our "everyday" lives.

Steve Jones

IMAGINING AN ASSOCIATION

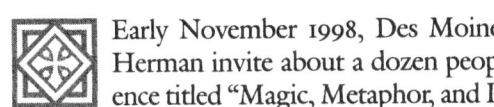 Early November 1998, Des Moines, Iowa. Thomas Swiss and Andrew Herman invite about a dozen people, including me, to speak at a conference titled "Magic, Metaphor, and Power: The World Wide Web and Contemporary Cultural Theory" at Drake University (Herman & Swiss, 2000). The talk that I had agreed to give was about online journalism, specifically about the experience of reading journalism on the Web (Jones, 2000). But as I looked at those assembled, presenters and participants, it was clear that there was more, much more, about which I wished to speak. Why, for example, did I know so many of those who gathered from research they had done that had nothing to do with the Internet? Indeed, it was a surprise to see some of them there, as I had no idea they were seriously interested in the Internet's social impacts. I knew most of the attendees from popular culture, popular music, sociology, anthropology, and art conferences and publications. Why had we all coalesced around a conference about the Web?

One obvious reason was that (thankfully) Swiss and Herman brought us together, but I did wonder why virtually none of us had taken the opportunities at the various other conferences at which we saw one another to present research about the Internet and the Web. In conversations at meals and between presentations, it became clear that no one felt there was great interest in our respective disciplinary associations for such research. It became even clearer that the energy generated at Drake those couple of days would not and should not dissipate.

I had already been thinking about the possibility of organizing an Internet interest group within one of the communication associations, but the interdisciplinarity of the conference at Drake quickly convinced me that building on traditional disciplinary foundations was not sufficient. A new organization, one that would be interdisciplinary and international, seemed appropriate, and needed.

Stefan Wray, then a doctoral student at New York University, was one of the first people with whom I spoke about the idea. He summed up the general sentiment about forming an organization in an e-mail written and sent at the end of the conference: "Right now there seems to be little reason to spend time making an argument for the need or necessity of an international academic association devoted to scholarly work and research on the Web and the Internet. At this point the reasons for such an endeavor are self-evident" (Wray, 1998).

Having had some experience with the International Association for the Study of Popular Music in its formative years, I knew that much planning was needed. Terri Senft, a colleague of Stefan's and a fellow doctoral student at New York University, and Stefan suggested a follow-up conference in New York. Greg Elmer, then a doctoral student at the University of Massachusetts, volunteered to help, but given that Stefan, Terri, and Greg had dissertations to write and degrees to earn I took on most of the tasks involved in starting up a scholarly association (ranging from creating an e-mail list to applying for tax-exempt status from the U.S. Internal Revenue Service), although I was reluctant to jump into conference organizing until some details were sorted out.

One detail had to do with the association's name. The conference at Drake University was focused on the Web, but rather than focus on a specific aspect of Internet technology or use we found ourselves discussing names with "Internet research" in them. Ultimately we opted for the simplest, most direct name we could come up with—the Association of Internet Researchers.[1] The association's mission statement today is essentially the same as the one we came up with in 1998, reflecting a spirit of inclusiveness, curiosity, interdisciplinarity, and openness.

The National Communication Association's annual convention in 1998 was in New York City, so we used that opportunity to have a planning meeting. We also arranged for an open meeting and hastily (perhaps even haphazardly) put out a call to those interested in forming an association. About a dozen people turned out for the open meeting.

Many mundane administrative tasks were then undertaken, but two stand out. One was creation of an e-mail list registration of the domain name aoir.org (air.org, air.com, air.net, etc., having all been reserved by others at that time). The new e-mail list, air-l, began in November 1998 with eight subscribers. Two weeks after that, it had 16 subscribers; a year later in 1999 there were 160, and by November 2000 there were 630 subscribers (at the time of this writing, April 2003, there are over 1,300 subscribers).

Why such a rapid increase in subscribers? To some extent it was because of the spread of knowledge about the association. But the truest answer to that question lies in the second key task that was undertaken, namely the association's first conference. Nancy Baym was one of those who attended the open meeting in New York. Her enthusiasm for the association never waned, and she was quick to offer up the possibility that the association's first conference be held at her institution, the University of Kansas. After that initial conference in September 2000 air-l subscriptions jumped, and what had been for all intents and purposes a "virtual" association quickly became very real for all involved in it.[2]

To date AoIR conferences have been, in my experience, part scholarly meeting and part a reunion of old friends. Strikingly, even new friends seem like old friends, perhaps because of the online interactions on air-l. The spirit of collegiality and interdisciplinarity has been nothing short of amazing. Although it can be difficult for people from various disciplines to communicate given the tendency to lapse into the familiar language of one's own discipline (if not into jargon), it has been a characteristic of AoIR conferences that attendees go to great lengths to understand and be understood. The extra effort required to go beyond the boundaries of one's "home" discipline is richly rewarded by the intellectual and personal connections that are made among the people and ideas present.

There are a few points that follow from this quick and incomplete history and description of AoIR. One is that creating an association is a lot of fun, but maintaining it is a lot of work (and a lot of fun). There are many people I should thank who should get credit for AoIR's success in addition to ones I have already mentioned but I would quickly use up most of the pages allotted to this book in so doing. AoIR has had first-rate executive officers who volunteered to help guide it through its formative years, top-notch conference coordinators and program chairs, and terrific members.

Another point is that associations need multiple means of getting together, of associating. Although air-l is an excellent medium of communication and source of information, meeting face to face is important. Were it not for the annual AoIR conference, it is highly unlikely the association would be as vibrant or as collegial as it has become. That is why I am particularly pleased that AoIR has a research annual as another means of sharing and remembering some part of its conferences, and I am grateful to Peter Lang Publishing, Inc., for their enthusiasm for this project, and very grateful to Mia Consalvo for leading the effort as the annual's executive editor.

Reviewing the e-mails from 1998 that I had saved, I am particularly struck by one of the earliest I sent to Stefan, Greg, and Terri in which I asked, in the context of believing in the association's future growth, "What do we want to be like?" (Jones, 1998). Most scholarly organizations do relatively predictable things, as I noted in that e-mail:

- Publish newsletters/journals/Web sites
- Hold conferences
- Provide job-hunting services
- Provide accreditation services
- Give awards for research, service

The Association of Internet Researchers does some of those things, and will do others (on that list or not on it) in the future. What caused me to bring the question up in 1998 causes me to ask it over and over again: What do we want to be like? There is no necessary reason to recreate all of the trappings of other scholarly associations, just as there is no necessary reason to do away with them all. Creating a scholarly association is not something that happens every day, and it ought to give us an opportunity to reassess and rethink what we would like a scholarly association to be. Furthermore, there is no reason to end such reassessment and rethinking. Although AoIR is now several years old and has a very promising future ahead of it, change may be as constant as it is in the field of research AoIR encompasses. I hope we can embrace it, and consider AoIR in somewhat the way we might consider the Internet, as a medium of communication and exchange, rather than as a fixed, inflexible object.

Creating "Internet Research 1.0: The State of the Interdiscipline" in Lawrence, Kansas, September 14–17, 2000

Nancy Baym (Conference Chair) and Jeremy Hunsinger (Program Chair)

JEREMY AND NANCY: In 1999, there was a conversation in a hotel lobby in New York City that became a mailing list. On this list was presented the idea for a conference, and the enthusiasm hit several members like a bolt, and this is what happened. Over time some things, people, and tools came together, and the thought was, "We can do this," and then we did and it was definitely a "We" effort.

NANCY: Some might say that Lawrence, Kansas (wonderful a town though it is), is the middle of nowhere. It seemed wildly ambitious to imagine that we could pull off an international conference sponsored by an association no one had ever heard of here. Indeed, our ambitions were modest. Although we presented it as the international event we dreamed it could be, among ourselves during the planning we hoped that our first conference might draw 100 people, and assumed they would probably all be American. Those assumptions were wrong, but this was what we thought.

I had just joined the faculty at Kansas in the fall of 1999. I spent my first year knocking on doors introducing myself, describing the event, and asking for sponsorship. The University of Kansas was amazingly supportive. Nearly everyone on campus that I spoke with got excited about the event. From upper administration to graduate students, everyone did what they could to make it happen.

JEREMY: I had just taken my administrative faculty appointment in the fall of 1998 as Director of VTOnline, having just finished my M.A. I had been working on a variety of Internet education projects. I had a variety of resources at my disposal and had just launched the Center for Digital Discourse and Culture at Virginia Tech with some colleagues. One of the things that I had done with an assistant was to develop a peer reviewing system; that system would become what AoIR has used in each of its conferences. That was my tool, and as the list had it, the developer of the tool was the one that had to deal with it. My role as program chair was ascertained. I volunteered and thus I was chosen. No one really knew me at that time, but I guess they know me now.

NANCY: Jeremy was as speedy, steadfast, and productive a planning partner as anyone could ever hope for, something he's continued through all our conferences since. We exchanged thousands of e-mails. Between the two of us and our conference planning list (air-meet), the whole conference was created, promoted, and managed online. If anyone ever wants to examine distributed collaborative work conducted via the Internet, we could dig those e-mails out for you.

Meanwhile, I was having a baby. If I can offer some advice to other women planning conferences it would be this: DON'T give birth three weeks before the big event, even if having a cute newborn on hand does give a conference a sort of cozy touch.

In the end, over 250 people from 20 countries and all across the United States converged in Lawrence and I think we all had a fantastic time. There were people I had heard of and admired for years, people I've only gotten to know since, and people I still haven't met. As one colleague said, "There are more people here that I cite than any conference I've ever been to!" I was, and remain, genuinely grateful to everyone who made the journey. I put the effort into creating this conference because I wanted to go to it. I didn't expect the turnout, the internationalism, or the disciplinary breadth. Those were thrilling surprises. But the best surprise of all was the tremendous sense of community. I felt like I'd found all the best friends I'd never met, as did many of the people there with whom I spoke. In the time and conferences since, there have been books, journal issues, collaborative projects, and information exchanges stimulated by AoIR. These are the academic rewards. But for me, the fact that we created a warm home full of friends for so many who felt marginalized in their disciplines has been the conference's greatest reward.

JEREMY: The conference is one of the highlights of my career. As program chair I learned quite a few names very quickly, and at the conference I met the people behind the names. Some of those were not quite what I expected, but that kept it interesting. Of course the strange thing is that this was not the only conference that I was working on in a significant capacity: two weeks after Internet Research 1.0, I was managing, with Tim Luke and Len Hatfield, the Learning 2000 conference. My advice is never to work on two conferences at once. The only reason that I could do both conferences was because of the program committee's efforts. Along with Nancy and her local committee, they made this conference possible. One of the important aspects of 1.0 was its open and collegial nature, and in that is founded the sense of community that makes these conferences so special to so many people. I share Nancy's joy in its success, and look forward to many more.

Building "IR 2.0: InterConnections" in Minneapolis, Minnesota, October 10–14, 2001

John Logie (Conference Chair) and Leslie Regan Shade (Program Chair)

Building the Association of Internet Researchers' second conference seemed, at the outset, a reasonable task. After all, Nancy Baym and her colleagues had invented most of the "wheels" for the first conference. It fell to us to adapt (rather than reinvent) those wheels to the particularities of the site on the campus of the University of Minnesota, and we had considerable support. The program committee achieved a remarkable degree of interdisciplinarity, in keeping with the conference theme: "INTERconnections." On the local side, a crew of talented graduate students and techies from Apple were committed to delivering wireless access throughout the main conference site. About a month before the conference, we were just beginning to get a clear picture of how it just might work.

And then planes crashed into the World Trade Center.

And within a few days, the Association and the conference organizers made a determination to press on because it somehow felt important to press on. The conference was transformed by its time, no question, but many members felt a special commitment to pursing the opportunities for discussion, exchange, and community that we find in AoIR. One correspondent wrote hopefully of "the potential for small islands of normalcy" at the Conference. With extra measures of tolerance and goodwill all around, IR 2.0 often achieved those small islands, even as we came to understand the Internet's developing role in a sadly transformed global circumstance. IR 2.0 should be remembered as a point in time where this organization's members were forced to weigh their willingness to assume an added measure of risk in order to meet with their colleagues and pursue their work. In overwhelming numbers, we chose to meet in Minneapolis, and the Association is stronger because we made that commitment to our work, and to one another.

Crafting "IR 3.0: Net/Work/Theory" in Maastricht, the Netherlands: Theoretical, Methodological and Empirical Approaches to Internet Research, October 13–16, 2002

Monica Murero (Conference Chair) and Klaus Bruhn Jensen (Program Chair)

The IR 3.0 theme was Net/Work/Theory. Contributors were called to reflect on "how to theorize what we know about the Internet and on how to apply what we know theoretically in practice," combining the best traditions of the American and

European schools of thought. This theme was particularly appropriate for such a conference to be held for the first time in Europe, whose intellectual environments have traditionally been a source of social and cultural theory.

The decision to hold the AoIR conference in Europe, in The Netherlands, was a sign of tremendous growth and international expansion of AoIR. The appropriateness of this decision was confirmed by the great success in terms of attendance, the quality of the scientific program, and the significance of international collaborations. Internet researchers, some for the first time, came to AoIR from 50 countries, including from Africa and Asia.

The proceedings of IR 3.0 marked two events in the history of Internet Research: (1) The AoIR Ethical Guide, and (2) The founding of the International Network of Excellence in Internet Research for e-health studies (NoERH).

1. The first AoIR Document on Internet Research Ethics was approved in Maastricht (see also Charles Ess's chapter in this volume).
2. The International Network of Excellence in Internet Research for e-health studies (NoERH) was founded by Monica Murero (University of Maastricht) and Susannah Fox (Pew Internet) during the proceedings of IR 3.0. A mailing list was created to continue the fervid intellectual debate started at the conference, and several international collaborations have been activated since then (to subscribe to the list: air-e-health@aoir.org).

The conference provided opportunities to network, learn from other researchers, hear from leading players in Internet development, and enjoy the "art of fine living" of Maastricht, in the south of the Netherlands. Building on the previous well-attended AoIR conferences, IR 3.0 in Europe brought together prominent scholars such as William Dutton, Director of the Oxford Internet Institute, Robin Mansell, professor at the London School of Economics, Cees Hamelink, professor at the University of Amsterdam, and many others. The event attracted researchers and practitioners from many disciplines, fields, and countries for a program of presentations, panel discussions, and informal exchanges.

The "informal character" of AoIR conferences and scholars was maintained in Europe, continuing a tradition of friendly and informal exchange. IR 3.0 was hosted in the beautiful city of Maastricht in the Netherlands, and many of the participants have enjoyed the city "by bicycle." As the city in which one of the key treaties of the European Union was signed (Euro currency), Maastricht also symbolizes a changing Europe in a changing international setting.

The IR 3.0 conference was organized entirely online, which required a lot of dedication, fast feedback, mediation, and a problem-solving attitude. More than 50 people from all over the world contributed to the AoIR planning and paper revision processes, and to them we'd like to address our deepest thanks. The air-list and the conference Web site (<http://www.aoir.org/2002>) have certainly played a fundamental role in the diffusion of information. Outstanding people, like Steve Jones, helped a lot during the whole process, and as contributors live in different parts of the world the Internet was certainly a great convenience for all of us!

Notes

1. Initially the name the Association took on, as suggested by Stefan Wray, was association(of).internet.researchers—a(o).i.r.—reflecting the exuberance of the period and fascination with computer code, but through use it became the common Association of Internet Researchers and was abbreviated AoIR.
2. For no one more so, I suspect, than for Nancy Baym!

References

Herman, Andrew, & Swiss, Thomas. (2002). *The World Wide Web and Contemporary Cultural Theory: Magic, Metaphor, Power.* London: Routledge.

Jones, Steve. (1998). E-mail correspondence with Greg Elmer, Terri Senft, Stefan Wray, November 12.

Jones, Steve. (2000). "The Bias of the Web." In Herman, Andrew and Swiss, Thomas (Eds.), *The World Wide Web and Contemporary Cultural Theory: Magic, Metaphor, Power* (pp. 171–182). London: Routledge.

Klaus Bruhn Jensen and Monica Murero Section One

The Internet as an Area of Research

One of the insights of contemporary social theory has been that the interpretations that humans make of themselves and of their everyday lives make a very real, practical difference. Although an early statement of the general insight was the familiar dictum by the American pragmatist philosopher, W. I. Thomas, "If men [*sic*] define situations as real, they are real in their consequences," more recent contributions have also been made under a heading of "double hermeneutics" (for an overview, see Alvesson and Sköldberg, 2000). This term suggests that researchers, in particular, perform a specific social role as they reinterpret the "lay theories" of "ordinary" social agents, and feed those reinterpretations back into society. Two historical examples are the works of Sigmund Freud and Karl Marx. Because of Freud's intervention into psychology, a significant proportion of the world's population regularly ask themselves whether other people's actions (or even their own actions) might be guided by subconscious motives. Because of Marx's interpretation of political economy, and despite its appropriation by political elites for purposes of control and oppression for much of the 20th century, a similarly significant group of people will ask themselves whether there is such a thing as a common interest or only conflicted social or class interests.

The terminology of double hermeneutics grows out of the publications of Anthony Giddens (e.g., Giddens, 1984). Building on the philosophical groundwork of Winch (1963), who had challenged a natural-scientific conception of social science and, indeed, of social action, Giddens (in Giddens, 1979) developed the point that social and cultural research engages a preinterpreted reality and that, hence, scholarly interpretations are likely, to a greater or lesser extent, to change that reality, as lived and enacted by social actors. Interpretations make a difference in science as well as in the rest of society.

Perhaps less central to considerations about double hermeneutics has been the other side of the coin of exchange—how the course of social reality informs social and cultural research, from the choice of problem areas to the constitution of new research fields. The general point of hermeneutics in this regard is that all social practice is informed by "theories," defined as generalized conceptions of what the world is like, and how things can be done. When research communities witness major social developments, questions inevitably arise as to the appropriate scholarly response, in terms of theories, methodologies, as well as institutional frameworks. The development of the Internet as a general medium of communication represents such a major social development, arguably the epochal development of the past decade.

This volume takes stock of the rise of Internet research as one engagement of science with contemporary society; the present section attempts to delineate the preliminary contours of Internet research as a field. In doing so, the contributions participate in an ongoing double hermeneutic regarding the Internet.

Dan L. Burk confronts the social consequences of interpretation and terminology head-on in "Legal Consequences of the Cyberspatial Metaphor," arguing that the prevalence of spatial metaphors regarding the Internet has produced unintended and adverse legal consequences. With detailed attention to concrete court cases, he shows how cyberspace tends to be conceived as land and, more important, as property, and that property traditionally implies rights of exclusion—"you cannot be on or use my land." An important question for the courts as well as for research is how cyberspatial rights may be defined in the future, taking into account the fact that, also for real property, absolute rights of exclusion have rarely been the norm.

The social and historical definition, not just of cyberspace but also of computers as such, is explored by Philip E. Agre under the heading of "Internet Research: For and Against." He makes the argument that the main impact of the Internet is, and will be, felt at the level of social institutions, not at the level of, for example, specific applications, information systems, or networks. In order to examine this institutional impact, researchers may need a great deal of hermeneutic labor to "dig our way from the landslide of ideology that engulfed public discourse about computing during the Internet bubble of the 1990s." Having emerged, researchers will be equipped to show, Agre suggests, that, historically, institutions have tended to shape information technologies, not vice versa.

The discussion about technology and its powers to shape society, and even replace humans, is continued by Barbara Warnick in her contribution, "Dangerous Futures: Artificial Intelligence and Scientific Argument." With reference to a case study, she revisits the debate concerning artificial intelligence (AI) and the nature of scientific argument for and against. AI remains one of the most richly suggestive implications of computers, and one that occupies both scientific research and popular culture. Whereas skeptics with regard to the potential of AI may have been in the majority for some time, Warnick suggests that the books and Web sites at the center of the case study have reopened the debate on AI.

Like AI in the past, the dot-com phenomenon has served, more recently, as a public backdrop to research on the social consequences of the Internet. The director of the Oxford Internet Institute, Bill Dutton, argues that, despite doom-laden predictions, Internet research has, indeed, come "Out of the Dot-com Bubble." Reviewing the broadening focus of Internet research, he goes on to suggest a number of key priorities for future research at Oxford and elsewhere, noting, as well, the importance of teaching for public understanding and uses of the Internet.

In "Constructs in the Storm," Sheizaf Rafaeli revisits the presentation he gave in October 2001, a month after 9/11, and that he updated during the first week of what was proving to be the second Gulf War. Suggesting that "the storm outside is echoed by the storm within" the research field, he explores this parallelism in a scholarly spirit of "infinite inquisitiveness," which might replace the quest and claim for "infinite justice" that was the military code of the 2001 war in Afghanistan. Outlining a "theoretical compass" for Internet research—multimedia, synchronicity, hypertextuality, packet switching, interactivity, logs and records, simulation and immersion, and the value of information—Rafaeli gives special attention to the last concept of information value and its subjective dimension, as illustrated by his own research with colleagues and students.

The following contributions turn their eyes inward, onto the field of research itself. Not only has the Internet raised important new research questions, but the spread of information and communication technologies (ICTs) has also served to reshape the instruments and practices of research. Thus, ICTs may be changing the very conditions under which researchers undertake their hermeneutic endeavors.

Susan C. Herring shares her experience of coming to the field of computer-mediated communication (CMC) and seeking appropriate methods in "Online Communication: Through the Lens of Discourse." Drawing on discourse analysis as a set of "tried and true methods for analyzing spoken and written communication," she shows how this approach has proven valuable for the study of new technologies and genres of communication, as well. In addition to illustrating how Internet discourses reflect on wider issues of social interaction and social structure, Herring also duly notes multimedia discourses, not least their visual component, as one current challenge for discourse analysis and for Internet research as such.

In "Cyberscience, Methodology, and Research Substance," Michael Nentwich asks whether an ICT-based scholarly communication system may be changing the core of the research substance. Drawing on interview evidence from a wide range of scientific disciplines, he finds several methodology-related types of impact, including a different choice of topics and the production of results that, without ICT, would simply have been impossible. Nentwich makes the case that Internet researchers need to be alert to technology, not just as an object of analysis but also as an implicit condition of their daily work.

Irene Berkowitz, the winner of the AoIR Student Award for 2002, extends the argument concerning "The Effects of New Communication and Information Technologies on Academic Research Paradigms." Like Nentwich, she draws on the testimony of scholars in various disciplines—as the research area is still in the making, being made by these very scholars, active researchers present themselves as a natural, and sometimes the only, source of evidence. Drawing on the theoretical framework of Harold A. Innis, and relying on a Delphi technique, Berkowitz concludes, among other things, that ICTs may contribute to an increase in interdisciplinary and multidisciplinary work.

Finally, under the heading of "The Cathedral or the Bazaar?," Charles Ess charts the development of the AoIR document on Internet Research Ethics. Being the product of a collective endeavor over several years, the document represents an exercise in open source principles, as applied to the development not just of technologies, but of research strategies, as well. The document is addressed to professional researchers, as well as to all those students and institutional authorities that increasingly need to consider the benefits as well as the problems of working online. As noted by the author, the document suggests that "ethical reflection can, if properly fostered, more or less keep pace with technological advancements and developments."

The Internet has become an integral, ubiquitous part of everyday life in many social domains and international contexts. Yet, most of the public attention remains fueled by either utopian or dystopian visions, rather than being informed by the growing body of research on the Internet as a complex fact of modern life. In the first part of the book—"the Internet as an Area of Research"—contributors to the first three conferences of the Association of Internet Researchers invite readers into a virtual, hermeneutic process of asking, what is the Internet, and how should one study it?

References

Alvesson, M., & Sköldberg, K. (2000). *Reflexive Methodology: New Vistas for Qualitative Research*. London: Sage.
Giddens, A. (1979). *Central Problems in Social Theory*. London: MacMillan.
Giddens, A. (1984). *The Constitution of Society*. Berkeley: University of California Press.
Winch, P. (1963). *The Idea of a Social Science*. London: Routledge.

Dan L. Burk 1

LEGAL CONSEQUENCES OF THE CYBERSPATIAL METAPHOR

 Like all new technologies, the Internet has been comprehended by metaphorical relation to familiar or established social icons. A variety of metaphors, such as the "information superhighway" and the "virtual community" have competed for conceptual preeminence. But the metaphor of space and territory has been ubiquitous in conceptualizing the Internet. In this short essay, I will argue that the metaphorical equation of the Internet with space has become an equation of the Internet with land. Because land is the paradigmatic type of property in law, these associations lead to an equation of the Internet with property, and most especially with strong property rights of an exclusionary nature. This in turn has profound implications for the configuration of power and control over network resources, outcomes being driven by a chain of metaphorical associations that have been adopted without full examination of their consequences.

The Internet and Space

The metaphorical equation of the Internet with space is most famously apparent in the term "cyberspace." But this association is not confined to a single idiom. As previous commentators have noted, such terminology is endemic to Internet nomenclature. Internet users frequent chat *rooms* or *home* pages located on Web *sites*, finding content on the electronic *frontier* by means of *domain* names that are associated with certain IP *addresses* (Adams, 1997; Chesher, 1997). Even the applications by which Internet files are accessed files are denominated "Navigator" or "Explorer" (Strate, 2000, p. 268; Nunes, 1997, p. 165).

Much of the impetus for this view of the network has been attributed to William Gibson, for coining the term "cyberspace" (1986a; 1986b). No doubt Gibson's description of the future network data had a powerful influence on how current data networks are conceptualized, influencing a generation of commentators, including architects who furthered the metaphor of network as social space (Benedikt, 1992; Mitchell, 1995). But Gibson's vision of the future, however compelling, cannot account for the association of the Internet with spatial tropes. Previous commentators have noted that spatial metaphors are integral to the human condition, or to the workings of the human mind (Chesher, 1997; Dallow, 2001). Kant long ago argued that the nature of human experience compels conceptualization in terms of space (1781, 1787/1929, p. A/24, B/39). The user's sense of inhabiting digital media or experiencing it spatially may flow inevitably from cultural ordering of information (Dallow, 2001).

But inevitable or not, conception of the Internet as spatial is not a culturally neutral phenomenon. Rather, because "space is political and ideological ... a product literally filled with ideologies" (Lefebvre, 1991, p. 31), the spatial metaphor imbues the Internet with an array of political and ideological consequences. Thus, "virtual spaces" are likely to reflect, and to perpetuate, the power structure of real spaces, including geopolitical spaces. Additionally, the connotative power of certain spatial associations may propagate past social consequences, either intended or unintended. For example, the metaphor of the "electronic frontier" carries with it Fredrick Turner Jackson's exposition of the American mythos of new challenges and endless opportunity (Healy, 1996; Adams, 1997, p. 161). At the same time, it may perpetuate attitudes of lawlessness and "wild west" anarchy that demean women or other disempowered users (Miller, 1995).

Metaphor and Law

Such latent cultural assumptions may become especially pernicious when they infect legal decisions. Particularly in common-law systems, legal decision-making rests on notions of precedent. Under the rule of *stare decisis,* courts are expected to apply the rules established in previous cases to subsequent cases presenting the same fact pattern (Schauer, 1987). Yet history never repeats itself exactly, and no two situations are ever precisely the same. This necessarily means that any system based on precedent is ultimately based on analogical reasoning, on a conclusion that the current situation is sufficiently similar to a previous situation. Thus analogical reasoning necessarily incorporates a form of metaphorical classification, mapping one concept onto another to reach the conclusion that they are analogous: *this* thing is like *that* thing in some significant aspect (Hunter, 2001).

Thus, for example, the juridical principles governing capture of a wild fox *(Pierson v. Post)* may evolve into the governing principles for ownership disputes over underground natural gas reservoirs, as the appropriation of an elusive and transient animal is analogized to appropriation of fossil fuel *(Westmoreland & Cambria Natural Gas Co. v. DeWitt).* Or, the principles governing compensation for harm done by flooding a neighbor's land may evolve into the principles governing compensation for harm done by high explosives detonated on a neighbor's land, as destructive escape of water is analogized to the destructive escape of blasting shocks *(Rylands v. Fletcher)*. The freely roaming nature of the fox becomes a metaphor for the elusive nature of natural gas; the destructive nature of flooding becomes a metaphor for the destructive potential of high explosives.

This approach has been justified in part on a deontological theory of fairness, treating like situations alike (Brewer, 1996; Sherwin, 1999). Additionally, reliance on precedent has been justified as efficient, in that courts facing factually familiar disputes need not develop new resolutions, but can instead rely on previous similar resolutions, saving unnecessary repeated effort. Finally, precedential decision making entails a utilitarian virtue of stability, as citizens both recognize that adjudicatory institutions will treat their cases fairly, and can come to rely on and predict the treatment of foreseeable factual patterns.

The drawback to the system is of course that, given the inevitable differences between any two situations, the similarities on which a decision is based must be considered more significant than the differences. The criteria by which significance is decided are ultimately ideological and political, and always potentially suspect. The admonition that use of legal metaphor is "wholly safe only when it is used with a complete awareness of its falseness" (Fuller, 1967, p. 10) serves as a useful but inadequate warning. Even when courts are cognizant that *this* thing is not entirely like *that* thing, the mechanics of analogical reasoning entail comparisons that may be silent or unhelpful on social consequences (Sunstein, 1993, p. 758).

This results in part from the tendency for analogical reasoning to degenerate into what Sunstein dubs "bad formalism" (p. 756). As a form of reasoning by comparison, analogy may treat new situations like old situations simply because they have been shoehorned into the same category. Thus, Judge Cardozo warns that "Metaphors in law are to be narrowly watched, for starting as devices to liberate thought, they end often by enslaving it" *(Berky v. Third Ave Railway)*. This is precisely the danger attending judicial adoption of the cyberspatial metaphor.

Space and Property

Analogical reasoning has been central to the development of Internet law, as U.S. courts sought to fit legal known principles to the characteristics of the new medium. In early Internet libel cases, Internet Service Providers (ISPs) drew on previous media analogies to characterize themselves as mere conduits for content, seeking the immunity of "distributors" such as bookstores or telephone exchanges before them *(Cubby v. CompuServe)*. Similarly, the U.S. Supreme Court analogized the Internet to print media, rather than to broadcast, telephone, or cable, thereby placing it in a category receiving the highest degree of First Amendment protection from government regulation *(Reno v. ACLU)*.

Each of these analogies has brought with them some precedential baggage, but none more so than the metaphorical trope of Internet and space. This metaphor carries with it an association of space with territory, and of territory with power.

As Keith Aoki observes, exclusive control or sovereignty over territory is deeply rooted in Anglo-American conceptions of ownership (Aoki, 1996, p. 1337). Thus, property is classically described by Blackstone as "that sole and despotic dominion which one man claims and exercises over the external things of the world, and in total exclusion of the right of any other individual in the universe" (Blackstone, 1766, p. 2). Blackstone was of course talking about land, which is the paradigmatic form of legal property. Property carries with it a long chain of rhetorical associations extending back into medieval jurisprudence (Parisi, 2002). Central to those associations is the equation of property with real property, which is to say with land (Rose, 1996, p. 351). Property equals land, and land equals exclusive power.

Carol Rose points out that Blackstone's commentary was less descriptive than mythological; he was consciously constructing paradigmatic forms of law rather than describing actual practice (Rose, 1990). Nonetheless, this characterization of property lives on in the form of frequent judicial pronouncements that the right to exclude is the essence of property, and in a scholarly tradition primacy (Merrill, 1998). Indeed, Calabresi and Melamed famously categorized exclusive legal regimes under the rubric of "property rules," as opposed to liability rules based on damages, or inalienability rules. In the rhetoric of the law, property is firmly associated with exclusivity.

The Internet and Land

The transition from metaphorical space to land to property is nowhere more apparent than in the series of American cases holding that unwanted Internet communications constitute trespass. Such holdings are ostensibly based on the ancient doctrine of trespass to chattels, a legal claim for compensation when movable property is damaged or interfered with by some unauthorized action (Burk, 2000; O'Rourke, 2001). But in cases of Internet trespass, courts have treated the trespass to computers as essentially a form of trespass to land, granting the kind of exclusive rights that attend trespass to land. Analogizing to cases in which dust or other particulate pollutants were held to constitute a trespass to land, the courts held that passage of unwanted electrons could constitute a trespass to computers.

Courts in these cases have either dispensed with any necessity to find harm, or have found "harm" in the storage of unwanted communications on the plaintiffs server, which deprived the computer owner of some number of processing cycles and some amount of storage space that could otherwise have been used for a purpose more to the ISP's liking *(CompuServe v. Cyberpromotions)*. But this combination of unwanted actions—the passage of electrons and the consumption of some computer memory or processing capacity—is common to every use of the Internet. Thus, unwanted e-mail, unwanted hypertext linking, or unwanted "crawling" of Web sites by automated data indexing "spiders" have all been asserted to constitute trespass *(eBay v. Bidders Edge)*.

The property metaphor appears again in the case against operators of the Napster file-sharing service *(A&M Records v. Napster)*. Although the operators of the service did not themselves reproduce or distribute unauthorized files, they were charged by the music industry with contributory infringement, which is to say knowingly assisting unauthorized copying and distribution of music files. Despite the operators' protests that it was implausible to monitor the millions of files on their system for illegal content, the court held that the service providers had a responsibility to do just that. The court reached this result by relying on earlier cases holding a landowner, on whose grounds a flea market was conducted, responsible for the sale of pirated cassette tapes on the market grounds. The earlier case rested on the assumption that the owner could have excluded or ejected the sellers of the illegal merchandise from the land. The court in *Napster* found that the operators had an analogous responsibility to "police" the boundaries of the peer-to-peer service, excluding or ejecting any subscribers who were purveying illicit music files.

The real property analogy appears yet again in conjunction with the anticircumvention provisions of the Digital Millennium Copyright Act. This statute was designed to prohibit circumvention of technological protections restricting use of digital works. Among the most troubling implications of such legislation has been its potential to stifle legitimate unauthorized uses of protected files. For example, the U.S. Copyright Act grants users a wide variety of privileges, including a broad and flexible privilege of fair use, allowing unauthorized uses of copyrighted works. Such uses could be blocked by technical measures, and the anticircumvention statute makes little provision for a user's motive in circumvention the technological restrictions. Circumvention for legal, legitimate uses is treated under the statute in the same fashion as circumvention for illegal and illegitimate purposes.

This problem was raised during the debates surrounding passage of the legislation (U.S. Congress, 1998). But industry representatives asserted the metaphor of a locked room, analogizing the circumvention of digital safeguards to breaking and entering another's secured physical space. They argued that there should be no privilege to circumvent technical measures in order to make fair use, just as there is no privilege to break and enter another's home in order to acquire a physical copy for fair use. The incongruities in the analogy are blatant, particularly given that fair users of a technologically protected work would be trying to access their own lawfully purchased copy, not the physical property of another. Nonetheless, the breaking and entering metaphor appears to have convinced Congress not to add a fair use exemption to the anticircumvention statute.

The Internet and Property

Each of these examples treats cyberspace as not only a place but also as land. Even in the case of Napster, where sovereign control inures to the liability of the system operators, such sovereignty is still recognized. Indeed, the *Napster* opinion highlights the disturbing implications of attributing such control to purveyors of digital information. Because the "space" of the Internet is for the most part metaphorical, the rights at issue are rights in intangible assets; thus much of the discussion is grounded in the language of intellectual property. Consequently, in each of the examples discussed, the rhetoric of property and dominion elevates the control of private information owners over the rights of access or use by the public.

This view of the Internet reflects in part a more general impetus toward a rhetoric of property, and of "sole and despotic dominion" over property (Lemley, 1997). Intellectual property rights generally are in a period of expansion, as courts and legislatures allocate the newly realized value of information. The metaphor is so pervasive that even commentators contesting the headlong rush toward propertization have adopted it. They speak of the digital "commons" and preservation of the public "domain." They speak in terms of a "second enclosure" movement, comparing the expansion of intellectual property rights with the aggregation of real property parcels in eighteenth- and nineteenth-century Britain (Boyle, 2002). Indeed, seemingly aware of the framework into which they have been subsumed, they look to the environmental movement as an example of successful resistance to excessive privatization of property—which is to say, excessive privatization of land (Boyle, 1997).

Even where courts have ostensibly have departed from the trope of property, the bias against public access remains dominant. In *Access Now, Inc. v. Southwest Airlines*, a federal court rejected the plaintiff's claim that an airline Web site, southwest.com, constituted a "place" of public accommodation for purposes of the Americans with Disabilities Act (ADA). According to the court, the Web site neither constituted a "specific, physical, concrete, space" for purposes of the statute nor did it have a sufficient operative nexus with such a space to fall under the statute. Neither would the court consent to extend the reach of the statute into "virtual spaces."

This result seems counter to the thesis of the Internet as land. But even though the opinion rejects classification of websites as places for purposes of the ADA, the discourse of the opinion is framed in terms of space, place, and land. The court merely refuses to map the Internet onto physical space, relying on the language that the Internet has no "fixed" geographic boundaries. The result indeed reaffirms the particular ideological construction of cyberspace as land, and land as sovereignty or dominion. The disabilities mandate of the ADA is in fact a challenge to the paradigm of sole and despotic control over property. In rejecting the ADA claim, the court in a very real sense treats Web sites as more propertized than real property.

But this points us toward some resolution of the pernicious legal effects of the cyberspatial metaphor. To categorize exclusionary rights as property rules need not imply that property constitutes an absolute right of exclusion. The right to exclude is only one of the rights associated with property, and Blackstone's hyperbole notwithstanding, the right has never been absolute. Even in the case of real property, the right to exclude has been riddled with easements, takings, adverse possessions, zoning, and exceptions of every kind imaginable, allowing both necessary private and public uses (Burk, 1999). Cyberspace may be associated with property, but this need not mean it entails absolute rights of exclusion; if the analogy is one of the Internet to land, then it must be to rights in land as actually practiced, not as paradigmatically idealized.

References

A&M Records, Inc. v. Napster, Inc., 239 F.3d 1004 (9th Cir. 2001)
Access Now, Inc. v. Southwest Airlines, Co., 227 F. Supp. 2d 1312 (S.D. Fla. 2002).
Adams, P. C. (1997). Cyberspace and virtual places. *The Geographical Review, 87,* 155-171.
Aoki, K. (1996). (Intellectual) property and sovereignty: Notes toward a cultural geography of authorship. *Stanford Law Review, 48,* 1293-1355.
Benedikt, M. (ed.) (1992). *Cyberspace: First Steps.* Cambridge, MA: MIT Press.
Berky v. Third Ave Railway, 155 N.E. 58, 61 (N.Y. 1926).
Blackstone, W. (1766). *Commentaries on the Laws of England,* vol. 2. Oxford: Clarendon Press.
Boyle, J. (2002). Fencing off ideas. *Daedalus,* spring, 13-27.
Boyle, J. (1997). A politics of intellectual property: Environmentalism for the net. *Duke Law Journal, 47,* 87-116.
Brewer, S. (1996). Exemplary reasoning: Semantics, pragmatics, and the rational force of legal argument by analogy. *Harvard Law Review, 109,* 925-1028
Burk, D. L. (1999) Muddy Rules for Cyberspace. *Cardozo Law Review, 21,* 121-179.
Burk, D. L. (2000) The trouble with trespass. *Journal of Small & Emerging Business Law, 4,* 27-56.
Calabresi, G., & Melamed, J. (1972). Property rights, liability rules, and inalienability: One view of the cathedral. *Harvard Law Review, 85,* 1089-1128.
Chesher, C. (1997). The ontology of digital domains. In D. Holmes (Ed.), *Virtual Politics: Identity and Community in Cyberspace* (pp. 79-92). London: Sage.
Compuserve Inc. v. Cyber Promotions, Inc., 962 F. Supp. 1015 (S.D. Ohio 1997).
Cubby, Inc. v. CompuServe, Inc., 776 F. Supp. 135 (S.D.N.Y. 1991).
Dallow, P. (2001). The space of information: Digital media as simulation of the analogical mind. In S. Munt (Ed.), *Technospaces: Inside the New Media* (pp. 57-70). New York: Continuum.
Digital Millennium Copyright Act, Pub. L. No. 105-304, Title I, 112 Stat. 2860 (1998), codified at 17 U.S.C. § 1201(a)-(b)
eBay Inc. v. Bidder's Edge, Inc., 100 F.Supp.2d 1058 (N.D. Cal. 2000).
Fuller, L. (1967). *Legal Fictions.* Palo Alto, CA: Stanford University Press.
Gibson, W. (1986a). *Burning chrome.* In *Burning Chrome.* New York: Arbor House.
Gibson, W. (1986b). *Neuromancer.* West Bloomfield, MI: Phantasia Press.
Healy, D. (1996). Cyberspace and place: The Internet as middle landscape on the electronic frontier. In D. Porter (Ed.), *Internet Culture* (pp. 54-68). New York: Routledge.
Hunter, D. (2001). Reason is too large: Analogy and precedent in law. *Emory Law Journal, 50,* 1197-1264.
Kant, E. (1929) *Critique of Pure Reason.* (N. Kemp Smith, trans.) London: Macmillan Press (originally published 1781, 1787).

Lemley, M. (1997). Romantic authorship and the rhetoric of property. *Texas Law Review, 75*, 873–906.
Lefebvre, H. (1991): *The Production of Space*, translated by D. Nicholson-Smith, Blackwell: Oxford.
Merrill, T. (1998). Property and the right to exclude. *Nebraska Law Review, 77*, 730–755.
Miller, L. (1995). Women and children first: Gender and the settling of the electronic frontier. In J. Brook & I. Boal (Eds.), *Resisting the Virtual Life: The Culture and Politics of Information* (pp. 49–57). San Francisco: City Lights Books.
Mitchell, W. (1995). *City of Bits: Space, Place, and the Infobahn*. Cambridge, MA: MIT Press.
Nunes, M. (1997). What place is cyberspace? The Internet and virtuality. In D. Holmes (Ed.), *Virtual politics: Identity and Community in Cyberspace* (pp. 163–178). London: Sage.
O'Rourke, M. (2001). Property rights and competition on the Internet: In search of an appropriate analogy. *Berkeley Technology Law Journal, 16*, 561–629.
Parisi, F. (2002). Entropy in property. *American Journal of Comparative Law, 50*, 595–630.
Reno v. ACLU, 521 U.S. 844 (1997).
Rose, C. (1990). Property as storytelling: Perspectives from game theory, narrative theory, feminist theory. *Yale Journal of Law & Humanities, 2*, 37–58.
Rose, C. (1996). Property as the keystone right. *Notre Dame Law Review, 71*, 329–365.
Ross, T. (1989) Metaphor and paradox. *Georgia Law Review, 23*, 1053–1084.
Rylands v. Fletcher, L.R. 3 H.L. 330 (1868).
Schauer, F. (1987). Precedent. *Stanford Law Review, 39*, 571–605.
Sherwin, E. (1999). A defense of analogical reasoning in law. *University of Chicago Law Review, 66*, 1179–1197.
Strate, L. (2000). Hypermedia, space, and dimensionality. In S. Gibson & O. Oviedo (Eds.), *The Emerging Cyberculture: Literacy, Paradigm, and Paradox* (pp. 267–286). Cresskill, NJ: Hampton Press.
Sunstein, C.R. (1993). On analogical reasoning. *Harvard Law Review, 106*, 791–741.
United States Congress House of Representatives. (1998). WIPO Copyright Treaties Implementation Act: Hearing on H.R. 2281 before the Subcommittee on Telecommunications Trade & Consumer Protection of the House Committee on Commerce, 105th Congress. Washington, DC: U.S. Government Printing Office.
Westmoreland & Cambria Natural Gas Co. v. DeWitt, 130 Pa. 235, 18 A. 724 (1889).

Philip E. Agre 2

INTERNET RESEARCH:
FOR AND AGAINST

 When I was going to graduate school at MIT, most of the professors around me were embarrassed to be called computer scientists. Their complaint was this: why should there be a separate field of computer science, any more than there is a separate field of refrigerator science? In their view, computers were just complex physical artifacts like any others. Following Simon (1969), they argued that design principles such as modularity are not specific to software, but are properties of the universe in general. The structures that evolve are modular because modular structures are more stable than others. Computers were simply a special case of these universal laws.

This perspective on computer science differs from the view in most textbooks. In the textbooks, a computer is a device that can compute any function that any particular Turing machine can compute. The professors at MIT would have none of this. Of course the mathematics of computability was interesting, but it reflected only one corner of a much larger space of inquiry. What they found most interesting was not the mapping from single inputs to single outputs but the relationship between the structure of a computational device and the organization of the computational process that arose when the device was set running.

The physical realization of computational processes was, however, only half the story. The other half lay in the analysis of problem domains. This is a profound aspect of computer work—and all engineering work—that is almost invisible to outsiders. Computers are general-purpose machines in that they can be applied to problems in any sphere. A system designer might work on an accounting application in the morning and an astronomical simulation in the afternoon. As the problems in these domains are translated into computational terms, certain patterns recur, and engineers abstract these patterns into layers of settled technique.

Here is an example. I once consulted with a company that wanted to automate the design of some complex mechanical artifacts. The designer of these artifacts might have to make several dozen design decisions. I spent several weeks sitting with an engineer and marching through a stack of manuals for the design of this category of artifacts. We needed the answer to a critical question: in working forward from requirements to design, does the designer ever need to backtrack? Is it ever necessary to make a design decision that might have to be retracted later? If backtracking was required, the company's task would become much harder. After working several cases by hand, it became clear that backtracking was not only necessary but ubiquitious, and that the company needed to hire someone who could build a general-purpose architecture for the backtracking of parameterized constraints. Backtracking is an example of a structure that recurs frequently in the analysis of problem domains. The resulting analogy among domains can be pursued, and might be illuminating all around.

For the professors at MIT, then, engineering consists of a dialectical engagement between two activities: analyzing the ontology of a domain and realizing that domain's decision-making processes in the physical world. ("Realize" here means "make physically real" rather than "mentally understand.") Ideas about computational structure exist for the purpose of translating back and forth between these two aspects of the engineer's work. This is a profound conception of engineering. And nothing about it is specific to computers.

This story is appealing because it dissolves the concept of the computer, which normally connotes a sharp break with the past, into the great historical tradition of engineering design. It is certainly an improvement on the standard story based on computability theory. Still, I believe that both stories overlook one area in which design is different for computers than for anything else. That area pertains to language.

Computers, whatever their other virtues, at least give people something to talk about. Your friends in China may not be having the same weather, but they are having the same virus outbreaks. Computers not only transcend geographical boundaries; they also bridge disciplines. Physicists and literary critics may not be able to discuss their research, but they can discuss their computers. Soldiers and media artists struggle with the same software. This kind of universality arises precisely from the analytical phase of the design process. Computers, in this sense, provide a "trading zone" (Galison, 1997) for discussions across different disciplinary languages. Computers are a shared layer in a wide variety of activities, and many activities have been reconstructed on top of the platform that computer standards provide. In these ways and more, computers are densely bound up with language (Hirschheim, Klein, and Lyytinen, 1996; Swanson and Ramiller 1997; Theoharakis & Wong, 2002; Weill & Broadbent, 1998).

Saying this, however, does not identify what is distinctive about computers. The answer is: computers are distinctive in their relation to discourse. Discourses about the world—that is, about people and their lives, the natural environment, business processes, social relationships, and so on—are inscribed into the workings of computers. It does not follow, of course, that computers then turn around and reinscribe those discourses into the activities of the people who use them.

Every social setting takes hold of its computers in its own distinctive way (Orlikowski, 2000). But neither is a computer a blank slate. Every system affords a certain range of interpretations, and that range is determined by the discourses that have been inscribed into it. To understand what is distinctive about the inscription of discourses into computers, as opposed to their inscription into other sorts of artifacts, it helps to distinguish among three progressively more specific meanings of the idea of inscription.

1. Shaping. Sociologists refer to the "social shaping of technology" (Dierkes & Hoffman, 1992, MacKenzie & Wajcman, 1985, Wiebe & Bijker, 1992). Newly invented technologies typically exist in competing variants, but political conflicts and other social processes eventually settle on particular designs. One prototype of social shaping is "how the refrigerator got its hum" (Cowan, 1985): early refrigerators came in both electric and gas varieties, but the electric variety won the politics of infrastructure and regulation. Social shaping is also found in the styling of artifacts, for example, tailfins on cars, and elsewhere. Social shaping analyses can be given for every kind of technology, and while language is certainly part of the process, the concept of social shaping does not turn on any specific features of language.

2. Roles. One type of social shaping is found in the presuppositions that a technology can make about the people who use it. Akrich (1992a, 1992b) gives examples of both successes and failures that turned on the designers' understandings of users. A company created a device consisting of a solar cell, a battery, and a lamp, intended for use in countries with underdeveloped infrastructures. Rather than study the web of relationships in which those people lived, however, the company sought to make its device foolproof, for example, by making it hard to take apart and by employing components that were not available on the local market. When ordinary problems arose, such as the short wire between the battery and the lamp, the users were unable to adapt it. By contrast, a videocassette player embodied elaborate ideas about the user, for example, as a person subject to copyright laws, that its very design was largely successful in enforcing. In each case, the designer, through a narrative that was implicit or explicit in the design process, tried to enlist the user into a certain social role. And language is geared to the construction of narratives about roles and relationships. (See also Barley 1990; Feenberg, 1991, pp. 80–82; Latour, 1996; Lea & Giordano, 1997; Mackay, Carne, & Beynon-Davies 2000; Sharrock & Button, 1997; and Woolgar, 1991.) Even so, nothing here is specific to computers either.

3. Grammar. Where computers are really distinctive is in their relationship to grammar. Systems analysis does not exactly analyze a domain, as the professors at MIT would have it. Rather, it analyzes a discourse for *talking about* a domain. (Or perhaps a domain must be understood as a discourse bound up with the objects it describes.) To be sure, much of the skill of systems analysis consists in assimilating this discourse to known techniques for realizing a decision-making process

in the physical world (Suchman & Trigg, 1993). But the substance of the work is symbolic. Computer people are ontologists, and their work consists of stretching whatever discourse they find on the ontological grid that is provided by their particular design methodology, whether entity-relationship data models (Simsion, 2001), object-oriented programming (Booch, 1996), or the language-action perspective (Winograd & Flores, 1986). In each case, the systems analyst performs a profound transformation on the domain discourse. The discourse is taken apart down to its most primitive elements. Nouns are gathered in one corner, verbs in another corner, and so on, and then the elements are cleaned up and reassembled to create the code. In this way, the structure of ideas in the original domain discourse is thoroughly mapped onto the workings of the computational artifact. The artifact will not capture the entire meaning of the original discourse, and will distort many aspects of the meaning that it does capture, but the relationship between discourse and artifact is systematic nonetheless.

Computers, then, are a distinctive category of engineered artifact because of their relationship to language. So it is striking that computer science pays so little explicit attention to discourse as such. Of course, computer science rests on formal language theory, which began as a way of analyzing the structure of natural languages (Chomsky, 1957). But there is more to discourse than the formal structures of language, and more to grammar than the structures of formalist linguistics. The discourses with which computer science wrestles are part of society. They are embedded in social processes, and they are both media and objects of controversy. Computers are routinely shaped through these controversies (Lessig, 1999; Mansell & Silverstone, 1996; Reidenberg, 1998). This is the great naiveté of computer science: by imagining itself to operate on domains rather than on discourses about domains, it renders itself incapable of seeing the discourses themselves, or the social controversies that pull those discourses in contradictory directions.

To understand the actual place of computing in the social world, it helps to take an institutional approach. An institution is a stable pattern of social relationships. Every institution defines a categorical structure (a set of social roles, an ontology and classification system, etc.), a terrain of action (stereotyped situations, actions, strategies, tactics, goals), values, incentives, a reservoir of skill and knowledge, and so on (Commons, 1970 [1950]; David, 1990; Fligstein, 2001; Goodin, 1996; Knight, 1992; March & Olsen, 1989; North, 1990; Powell & DiMaggio, 1991; Reus-Smit, 1997). The main tradition of computer system design was invented for purposes of reifying institutional structures (cf. Callon, 1998).

Institutional study of computing begins in earnest with research at UC Irvine in the late 1970s (e.g., Danziger, Dutton, Kling, & Kraemer, 1982). These researchers were interested in the organizational dynamics of computing at a time when computing was new. They worked in an intellectual climate that was far too credulous about the claims of rationalism, and sought to reassert the political and symbolic dimensions of computing in the real world.

Since that time, the world has changed a great deal in some ways—and very little in others. The Internet changed the technology of computing, for example, the practical possibility of interorganizational information systems. The Internet also changed the ideological climate around computing. It was no longer necessary to persuade anyone of the significance of computing as a topic of social inquiry, even if the social sciences proper have not exactly made computing central to their view of the world. Rationalism is out, and the central authorities that had long been associated with mainframe computing have been replaced by an ideal of decentralization. Of course, ideology should be distinguished from reality, and in the real world computing is still heavily political and symbolic. The institutionalist research program of the 1970s is still alive and well, and twenty years of technological change have done little to outdate it.

To examine in detail how the world has changed, we must dig our way from the landslide of ideology that engulfed public discourse about computing during the Internet bubble of the 1990s. We must return to the starting point of all serious social inquiry into computing: the evils of what Veblen (1921) called "technological determinism." Technological determinism—which can be either an openly avowed doctrine or an inadvertent system of assumptions—is usefully divided into two ideas: (1) that the directions of technical development are wholly immanent in the technology, and are not influenced by society; and (2) that the directions of social development are likewise entirely driven by the technology. These two ideas are both wrong. Social forces shape technology all the time. And the directions of social development are not driven by the technology itself, but rather by the incentives that particular institutions create to take hold of the technology in particular ways (Agre, 2002; Avgerou, 2002; Bud-Frierman, 1994; Dutton, 1999; Gandy, 1993; Kling, 1989; Mansell & Steinmuller, 2000; Preston, 2001).

Progress in the social study of computing requires us to discover and taxonomize the forms that technological determinism takes in received ways of thinking. Two of these might be called discontinuity and disembedding (cf. Brown & Duguid, 2000). Discontinuity is the idea that information technology has brought about a sudden change in history. We supposedly live in an "information society," a "network society," or a "new media age" whose rules are driven by the workings of particular technologies. These theories are wrong as well. Of course, new information technologies have participated in many significant changes. But many other things are happening at the same time, yet other things are relatively unchanged, and the changes that do occur are thoroughly mediated by the structures and meanings that were already in place. It is easy to announce a discontinuity and attribute it to a single appealing trend, but doing so trivializes a complex reality.

Disembedding supposes new technologies to be a realm of their own, disconnected from the rest of the world. An example is the concept of "cyberspace" or the "online world," as if everything that happened online were unrelated to anything that happened offline. The reality is quite different. The things that people do on the Internet are almost always bound up with the things that they do elsewhere (Friedland, 1996; Miller & Slater 2000; Wynn & Katz 1997). The "online world" is not a single place, but is divided among various institutions—banking sites, hobby sites, extended family mailing lists, and so on, each of them simply annexing a corner of the Internet as one more forum to pursue an existing institutional logic, albeit with whatever amplifications or inflections might arise from the practicalities of the technology in use. People may well talk about the Internet as a separate place from the real world, and that is an interesting phenomenon, but it is not something that we should import into serious social analysis.

Institutional analysis thus encourages us to make distinctions. If we do not enumerate institutions (education, medicine, family, religion, politics, law), then the temptation to overgeneralize is overwhelming. We will start from the single case that interests us most, and we will pretend that the whole world worked that way.

Consider, for example, the famous cartoon in which a computer-using dog asserts, "On the Internet, nobody knows you're a dog" (Steiner, 1993). Unfortunately, the cartoon dog's assertion has often been taken seriously by scholars even though it is not true. When people think about identity on the Internet, they generally think of games where people adopt fictional personae, trading sites such as eBay where most people use pseudonyms, or loosely woven discussion forums where people never learn much about one another as individuals. But these contexts represent only part of the Internet, reflecting the workings of certain kinds of institutions. Many other institutions work in other ways. In academia, for example, researchers are generally well identified to one another. They meet at conferences, read one another's research, and so on. They are not interested in being anonymous online; indeed, the institutions of research create incentives for promoting one's work, and thus one's identity, at every turn.

Institutional analysis, by applying the same concepts in several contexts, also captures important commonalities. An investigator can apply a given framework to the analysis of a given case, extend the framework by making bits and pieces of novel observation, and then advertise that novel result as a heuristic resource for the analysis of other cases in the future. Investigators can read one another's analyses, and in this way they can build up a toolkit of concepts and precedents, each of which stimulates research by posing questions to whatever case is studied next. That is how interpretive social science works. It is similar to the methods of engineering that I described at the outset, except that it has not been so intricately constrained by the demands of physical realization.

How, then, from an institutional point of view, does the world change with the advent of the Internet? One answer lies in the exact relationship between information technology and institutions. Recall that information technologies are designed by starting with language, and that this language has generally originated with the categorical structures of an institution. Information technology is often said to be revolutionary—that much is constant in the ideology from the late 1970s to the present—but as the UC Irvine group pointed out, the actual practice of computing is anything but. Indeed the purpose of computing in actual organizational practices is often to conserve and even to rigidify existing institutional patterns (cf. Cornford, 2001). As studies of print (Zaret, 2000) and the telephone (Fischer, 1992) have shown, media are often taken up to good effect by people who are trying to be conservative. Yet history is not just the story of people's intentions. History is a story of local initiative and global emergence that needs to be investigated concretely in each case (Marvin, 1988; Orlikowski, 2001).

The specific role that the Internet has played in this story is illustrated by the concept of layering (Messerschmitt, 1999). The Internet is a layered protocol, and the layering principle is partially credited with the Internet's success. But the Internet hardly invented layering, and is best seen as one more expression of a pervasive principle of order. If a complex functionality is broken into layers, then the bottom layers can be shared among many purposes. That helps them to propagate, and to establish the economies of scope and network effects that make them work as businesses for the industrial ecosystem around them. The argument is roughly Simon's, except that it is the whole ecosystem that is stable, not just the Internet as a modular artifact.

The principle of layering operates in a wide range of digital communication technologies, even if the bundling imperatives of companies such as Microsoft provide a countervailing force. Layers have an important property: they are appropriable. Layers of nonproprietary public networks are especially appropriable (Feenberg, 1995), and the appropriability of the Internet is a miracle in many ways and a curse in others. To analyze the social and technical dynamics that result, we need serious concepts. The traditional institutional studies of computing assumed that these matters were fought out in the architecture of computing in a given organization. This analysis works best in the context of bespoke organizational applications, especially ones that affect the resource allocations and political positions of diverse organizational players. It can also be generalized to applications that are relatively specific to the workings of a given institutional field, for example in the work by Kling, Fortuna, and King (2001) on emerging architectures for scholarly publishing in medicine. Standard political issues arise: collective action problems among the authors, professional society staffs pursuing their own interests instead of those of their constituencies, copyright interests and their influence on the legislative system, cultural norms that stigmatize change, and the practical difficulties facing would-be change entrepreneurs. This is the institutional politics of technology-enabled institutional change. Meanwhile, new technologies mediate the political process in new ways, and the cycle closes completely.

The dynamics of these conflicts change when individual parties can go off and change the world on their own. When new systems cannot be built without large organizations, politics still has a central focus. In a world of appropriable layers, however, it is easier to create facts on the ground. The decision-making process changes. It is no longer a debate about how to design a single system but a competition among multiple systems. Of course, technical innovations have always led to competing designs. In a world of layers, however, the costs of joining the competition are reduced.

The point is not exactly that the institution is an arbitrary authority that has been circumvented. Somebody's new back-room invention will only change anything if it is aligned to some degree with real forces operating within the institution, such as the incentives that the researchers experience to publicize their research. In a sense the institution splits: its forces are channeled partly through the established mechanisms and partly through the renegade initiatives that someone has built on the Internet. That is when the politics starts, itself structured and organized within the framework of the institution—after all, institutions are best understood not as zones of mindless consensus but as stabilized mechanisms for the conduct of disputes over second-order issues (Holm, 1995).

The Internet, from this perspective, does not so much replace institutions as introduce new elements into the ongoing dynamics of controversy within them. The possibility of creating new technologies on top of open network layers simply represents a wider range of potential tactics within an existing and densely organized logic of controversy. Creating new technologies does create new facts on the ground, but it does not, of itself, create new institutions. The gap between technologies and institutions is large, and many institutional arrangements will need to be settled aside from the system architecture.

But this is where the impact of the Internet is greatest: in the relationship between information technologies and institutions. Historically, systems analysts have been taught to transcribe institutional orders directly onto the applications they build. One reason for this was organizational: an application may fit better into an organization if it is aligned with the existing ecology of practices. Of course, the process of appropriating a new technology routinely shifts an ecology of practices into a new and perhaps unanticipated equilibrium (Berg, 1999; Orlikowski, 2001). But precisely because the shifts are hard to anticipate, aligning the categorical structure of the technology with that of the existing institution may be almost the only practical strategy (cf. Bourdieu, 1981). Another reason is pure conservatism: organizational practices evolve at a deeper level than anyone can explain or rationalize, and it is often better to transcribe these practices with a certain willful superficiality than to follow the advice of the "reengineering" revolutionaries (Hammer, 1990) by trashing history and starting over.

A final reason pertains to social relations: computer systems by their nature entrain their users to the categorical structures that they embody, for example by requiring the users to swipe their magstripe cards every time they undertake particular sorts of transactions, and a computer system whose categories map directly onto the categories of the institution will thereby, other things being equal, make people easier to control. And this last point is key: the Internet, by providing an extremely generic and appropriable layer that other systems can easily be built upon, disrupts this classic pattern of social control. The gap between technology and institution yawns, and into the gap pour a wide variety of institutional entrepreneurs, all trying to create their own facts on the ground.

Fortunately for the powers that be, these would-be entrepreneurs often fail to understand the opportunity that has been handed to them. For example, many of them overestimate what can be accomplished by writing code. Programmers build exciting new systems and then they watch in dismay as they fail to mesh with the institutional orders around them. The understanding is perhaps now dawning that architecture, while certainly a variety of politics, is by no means a substitute for politics.

Precisely through its explosive success, the Internet has disserved us, teaching us a false model of institutional change. The appropriability of layered public networks is indeed a new day in the dynamics of institutions, but it is not a revolution. It brings neither a discontinuous change nor a disembedded cyber world. It is, to the contrary, another chapter in the continuous renegotiation of social practices and relationships in the world we already have. The organized social conflict that is endemic to democracy has not gone away, and the lessons of democracy are as clear as they ever were.

References

Agre, Philip E. (1998). Yesterday's tomorrow, *Times Literary Supplement*, July 3, 3–4.

Agre, Philip E. (2002). Real-time politics: The Internet and the political process, *The Information Society* 18(5), 311–331.

Akrich, Madeleine. (1992a). The description of technical objects. In Wiebe E. Bijker and John Law (Eds.), *Shaping Technology/Building Society: Studies in Sociotechnical Change* (pp. 205–224). Cambridge, MA: MIT Press.

Akrich, Madeleine. (1992b). Beyond social construction of technology: The shaping of people and things in the innovation process. In Meinholf Dierkes and Ute Hoffman (Eds.), *New Technology at the Outset: Social Forces in the Shaping of Technological Innovations* (pp. 173–190). Frankfurt: Campus Verlag.

Avgerou, Chrisanthi. (2002). *Information Systems and Global Diversity*, Oxford: Oxford University Press.

Barley, Stephen R. (1990). The alignment of technology and structure through roles and networks. *Administrative Science Quarterly*, 35(1), 61–103.

Berg, Marc. (1999). Accumulating and coordinating: Occasions for information technologies in medical work. *Computer Supported Cooperative Work*, 8(4), 373–401.

Bijker, Wiebe E., & Law, John (Eds.). (1992). *Shaping Technology/Building Society: Studies in Sociotechnical Change*, Cambridge, MA: MIT Press.

Booch, Grady. (1996). *Object Solutions: Managing the Object-Oriented Project*, Menlo Park, CA: Addison-Wesley.

Bourdieu, Pierre. (1981). Men and machines. In Karin Knorr-Cetina and Aaron V. Cicourel (Eds.), *Advances in Social Theory and Methodology: Toward an Integration of Micro- and Macro-Sociologies* (pp. 304–317). Boston: Routledge and Kegan Paul.

Brown, John Seely, & Duguid, Paul. (2000). *The Social Life of Information*. Boston: Harvard Business School Press.

Bud-Frierman, Lisa. (Ed.). (1994). *Information Acumen: The Understanding and Use of Knowledge in Modern Business*. London: Routledge.

Callon, Michel. (Ed.). (1998). *The Laws of the Markets*. Oxford: Blackwell. .

Chomsky, Noam. (1957). *Syntactic Structures*. Gravenhage: Mouton.

Commons, John R. ([1950] 1970). *The Economics of Collective Action*. Madison: University of Wisconsin Press.

Cornford, James. (2001). The virtual university is . . . the university made concrete? *Information, Communication, and Society*, 3(4), 508-525.

Cowan, Ruth Schwartz. (1985). How the refrigerator got its hum. In Donald MacKenzie and Judy Wajcman (Eds.), *The Social Shaping of Technology: How the Refrigerator Got Its Hum* (pp. 202-218). Milton Keynes: Open University Press.

Danziger, James N., Dutton, William H., Kling, Rob, & Kraemer, Kenneth L. (1982). *Computers and Politics: High Technology in American Local Governments*, New York: Columbia University Press.

David, Paul A. (1990). The dynamo and the computer: An historical perspective on the modern productivity paradox. *American Economic Review*, 80(2), 355-361.

Dierkes, Meinholf, & Hoffman, Ute. (Eds.). (1992). *New Technology at the Outset: Social Forces in the Shaping of Technological Innovations*. Frankfurt: Campus Verlag.

Dutton, William H. (Ed.). (1999). *Society on the Line: Information Politics in the Digital Age*. Oxford: Oxford University Press.

Feenberg, Andrew. (1991). *Critical Theory of Technology*. New York: Oxford University Press.

Feenberg, Andrew. (1995). *Alternative Modernity: The Technical Turn in Philosophy and Social Theory*. Berkeley: University of California Press.

Fischer, Claude S. (1992). *America Calling: A Social History of the Telephone to 1940*. Berkeley: University of California Press.

Fligstein, Neil. (2001). *The Architecture of Markets: An Economic Sociology of Twenty-First-Century Capitalist Societies*. Princeton, NJ: Princeton University Press.

Friedland, Lewis A. (1996). Electronic democracy and the new citizenship. *Media, Culture and Society*, 18(2), 185-212.

Galison, Peter. (1997). *Image and Logic: A Material Culture of Microphysics*. Chicago: University of Chicago Press.

Gandy Jr., Oscar H. (1993). *The Panoptic Sort: A Political Economy of Personal Information*. Boulder, CO: Westview Press.

Goodin, Robert E. (Ed.). (1996). *The Theory of Institutional Design*. Cambridge: Cambridge University Press.

Hammer, Michael. (1990). Reengineering work: Don't automate, obliterate. *Harvard Business Review*, 68(4), 104-112.

Hirschheim, Rudy, Klein, Heinz K., & Lyytinen, Kalle. (1996). Exploring the intellectual structures of information systems development: A social action theoretic analysis. *Accounting, Management and Information Technologies*, 6(1-2), 1-64.

Holm, Petter. (1995). The dynamics of institutionalization: Transformation processes in Norwegian fisheries. *Administrative Science Quarterly*, 40(3), 398-422.

Kling, Rob. (1989). Theoretical perspectives in social analysis of computerization. In Zenon W. Pylyshyn & Liam J. Bannon (Eds.), *Perspectives on the Computer Revolution*, second edition (pp. 459-518). Norwood, NJ: Ablex.

Kling, Rob, Fortuna, Joanna, & King, Adam. (2001). The real stakes of virtual publishing: The transformation of E-Biomed into PubMed Central. Working Paper 01-03, Center for Social Informatics, Indiana University. Available on the Web at < http://www.slis.indiana.edu/CSI/wp01-03.html >.

Knight, Jack. (1992). *Institutions and Social Conflict*. Cambridge: Cambridge University Press.

Latour, Bruno. (1996). Social theory and the study of computerized work sites. In Wanda Orlikowski, Geoff Walsham, Matthew R. Jones, & Janice I. DeGross (Eds.), *Informa-

tion Technology and Changes in Organizational Work (pp. 295–307). London: Chapman and Hall.

Lea, Martin, & Giordano, Richard. (1997). Representations of the group and group processes in CSCW research: A case of premature closure? In Geoffrey C. Bowker, Susan Leigh Star, William Turner, & Les Gasser (Eds.), *Social Science, Technical Systems and Cooperative Work: Beyond the Great Divide* (pp. 5–25). Mahwah, NJ: Erlbaum.

Lessig, Lawrence. (1999). *Code: And Other Laws of Cyberspace*. New York: Basic Books.

Mackay, Hugh, Carne, Chris, & Beynon-Davies, Paul. (2000). Reconfiguring the user: Using Rapid Application Development. *Social Studies of Science*, 30(5), 737–757.

MacKenzie, Donald, & Wajcman, Judy. (Eds.). (1985). *The Social Shaping of Technology: How the Refrigerator Got Its Hum*. Milton Keynes: Open University Press.

Mansell, Robin Mansell, & Silverstone, Roger. (Eds.). (1996). *Communication by Design: The Politics of Information and Communication Technologies*. Oxford: Oxford University Press.

Mansell, Robin, & Steinmueller, W. Edward. (2000). *Mobilizing the Information Society: Strategies for Growth and Opportunity*. Oxford: Oxford University Press.

March, James G., & Olsen, Johan P. (1989). *Rediscovering Institutions: The Organizational Basis of Politics*. New York: Free Press.

Marvin, Carolyn. (1988). *When Old Technologies Were New: Thinking About Electric Communication in the Late Nineteenth Century*. New York: Oxford University Press.

Messerschmitt, David G. (1999). *Networked Applications: A Guide to the New Computing Infrastructure*. San Francisco: Morgan Kaufman.

Miller, Daniel, & Slater, Don. (2000). *The Internet: An Ethnographic Approach*. New York: New York University Press.

North, Douglass C. (1990). *Institutions, Institutional Change, and Economic Performance*. Cambridge: Cambridge University Press.

Orlikowski, Wanda J. (2000). Using technology and constituting structures: A practice lens for studying technology in organizations. *Organization Science*, 11(4), 404–428.

Orlikowski, Wanda J. (2001). Improvising organizational transformation over time: A situated change perspective. In JoAnne Yates and John Van Maanen (Eds.), *Information Technology and Organizational Transformation: History, Rhetoric, and Practice* (pp. 223–274). Thousand Oaks, CA: Sage.

Powell, Walter W., & DiMaggio, Paul J. (Eds.). (1991). *The New Institutionalism in Organizational Analysis*. Chicago: University of Chicago Press.

Preston, Paschal. (2001). *Reshaping Communications: Technology, Information and Social Change*. London: Sage.

Reidenberg, Joel R. (1998). Lex Informatica: The formulation of information policy rules through technology. *Texas Law Review*, 76(3), 553–593.

Reus-Smit, Christian. (1997). The constitutional structure of international society and the nature of fundamental institutions. *International Organization*, 51(4), 555–589.

Sharrock, Wes, & Button, Graham. (1997). Engineering investigations: Practical sociological reasoning in the work of engineers. In Geoffrey C. Bowker, Susan Leigh Star, William Turner, and Les Gasser (Eds.), *Social Science, Technical Systems and Cooperative Work: Beyond the Great Divide* (pp. 79–104). Mahwah, NJ: Erlbaum.

Simon, Herbert A. (1969). *The Sciences of the Artificial*. Cambridge, MA: MIT Press.

Simsion, Graeme. (2001). *Data Modeling Essentials*, second edition. Scottsdale, AZ: Coriolis.

Steiner, Peter. (1993). untitled cartoon, *The New Yorker*, July 5, 61.

Suchman, Lucy A., & Trigg, Randall H. (1993). Artificial intelligence as craftwork. In Seth

Chaiklin & Jean Lave (Eds.), *Understanding Practice: Perspectives on Activity and Context*, Cambridge: Cambridge University Press.

Swanson, E. Burton, & Ramiller, Neil C. (1997). The organizing vision in information systems innovation. *Organization Science*, 8(5), 458–474.

Theoharakis, Vasilis, & Wong, Veronica. (2002). Marking high-technology market evolution through the foci of market stories: The case of local area networks. *Journal of Product Innovation Management*, 19, 400–411.

Veblen, Thorstein. (1921). *The Engineers and the Price System*. New York: Viking.

Weill, Peter, & Broadbent, Marianne. (1998). *Leveraging the New Infrastructure: How Market Leaders Capitalize on Information Technology*. Boston: Harvard Business School Press.

Winograd, Terry, & Flores, Fernando. (1986). *Understanding Computers and Cognition: A New Foundation for Design*. Norwood, NJ: Ablex.

Woolgar, Steve. (1991). Configuring the user: The case of usability trials. In John Law (Ed.), *A Sociology of Monsters: Essays on Power, Technology and Domination* (pp. 57–99). London: Routledge.

Wynn, Eleanor, & Katz, James E. (1997). Hyperbole over cyberspace: Self-presentation and social boundaries in Internet home pages and discourse. *The Information Society*, 13(4), 297–327.

Zaret, David. (2000). *Origins of Democratic Culture: Printing, Petitions, and the Public Sphere in Early-Modern England*. Princeton, NJ: Princeton University Press.

Barbara Warnick

DANGEROUS FUTURES: ARTIFICIAL INTELLIGENCE AND SCIENTIFIC ARGUMENT

Communication with the public about scientific research and technology development subsumes a number of different genres of discourse. Some of these include scientific reports in such periodicals as *Scientific American* and *Science,* while others take the form of trade books or online resources intended for nonspecialist readers. This essay considers a particular example in one subgenre of this category—publications for general consumption that promote technology development. I am specifically concerned with the problematic nature of some scientific publications that exaggerate the expected benefits of developing technologies, fail to consider dangers in their development, and avoid discussion of their ethical implications.

The present study corroborates Robert C. Goldbart's claim (1998) that many scientists are not explicitly trained to communicate their findings or to mount arguments effectively designed for lay consumption. It also supports the work of Jeanne Fahnestock (1998) who noted that much public discourse about scientific research is disproportionately favorable. Fahnestock compared argumentation and language use in scientific reports on a set of topics with popular press accounts of the same topics and found that the latter were overwhelmingly celebratory, oversimplifying the research and exaggerating its benefits.

Artificial intelligence is a frequently discussed topic in trade books, periodicals, public symposia, and on the World Wide Web. In these forums, researchers in computer science, artificial intelligence, and other fields engage in debates about the future of the human race and envision a world where machine intelligence may (or may not) equal or surpass human intelligence. Because of their successes in product development and research, spokesmen such as Ray Kurzweil, Marvin Minsky, Hans Moravec, and others have a certain cachet with readers interested in

AI-related issues. In this essay, I will focus on the work of one of these authors, the quality of his arguments, and responses made to them. My emphasis will be on the nature and character of public arguments made by AI advocates rather than on the substantive merits of their claims, which have been discussed at length elsewhere (Crevier, 1993; Turkle, 1995; Ekbia, 2001, 2002).

By virtue of their placement in books, general periodicals, and on Web sites intended for the lay reader, writings on AI take the form of public argument. That is, they are addressed to nonspecialists, make claims that can potentially be empirically substantiated, present evidence to support their claims, and are designed to persuade their reading audiences. As many argument theorists have observed, public argument is a genre of discourse that, in order to qualify as argument *per se* (rather than mere hype or fantasy or propaganda), should fulfill some obligations to its readers. In particular, arguments addressed to the public should position readers in such a way as to enable them to make an independent judgment of the merits of their claims.

In part, this means presenting reasoning and evidence on both sides of a question. For example, in writings about AI, open argumentation would mean citing failures as well as successes in AI research, discussing dangers and risks as well as future promise of the work, and reporting on factors that impede as well as those that promote future research progress. In part also, this means implementing an ethical standard for the conduct of an argument. In principle, such argument would leave room for interlocutors to disagree and should leave open the possibility that one or both parties to an argument might change their mind about the issue in question.

It is important to think about these ethical standards in judging many of the public discussions about technology development. Experts in technoscience should be held all the more to these standards because they often write for publics who are not positioned to judge the technical merits of what they say. The only way that publics can make informed decisions about technology development is in a public sphere where all the dangers, risks, social implications, and ethical issues relevant to a question are weighed. In the example that follows, I will briefly consider a case study in which an author initially failed to place his readers so as to make a considered judgment about the merits of what he had to say. After the initial publication of his argument, however, he followed up by posting a website that included both arguments against his original position by scientific experts and message boards in which respondents to his book could openly discuss the issues pro and con.

Ray Kurzweil's *The Age of Spiritual Machines: When Computers Exceed Human Intelligence* was published in 1999 by Penguin Putnam. Kurzweil there argued that in the first half of the 21st century, machine intelligence will come close to equaling human intelligence, and that before the century is over, machine intelligence will exceed human intelligence. To support his claim, Kurzweil noted that in light of Moore's Law (Miller, 1996) concerning the exponential increases in the speed and density of computing, computers can be expected to achieve the memory capacity and computing speed of the human brain by around the year 2020. Once computers have become capable of independent thought and can communicate that to humans, Kurzweil predicted that they will come to be viewed as conscious entities. In his view, the increasing rapprochement of human and machine intelligence will be reciprocal; that is, machine intelligence will be developed through reverse engineering human brains so as to design machine prototypes of human intelligence, and once that has been successfully completed, people will be able to download their minds into machines.

Although some readers might have had difficulty taking Kurzweil's predictions seriously, their credibility was buttressed by his past record of innovation and invention. As he reminded readers, his accomplishments included invention of the Kurzweil Reading Machine and pioneering work in speech recognition systems and digital music synthesis. Furthermore, many of his short-term predictions in an earlier book, *The Age of Intelligent Machines* (1990) (e.g., development of a global information network, cyberterrorism, surveillance technologies) have turned out to be true. However, many observers, including reviewers of the book and Kurzweil's own colleagues, questioned his vision and his assumptions as he looked further into the future (Shaffer, 1999; Proudfoot, 1999; Muska, 2000; Lanier, 2000a; 2000b).

What is it about the writings of Kurzweil and other artificial intelligence researchers that evokes either the incredulity of skeptics or the fascination of admirers? Why does public discourse on such topics seem to split into opposing camps without the moderating influence of serious deliberation about the merits and ethical implications of the claims that are made? As an argument theorist, I am very interested in the narrative and argument structures used in *The Age of Spiritual Machines*. Considering their rhetorical features, as well as the arguments posed by his critics, might help us to better understand how public discourse proceeded in this case.

To support his views, Kurzweil worked through various topics using a limited number of patterns of thought. These include deductive, analytical reasoning; use of algorithms; and progressive narratives with a predetermined conclusion. For readers used to thinking in these ways, Kurzweil's arguments probably seemed compelling and forceful. Analytical reasoning as exemplified in formal logic includes categorical, disjunctive, and conditional syllogisms. These work well so long as the premises are taken as true and the terms are reduced and unequivocal in meaning. So long as one stays inside the universe of formal validity, the conclusion of such reasoning is unquestionable. An example (and an important move in Kurzweil's discussion) is:

> Evolutionary processes build on themselves.
> Technology is an evolutionary process.
> Therefore, technology development builds on itself.
> (Kurzweil, 1999, p. 32)

So long as the major and minor premises are taken as true, the conclusion follows logically. Conditional syllogistic forms relying on if/then relationships are also frequently used in Kurzweil's book. Because of their simplicity and clear logic, these categorical and conditional forms of argument appear to be persuasive on their face.

Kurzweil's use of algorithmic thinking is of real interest. This mode of reasoning, not often covered in texts on informal or practical argument (van Eemeren, Grootendorst, & Henkemans, 1996; Inch & Warnick, 2002) seemed to be Kurzweil's favored form of thought, both in his own practice and in the sort of thinking he expected artificial intelligence agents to perform. Algorithmic thinking uses a step by step procedure in which answers to initial questions determine the next question to be asked in the sequence ("Algorithm," 2001). Algorithmic thinking serves well for many purposes to which computing is well suited. For example, in warfare it can be used to control weapons deployed for strategic action; in medicine, to assist physicians in diagnosing and treating patients; in education, to teach students some of the basic skills and elements of critical thinking. There are other contexts, however, to which it is poorly suited. These are situations in which what Aristotle called *phronesis* or practical wisdom is needed (Kennedy, 1991). For example, algorithmic thinking will not help us to decide whether to attack a military target where civilians are present, or to decide whether an already terminally ill patient should receive a particular medical treatment, or to teach students how to make principled, ethical, moral choices. The problem, then, is with equating certain, limited forms of thinking with *all* thinking. Kurzweil does this, and because he reduces thinking to only some of its forms, he makes the view that computers will achieve human intelligence logically supportable.

A third mode of thought at the organizational or macro level in Kurzweil's book is the progressive narrative. This narrative form sets a pattern, gains momentum as it unfolds, and its structure seems to discredit any possible objections or counter narratives. As with the premises of deductive arguments, so long as one anticipates and accepts the foregone conclusion of the narrative that is implied in its telling, the conclusion is inevitable. For example, early in his book, Kurzweil sets up a pattern of seven stages in technological development. These include the precursor stage in which the technology is imagined, the invention stage where it first appears, the development stage, the stage of maturity, the stage of pretenders where an upstart threatens to eclipse the older technology, followed by obsolescence and antiquity (1999, pp. 19–20).

Reading this apparently seamless account of the progressive and nearly inexorable development of technology might cause one to wonder whether there have ever been instances of technological development that might not have followed Kurzweil's progressive narrative pattern. Elsewhere in the book, Kurzweil lists a number of past negative predictions regarding future technology development that now seem ludicrous. Here are some examples:

> Heavier than air flying machines are not possible.
> Lord Kelvin, 1895

> I think there is a world market for maybe five computers.
> IBM Chairman Thomas Watson, 1943

> The Internet will catastrophically collapse in 1996.
> Robert Metcalfe, n.d. (1999, pp. 169–170)

There are, by contrast, other optimistic predictions specifically regarding AI that were not mentioned by Kurzweil and have not come to pass within their predicted time frames. Two examples are:

> Machines will be capable within twenty years of doing any work that a man can do.
> Herbert A. Simon, 1965 (Crevier, 1993, p. 109)

> Within a generation . . . few compartments of intellect will remain outside the machine's realm—the problem of creating "artificial intelligence" will be substantially solved.
> Marvin Minsky, 1967 (Crevier, 1993, p. 109)

One would like to think that critical readers of Kurzweil's book would pause to think of the opposite case, but it could be that many of them might not do so.

After its publication, discussions of and responses to *The Age of Spiritual Machines* occurred in many venues; the book became a topic of serious discussions; and Kurzweil's treatment seemed to rekindle interest in the field of artificial intelligence. In April 2000, Bill Joy published a lengthy essay in *Wired* that was intended in part to respond to some of the issues raised by Kurzweil. Joy was particularly struck by Kurzweil's prediction that humans in the future will concede social control to robots. For Joy, this raised the specter of a future in which a small human elite might retain control of large robotic systems and also control the lives and society of the human race. Joy argued that those who develop technologies are responsible for their later use (2000, p. 243). Joy's attitude and concern contrast sharply with the views of many technophiles who have seemed fatalistic or unconcerned about such matters. Furthermore, Joy raised other ethics-based questions about Kurzweil's proposed program for AI development. Whose brains will be destructively scanned so that the brain can be reverse engineered? How much will it cost to upload one's mind into a form of machine intelligence? What will become of humans who are not placed so as to benefit from machine intelligence? What might be the implications of disembodied intelligence? And, eventually, what will become of the human race if it is superseded by forms of inorganic machine intelligence?

Elsewhere, the discussion continued into late 2000 and early 2001 on the Web site Edge (<http://www.edge.org>) and included Kurzweil's defense of the ideas in *The Age of Spiritual Machines* as criticized by Jaron Lanier (2000a) in a commentary on Joy's essay. Edge is a by-invitation Web forum self-described as "an informal salon, a forum for eminent scientists, members of the digerati and science journalists from all over the world" (Mundy, 2000). It is edited by Jon Brockman who in September 2000 decided to publish Jaron Lanier's "One Half of a Manifesto"—a refutation of what Lanier viewed as "Cybernetic Totalism" and, in particular, AI research. Since Lanier is a pioneer in virtual reality and lead scientist for the National Tele-Immersion Initiative, other Edge participants took his remarks seriously.

Lanier argued that AI enthusiasts such as Kurzweil and Hans Moravec confuse ideal computers with real computers that behave differently. Real computers run on software rendered inadequate to keep pace with hardware advances because of a "legacy" effect—the disruptive influence of underlying code on which later code and code components depend. This is what leads to brittleness—the subtle incompatibility between chunks of software that were originally created in different times and contexts.

Lanier furthermore argued that many AI researchers have a limited view of human thought. He maintained that we still do not fundamentally understand the processes of rational thought—in particular, humans' ability to build abstract representations of the world and to enact common sense. This is often unrecognized by the general public because, as Lanier noted, thinkers who "place what is essentially a form of algorithmic computation at the center of reality . . . tend to be confident and crisp and to occasionally have new and good ideas" (Lanier, 2000a). Lanier subsequently wrote a postscript to his "Manifesto" specifically addressed to Kurzweil. In it, he emphasized Kurzweil's tendencies to make no distinction between quantity (Moore's Law) and quality, to blend phenomena in different categories together indiscriminately, and to cite only those examples and facts that supported his own predictions (Lanier, 2000b).

Kurzweil (2001) responded by characterizing Lanier's concern about bad software as "engineer's pessimism"—a trait causing Lanier to lose sight of the long-term implications of technology growth. He noted that similar forms of pessimism had earlier plagued the human genome project and early views of the Internet's potential. In response to the software issue, Kurzweil argued that he viewed reverse engineering of the human brain as the solution. He cited recent advances in improved understanding of the brain's physical structure and its function, and he insisted that advances in brain research enable us to "observe the brain's massively parallel methods . . . scan and understand its connections . . . and replicate its methods" (Kurzweil, 2001). He said that he viewed the subsumption of human intelligence by machine intelligence as "neither utopian nor dystopian" but as the logical outcome of an evolutionary process.

Subsequent to Joy's public indictment of his views and Lanier's discussion of his book on Edge.org, Kurzweil launched a new Web site—kurzweilai.net—on February 22, 2001. The express purpose of this site was to provide an open forum for his and his critics' ideas on AI. On this site, which has been assiduously maintained and upgraded since its inception, Kurzweil has frequently responded to the views of some of his critics. In particular, the site contains the entire text of a book—*Are We Spiritual Machines: Ray Kurzweil vs. the Critics of Strong AI*, published in Spring 2002 (Richards, 2002).

One of Kurzweil's respondents in *Are We Spiritual Machines* was William A. Dembski, a mathematician and philosopher and research associate professor at Baylor University. Dembski noted that Kurzweil's aim of reverse engineering the human mind and his descriptions of intelligence and brain function indicate that he is a materialist who believes that "mind must, in some fashion, reduce to matter." Dembski notes that Kurzweil's view aligns with neuroscience, which holds that mind does ultimately reduce to neurophysiology. Dembski observes that many neuroscientists describe ordinary psychology as "folk psychology" as opposed to a revamped psychology grounded in neuroscience. The view is that eventually, "in place of talking cures that address our beliefs, desires, and emotions, tomorrow's healers of the soul will manipulate brain states directly and ignore such outdated categories as beliefs, desires, and emotions" (Dembski, 2002).

Dembski offers a number of interesting arguments against a materialist view of the mind's function. Among them are examples of people with badly damaged brains, such as Louis Pasteur, who continued to function optimally. He asks how one can explain a flourishing intellectual life despite a damaged brain if mind and brain coincide. He also notes that actual neuroscience research is a modest affair and "fails to support materialism's vaulting ambitions" (Dembski, 2002). He then proceeds to note that whereas the goal of neuroscience is to reduce intelligent agency to neurophysiology, the goal of AI is to reduce it to computation. He concludes that cognitive scientists still have the task of showing in what sense brain function is computational.

Kurzweil's lack of concern about "everything else but matter" is reflected in his discussions of consciousness and of ethics. He admits that we really have no idea of what consciousness is: "It's hard even to define what each object or thing is that might be conscious, as there are no clear boundaries. Or maybe there's more than one conscious awareness associated with my own brain and body. There are plenty of hints along these lines with multiple personalities, or people who appear to do fine with only half a brain (either half will do)" (International Society, 2002). He is not concerned with consciousness in his discussions, and he focuses on those portions of the brain structure and neurological activity that can be objectively measured. "It's the difference between the concept of 'objectivity,' which is the basis for science, and 'subjectivity' which is a synonym for consciousness" (Kurzweil, 2001). Because of the fact that we cannot resolve the issues of consciousness entirely through objective measurement and analysis, "there is a critical role for philosophy, which we sometimes call religion" (Kurzweil, 2001). In Kurzweil's view, the question of consciousness is therefore assigned to the nonscientific disciplines and is not an issue he wishes to engage.

If a necessary aim of public discussion about technology development is to promote rather then inhibit critical discussion, then Kurzweil's work in publishing his website and his critics' views has been successful. In its conception, design, and substance, kurzweilai.net affords its users a valuable opportunity to read, consider, and debate a range of issues pertinent to AI development. Although Kurzweil's own lack of concern about dystopic scenarios of the AI future may be disappointing, such concern would be out of alignment with his faith in the inherently meliorative force of science and technology development. In any case, Kurzweil seems to have rekindled public interest in AI and mounted a successful defense of it as a viable, albeit risky, technology.

References

"Algorithm." (2001). *Oxford English Dictionary*. Oxford: Oxford University Press.
Crevier, D. (1993). *AI: The tumultuous history of the search for artificial intelligence*. New York: Basic Books.
Dembski, W. A. (2002). Kurzweil's Impoverished Spirituality. In J. W. Richards (Ed.) *Are We Spiritual Machines: Ray Kurzweil vs. the Critics of Strong AI*. Seattle, WA: Discovery Institute Press. Retrieved September 8, 2002, from < http://www.kurweilai.net/meme/frame.html?main=/articles/art0497.html >.
Ekbia, H. R. (2001, November). *Artificial intelligence at a crossroads*. Paper presented at the Society for Social Studies of Science Conference, Cambridge, MA.
Ekbia, H. R. (2002). *Artificial intelligence: Hype versus hope*. Unpublished doctoral dissertation, Indiana University, Bloomington.
Fahnestock, J. (1998, July). Accommodating science. *Written Communication 15*.
Goldbart, R. C. (1998, April). Scientific writing: Three neglected aspects. *Journal of Environmental Health 60*. Expanded Academic Index, File A57533204.
Inch, E. S., and Warnick, B. (2002). *Critical thinking and communication: The use of reason in argument*. Boston: Allyn and Bacon.
International Society for Complexity, Information, and Design. (2001, July 19). 'Live Moderated Chat: Are We Spiritual Machines?' Retrieved September 11, 2002, from < http://www.kurzweilai.net/meme/frame.html?m=17 >.
Joy, B. (2000, April). Why the future doesn't need us. *Wired 8.04*, 288–245, 248–263.
Kennedy, G. A. (1991). *Aristotle on rhetoric*. New York: Oxford University Press.
Kurzweil, R. (1999). *The age of spiritual machines: When computers exceed human intelligence*. New York: Viking.
Kurzweil, R. (2001). One half of an argument. *Edge*, August 4. Retrieved March 19, 2003, from < http://www.edge.org/3rd_culture/kurzweil/kurzweil_print.html >.
Lanier, J. (2000a). One half of a manifesto. *Edge 74*, September 25. Retrieved March 19, 2003, from < http://www.edge.org/documents/archive/edge74.html >.
Lanier, J. (2000b). Postscript re: Ray Kurzweil. *Edge*, November 20. Retrieved March 19, 2003, from < http://www.edge.org/discourse/jaron_answer.html >.
Miller, S. E. (1996). *Civilizing cyberspace: Policy, power, and the information superhighway*. New York: Addison-Wesley.
Mundy, T. (2000). The edge of science. *Edge 74*, September 25. Retrieved March 19, 2003, from < http://www.edge.org/documents/archive/edge74.html >.
Muska, R. (2000). Created laws and spiritual machines. [Review of *The age of spiritual machines*]. *The Skeptical Inquirer 24*: 56.
Proudfoot, D. (1999). How human can they get? [Review of the book *The age of spiritual machines*]. *Science 284*: 745.
Richards, J. W. (Ed.). (2002). *Are We Spiritual Machines: Ray Kurzweil vs. the Critics of*

Strong AI. Seattle, WA: Discovery Institute Press. Retrieved September 8, 2002, from <http://www.kurweilai.net/meme/frame.html?main=/articles/art0497.htm>.

Shaffer, R. A. (1999). Pundit forecasts portable, praying PCs in *The age of spiritual machines*. [Review of the book *The age of spiritual machines*]. *Fortune* 139, 124.

Turkle, S. (1995). *Life on the screen: Identity in the age of the Internet*. New York: Simon and Schuster.

William H. Dutton 4

OUT OF THE DOT-COM BUBBLE: A NEW OPPORTUNITY FOR INTERNET RESEARCH

Internet Research Before and After the Dot-com Crash

Time and change move fast in the world of information and communication technology (ICT) innovation—leading many pundits to speak of "Internet time." For instance, the dot-com crash at the turn of the century raised the specter of the Internet becoming such a quickly falling star that there would be no point in considering it a subject for long-term social research. Yet it was the almost unrestrained enthusiasm for the Internet just a few years earlier that fueled the unrealistic dot-com boom preceding the crash.

These extremes of optimism and pessimism continue the ongoing debate between utopian and dystopian visions that has characterized the study of technology and people since the 1950s (Mesthene, 1969; Dutton, 1999a). The reality has typically been more muddled, varied, and uncertain than predictions based on either extreme position. Yes, we've seen videotext, the videophone, the paperless office, and other bullish predictions turn into passing fads, so it was not unreasonable to ask if the Internet also might be a more ephemeral technology than was once contemplated. But despite the dot-com crash, growth has continued in the use and capabilities of the Internet and related ICTs, which is evidenced by the continued diffusion of the Internet, the accelerating pace of broadband Internet take up, and the convergence of mobility and the Internet as with the excitement over wireless broadband access, such as with "Wi-Fi."[1]

Almost every sector of society is touched by the ever-expanding options these technologies open for new ways of learning, relaxing, doing business, governing, and carrying out other activities of real value to millions of people. This entails a coevolution of people and social structures in a "network of networks" encompassing an interwoven web of people and technology (Dutton, 1999b). The pervasiveness of networks interconnecting technology and people in everyday life as well as in once-in-a-lifetime decisions convinces me and others that the Internet, the social issues it will raise, and the social research that should address it, are not likely to fade away (Dutton, 1999b; Teich, 2000).

In fact, the contrary is more probable: The dot-com boom tended to deflect attention from social issues and research, whereas the bursting of the bubble has tended to refocus attention on the need to understand users, along with the many interconnected social and economic aspects of technological change (Dutton, 1999b). However, the future of social research on the Internet is not on a deterministic path, and its continued strength is not a fait accompli.

Real developments are occurring, there are changes in perception about the Internet and other new ICTs, and there are many different players, with many different goals and strategies. This "ecology of games" (Dutton, 1995) in which multiple actors interact in fairly complex ways will shape the quite unpredictable outcomes for the Internet, research about it, and the evolution of related public policies. This means Internet researchers should think strategically in order to maintain the significance of this field.

Broadening the Focus of Internet Research

Much past research into the Internet has adopted a narrower, more inward-looking focus than the view outlined above of the Internet as a network of networks. Most centers of Internet studies have a more technical emphasis and a concentration on the development of applications and related technologies. There has been a great deal of research looking historically to the Internet's origins, which has shown its links with the evolution of ICTs in general and with a culture promoting the free exchange of ideas and information (Lessig, 1999). This is of considerable interest as far it goes—but does not generally go far enough in recognizing the full breadth of the Internet as a network of intertwined social and technological networks.

Eli Noam, a leading economist of communication, is fond of saying that social scientists are too often the cheerleaders and not the leaders. I don't think that's entirely right, as many have been among the first to identify the reality behind new technologies, for example how people actually adopt, reject, and use the Internet (Dutton, 1996; Woolgar, 2002). Some were cheerleaders, but many were not and tried to do something else by understanding emerging trends and warning against the kind of hype that preceded the dot-com frenzy (e.g., Dutton, 1999b). This had made everything "e" seem such an unrealistic "slam dunk" success that issues such as the "digital divide" were expected to disappear when the Internet facilitated the ubiquitous availability of ICTs.

We now know that did not happen. The digital divide not only remained, but new divides have emerged over broadband and other ICT innovations. It was the narrowness of the technological vision that led to the common fallacy that confused the fate of dot-coms with the fate of the Internet per se. The dot-com crash was not a failure of the technology. It was a market failure resulting from poor business and financial decision making. It dramatically demonstrated that even magnificent technical and engineering feats do not in themselves translate into innovations in real social settings.

If the dot-com crash means anything, it is that technology cannot be understood without a good understanding of the role played in change processes by people and institutions as well as technology. This lends fresh weight to the need to understand and value research encompassing the social sciences. The Internet's pivotal role in the coevolving web of people and technology means this broad social research focus is essential to any studies of its implications that hope to exert real influence on policy and practice around the world.

However, it is not sufficient just to recognize the need for multidisciplinary research to address the vast range of social and technological factors that can be tied to the Internet. In the past, multidisciplinary teams studying outcomes tied to technology have usually entailed an A-team of scientists and engineers, complemented by a B-team of social scientists. If Internet research is to continue to thrive, there must be only an A-team, with social researchers at its core.

A Framework for Integrating Research about Society and the Internet

Internet studies can draw on a rich tradition of research on the societal implications of ICTs whose roots go back to work on society and technology in the 1950s.[2] Social research on technology has evolved and expanded since then to take account of rapid technological advances. The explosive growth that has made the use of ICTs an intrinsic aspect of everyday life in many countries stimulated much interest in what innovations like the Internet, Web, and other ICTs mean for society as a whole, not just specific sectors within it (Dutton, 1999a; Castells, 2001).

At first, studies of technology and people focused rather deterministically on the impacts of technology on society, for instance, in the emergence of the idea of the "information society" (Bell, 1973). Over time, social research increasingly revealed that technology is inherently social, in that it is designed, produced, and used by people. This shifted attention from technological impacts to an understanding of the underlying processes in which a variety of actors make choices that shape technologies and the outcomes of innovation, as well as being shaped by those outcomes.

I built on this emerging view in directing attention on the "shaping of tele-access" as a means to conceptualize how technical and social choices regulate access to information, people, services, and technology in ways that reconfigure the relative communicative power of different actors in households, communities, and society at large (Dutton, 1999a). Shifts in tele-access—and the relative communicative power of actors—reshapes the consumption, production, utilization, and governance of emerging technologies. I believe this notion offers an integrative framework that can help to draw together the diverse streams of Internet research. It moves attention away from conceptions of "information" as the key element in ICTs toward an appreciation of the significance of "access" and how the Internet's network of networks reshapes access to people, services, and technologies, as well as to information.

In addition to developing more integrative frameworks, it is important for Internet researchers to build a stronger global network focused on social aspects of ICTs. This will be an important step in overcoming some problems with the fragmentation and limited size of this emerging field. Technological producers and users are already organized globally, but social researchers have remained relatively national and regional in their outlooks and networks.

In thinking about the future of Internet studies, individuals clearly have to follow their own stars and focus on what they think is important. At the broader level of a research center or program, thinking more strategically will enhance the likelihood of individual efforts having greater impact and significance. When I became the Director of the Oxford University's Oxford Internet Institute (OII) in the summer of 2002, I was in the fortunate position of being able to formulate and implement such a strategy. I have based this on the vision and agenda outlined above. I hope the following summary of the Institute's plans and progress will assist others to think through their own plans for social research on the Internet.

The Oxford Internet Institute's Social Research Strategy

A Sound Base in the University of Oxford

Oxford University is an ideal home for a multidisciplinary Internet institute. It has a long tradition of innovation; all the colleges at Oxford are interdisciplinary in a true sense—and it can even claim to be a pioneer in this area, as it was one of the first universities to establish a major publishing operation with Oxford University Press. However, Internet Studies is new to Oxford, and much credit for its far-reaching outlook is due to those at the University, particularly the Master of Balliol, Andrew Graham, who originally conceived its ambitious plan to encompass economic, political, institutional, scientific, legal, and other social factors influencing the Internet and its implications for society. Their innovative proposal quickly became a reality through a generous endowment from The Shirley Foundation, augmented by a grant from the Higher Education Funding Council for England.

The OII's physical home is in the heart of Oxford, within Balliol College at 1 St Giles, an early-19th-century building we have internally redeveloped to create a modern Internet center within a traditional setting. Organizationally, we are an independent unit within the University's Social Sciences Division. This enables us to draw on all the University's other colleges and divisions to enrich the work of our own researchers. From this base, we are well positioned to build on the United

Kingdom's lively tradition of scholarly research and debate over the societal implications of technology and to forge partnerships with other researchers in the United Kingdom and around the world.

Focusing on Key Research Priorities

The OII is committed not just to world-class research but also to taking a positive role in the United Kingdom, regionally, and globally in shaping policy, practice, and research on the social implications of the Internet. Four activities are critical to doing this: high quality research; collaboration; "net-working" using the Internet in a myriad of imaginative ways to support our work; and teaching.

In the long term, teaching might be our most important contribution to improving understanding of the Internet. However, we are acutely aware that we cannot address everything at once, because the array of possibilities is enormous. As world-class research will underpin all our teaching and collaborative efforts, our initial priorities have targeted five strategic research focal points: governance, including issues of e-Democracy and e-Government; learning and education across all levels; science and networks; the social role of the Internet in the household, community, including virtual communities, work, commerce, arts, and entertainment; and policy issues that cut across all these social settings. One of the factors in defining these was the people we knew were on board. But we primarily chose areas where particularly critical social implications are at stake, and where we think there is less likelihood of support from commercial and business interests.

In order to build up our own academic resources, we also devoted much early effort to recruiting top-drawer OII and Visiting Professors, Senior Fellows, and researchers, with many appointments affiliated with other University of Oxford Colleges. We believe our appointment in 2002 of Dr Stephen Coleman as Cisco Visiting Professor of e-Democracy, in affiliation with Jesus College, was the first such professorship. We also have established professorships in Internet Governance and Regulation (with Keble College) and in Society and the Internet (with Mansfield College). We are therefore well on our way in building a small academic team of the highest quality. In addition to social scientists, the OII includes individuals with economic, political, institutional, computer science, engineering, legal, and other expertise.

Our governance stream investigates the criteria and processes by which public policy and regulation balance competing values and interests. Plans include a qualitative longitudinal study of how parliamentarians and their staff incorporate ICTs into their roles and a global survey of leading local and national government initiatives in e-Democracy. Collaboration with other digital government research programs and case studies of the role of the Internet in particular political campaigns and elections are also being considered.

The OII has a cluster of scholars interested in innovation in all areas of education and learning using new media, online links, and other emerging e-capabilities. Our first study in this area was of the use of broadband in schools in the county of

Oxfordshire. Close observation of the interactions of teachers, students, and technologies in this broadband environment could develop an understanding of the mechanisms linking the Internet with learning objectives, which could extend well beyond the confines of this case. It also aims to develop proposals that could extend its scope beyond this initial case to different educational contexts around the world. Other initiatives here include a cross-national comparison of educational innovation and investigation into the role of new media in reconfiguring libraries and information services within higher education, including early proposals to study the role of ICTs in such traditional Oxford institutions as the tutorial and collegiate system.

We have vigorously advanced our research activities on the role of electronic networks in the conduct of science. This includes collaboration with Oxford University's Law Faculty to examine how the legal-institutional settings of scientists are likely to influence the incentives for collaboration within and across universities in ways enabled by e-Science and envisioned by its proponents. Discussions are also underway on the formation of a virtual network among the University's researchers involved in the study of e-Science. And interviews have been conducted to understand the extent to which the Internet affects ethical issues about the rights of participants in social science research.

Our main early initiative in studies of electronic media in everyday life has been the development of our Oxford Internet Surveys (OxIS), which will be launched by a large-scale survey of U.K. households that focuses on transnational and local impacts of the Internet. OxIS will be embedded within the World Internet Project, which involves 23 nations in detailed household surveys to help understand how individuals adopt and use the Internet in their everyday lives. This will enable the OII to develop data sets and inquiries that are comparative and cross-national in scope. All these survey efforts will be enhanced by a program of qualitative research, including studies of leading-edge developments, such as "Wi-Fi" and other broadband households, but also studies of less affluent groups using the Internet, such as a study of teenagers involved in producing their own digital radio station.

Issues cutting across the Institute's strategic priorities are being pursued in a variety of ways. Intellectual Property Rights (IPR) and the way standards affect technical choices are among the cross-cutting issues we are studying.

Criteria for Research Activities

Four common dimensions characterize the distinctive nature of all OII research activities. First, we are not wedded to any single methodological or theoretical approach. The OII fosters quantitative as well as qualitative studies, ranging from our survey research on households to ethnographies of scientists. Whether quantitative or qualitative, we foster innovative and critical approaches that question the taken-for-granted assumptions about societal implications of the Internet.

Second, we aim to address a global audience, shaping and informing debate within the United Kingdom and elsewhere. All our projects are assessed in terms of their global significance. We believe it is often by joining analytically sophisticated and richly descriptive studies of local processes, such as the Internet in households or broadband in Oxfordshire schools, that insights emerge that can be communicated and examined in broader global arenas.

Third, our research seeks to use theoretically powerful concepts and frameworks, such as the shaping of access, to integrate the discussion of the huge spectrum of issues and policy dimensions that could fall within our area of inquiry. The impact of OII research will depend less on the number of topics we explore than on the degree to which the concepts and theoretical frameworks we develop can be used across a number of topics by a wide variety of scholars in different settings. This will enable OII research to be empirically anchored in specific cases and settings, while being able to generate insights that reach across different disciplines and contexts of ICT use.

Finally, the OII is committed to pursuing vigorously Oxford University's tradition of independence from government or commercial influence. This will be accomplished not by being distant from government and industry—who also need and value independent, disinterested research—but by developing patterns of support and collaboration that free the OII from being too dependent on any one source of support.

Collaboration

We want to avoid the "trickle down" theory of disseminating social science research: the idea that we publish in journals and pretty soon the wisdom trickles down to users and somehow gets employed in policy and practice. Instead, the OII wants to collaborate directly with people in the policy world and industry, as well as in academe, in a variety of venues. These include the encouragement of visiting research scholarships from industry or government, the organization of policy forums that explore key aspects of policy and practice, such as the implications of broadband on social and economic divides, and the involvement of leaders from business, industry, and the policy community in many of our research efforts.

Oxford has, for hundreds of years, been much more of a networked organization than most other universities. But effective collaboration is still not easy, as at all universities. That is why we always seek to have a unified A-team in which social scientists are equal partners in forging connections across disciplinary boundaries, not the "token" social scientist or evaluation person as has too often happened.

Net-working

Retrofitting 1 St Giles allowed us to think about our use of the Internet in every aspect of our operation, from dissemination of our research and work with partners around the world to designing our library requirements and shared office spaces.

Integrating the Internet into a 19th-century building in a way that fits and works also emphasized the importance of not just pushing new technology for its own sake, but really trying to envelop new technology into best practice. To ensure we exemplify excellence in the use of the Internet, we regard the recruitment of exceptionally qualified technical and Web officers as central to our academic mission, rather than as an administrative overhead.

Teaching

We have put in place an exciting array of short-term and long-range initiatives to make the Institute a magnet for students undertaking studies at all levels at Oxford University. For instance, the first of a planned annual series of Summer Doctoral Programmes is arranged for July 2003. At these, top doctoral students from around the world will receive support for their Internet research from leading scholars in the field as well as from their fellow students. We also hold a variety of open seminars and lectures, as well as experimenting with innovative mechanisms for reaching new audiences through the Internet. Proposals for a paper that could be incorporated within a variety of Master's-level degree programs is being explored as one mechanism to reinforce our multidisciplinary makeup and to support the variety of degree programs already in place at Oxford. In due course, doctoral students will study with OII staff, work on OII research grants, contribute to our research, and be active in teaching at Oxford.

Getting in Touch

The future of the OII is relevant to Internet Studies as a whole, but I believe that many of our strategies are applicable well beyond the Institute. Out of the dot-com bubble has come a new appreciation for the important role that social research could play in shaping the future of communication and society. It is important that social researchers of the Internet seize this newfound recognition to build a stronger base of theory and research from which to shape policy and practice in the years to come.

Notes

This chapter has been developed from the keynote talk at the 2002 AoIR Conference in Maastricht. The author thanks Denise N. Rall for preparing a verbatim transcript of the talk and Malcolm Peltu for his editorial assistance in adapting it for publication in this edited collection.

1. Wireless Fidelity (Wi-Fi) connotes IEEE 802.11a, or b-based technologies that have passed "Wi-fi" certification. They enable wireless broadband Internet access.
2. See Dutton (1999a) for a synthesis of decades of research on ICTs.

References

Bell, D. (1973, 1999). *The Coming of Post-Industrial Society: A Venture in Social Forecasting*. New York: Basic Books.

Castells, M. (2001). *The Internet Galaxy Oxford: Reflections on the Internet, Business and Society*. Oxford: Oxford University Press.

Dutton, W. H. (1995). The Ecology of Games and its Enemies. *Communication Theory*, 5(4), 379–92.

Dutton, W. H. (1996). (Ed.). *Information and Communication Technologies — Visions and Realities*. Oxford: Oxford University Press.

Dutton, W. H. (1999a). *Society on the Line: Information Politics in the Digital Age*. Oxford and New York: Oxford University Press.

Dutton, W. H. (1999b). The Web of Technology and People: Challenges for Economic and Social Research. *Prometheus*, 17 (1), 5–20.

Lessig, L. (1999). *Code and other Laws of Cyberspace*. New York: Basic Books.

Mesthene, E. G. ([1969] 2000). The Role of Technology in Society. In A. H. Teich, *Technology and the Future* (pp. 61–70). Boston: Bedford/St. Martin's Press.

Teich, A. H. (2000). *Technology and the Future*, Eighth Edition. Boston: Bedford/St. Martin's Press.

Woolgar, S. (2002). (Ed.). *Virtual Reality? Technology, Cyberbole, Reality*. Oxford, Oxford University Press.

CONSTRUCTS IN THE STORM

The following is based on a talk given in the Second AoIR conference, the University of Minnesota campus, October 2001. That conference was overshadowed by the events of the preceding September, etched in public memory as 9/11. I started my talk then commenting that the times were scary. I am updating my comments for the purposes of this chapter during the first week of what is proving to be the second Gulf War, and may yet spread into something even more momentous. In any event, it is already just as scary. Ostensibly, neither consequence seems auspicious for theoretical work, or thoughtful research. Yet, on second thought, these conflict-ridden, stormy times are somehow quite fitting. The storm outside is echoed by the storm within the domain of those interested in the Internet and computer-mediated communication. Can one conjure up a more appropriate backdrop for a discussion of a medium conceived and constructed in discord?

 Many think of the Internet and public networks in utopian terms. The communal, reaching-out, democratizing potentials of the Net have ignited many an imagination. Yet the Net was actually conceived by military planners in the context of wars and conflict. It has been led and funded by interesting combinations of profit and power motivations, probably much removed from the rosier views of optimists.

The Net is a land of paradoxes. Tensions between extremes abound.

Our newspapers had the current (2001) war going on in Afghanistan codenamed "infinite justice." As researchers, perhaps we can strive for "infinite inquisitiveness?" What will the inquisitive quest seek?

The storm I refer to in the title to this talk has had many clouds in the arenas of the Net, perhaps echoing real world claps of thunder. We've weathered quite a few tempests in the last few years. The blizzards in question include the blossom and burst of the Internet and e-commerce stock bubble, known to one and all.

But even in our own, intellectual front yard, there have been major earthquakes. Excitement with the Internet in the early 1990s probably went overboard with overly optimistic predictions. Thus, the end of the printed book was promised "very soon now." Universities, and perhaps other forms of traditional structured education as well, were said to be on their way out. Business as we've known it was eulogized. In fact, all mediators were said to be made obsolete by the great power of "disintermediation." These include the rise and fall of fascination with technological determinism theory, beliefs, and oratory. Remember, each had its turn, the short-term excitements over "content is king," and over "pull is over, now push is the way to go," then, most recently, the "wireless" wave crowned by the bandwidth mega-auctions. Instead of disintermediation we have rediscovered "reintermediation," have we not? We focused on gender gaps as being major role players in Internet use. The belief, theory, and focus on age gaps as major forces in understanding Internet use, and the focus on the socioeconomic digital divide.

So the Internet may not have proven up to Wall Street's expectations—or maybe just failed the inflated fantasies of some misled investors. Developments in the first two or three years of the new century indicate that the old economy was and still is rather shaky too, so not all the blame is on the ephemerality of new economy promises. The Internet itself has also evolved in nature, course, and control. Much of the early pioneering flavor has evaporated. The Internet is more corporate, more mainstream, less experimental. But it is also ever growing, ever more central to ever more people and their lives. Therefore deserving of attention, despite the dizzying switchbacks along the "information highway."

Such switches are not so surprising. I would even suggest that swinging between rhetorical extremes is both endemic and natural to our field. Back in the early 1980s we witnessed religious wars about the "best" operating system, between Mac aficionados and IBM PC devotees. I use the term "religious wars" judiciously, following a classic article that spoofed the vehemence, intensity, fervor, and orthodoxy invested in choosing and defending the choice of computer. This, for those who have been around long enough, was Umberto Eco's essay on the Mac as Catholicism, DOS as Protestantism, and Unix's Talmudic/Jewish nature. In the 1990s, the same sort of pietistic polemic polarity appeared in the shape of Eric Raymond's Cathedral and Bazaar metaphors surrounding open source issues.

So our field may have a tradition of overstating theoretical positions. It also has a history of interesting reversals. Take the "Negroponte Switch," for example. This is the classic antitechnological determinism observation. Dredging up old patent application forms Negroponte reminded us how tenuous a grasp the technological view on technology may be. That which was originally thought of as destined to be wired would be wireless, and vice versa. Both Marconi and Bell misinterpreted the core contribution of the respective technologies they constructed. They predicted uses of terrestrial phone lines for public one-to-many communication, and over-the-air radio for intimate, one-to-one contacts. Actually, during most of the 20th century, things turned out transposed—phones were the quintessential intimate technology while radio heralded mass audiences. And then, a century or more later, wired and wireless are switched again. Wireless and cellular beepers and phones and personal computers vindicated Marconi's original forecast. Cable television finally bears out Bell's projection.

I would like to suggest an antidote to a fashionable surge and fade-out of opinions that are sharper than their support. Instead of positions or right beside these positions, I wish to propose some *constructs* to guide our thinking and study. These constructs, I hope, should shed some light on what can be investigated, and suggest manners to do so. Constructs can suggest what should be asked. And they can illuminate, so I hope, a view into the future of our field. In the following, I will list several such constructs as a proposed shorthand map of communication-related phenomena represented by the Net.

I propose focusing on several defining qualities of *communication* on the Net: multimedia, synchronicity, hypertextuality, packet switching, interactivity, logs and records, simulation and immersion, and the value of information. To me, these qualities capture what is, or can be, different, new and intriguing about Net-based communication. None of these qualities is mandated or necessarily realized by any one instance of behavior or application on the Net. None is necessarily good or bad. However, Net-based communication offers up these constructs as options to think about, and highlights these dimensions and areas of potential change. Each of these constructs alone, and taken together, essentially "beg the questions" research should try to answer.

Multimedia/MultiSense

For its audience, the Net is a breed apart. It is clearly not printed matter, televised, staged, filmed, or broadcast. It can be a new sensory experience: Text, voice, pictures, animation, video, virtual-reality motion codes, tactile output, even smell, are all already being conveyed on the Net. What journalists used to call "the news hole" has simply expanded into an unprecedented potential sensory vastness. It could be embarrassing to be a designer on the Web nowadays. As far as technology is concerned, anything can go. Much does, and, by the time it does, it could be overshadowed by new capabilities. The Net's capacity for addressing senses far surpasses that of any other medium. The CMC medium serves less than ever before in a constraining, or guiding role. Instead, the medium affords rather than limits. Technological determinism? I suspect not. More often than not, affordances are ignored, and traditional modes are perpetuated, even on the Net. But the avalanche of technology brings with it an embarrassment of riches: we can convey more cues than we actually need. Remember how early research about the Net was driven by a set of "reduced cues" hypotheses? The convergence of broadband and new output devices is about to turn this around. We may even end up studying a set of "cue overload" hypotheses instead.

Switching: The Topology of Communication

The organizing principle for routing traffic ("switching") has always been a focus of social, behavioral, and communication research. This is the description of how messages get pointed to their intended recipients, queued in delivery, and ordered in the use of the available channels. Route switching is, for example, a cornerstone of telephony and the social reality it avails. In mass media research the notion of switching was called "gatekeeping." In interpersonal communication research, much is made of "turn taking." In political science, switching is one way to view the distribution and management of power and control.

On the Net, because of historical reasons perpetuated by the discovery of other functions, the organizing principle is to have limited or reduced organization and central control. Packet switching was understood by some as deliberate anarchy. Packet switching was in fact invented to reduce centralization and the vulnerabilities it entails. In packet switching, the message keeps its own gate, carries its own homing device. The Net treats censorship as noise and is designed to work around it. Most other (and all earlier) communication is or was either route directed (I talk to you, she broadcasts at us) or (at least) misdirected (he eavesdrops, they try to block transmission). By contrast, much of the Net is designed to be route oblivious. Instead, it is packet switched.

The technical fact of packet switching has content, social, and sender-and-receiver implications. It affects the kind of legislation that can be imposed on the Net, determines much of the pricing of information, and plays a big role in restructuring the social relations of "Netizens," or citizens of the Net.

The Elasticity of Synchronicity

All communication is temporally sensitive. How fresh is communication when it is "served"? How quickly does it go stale? Are we becoming an impatient species? Do we have preferences for the old, tried, and true? Naturally, communication is synchronous, but how likely are we to want to communicate asynchronously? The phone has its answering machine. Theater has film and video. TV has VCR. Even interpersonal communication has memories.

The Net stretches the edges of the synchronicity continuum. Communication on the Net travels at unprecedented speed. It also can be consumed at unprecedented delays. Messages have time stamps, accurate to one hundredth of a second. A whole generation now knows what "GMT" stands for. Bandwidth has become the new gold. Archives confront us with the possibility and threat of longer memories. Remember the surprise value in dredging up White House electronic mail records during "IranGate"? Witness the use of Usenet logs in various court cases.

Communication used to be segregated between the immediate and the delayed. The Net seems to stretch the temporal overlaps and discrepancies between time zones. Interpersonal communication, once either face-to-face or time delayed, can now be both at once. For instance, there are amazing time warps introduced by discussion groups, videoconferencing, IRC, MUD/MOOs, and so on. All of this makes synchronicity both a process and an effects concern.

Is Communication Linear? Hypertextuality

Large parts of the net are nonlinear. The Web was designed to highlight a reality based on many interconnected little pieces. Its manifesto is about content being "loosely linked." Hypertext is not just a data structure, it is an ideology. The "shackles" of linearity can be shed. Linearity has traditionally bound communication into a procrustean bed of predetermined order and a tyranny of writer over reader. Because of hypertext, neither author nor document or genre structure hold that much authority any more. The reader-audience member-receiver shoulders a lot more responsibility now. The World Wide Web is hypertextual, as is the special structure of threads that organize Usenet. The hypertext idea has been with us since before print. Religious scripture, political tracts, musical pieces, and other content have been composed in nonlinear fashion for centuries. But hypertext has come so much closer to becoming the dominant content structure that it deserves to become a focus of communication research. Nonlinearity can affect rhetoric, perception, modes of thinking, degrees of understanding, culture, and its institutions. Does it?

Interactivity

By interactivity, I mean the extent to which communication reflects back on itself, feeds on and responds to the past. Interactivity is the degree of mutuality and reciprocation present in a communication setting. The term interactivity is widely used to refer to the way content expresses contact, and communication evolves into community.

Communication on the Net serves to highlight the role of interactivity. It can be consciously "programmed in" or kept out. Interactivity is behind the issues of moderated or unmoderated virtual groups. Interactivity is an operating force in the allure of virtual communities in forums, IRC and MUDs. Good choices and crafty implementation of interactivity are often the difference between successful and failing Web sites. But do the genres residing on the Web live up to the promise of interactivity? Are there costs to interactivity, or is it all rosy? When and where is interactivity achievable, and when should it be avoided?

Logs and Records

Web use leaves behind a variety of written tracks in the form of copies of what was said, but also quantitative, orderly time-stamped meticulously byte-counted logs of who accessed or sent what, to or from whom, when and whence. These logs and records have been enhanced, recognized, and pounced on by marketers. As is the case with rich sensory appeals (multisense), intricate nonlinear context structures (hypertext), ornate and ingenious organizational designs (packet switching), sophisticated temporal relations (elastic synchronicity), and choices regarding interactivity—exploitation of the data that are collected in logs is a matter of choice. There are serious issues of privacy and autonomy involved. The logs, records, and tracks are unprecedented in magnitude.

Never before have so many data points been available, at such a detailed level of granularity, about the behavior of so many people. Logs can be a nightmare in terms of individual rights. They also can be a dream for the researcher who believes in the value of unobtrusive measuring and study. Either way, they are an important and unique characteristic of networked communication.

Simulation and Immersion

Both the research and training fields know about the opportunities hidden in simulation. Learning and investigation can be done in real life, but often are just as useful if done in artificial environments that imitate reality. Computer mediation provides numerous occasions for simulation. The sensation of immersion that is part of the fascination of CMC in general can be put to very good use in the form of simulation. The online gaming industry has recognized this. Marketing, educational, persuasive, and political uses of simulation are sure to follow.

Value of Information and Privacy

CMC is about the flow of information, its exchange, and the acts of sharing it. While technological arrangements ease the flow and make for an "information wants to be free" atmosphere, increasingly, we are discovering barriers. Often, the flow of information prefers making money for those producing it over being free. At other times, the free flow of information is curtailed as people or organizations would rather it not flow at all. Privacy (another term for less than free flow of information) is considered in some cultures and legal settings to be an inalienable right.

The tension is between expensive production and cheap dissemination of this unique "thing" called information. At one and the same time there are vast markets, legal arrangements and norms and traditions regarding ownership and transmission of information, as well as concomitant powerful human tendencies to spread information (gossip, give and take advice, eavesdrop, imitate, etc.). So, will it be Time/Warner or Napster, Bertellsmann, or Gnutella? One central determinant in this tug-of-war is and will be the subjective positions we take vis-à-vis information. How do we value information? Do we instinctively treat information as a public or as a private good? Is its induced value high or low?

To summarize: I proposed the constructs of multimedia, synchronicity, hypertextuality, packet switching, interactivity, logs and records, simulation, and immersion, and the value of information as compass points in the study of the Net. Let me repeat that none of these is necessarily realized, optimized, or maximized by any one instance of behavior or application on the Net. Furthermore, none of these constructs is value laden. No claim is made that either is necessarily good or bad. However, Net-based communication evokes these concepts, and offers them up for designer, participant, and onlooker. Understanding these dimensions is important for the evolution of systems, norms, scholarship, and critique. These constructs are crucial for scholars. I propose that these dimensions are the communication-specific stepping-stones we need to climb to seriously examine behavior and consequences in and of CMC.

Three important observations: First, some of these proposed qualities (multimedia, hypertextuality, packet switching, synchronicity, interactivity, logs and records) have an engineering nomenclature "sound." Engineering, indeed, is their origin. Not surprisingly, much of "Net culture," perhaps more than other cultures, is influenced by engineering. Maybe this is an echo of the (virtual?) reality that re-dredged McLuhanistic rhetoric, but the sense in which I use each of these terms is removed from the original, engineering-technological intent. This is one way to conceptualize the role of communication research with the Net: fortify unidimensional engineering concepts with social science thinking and study.

Second, and perhaps related to this, is the inviting empiricism inherent in Net behavior. Not only does it occur on a computer, communication on the Net leaves tracks to an extent unmatched by that in any other context—the content is easily observable, recorded, and copied. Participant demography and behaviors of consumption, choice, attention, reaction, learning, and so forth, are widely captured and logged. Anyone who has an opportunity to watch logs of WWW servers, and who is even a little bit of a social scientist, cannot help but marvel at the research opportunities these logs open.

Third, what aspects of the Net can we study? Almost everything. The same things we studied before and more. Each of the qualities outlined above deserves descriptive scrutiny to establish to what extent it is present. As dependent variables, we would be interested in what brings about optimal levels of each (e.g., how do you get the most interactive group discussion, what causes a preference for synchronicity, etc.). How does each perform as an independent or intervening variable?

In recent years, we have been attempting to apply these concepts to empirical situations and opportunities in the course of our research. These research efforts, conducted with doctoral students and other colleagues, are my humble effort to mine the theoretical hints folded inside the constructs I just surveyed. Among other efforts, we look at simulations in the study of the subjective value of information.

The Subjective Value of Information

Numerous voices in both the public and intellectual arena have expressed the sentiment best captured in the slogan "information wants to be free." This view has been related to different incarnations of information: operating systems, software, business information, news, or academic knowledge. The value of information is a major underpinning of the importance and the dynamics of the Net. The implications of the "information wants to be free" position, as well as its critiques vary from political ideology through novel business models to an upheaval in the established order of academe. The term "Free" means different things in different contexts. It includes arguments against copyright law, in favor of collaborative development of software or support for unmitigated proliferation of content, often using information as attention grabbing inducements ("information freebies"). The evolution of media that erase the distinction between author and audience accelerate these notions of free information. Of course, the popular "information wants to be free" slogan cannot be evaluated apart from the fact that producing, manipulating, and searching information can be very costly. The issue is not just philosophical: business and markets promise and perils have fluctuated widely around the divergent conception of the value of information.

Information is costly to produce, but very cheap to reproduce. It is therefore difficult to assess its value. There are three ways to assess the value of information: Normatively, realistically, and subjectively. Whereas user utility should be the base for calculating the price of information, utility varies by person and circumstance. Information is an "experience good," the value of which is revealed only after use. Normative and realistic methods are ex post and consequently inappropriate for evaluating information content. We are, therefore, focused on the subjective value of information.

We try to measure the value of information, as well as manipulate and investigate the propensity to share information in a series of simulations and experiments.

- When do individuals tend to share information? What is it, in the communication context, that encourages or inhibits information sharing?
- When and why do groups share information?
- What is the topology of information sharing? Is it hublike (with everyone communicating with everyone) or is it focused?
- Is networked information sharing efficient?
- How do group crises affect information sharing?
- Which (what) information gets shared?

We construct networked settings in which, in the context of an ostensible business game, players are pressed to "need" information, and offered chances to buy, sell, share, or ask for shared information. Empirically, we focus on disintermediation, Willingness to Purchase, that is the highest amount you will agree to pay, and Willingness to Accept, that is the lowest amount you are willing to accept in exchange for information. The ratio of WTP/WTA is a long-standing focus of study. One main finding is that ownership matters. And the perception of ownership can be manipulated by communication arrangements.

In Rafaeli and Ravid (2001; 2003) we present a broad conceptual map of our project. It encompasses over 25 characteristics and 40 links. Such a broad research program can be approached either reductively or broadly. We have chosen to cast as wide a net as possible to study this issue in the broadest possible sense. There are numerous appropriate levels of analysis: individual, individual and group, the group, and of course varying analyses of inter- and intragroup communication. In Rafaeli and Raban (2003) we describe an individual level simulation and report some findings regarding the subjective value of information.

We found that group, synchronous, distributed Java-based simulations are both feasible and useful for gaming and management simulation processes in both learning and research capacities (Ravid and Rafaeli, 2000; Rafaeli, Raban, Ravid, and Noy, 2003). Moreover, we found that online simulations offer a unique opportunity to study the message, the individual, dyads, and teams as units of analysis. As we have run the simulations and collected data on many dozens of teams with hundreds of participants, we are interested in harvesting group and team-related research opportunities presented by this simulation.

Several fairly reliable outcomes have been repeatedly uncovered when groups or teams are engaged in supply chain management tasks. Reliably across repeated runs, the game results in negative feedback and time delays in communication that cause oscillation, amplification and unrealistic decisions made in the group level (echoing earlier work in the field). Players' excitement and motivation fuel learning, group and team pressure rise very rapidly. Under these stimuli, we measured and reported the tendencies of individuals to share information, and the variability of knowledge sharing at the group level. As we have controlled experimental settings, we report the differences found between performance and behavior patterns under conditions with and without access to electronic mail.

Team sharing of information is related to team and task characteristics, as well as communication setting modalities. Increased and improved information sharing enriches both the team and the organization. Information sharing helps team members' understanding of the organization and participation. A local instance of these connections is the parallelism in team discussion affecting the efficiency and amount of information sharing, which in turn both affects and is affected by work habits.

Summary

In summary, our approach attempts to untangle the technological determinism limitation by examining the broad and complex interconnecting effects of social behavior in virtual communities. We try to take the broadest possible view by incorporating views of the effects of group structure, and the nature of both the task and communication process and modality. As the Net is still in its infancy, I believe these constructs can point the direction for quite a few research programs yet to evolve.

Bridging back to the real world turbulence with which I opened: reminisce on communication diets during the "first" (?) Gulf War, and contrast with today. That war was dubbed "the first cable TV" war. CNN was the novel medium of choice. Audience research as we knew it in the late 20th century may have been the appropriate mode of thought and inquiry for that era. During that same war, some of us tuned old shortwave radios to pull in news from afar. And, at the other end of technology/history spectrum, that war already had its first online "bloggers" (though not called that yet, e.g., Werman, 1993). The events of early 2003 are already termed by some to be the first "Internet war." What I have proposed here is that we think about and critique the new communication realities and opportunities through these unique communication and Net-appropriate lenses of senses addressed, time and synchronicity, linearity in reporting and discussing, interaction, logs, simulation, and value of information.

References

Rafaeli, S. & Raban, D. (2003). Experimental investigation of the subjective value of information in trading. *Journal of the Association of Information Systems* (available from < http://jais.isworld.org >)

Rafaeli, S., Raban, D., Ravid, G., & Noy, A. (2003). Online Simulation in Management Education about Information and its Uses, in Charles Wankel and Robert Defillipi, *Rethinking Management Education for the 21st Century*, Information Age Publishing. (available from < http://sheizaf.rafaeli.net/publications/EducatingManagersSimulations20030210 RRRN.pdf>).

Rafaeli, S., & Ravid, G. (2003). Information sharing as enabler for the virtual team: an experimental approach to assessing the role of electronic mail in disintermediation. In *Information Systems Journal*, 13.

Rafaeli, S., & Ravid, G. (2001). Research through online simulation of team coordination, communication, and information sharing, INFORMS Section on Group Decision and Negotiation and EuroGDSS Group Decision and Negotiation 2001 (available from < http://sheizaf.rafaeli.net/publications/gdn2001.pdf>).

Ravid, G., & Rafaeli, S. (2000). Multi Player, Internet and Java Based Simulation Games: Learning and Research in Implementing a Computerized Version of the "Beer-Distribution Supply Chain Game". Paper presented at the Web-based Modeling and Simulation WEBSIM 2000, San Diego, CA.

Werman, Robert. (1993). *Notes from a Sealed Room: An Israeli View of the Gulf War*. Carbondale: Southern Illinois University Press.

Susan C. Herring 6

ONLINE COMMUNICATION: THROUGH THE LENS OF DISCOURSE

Data in Search of a Method

Online communication is easy (almost too easy) to collect, be it postings to international newsgroups, e-mail exchanges, chat logs or blog entries. Such data are a potentially rich source of insight into human behavior. Yet, for all their ready availability, the cognitive, cultural, expressive, political, and social meanings of online data are not transparent; structured methods and theoretical frameworks are necessary in order to analyze them. What methods and theories are most appropriate to extract patterns and insights from computer-mediated text?

When I first became interested in researching computer-mediated communication (CMC) some 13 years ago, I turned to discourse analysis for methodological inspiration. As a linguist, I knew that the study of discourse—or what Rice and Gattiker (2000) call the "microprocesses of human communication"—offered tried and true methods for analyzing spoken and written communication. It seemed only natural to extend this approach to discourse on the Internet. Yet, as I soon learned, the academic fields with which discourse analysis has been most closely associated—linguistics, psychology, and sociology—tend not to theorize about technologically mediated communication, and their purists discourage the study of "popular" cultural phenomena (as the Internet is sometimes considered) as less interesting or worthwhile than traditional problems in each field. As a result, relatively little methodological guidance can be found in mainstream discourse analysis literatures for researchers seeking to analyze CMC.

In an effort to bridge this gap, in the mid-1990s I began adapting discourse analysis methods to the study of computer-mediated interaction.[1] The resulting paradigm, computer-mediated discourse analysis (CMDA), is a language-focused specialization within the broader interdisciplinary study of computer-mediated communication (Herring, 1996, 2001, in press). CMDA differs from other forms of discourse analysis in that its descriptive and interpretive apparatus crucially takes into account the technological affordances of CMC systems. Moreover, its methodological "toolkit" is customized to address common phenomena in CMC, and its analyses are socially, culturally, and historically situated in the larger Internet context. At the same time, CMDA shares with other forms of discourse analysis the theoretical premise that choice of word and expression is potentially significant, beyond the requirements of lexicon and grammar. It seeks to identify patterns in language structure and use that may have been produced unconsciously, yet shed light on broader phenomena such as decision making (Condon & Cech, 1996), gender ideology (Herring, 1999), cultural identity (Paolillo, 1996), and the social construction of knowledge (Paulus, 2003).

This essay provides an overview of CMDA.[2] After describing the methodological underpinnings of the approach, it illustrates how computer-mediated text appears when viewed through the lens of discourse analysis. It does this by advancing observations about a sample e-mail message that I received in June 2000, in preparation for the first conference of the Association of Internet Researchers, at which I delivered a version of this essay as a keynote presentation. I conclude by discussing a challenge currently faced by the CMDA research paradigm: the analysis of multimedia messages.

The CMDA Paradigm

In the most general sense, any analysis of computer-mediated text can be considered computer-mediated discourse analysis. In this broad sense, CMDA is employed by researchers in a range of disciplines including anthropology, communication, education, library and information science, linguistics, management, rhetoric, sociology, and women's studies, although they may not call what they do CMDA. The linguistic approach described here is further characterized by an empirical methodological orientation and a focus on language-related behaviors.

Methodological Orientation

CMDA, like other forms of discourse analysis, can be considered a subtype of content analysis (Bauer, 2000) that seeks to extract patterned regularities from text, and in which the units of analysis are elements of computer-mediated language (letters, words, sentences, messages, turns, exchanges, threads, archives, Web pages, etc.). Beyond this, CMDA approaches vary: they can be qualitative or quantitative; case studies or corpus-based; and the data can be naturalistic or produced in experimental settings. The linguistic variant of CMDA tends to draw its coding categories and research questions from linguistic discourse analysis, for example, Conversation Analysis, Text Linguistics, Critical Discourse Analysis, Interactional Sociolinguistics, and Pragmatics (see Herring, in press, for a fuller discussion), although it is also common for researchers to allow the phenomena of interest to emerge from the data themselves, in what is sometimes called the grounded theory approach (Glaser & Strauss, 1967). CMDA may be supplemented with surveys, interviews, ethnographic observation, historical/comparative analysis, sociopolitical criticism, and the like. However, such methods do not in and of themselves constitute CMDA, unless of course they involve the analysis of computer-mediated text.

In my own research, I have found it useful to specify two types of interpretive apparatus, which can be considered part of the methodology of CMDA. The first is a classification scheme for contextual variables that potentially account for variation in CMC (Herring, under review). These variables are of two broad types: technological and situational.

Technological Variables

- synchronicity
- message-by-message versus keystroke-by-keystroke transmission
- size of message buffer
- persistence of transcript
- channels of communication (text, audio, video, graphics)
- anonymous messaging
- automatic filtering
- etc.

Situational Variables

- participation structure (number of participants; public or private, etc.)
- participant characteristics (demographics; experience, etc.)
- setting
- purpose
- topic
- tone
- norms (of participation, behavior, language use)
- linguistic code (language; writing system, etc.)
- etc.

The second interpretive apparatus is the operationalization of the concepts of interest in terms of specific discourse features (Herring, in press). Suppose a researcher is interested in determining whether an online communication environment is "empowering" to participants—what kinds of discourse behavior should she look for as evidence of "empowerment"? As in other forms of content analysis—particularly if the goal is to quantify the results—it is essential to define precisely (and argue for, in case it is not obvious) what "counts" as empowering behavior.

Language-related Behaviors

Language, even written language, is very rich. Text producers make numerous choices (mostly unconscious) regarding word selection and grammatical expression, depending on their purpose, their audience, and their linguistic and rhetorical skills. When confronted with computer-mediated text, the researcher must decide which features to analyze. Language communicates at multiple levels: structural (form), semantic (meaning), interactional (conversation management), and social (activities and functions). Some specific phenomena associated with each level are listed below.[3]

Structure
typography, spelling, word choice, sentence structure, message organization, etc.

Meaning
of symbols, words, utterances, exchanges, etc.

Interaction
turn-taking, topic development, back-channels, repairs, etc.

Social Function
identity markers, humor and play, face management, conflict, use and abuse of power, norm articulation and enforcement, etc.

The following section illustrates how linguistic features at each level can potentially reveal information of a nonlinguistic nature.

An Example of CMDA

Consider the following e-mail message sent to me by one of the conference organizers regarding the scheduling of a keynote presentation and a workshop I had agreed to give at the first Association of Internet Researchers Conference. (The message is used with the permission of the author.)

Date: Thu, 1 Jun 2000 10:03:13 -0500
To: HERRING SUSAN <herring@uta.edu>
From: Nancy Baym <nbaym@ukans.edu>
Subject: Re: keynote scheduling

HI Susan, the last day is Sunday and we're having no keynoters at all, so not to worry about that. Appreciate your flexibility, and expect we'll be able to work within such lax parameters! Plenary topic and title sound great, as does the workshop idea (you might want to call that one gender and the internet, just to hit the broader population a bit). Look forward to meeting you f2f and will stay in touch as things progress,
Nancy

A number of observations can be made about this message, which I selected as a typical example of my professional e-mail correspondence at the time. In an actual discourse analysis, we would probably not restrict ourselves to such a small sample of data, but for the purpose of illustration a single e-mail message will serve.

A first step is to apply the classification scheme presented above to the sample message. For the list of technological variables, this yields the following values:

Technological Variables

- asynchronous
- message-by-message transmission
- unlimited message buffer
- persistent (must be deleted or will remain)
- text only
- anonymous messaging not readily available from sender's university account
- filtering may or may not be available (depends on e-mail system)

These values would be the same for most messages sent from university e-mail accounts, however, and as such are not likely to explain much of interest about the message. More potentially explanatory in this case are the values for the situational variables:

Situational Variables

- One-to-one; private; real identities
- Sender and receiver are white, female, 35–45; native speakers of U.S. English; experienced e-mail users; professors and CMC researchers; S is senior to N; S and N have e-mailed before but never met face-to-face
- Setting is academic (messages are exchanged between university accounts)
- Purpose is communication re: upcoming conference to which S is an invited speaker
- Topics are scheduling S's presentation and title of workshop S has agreed to give before the conference
- Tone is professional yet friendly

- Norms (of academic e-mail in the United States) are semiformal, polite
- Code is written U.S. English; ASCII text

Of particular interest are the participant characteristics and the purpose/topic of the message, since these are specific to the exchange in question. We might expect these circumstances to be reflected in discourse choices that set this message apart from other e-mail messages.

Let us proceed by considering the *structural* properties of the message. The accurate spelling, grammatically well-formed sentences, and varied and sophisticated vocabulary (e.g., "lax parameters") reveal that N is an educated writer, and probably a native speaker, of English. Moreover, the message is well organized, following the basic e-mail message schema described in Herring (1996): Greeting-Message Body-Closing. At the same time, the style of the message is somewhat informal, as indicated by the casual greeting "HI," the abbreviation "f2f," and the repeated ellipsis of subject pronouns and articles (e.g., "Plenary topic and title sound great"), lending the message a "telegraphic" feel. This, taken together with the fact that the greeting and the message body are run together without a paragraph break and the fact that the word "HI" contains an uncorrected typo, suggests that the sender was in somewhat of a hurry or otherwise preoccupied.

As an example of analysis at the *meaning* level, let us consider what actions are performed by the propositions of the message. We borrow here from linguistic pragmatics the notion of "speech acts" (Austin, 1962) or what Herring (1996) calls "functional moves." In what follows, the message is broken into propositions in the left column, which are assigned speech act labels in the middle column. The right column labels the macrosegments (cf. Longacre, 1992), or larger functional units, of the message.

Functional Moves

1.	HI Susan,	Greeting	OPENING
2a.	the last day is Sunday...	Explanation	
2b.	so not to worry about that.	Reassurance	ACCEPTANCE OF
3a.	Appreciate your flexibility...	Thanks	S's PROPOSALS
3b.	and expect we'll be able to...	Promise (mitigated)	
4a.	Plenary topic and title sound great...	Evaluation	
4b.	you might want to call that...	Suggestion	REQUEST FOR FUTURE ACTION
5a.	Look forward to meeting you f2f	Assertion (formulaic)	
5b.	and will stay in touch...	Promise (formulaic)	CLOSING
6.	Nancy	Signature	

The macrosegmentation column suggests that the message is task focused and involves negotiation. The speech act column reveals the meaning of each utterance in context: for example, that proposition 3b functions as a promise, although it does not superficially resemble one. It further suggests that the sender is somewhat indirect in communicating her meanings, in as much as the promise must be inferred (rather than being stated directly), and in that the sender uses conventionally indirect speech acts such as politeness formulas. Indeed, an indirect speech act in this message results in a misunderstanding on the part of the receiver, as will be noted below.

To analyze *interaction* we must situate this message in relation to other messages in the same exchange sequence, of which there are a total of four. We may then characterize the exchange structure (cf. Sinclair & Coulthard, 1975) as follows:

Exchange Structure

N (30 May 20:35)	Initiation	[Request time preferences]
S (1 Jun 2:19)	Response	[Suggest preferred times]
N (1 Jun 10:03)	Follow-up/ Initiation	[Approve times/Request modification to workshop title]
N (17 Jul 15:07)	Re-initiation	[Request workshop title + abstract]

This analysis reveals the function of the target message in a longer sequence of messages: as a follow-up to a previous response, and as an initiation of a new exchange. Furthermore, it exposes a breakdown in the expected exchange structure: S doesn't respond to N's 2nd initiation, so N reinitiates her request a month and a half later. Closer inspection reveals the probable reason for S's failure to respond: N's request for a modified workshop title was phrased indirectly, as a suggestion (see proposition 4.b). The problem becomes further apparent when we examine the use of cohesive elements (cf. Halliday & Hasan, 1976) that refer to previous and anticipated messages in the exchange sequence. The message contains several cohesive links to S's previous message ("that"; "your flexibility"; "such lax parameters"; "the workshop"), but only one link that (weakly) suggests a future response ("you might want . . ."). This minimal linkage, in combination with the indirectness of the speech act, does not clearly communicate that a response is expected. Fortunately, the misunderstanding had no adverse consequences beyond requiring N to send a follow-up message.

Finally, although the message is short, it is possible to identify features in it that perform *social functions*. The sender indexes her identity as an Internet-savvy communicator by her use of the abbreviation "f2f." By displaying knowledge of conference conventions, she shows that she is an academic professional, and her choice of topic and assumed authority to influence scheduling decisions reflect her conference organizer role. At the same time, she performs a female identity by attending repeatedly to her addressee's social face. In the terms of Brown and Levinson (1987), she employs both positive politeness ("appreciate," "sound great," "look forward to meeting you," "will stay in touch") and negative politeness ("not to worry"; "you might want"; "a bit"), consistent with research that finds that women (in CMC, as in face-to-face communication) tend to make greater use of linguistic politeness than do men (Herring, 1994; cf. Tannen, 1990). Consistent with this interpretation, power relations are backgrounded: although S is senior to N (S > N) and N is a conference organizer (N > S), N addresses S in an informal, friendly style, as her equal, as has been described for face-to-face female-female interaction (Coates, 1993).

This simple example illustrates how an e-mail message might appear through the eyes of a discourse analyst, and suggests how broader concepts might be operationalized in terms of specific linguistic features. Education level, state of mind, purpose of communication, directness, and social identity can all be read off of computer-mediated text—even from a short message that does not strike one as particularly revealing at first glance.

Of course, an actual analysis would consider a larger sample of data and focus on developing a coherent analysis around a particular research question. The following table lists examples of actual CMDA research.

Table 1: Other CMDA Research

Structure	• Abbreviations as community markers in a social MUD	Cherny, 1999
	• Structural features of private e-mail compared with written memoranda in a workplace setting	Cho, in press
	• Schematic organization of e-mail messages posted to academic listservs	Herring, 1996
Meaning	• Content of Instant Messages exchanged among co-located students in a Swedish computer lab	Hård af Segerstad, 2002
	• Information exchanged in computer-mediated library reference interviews (analysis of questions and responses)	Ford, 2003
	• Collaboration and the social construction of knowledge in a distance education course (speech act analysis)	Paulus, 2003
Interaction	• Effects of medium, task complexity, and number of participants on turn-taking strategies	Condon & Cech, 1996, 2001
	• Topical coherence in recreational and pedagogical Internet Relay Chat (IRC)	Herring & Nix, 1997
	• Agreements and disagreements in a soap opera fan newsgroup	Baym, 1996
Social function	• Expressive use of emoticons in IRC play	Danet et al., 1997
	• Language choice as a marker of ethnic identity among diasporic South Asians on Usenet	Paolillo, 1996
	• Rhetorical mechanisms of online gender harassment	Herring, 1999

Looking to the Future: Interactive Multimedia

Discourse analysis has traditionally been applied to verbal language, whether it be spoken or written. So, too, CMDA has thus far focused primarily on communication of a verbal nature. However, as CMC becomes increasingly multimodal, there is a growing need for systematic methods of analysis to extract pattern and meaning from communication produced by means other than typed text. In particular, images (graphics, photographs, animation, and video) are playing an increasingly important role in interactive media ranging from the World Wide Web to group videoconferencing to 3-D virtual worlds. Discourse analysis can be used to analyze images produced alongside, or in place of, text.

I have recently initiated several research projects that involve the development of methods to analyze images in multimodal CMC. The first is concerned with gender representation in video clips on a professional development Web site; qualitative methods were devised to analyze gestures and movement in the videos (Herring, Martinson, & Scheckler, 2002). The second project concerns gender representation in pornographic Web sites. This study makes use of quantitative content analysis and link analysis methods for Web pages containing mostly photographic images (Herring & Martinson, 2002). Concurrently, research is being conducted into the nature of communication in 3-D virtual worlds that is leading to the development of methods to analyze animated graphics and navigation in three dimensions (Herring, Börner, & Swan, under review).

We draw inspiration in this work from the social semiotic approach to the analysis of images articulated by discourse analysts Gunther Kress and Theo van Leeuwen (1996). Although Kress and van Leeuwen have not yet taken this step, their approach suggests the possibility of integrating methods of visual analysis with methods of textual analysis as part of a unified paradigm. In a similar vein, the not-too-distant future could see the emergence of CMDA techniques to address multimedia CMC, in which a common set of social semiotic principles informs the analysis of computer-mediated text and images.

Acknowledgments

Thanks are due to Nancy Baym for granting permission to use her e-mail message as an example. Zilia Estrada, Courtenay Honeycutt, Anna Martinson, and John Paolillo provided constructive feedback on an earlier version of this essay. Any remaining errors or infelicities are my own.

Notes

1. Other researchers were doing this more or less unconsciously around the same time, as they struggled with similar issues and concerns; see, for example, Baym (1996), Cherny (1995), and Yates (1993, 1996). Ferrara et al. (1991), Murray (1985), and Severinson Eklundh (1986) were pioneers in this regard.

2. For more extensive descriptions of the CMDA approach, see Herring (2001, in press, under review).
3. The choice of which features to focus on depends on one's research interests. For example, Herring (in press) discusses what discourse features one might analyze to address the question of whether a given online group is a "community."

References

Austin, J. L. (1962). *How to Do Things With Words*. Cambridge, MA: Harvard University Press.
Bauer, M. (2000). Classical content analysis: A review. In M. Bauer & G. Gaskell (Eds.), *Qualitative Researching with Text, Image and Sound* (pp. 131–151). Thousand Oaks, CA: Sage.
Baym, N. (1996). Agreements and disagreements in a computer-mediated discussion. *Research on Language and Social Interaction, 29* (4), 315–45.
Brown, P., & Levinson, S. (1987). *Politeness: Some Universals in Language Usage*. Cambridge: Cambridge University Press.
Cherny, L. (1995). The modal complexity of speech events in a social MUD. *Electronic Journal of Communication/La revue électronique de communication, 5* (4). Retrieved June 15, 2001, from the World Wide Web: <http://www.cios.org/www/ejc/v5n495.htm>.
Cherny, L. (1999). *Conversation and Community: Chat in a Virtual World*. Stanford, CA: Center for the Study of Language and Information.
Cho, N. (in press). Linguistic features of electronic mail. In S. Herring (Ed.), *Computer-mediated Conversation*. Cresskill, NJ: Hampton Press.
Coates, J. (1993). *Women, Men and Language*, 2nd ed. London: Longman.
Condon, S. & Cech, C. (1996). Discourse management strategies in face-to-face and computer-mediated decision making interactions. *Electronic Journal of Communication, 6* (3). Retrieved June 15, 2001, from the World Wide Web: <http://www.cios.org/www/ejc/v6n396.htm>.
Condon, S. C., & Cech, C. (2001). Profiling turns in interaction: Discourse structure and function. *Proceedings of the 34th Hawaii International Conference on System Sciences*. Los Alamitos, CA: IEEE Computer Society.
Danet, B., Ruedenberg-Wright, L., & Rosenbaum-Tamari, Y. (1997). Hmmm . . . where's that smoke coming from? Writing, play and performance on Internet Relay Chat. In S. Rafaeli, F. Sudweeks, & M. McLaughlin (Eds.), *Network and Netplay: Virtual Groups on the Internet* (pp. 41–76). Cambridge, MA: AAAI/MIT Press.
Ferrara, K., Brunner, H., & Whittemore, G. (1991). Interactive written discourse as an emergent register. *Written Communication, 8* (1), 8–34.
Ford, C. (2003). *An Exploratory Study of the Differences between Face-To-Face and Computer-Mediated Reference Interactions*. Unpublished Ph.D. dissertation, School of Library and Information Science, Indiana University, Bloomington.
Glaser, B., & Strauss, A. L. (1967). *The Discovery of Grounded Theory: Strategies for Qualitative Research*. Chicago: Aldine Publishing.
Hård af Segerstad, Y. (2002). *The Use and Adaptation of Swedish Written Language to Computer-Mediated Communication*. Unublished Ph.D. dissertation, Department of Linguistics, University of Göteborg, Sweden.
Halliday, M. A. K., & Hasan, R. (1976). *Cohesion in English*. London: Longman.

Herring, S. C. (1994). Politeness in computer culture: Why women thank and men flame. In M. Bucholtz, A. Liang, L. Sutton, & C. Hines (Eds.), *Cultural Performances: Proceedings of the Third Berkeley Women and Language Conference* (pp. 278–94). Berkeley, CA: Berkeley Women and Language Group.

Herring, S. C. (1996). Two variants of an electronic message schema. In S. Herring (Ed.), *Computer-Mediated Communication: Linguistic, Social and Cross-Cultural Perspectives* (pp. 81–106). Amsterdam: John Benjamins.

Herring, S. C., ed. (1996). *Computer-Mediated Discourse Analysis*. Special issue of the *Electronic Journal of Communication*, 6 (3). Retrieved March 23, 2003, from <http://www.cios.org/www/ejc/v6n396.htm>.

Herring, S. C. (1999). The rhetorical dynamics of gender harassment on-line. *The Information Society*, 15 (3), 151–167.

Herring, S. C. (2001). Computer-mediated discourse. In D. Tannen, D. Schiffrin, & H. Hamilton (Eds.), *Handbook of Discourse Analysis* (pp. 612–634). Oxford: Blackwell.

Herring, S. C. (in press). Computer-mediated discourse analysis: An approach to researching online behavior. In S. A. Barab, R. Kling, and J. H. Gray (Eds.), *Designing for Virtual Communities in the Service of Learning*. New York: Cambridge University Press.

Herring, S. C. (under review). A classification scheme for computer-mediated discourse.

Herring, S. C., Börner, K., & Swan, M. (under review). "There, you're right next to me": Spatial reference in a 3-D virtual world.

Herring, S. C., & Martinson, A. (2002). *Diversity and choice in Web-based pornography*. Paper presented at the Annual Society for the Study of Social Sciences Conference, Milwaukee, November 9, 2002.

Herring, S. C., Martinson, A., & Scheckler, R. (2002). Designing for community: The effects of gender representation in videos on a Web site. *Proceedings of the 35th Hawaii International Conference on System Sciences*. Los Alamitos: IEEE Press.

Herring, S. C., & Nix, C. G. (1997, March). *Is "serious chat" an oxymoron? Academic vs. social uses of Internet Relay Chat*. Paper presented at the annual meeting of the American Association of Applied Linguistics, Orlando, FL.

Kress, G., & van Leeuwen, T. (1996). *Reading Images: The Grammar of Visual Design*. London: Routledge.

Longacre, R. E. (1992). The discourse strategy of an appeals letter. In W. Mann & S. A. Thompson (Eds.), *Discourse Description: Diverse Linguistic Analyses of a Fund-Raising Text* (pp. 109–130). Amsterdam: John Benjamins.

Murray, D. (1985). Composition as conversation: The computer terminal as medium of communication. In L. Odell & D. Goswami (Eds.), *Writing in Nonacademic Settings* (pp.203–27). New York: Guilford.

Paolillo, J. (1996). Language choice on soc.culture.punjab. *Electronic Journal of Communication*, 6 (3). Retrieved June 15, 2001, from <http://www.cios.org/www/ejc/v6n396.htm>.

Paulus, T. (2003). *The Impact of Group Size and Synchronicity on Collaboration and the Social Construction of Knowledge in Online Learning Environments*. Unpublished Ph.D. dissertation, Department of Instructional Systems Technology, Indiana University, Bloomington.

Rice, R. E., & Gattiker, U. E. (2000). New media and organizational structuring. In F. Jablin & L. Putnam (Eds.), *The New Handbook of Organizational Communication* (pp. 544–581). Thousand Oaks, CA: Sage.

Severinson Eklundh, K. (1986). *Dialogue Processes in Computer-Mediated Communication: A Study of Letters in the COM system*. Linköping Studies in Arts and Sciences 6. University of Linköping.

Sinclair, J. M., & Coulthard, R. M. (1975). *Towards an Analysis of Discourse: the English Used by Teachers and Pupils*. Oxford: Oxford University Press.

Tannen, D. (1990). *You Just Don't Understand*. New York: Ballantine.

Yates, S. J. (1993). *The Textuality of Computer-Mediated Communication: Speech, Writing and Genre in CMC Discourse*. Unpublished Ph.D. dissertation, The Open University, UK.

Yates, S. J. (1996). Oral and literate linguistic aspects of CMC discourse: A corpus based study. In S. Herring (Ed.), *Computer-Mediated Communication: Linguistic, Social, and Cross-Cultural Perspectives* (pp. 29–46). Amsterdam: John Benjamins.

CYBERSCIENCE, METHODOLOGY, AND RESEARCH SUBSTANCE

Introduction

This paper builds on an ongoing research project[1] exploring the impact of information and communication technologies (ICT) on academia. We coined the term "cyberscience" (Nentwich, 1999) to depict the gradual move from traditional science (in a wide sense, including the social sciences and the humanities) where computers and telecommunication played only a marginal role toward a new type where, in particular, the Internet seems to have changed the way academics produce knowledge. Inter alia, we put forward a number of initial hypotheses about the qualitative impact of the advent of the new technology on how academics work and what they produce (Nentwich, 2001) and then tested them in a series of interviews.[2] This paper presents both the hypotheses and the empirical evidence gathered from the interviews on how ICT may affect the substance of research. We define substance of research as the essence proper of the research results, devoid of the form or representation.

Conceptually, ICT-induced changes of scholarly communication do not directly influence the substance of research. Rather, there are three possible routes how these changes may impact, namely, first, via changes of the *methodology*, defined here as the sets of rules of "how to" and standardized ways in which researchers carry out research; second, via changes in the *representation* of scientific knowledge (e.g., hypertext); and third, via changes in *work modes*, that is the practical, day-to-day, carrying out of research (e.g., collaboration). In this paper, we focus on the first of these impact routes (methodology). We found the following methodology-related types of impact: outcomes, otherwise impossible; changing initial input side; choice of topic; creative potential; inter- and transdisciplinarity. For reasons of space, we only discuss the first four types in the rest of this chapter.[3]

Outcomes, Otherwise Impossible

ICT is opening up new ways of producing results that could not have been produced before. I am not arguing here that different results are being produced, but that they *are* produced at all. In other words, these outcomes would otherwise be impossible, that is not feasible without ICT. Note that "impossible" has to be understood here in a broad sense including alongside impossibility in principle also practical impossibility because of restrictions of time and money. Obviously, this will be different in the various research fields. Indeed, many of our interviewees said that, in their field, ICT is not capable of producing new results. However, a number of starting points for innovation exist.

Access to data: In many circumstances, projects would not have been carried out if getting the necessary data had not been so easy because of remote, dispersed archives and databases for country or regional comparisons in the social sciences (e.g., panel studies, combining time series and cross-sectoral studies in economics). Comparative research and transnational questions are favored. Another example is the online availability of legal acts, which allows for statistical analysis of growth of legislative activity by political scientists. Furthermore, legal scholars seem to be more inclined to access a text in the original language if access is easy. Also in molecular biology, the combined computing of data of several sequence databases opens up new research questions. The same is true in papyrology, in which cross-database full-text search has led to new activity areas of papyrologists. One interviewee summarized that if a certain piece of information is not available in due time, it cannot be used, while if it is easily available, it will be used and we have to expect that the substance is altered.

Distributed computing enables researchers to fulfill tasks that would take much too long for single computers (or even local clusters of computers). Prime examples come from chemistry and mathematics, other fields may follow suit with a view to compute world-models (e.g., climatology, astronomy, economics).

Software for administering large *Internet surveys* allows for new ways of reaching research subjects around the globe and is transforming and revolutionizing (Bainbridge, 1999, p. 124) the methodologies of the human-related disciplines. Web-based surveys allow for dynamic "on the flight" analysis of the data as the input flows in in digital format.

Shifting the work through time zones may in some cases be a conditio sine qua non for a project to be carried out. An example is the coordination of astronomical projects in which scanning of a particular stellar region needs to be handed over from one observatory to the next.

To sum up, there are scientific results being delivered in the age of cyberscience, which would not have been possible without the help of ICT.[4]

Initial Input Side Changes

One of the most striking features of the emerging mode of doing research in the age of cyberscience is the improvement of direct access to relevant information. It is to be expected that sooner or later almost all written information necessary for research (in most fields) will be available online. Other material such as pictures, numerical data, audio, or video files will follow suit.

The networked environment with its multiplied opportunities to access and filter information may lead to a different starting point or initial input side of the research. Our interviewees almost univocally agreed with the thesis that cyberscience changes these starting conditions. This might be positive and negative at the same time: on the one hand, it may lead to a broader basement of the research. Research will start with more upfront information available and will be more broadly founded in the existing literature as well as empirical data. For instance, literature surveys are likely to be more comprehensive (bibliographies get larger). Another effect mentioned by our interviewees was that this triggers more variation, more selection opportunities, more information turn-around. For instance, it seems that cyberscientists are more inclined to use gray literature, that is not formally published papers and pieces of information found in the World Wide Web. Furthermore, structured full text databases with appropriate search-tools in place may help the researcher "to make a navigation chart, and avoid hazards, waste lands and culs-de-sac" (Davenport & Cronin, 1990, p. 182).

On the other hand, selection opportunities also may be interpreted in a negative way: the input may simply be too much to process adequately (problem of *information overload*). Interviewees pointed at the danger that the scientific products may become less concise and even spoke of the danger of stasis. The online availability of full text may lead to less original work when copying and pasting quotes into a new piece without much value added. Mittelstraß, a philosopher, argues that information technologies will not help much in the humanities (and elsewhere), because too much information, although easily accessible at one keystroke, is rather inhibitory for research than promotional because this is not the way our brain works (1996, 28f.). Therefore he asks for the preservation of the unforeseen, which is crucial for research. We think, however, that Mittelstraß is underestimating the potential of hyperbrowsing through the new electronic information bases (similarly Dicks & Mason, 1998, 6.5).

Furthermore, in the present time of transition, the selection criterion may be *biased toward availability through the electronic networks*. The early cyberscientist may remain negligent of literature and information that is not online. This has two aspects: First, keyword search in databases will let the cyberscientist find only what has been keyworded and indexed. How we will be "browsing" for information is about to change: we will not find any more the "book shelved next to the one we were searching for" because there are no physical shelves any more. In exchange, we might find other resources that were given the same keyword. Second, as regards access to full texts, one may argue that there might be a trend that only the most recent online publications will be quoted, because older publications, in particular from the printed world, "lose" their value in the sense that they may be considered as probably not containing the most recent data, information, arguments in an ongoing discussion (Mueller, 2000, p. 8; Odlyzko, 2000, p. 4). In the longer run, this will be no problem anymore as soon as most of the sources are indeed online. In some disciplines, however, there is a long way to go still and this may lead to blind spots. However, once all the material is available online, information-seeking behavior may change again (Odlyzko, ibid.)

In any case, what the scholar starts with before specifying the proper research question and elaborating the theme is changing (cf. also Bourguignon & European Mathematical Society, 1999, p. 113). In some respect, it is (a bit) less (what has not been keyworded or put online), in another it is (much) more (full-text search).

Impact on Choice of Topic

While in the previous section we did not discuss the choice of the research topic, but only how it will be treated, we may further ask whether different subjects will be chosen because of the different opportunities to organize scientific work. Do networked researchers do different things (ask different questions, treat different subjects) than those not working on the Net? Obviously, in a variety of disciplines, there is the new field of Internet research, that is, research on the Internet with the set of tools and concepts applied in the particular field (e.g., from the point of view of sociology, ethnography, or law). Here, we are instead interested in knowing whether researchers adapt their research topics and questions because of the new opportunities available.

One such mechanism may be the participatory nature of the new medium. The NRENAISSANCE Committee observes that "(q)ualitative benefits have arisen with changes in the nature of the work being done: broader interaction can change the questions being asked" (1994, p. 113). This may trigger interdisciplinarity as well as more collaborative work.

Another reason for changing or "adapting" topics is the structure of the digital information available. Brandtner gives us an example from the humanities:

> If literature science is in a position to revert to manuscripts and autographs, then the focus of research and theory as well as methodology building will shift and reconstitute. (. . .) Under today's conditions, [to provide optimal access to autographs] is only possible with the help of current information technologies. (. . .) The structure of the searchable categories defines also the topics of literature science. (1998, p. 2055 f., transl. MN)

The majority of experts included in our survey acknowledged the potential of the Internet to influence the choice of subject (and perhaps also the choice and perception of new/different methods). Although only philosophers hold that their choice of topic is not at all influenced by the new media, in all other fields the opinion was either univocally in favor of this effect or at least partly in favor. The reasons mentioned were the following: that new horizons are opened up, in particular, with regard to hot issues in related fields; that one is more up-to-date about what is going on in one's own field and what others are currently doing (orientation effect; this may avoid duplication and enhance connectivity of the research); that an international (and often comparative) perspective is added ("inbreeding" of ideas is less likely); that the ease with which projects with remote collaborators can be managed may often stand at the root of a decision to actually engage in it (even if it would be possible otherwise); that the Internet enables the establishment of a critical mass of researchers to lay the foundation of a new field.

Against these effects, some experts hypothesized that it would rather be the younger (and peripheral) scholars who are influenced by the available information on the Internet, while those with more experience and a better personal network are not. Obviously, individual habits and preferences play a role here, too. Furthermore, there is the argument that the choice of the research topic is mainly dependent on previous research done by the same person and comes, as it were, from "within" the research, not from outside impetus. In addition, the policies of research funds, the aims of the respective research institution and money play an important role.

To sum up, the net impact of the Internet could only be marginal in some cases, but there is evidence that ICT has an impact on the choice of subjects in other fields.

Creative Potential of the New Media

While some fear that the Internet brings chaos and less clarity (too much "background noise" in the words of Glanz, 2001), others point exactly at the creative potential for the research process of this very chaos produced by the wealth of information in the network, the various forms of interactivity and participation.

Written e-mail discussions are one such half-chaotic medium. Gresham speaks of idea generation through such discussions (1994, p. 48). Harnad predicts that what he calls "scholarly skywriting" will revolutionize how science is done. He suggests that there is "plenty of room on the net for exploring freer possibilities, and the collective, interactive ones, are especially exciting" (1993, p. 9). Harnad argues that the shift from P- to E-publishing is not only a change of medium but also a revolution in the way science is done, namely much more interactively, and concludes that "(s)cholarly inquiry in this new medium will proceed much more quickly, interactively, and globally; and it is likely to become a lot more participatory" (1990, p. 2). Based on his case study of the cold fusion newsgroup, Lewenstein (1995, p. 141), too, argues that this form of communication, despite all shortcomings, contributed to awareness building and information gathering and influenced "the process by which social consensus—knowledge—was produced."

In a similar line of argument, Harasim and Winkelmans argue that computer mediated communication offer the "opportunity for serendipitous contact" (1990, p. 397) and make "a near-immediate audience" available that those actively contributing a presentation to the extended discussion (conference) found "stimulating and motivating, enhancing their creativity and productivity" (ibid., p. 399). Therefore, the new media simultaneously support two thinking modes: "brainstorming, as ideas encountered online spark immediate responses; and reflection, as transcripts are studied and responses composed prior to uploading" (ibid., p. 401).

The creative potential has to be tamed, however. Winiwarter observed that one of the main problems of an interdisciplinary discourse is how to get hold of volatile creativity of the group, that is, the good ideas coming up and being forgotten as the process goes on. She proposes e-mail discussion forums with a searchable archive as a solution to this problem (2000, p. 6) and other forms of "collective memory" such as Krajewski's hypertextual slip box (Krajewski, 1997). Harasim and Winkelmans think in a similar direction: "Interactive information dissemination and exchange contribute to a synergistic relationship among the members of the group" (1990, p. 397). However,

> (a)n important part of scholarly collaboration is the need to move beyond "synergy" into organizing and managing the information generated by a synergistic encounter. (. . .) The convergence of these sociotechnological systems (computer conferencing and hypertext) will have significant implications for scholarly work in the future. (ibid., p. 405)

The answers of our interviewees in this context varied. While the political scientists, biologists, economists, and mathematicians were divided among themselves and rather skeptical, all others saw at least some creative potential in the information chaos produced by the Internet. While anthropologists, historians, and lawyers univocally acknowledged the big potential, most skeptics pointed to the danger of information overload, which may easily lead to the contrary of creativity. Some doubted that the effect, although certainly present, is really important.

Brainstorming (and reflection) may thus be raised to a new level, awareness of concurring approaches may rise and ideas may more easily influence each other. Borrowing Dennett's (1997) metaphor of the genelike "memes"—ideas that proliferate from brain to brain just as genes use living organisms to survive—one could formulate: the ecosystem for memes is improving because its viscosity is enhanced. However, making use of this ecosystem requires new and special skills, which not every researcher has mastered.

Summary

As regards methodology-related effects, we found, first, that ICT is opening up new ways of producing results that could not have been produced otherwise. This relates to new ways of accessing data, distributed computing, Internet surveys, and timezone shifting of research tasks. None of these ways is universal, but their applicability depends on discipline and research task. Second, the initial input to every research project is definitely changing because of the widespread instantaneous availability of information resources. At least for the phase of transition, we found that selection is an issue here: the wealth of information may lead to overload and the concrete selection may be biased toward availability through the electronic networks (later on sophisticated filters will be available and there will be an ever-diminishing share of material not yet online). Third, at least in some research fields, it seems likely that the choice of topic may be codetermined by the availability of up-to-date information in the Internet. Fourth, there is a potential that the chaos produced by the wealth of information in the network, the various forms of interactivity and participation lead to new creativity—but the potential still needs to be realized.

It seems impossible at this point in the development of cyberscience to do more than list these first assessments. Final conclusions cannot yet be drawn as there is not enough experience yet. A noteworthy potential is, however, there and it waits to be realized. The same holds for two other areas, not dealt with here, namely the impact of changed work modes and new kinds of knowledge representation on research outcomes (cf. Nentwich, 2003).

Acknowledgment

The author wishes to acknowledge the support of parts of the underlying project by the Austrian Research Fund (FWF) from January 2000 to December 2002 (project no. P14042).

Notes

1. The project homepage can be found at <http://www.oeaw.ac.at/ita/cyberscience.htm>; there you will also find a link to the extended version of this paper as well as to other related articles.
2. Fifty in-depth interviews on the basis of a semi-structured, open questionnaire with researchers in 13 disciplines (comprising 36 sub-disciplines) during winter 2001/02.
3. For the two other impact routes as well as a discussion of interdisciplinarity, see chapter 10 in Nentwich (2003).
4. This is not to deny that the computer as a (stand-alone) working tool has further considerable impact on substance (e.g., in the case of computer modeling or artificial intelligence). This study, however, focuses on communicative tools.

References

Bainbridge, W. S. (1999). Information Infrastructures in the Social Sciences. *Science Technology Industry Review* (OECD)(24), 123–135.

Bourguignon, J.-P., & European Mathematical Society. (1999). The Future of Mathematical Databases. *Science Technology Industry Review* (OECD)(24), 107–122.
Brandtner, A. (1998). Zur Vernetzung der österreichischen Literaturarchive. *Bibliotheksdienst*, 32(12), 2055–2064.
Davenport, E., & Cronin, B. (1990). Hypertext and the Conduct of Science. *Journal of Documentation*, 46(3), 175–192.
Dennett, D. C. (1997). Darwins gefährliches Erbe–Die Evolution und der Sinn des Lebens. Hamburg: Hoffmann und Campe (English: Darwin's Dangerous Idea: Evolution and the Meanings of Life, Touchstone Books).
Dicks, B., & Mason, B. (1998). Hypermedia and Ethnography: Reflections on the Construction of a Research Approach. *Sociological Research Online*, 3(3). Retrieved from <http://www.socresonline.org.uk/3/3/3.html>.
Glanz, J. (2001, June 19). The Web as Dictator of Scientific Fashion. *New York Times*.
Gresham, J. L. (1994). From Invisible College to Cyberspace College: Computer Conferencing and the Transformation of Informal Scholarly Communication Networks. *Interpersonal Computing and Technology*, 2(4), 37–52. Retrieved from <http://jan.ucc.nau.edu/~ipct-j/1994/n4/gresham.txt>.
Harasim, L. M., & Winkelmans, T. (1990). Computer-Mediated Scholarly Collaboration—A Case Study of an International Online Educational Research Workshop. Knowledge: Creation, Diffusion, *Utilization*, 11(4), 382–409.
Harnad, S. (1990). Scholarly Skywriting and the Prepublication Continuum of Scientific Inquiry. *Psychological Science*, 1, 342–343. Retrieved from <http://www.cogsci.soton.ac.uk/~harnad/Papers/Harnad/harnad90.skywriting.html>.
Harnad, S. (1993, 1.10.1993). *Implementing Peer Review on the Net: Scientific Quality Control in Scholarly Electronic Journals*. Paper presented at the International Conference on Refereed Electronic Journals: Towards a Consortium for Networked Publications—Implementing Peer Review on the Net: Scientific Quality Control in Scholarly Electronic Journals, University of Manitoba, Winnipeg. Retrieved from <http://cogsci.soton.ac.uk/~harnad/Papers/Harnad/ harnad96.peer.review.html>.
Krajewski, M. (1997). Käptn Mnemo–Zur hypertextuellen Wissenspeicherung mit elektronischen Zettelkästen. In M. Rost (Ed.), *PC und Netz effektiv nutzen* (pp. 90–102). Kaarst: bhv Verlag.
Lewenstein, B. V. (1995). Do Public Electronic Bulletin Boards Help Create Scientific Knowledge? The Cold Fusion Case. *Science, Technology & Human Values*, 20(2), 123–149.
Mittelstraß, J. (1996). Der wissenschaftliche Verstand und seine Arbeits- und Informationsformen. In Börsenverein des Deutschen Buchhandels e.V. (Ed.), *Die unendliche Bibliothek: digitale Information in Wissenschaft, Verlag und Bibliothek* (Vol. 2, pp. 25–29). Wiesbaden: Harrassowitz.
Mueller, M. (2000). *The library catalog, the word processor, and the digital archive: Three stages of information technology in humanities scholarship*. Retrieved 10-23, 2000 <not available any more at original URL>.
Nentwich, M. (1999). Cyberscience: Die Zukunft der Wissenschaft im Zeitalter der Informations- und Kommunikationstechnologien, Working papers of the Max Planck Institute for the Study of Societies, no. 99-6. Retrieved from <http://www.mpi-fg-koeln.mpg.de/pu/workpap/wp99-6/wp99-6.html>.
Nentwich, M. (2001). How online communication may affect academic knowledge production—Some preliminary hypotheses. *Trans, Internet-Zeitschrift für Kulturwissenschaften*(10). Retrieved from <http://www.inst.at/trans/10Nr/nentwich10.htm>.

Nentwich, M. (2003). *Cyberscience: Research in the Age of the Internet*. Vienna: Austrian Academy of Sciences Press. <http://hw.oeaw.ac.at/3188-7>.

NRENAISSANCE Committee, Computer Science and Telecommunications Board, Commission on Physical Sciences Mathematics and Applications, & National Research Council. (1994). *Realizing the Information Future–The Internet and Beyond–Chapter 3: Research, Education, and Libraries*. Washington, DC: National Academy Press.

Odlyzko, A. (2000). The Future of Scientific Communication. In P. Wouters & P. Schroeder (Eds.), *Access to Publicly Financed Research: The Global Research Village III* (pp. 273–278). Amsterdam: NIWI.

Winiwarter, V. (2000). Zur Rolle von Computer Mediated Communication (CMC) für interdisziplinäre Wissensarchitekturen am Beispiel der österreichischen Kulturlandschaftsforschung. *Landschaftsplanungnet*(2). Retrieved from <http://www.lapla-net.de/texte/02_00/winiwarter/winiwarter.pdf>.

Irene Berkowitz 8

THE EFFECTS OF NEW COMMUNICATION AND INFORMATION TECHNOLOGIES ON ACADEMIC RESEARCH PARADIGMS

Introduction

 The study focuses on evidentiary forms and contemporary academic research paradigms. It is exploratory and qualitative, resulted in conclusions that evidentiary bases and research paradigms are undergoing significant operational and philosophic shifts, and that corresponding changes in social and cultural markers can likely be attributed to the introduction of new ICTs into academic research. This study was guided by theories developed by Harold Innis, Elizabeth Eisenstein, and Walter Ong. The findings most strongly support the work of Innis.

The Theoretical Context

Innis's most significant contributions are found in *The Bias of Communication* and *Communications and Empire*. He makes two particularly important observations: (1) communication is biased either toward time or space and (2) the significance of a new communication technology is the expansion and maintenance of empire. Carey in *Communication and Culture* claims that Innis "pursued communications in a genuinely interdisciplinary way (Carey, 1989, p. 149)." Innis studied the relationship between communications technology and how time and space is manifested in economic and political relations.

> Innis argues that changes in communication technology affect culture by altering the structure of interests (the things thought about), by changing the character of sym-

bols (the things thought with), and by changing the nature of community (the area in which thought developed).... By a space-binding culture he meant literally that: a culture whose predominant interest was in space—land as real estate, voyage, discovery movement, expansion, empire control.... In the realm of symbols and conceptions that supported these: the physics of space, the arts of navigation and civil engineering, [and] the price system.... By a time-binding culture, he meant those interested in time—history, continuity, permanence, contraction; whose symbols were fiduciary—oral, mythopoetic, religious, ritualistic; and whose communities were rooted in place—intimate ties and a shared historical culture. He believed that structures of consciousness parallel structures of communication. (Carey, 1989, p. 156)

Ramos (2000, p. 48) suggests that the three key ideas of Innis are: (1) physical forms of media and their symbolic forms concentrate socioeconomic and political power in the hands of different groups and give rise to knowledge monopolies (2) communications media alters both cultural conceptions of reality and sociopolitical forms by changing the scope and scale of human associations, and (3) different media favors different cultural mind sets or epistemological biases.

Innis proposes:

The significance of a basic medium to its civilization is difficult to appraise since the means for that appraisal are influenced by the media and indeed the fact of appraisal seems to be peculiar to certain types of media. A change in the type of medium implies a change in the type of appraisal and hence makes it difficult for one type of civilization to understand another. (Innis, 1950, p. 10)

This last statement describes the situation that exists with respect to electronically produced academic research evidence and the current challenge to traditional positivist research paradigms. The confrontation with the "established" rules for scientific inquiry, and the creation of an "evidentiary dilemma" in contemporary critical method may be partially a response to the change in dominant media, as much as it is an ideologically or methodologically induced crisis.

Kuhn (1971, in Ramos, 2000, p. 48) provides a summary of the main conclusions from Innis's seminal work, *Empire and Communications:*

Innis suggests four basic ways in which control and authority over an empire are secured; systems for storing and continuing knowledge, organizations capable of dealing with the distinct features of the cultural bias, regulations to advance the check of newer media and the most important, the cultural conditioning that enables everyone to accept the boundaries imposed by the dominant medium.

The importance of Kuhn's summary, in relationship to evidence, is borne by the centrality of the type of social institutions that ensure the four basic ways that control and authority are secured. The social regulating function of the jurisprudential system and the knowledge producing, storage and transmission, cultural - conditioning, and credentialing function of the Academy are key components to the expansion and maintenance of the dominance of contemporary industrialized cultures.

Why Study Evidence?

This study is framed by the premise that evidence, in some form, lies at the foundation of our claims of "valid knowledge." Toulmin (1984) asserts that all arguments, regardless of the method used to construct the argument uses a primary, secondary or tertiary form of evidence to construct the logic by which we reach conclusions. The author of this study would further argue that in academic research, the questions of reliability and validity are continuously raised whether they have been formalized or operationalized scientifically. Even those who argue against the reliability of scientific method generally cite examples, do ethnographic or observational study, or examine cultural artifacts to warrant their claims (Latour & Woolgar, 1986, Ginzburg, 1999). Heather Dubrow (1996) raises philosophical questions regarding the status of evidence in special issues of the *Publication of the Modern Language Association* with leading humanities scholars. It can safely be assumed that evidence is central to evaluation of scientific work. Consciousness has been raised since the 1980s about the growing dilemma regarding evidence, objective standards of scholarship, and the rigor of method.

The Main Premise of the Study

The underlying premise of this study is: When our basis for validating evidence, or methods for ascertaining credibility and weight of evidence change, there will be a corresponding paradigmatic shift in our worldview.

Method

Participants

Ten renowned scholars from a wide range of academic disciplines participated. The term "expert" was operationalized by the following criteria: (1) The scholar was well published in his or her primary discipline in an area related to this study; (2) The scholar was considered renowned by his or her peers, determined by number of publications, and distinguished award(s) for his or her work; and (3) Practitioners were recognized by the academic community as being of high academic caliber, and well published.

Primary Research Themes

- The nature of the individual expert's work as it relates to the topic of study.
- The paradigmatic shift that s/he observes, which may be happening in his or her discipline. The observed impact of new communication technologies on paradigm shifts in response to: (a) Changes in temporal, spatial, organizational and visual aspects of information; and (b) Sensory impact on cognition and consequent changes in research paradigms.
- The anticipated affect on evidence in terms of the affect on credibility and weight, and consequent impact on the growth of knowledge.

Design and Procedure

A modified Delphi Technique was used to conduct this study. The Delphi technique allows knowledgeable individuals to work collaboratively to examine a complex problem and build consensus. Through iterations of data collection with the same participants, the problem is given increasingly more consensual focus by creating specific questions from an analysis of the previous questioning, ultimately organizing the discussion into meaningful categories that structure their relevance and significance.

The procedure:

Step 1: Development of a qualified expert's list and selection of participants.

Step 2: Development and distribution of a participant's guide, including main themes being researched, a list of interview probes, a synopsis of theoretical concerns, a synopsis of Ong, Eisenstein, and Innis's work, and a list of participants.

Step 3: An initial phase of questioning through extensive, individual interviews was conducted, audiotaped, and transcribed.

Step 4: Follow-up as necessary.

Step 5: A review of readings recommended by the participants to aid in interpretation.

Step 6: An analysis of the interviews.

Step 7: A synopsis of the results was presented to the participants using a private listserv for additional comment.

Step 8: The panel's comments were incorporated into the prior round of results.

Step 9: The results were reported by frequency that the topic was raised and by importance of the issue. The most illustrative examples are reported below.

Analysis

Major Findings

Major findings include: erosion of disciplinary boundaries and a corresponding increase in interdisciplinary and multidisciplinary work; a disjunction between contemporary organizational practices and the actual nature of contemporary research; impact from the spatial, temporal, and visual aspects of information as well as magnitude of information, and changes in the bases of evidence, producing observable paradigmatic shifts.

Finding #1. Academic research is becoming more multidisciplinary and more interdisciplinary. Mentioned by almost all participants is the breakdown of disciplinary boundaries. Where this phenomenon is manifest in the humanities, it tends to be toward interdisciplinary study. Science and technology oriented disciplines tend toward multidisciplinary study.

This is viewed as being influenced by two primary, driving forces, specifically related to computer and Internet technologies. The ease of access to the intellectual work in other disciplines through electronic search engines was the most frequently cited reason. The vulnerability of misguided appropriation was routinely mentioned. The second reason offered is the emergence of a common language across all disciplines that is computer and Internet related, and providing a common basis for communication between peers in different knowledge domains. There appear to be more opportunities for discovery of similar concepts in different fields that use different nomenclature and an observable increase in social interaction among peers as they experience common goals and problems associated with technology. In some cases, this interaction is formally planned through the nexus of disciplines into a single physical space.

Finding #2. There is a disjunction between the political and economic nature of the organization of the institutions associated with higher education and the actual research work being conducted by these institutions. This concern was raised by almost every interviewee and manifested itself it a wide variety of ways. The interviewees mentioned all of the key institutions directly related to academic research. The most focus was placed on the organizational boundaries of the University, itself. Concerns about research libraries, accrediting agencies, and funding agencies also were raised.

It can be difficult for faculty members whose work is highly interdisciplinary or multidisciplinary (and perhaps having the most contemporary focus) to comfortably fit within the hiring, appointment, and tenure structure. Funding agencies generally still are tied to paradigms that are more representative of print. This includes both the structure and nature of the work given serious review by agencies, and the nature of the review process itself. Businesses and applied governmental projects seem to be more flexible and adaptable to new models and are having considerable influence on research. Funding is becoming more complex as the research projects become more complex.

Libraries are experiencing particular dilemmas, related both to economics and organizational constraints. This is either in terms of the research itself or in terms of the administrative systems and infrastructure that support research. There are considerable competing objectives that appear primarily driven by economic and/or political motives.

1. Cost of print resources versus electronic resources.
   It is more economically viable to expand the resource base in libraries by increasing reliance on electronic resources in the long term. Unresolved issues exist regarding costing formulas, licensing, and copyright from publishers and the increasing monopolistic tendencies of commercial publishers, particularly as university-funded presses come under increased economic pressure.
2. Resistance to electronic resources, or conservation toward print/nonelectronic resources.
   - *Resistance that is politically tied to status or the status quo.*
   - Tenure is often related to publishing books or in high prestige journals. The highest prestige journals and books are often available in print medium only. Print was viewed as a superior format by custom. This also existed in other fields of study in which the product of research work is in alternate formats such as film or other forms of artistic expression. Resistance to electronic media was not universal across all fields.
   - Resistance may represent a time lag more than political resistance, but could have serious politically charged consequences. There is possibly more of a lag, by the accrediting agencies and other regulating agencies that rank university research libraries. Print models are still used to rate universities. At the same time, there are conflicting requirements relative to the number of available online resources from alternate accreditors.
   - *Some accrediting bodies raise questions about the ability of electronic systems to ensure the same level of integrity as manual and print systems.*
   - Resistance created by the research or programmatic needs for conservation of print and other nonelectronic materials. In many fields, the original source material is necessary as it provides information above and beyond the information that is strictly transmitted in a textual format. This creates difficult and complicated formulas for the allocation of resources. The general conclusion here is that the transmission of information is simply insufficient for the task at hand, even in the hands of the brightest and most qualified.
   - *Resistance created by the "social practice of research."* Mentioned more frequently by scientists and applied researchers, is the importance of telephone calls and personal face-to-face meetings. Those working with masses of data, ironically, appeared to have the most need for some type of personal contact to make "sense" of their research work. Humanists tended to express stronger sentiment about the differences between print and electronic media and

therefore, interpretative differences. Again, it appeared that the transmission of information was simply not completely sufficient for the task at hand.

Finding #3. Spatial, temporal, and visual aspects of information as well as the magnitude of information that can be analyzed in a practical manner have changed the nature and power of conclusions.

- *Speed and magnitude have the single most dramatic impact on the production of evidence in a practical manner.* This combined with worldwide accessibility of resources that previously required specialized or privileged access is having significant influence on the nature of research and on conclusions. The sheer magnitude of data that can be processed efficiently is allowing for the definition and treatment of research problems in ways that were not previously conceived or possible.

Discussion

Computational methods are replacing inferential methods, conclusions from evidence are becoming more certain and more uncertain simultaneously and it is likely that conclusions are becoming more robust and powerful at the same time that evidence perhaps is becoming more derivative.

Computational methods are becoming increasingly popular and are used over inferential methods when possible. There was more evidence of this trend in the sciences and technology, but it could be observed in the humanities, classics, architecture, and library science as well. In the majority of cases, both the capability of the personal computer and the Internet or networking capability is critically important. Many of the research problems might have been conceived under earlier paradigms, but there was no effective or efficient way to actually structure the research problem. This finding has had dramatic consequences on the types of problems that are researched, how problems are framed, and the nature of information that is derived, which in some cases is challenging fundamental assumptions of previous paradigms.

There also appears to be a shift in methods in the humanities toward perhaps more inferential methods, highly focused, deep bands of evidence, and the theoretical framework is relatively constrained within a more rigorously defined research community. Where there is evidence of more computational approaches there was also a tendency for informal a priori hypotheses to be structured into the research work. Information was computationally extracted and then used as "evidence" to build an argument or hypotheses.

Some principles of statistical evidence appear to operate to some degree across all disciplines, not only those that traditionally rely on statistics. The capability to derive conclusions from either very large data set(s) or from a small set, but with very precise observations within a relatively restricted set of assumptions and operating within a closely defined research community leads to an increasing sense of certainty.

Conclusions are becoming more robust and more powerful at the same time that evidence is becoming perhaps more derivative. This is because of the computational nature of methods and magnitude of observations made possible through computing. The analysis of several sets of data simultaneously, frequently with the computer spontaneously generating visual models and deriving patterns, does not necessarily produce evidence that is in a direct one-to-one relationship to the physical evidence used to produce the conclusion. Conclusions were derived through several levels of abstraction from the research problem, or there were several layers of data that produced a single set of conclusions.

Conclusion

The findings suggest that many of the conclusions reached by Innis regarding the cultural indicators of dominance of a new communication medium are supported by this study. There is strong confirmation for the argument that "the growth of long-distance communication is cultivating new structures in which thought is occurring; new things to think about, and new things to think with—increasingly abstract, analytic, and manipulative symbols" (Carey, 1989, p. 149). There are indications that new communication technologies favor a different cultural mindset or epistemological bias. Issues of appraisal and the means of appraisal are surfacing as various kinds of cultural resistance in a myriad of venues. It appears increasingly clear that "the fact of appraisal does seem to be peculiar to certain types of media and that a change in the type of medium implies a change in the type of appraisal" (Innis, 1950, p. 10).

Strict positivism is not embraced by any of the interviewees and yet there seems to be some tendency toward more scientific methods in a number of disciplines, including those that have not relied previously on these types of methods.

The accessibility and magnitude of data that can be processed has allowed for substantive changes in the evidentiary base that is used to conduct research. This appears to have direct affect on the research that is being conducted and the perceived power of conclusions.

References

Babe, R. E. (2000). *Canadian Communication Thought: Ten Foundational Writers*. Toronto: Toronto University Press.
Carey, J. W. (1988). *Communication as Culture: Essays on Media and Society*. Boston: Unwin Hyman.
Collins, H. M. (1992). *Changing Order, Replication and Induction in Scientific Practice*. London: Sage.
Dubrow, H. (1996). Introduction to the Status of Evidence, *Publications of the Modern Language Association* (111) 1, 7–19.
Dubrow, H. (1996). The Status of Evidence Roundtable, *Publications of the Modern Language Association* (111) 1, 21–31.

Edgar, W. (1980). *Evidence*. Lanham, MD: University Press of America.
Eisenstein E. (1979). *The Printing Press as an Agent of Change, Vol. 1*. New York: Cambridge University Press.
Gustason, W. (1994). *Reasoning From Evidence*. New York: Macmillan College Publishing Company.
Hacking, I. (1981). *Scientific Revolutions*. New York: Oxford University Press.
Hennings, U., Huber, R. P. O., & Stanke, F. (1973). Delphi interrogation concerning future possibilities of the employment of robots. In H. Blohm and K. Steinbuch (Eds.), in co-operation with the Research Group for Technological Forecasting, Karlsrube, *Technological Forecasting in Practice* (pp. 19-28). (F. and C. Crowley, Trans.), Westmead, England: Saxon House.
Innis, H. A. (1964, c. 1951). *Bias of Communication*. Toronto: University of Toronto Press.
Innis, H. A. (1950). *Empire and Communications*. Oxford: Clarendon Press.
Jones, Steven. (1999*)*. *Doing Internet Research*. Thousand Oaks, CA: Sage.
Kuhn, T. S. (1962*)*. *The Structure of Scientific Revolutions*. Chicago: University of Chicago Press.
Latour, B., & Woolgar, S. (1986). *Laboratory Life: The Construction of Scientific Facts*. Princeton, NJ: Princeton University Press.
Lum, C. M. K. (2000). Introduction: the Intellectual Roots of Media Ecology. The New Jersey Journal of Communication. 8(1): 1-7.
Ong, W. J. (1977*)*. *Interfaces of the Word: Studies in the Evolution of Consciousness and Culture*. Ithaca, NY: Cornell University Press.
Ong, W. J. (1983). *Orality and Literacy.* London: Methuen.
Pickering, A. (1992). *Science as Practice And Culture*. Chicago: University Of Chicago Press.
Ramos, L. (2000). Understanding Literacy: theoretical foundation for research in media ecology, *The New Jersey Journal of Communication*. 8(1): 46-55.
Reiss, T. Knowledge (1997). *Discovery and Imagination in Early Modern Europe*. Cambridge: Cambridge University Press.
Schum, D. A. (1994). *Evidential Foundations of Probabilistic Thinking,* New York: John Wiley.
Strate, L., & Lum, C. M. K. (2000). Lewis Mumford and the ecology of technics. *The New Jersey Journal of Communication*. 8(1): 56-78.
Toulmin, S. (1984). An Introduction to Reasoning. New York: Macmillan.
Trowler, P. (1998). *Academics Responding to Change: New Higher Education Frameworks and Academic Cultures*. Buckingham, UK: Society for research into higher education & Open University Press.
Turoff, M., Hiltz, S. R., Bieber, M., Fjermestad, J. and Rana, A. (1999). Collaborative Discourse Structures in Computer Mediated Group Communications. *JCMC* 4(4). Retrieved from < http://www.ascusc.org/jcmc/vol4/issue4/turoff.html >.
Weissenberger, G. (1987). *Federal Rules of Evidence, Rules, Legislative History, Commentary and Authority.* Cincinnati: Andersen.

THE CATHEDRAL OR THE BAZAAR? THE AoIR DOCUMENT ON INTERNET RESEARCH ETHICS AS AN EXERCISE IN OPEN SOURCE ETHICS

> *I believed that the most important software ... needed to be built like cathedrals, carefully crafted by individual wizards or small bands of mages working in splendid isolation, with no beta to be released before its time. Linus Torvalds' style of development—release early and often, delegate everything you can, be open to the point of promiscuity—came as a surprise... The Linux community seemed to resemble a great babbling bazaar of differing agendas and approaches.*
> —Raymond (2001, 21), in Floridi and Sanders (2004)

Origins

During the inaugural conference of AoIR at the University of Kansas (Lawrence) in September 2000, a scholarly panel organized by Steve Jones and peopled by Sarina Chen, Philip Howard, David Snowball, Barbara B. Lackritz, and Storm King attracted a standing-room-only crowd. Researchers and ethicists voiced a number of diverse responses to the AAAS report on "Ethical and Legal Aspects of Research on the Internet" (Frankel & Siang, 1999), a milestone document in articulating some of the ethical problems that emerge in online research. To begin with, the AAAS report stressed a *medical* model for human subjects' protection—that is, one based on the multiple ethical concerns that arise in direct intervention with human *bodies*. But for many online researchers, there is a range of ethically relevant *differences* between research on *embodied subjects* and research in the new environments of the Net and the Web—differences the report did not adequately acknowledge (see AoIR ethics working committee, 2001). Moreover, the AAAS report stressed the role of Institutional Review Boards (IRBs) in overseeing online research. This raised two issues. First, whereas the goal of such Boards to protect human subjects is clearly crucial—some researchers feared that IRBs, especially as guided by the medical model, would be unnecessarily restrictive. Others, however, saw no such threat, insofar as the report was "a very general overview of the area that provided no solutions but merely highlighted where further work was needed" (Amy Bruckman, personal communication, 3/10/03). Indeed, both Bruckman and Sanyin Siang rather agreed with the tone and approach of the AAAS report, and were rather ". . . concerned that these ideas were not being disseminated widely enough or taken seriously enough" (ibid). Second, U.K. researcher Kate S. O'Riordan noted that ". . . using these very terms of reference (IRB) conveys a message that the whole debate is an USA debate." To take the AAAS as its ethical starting point would be acutely problematic for AoIR as an organization stressing international participation and perspectives (personal communication, 3/11/03).

Amy Bruckman, Sarina Chen, and Sanyin Siang then petitioned the AoIR executive committee to create an ethics task force to develop an ethics statement. The AoIR executive committee, after debating their proposal and at the urging of Steve Jones, began to form a research ethics working group charged not only with developing an ethics statement but also making recommendations for member education, development of case studies, and education of nonmembers.

I (Charles Ess), a philosopher with a background both in applied ethics and computer-mediated communication, happily agreed to chair the group. In recruiting committee members, we stressed bringing together ethicists familiar with CMC and researchers from a range of disciplines who are prominent for both their research and published reflection on the ethical aspects of such research. Moreover, the global reach of the Web and the Net demanded that we ensure representation of a wide range of national and cultural traditions. At the same time, "AoIR's attempt to engage with/create/contribute to a global network of Internet Researchers requires that it create inclusive terms of reference and avoid exclusive ones where possible" (O'Riordan, ibid.). The original committee in fact represented some eleven cultures/nations, both East and West, and included at least one researcher familiar with the interactions between indigenous cultures and CMC.[1]

In Raymond's image, the impetus for the committee's formation came not from the cathedral, but from the bazaar of AoIR 1.0—the bazaar of engaged dialogue between researchers and ethicists from a wide diversity of disciplines, experiences, and perspectives. By the same token, we hoped to generate ethics from this thriving bazaar, as represented by our committee.

Charge of the Committee

The committee was charged to:

1. formulate a set of values that all Internet researchers should uphold when research involves humans;
2. pursue ongoing clarification and education regarding the ethical dimensions of human subjects research.

Process/Components of Discussion

In its first round of work—culminating in the document presented to AoIR 2.0 (AoIR ethics working committee, 2001)—the committee collected and reviewed a range of materials relevant to its charges, and discussed these via a closed e-mail list over a period of approximately nine months. Most of these materials were collected onto a Web site organized and maintained by committee member Jeremy Hunsinger (see < http://www.cddc.vt.edu/aoir/ethics/ >). The chair coordinated the process of collecting these, focusing discussion on a particular resource, topic, and so on, and occasionally summarizing the highlights of our discussion before moving on.[2]

Our initial materials included both published and prepublication papers (e.g., Feenberg & Bakardjieva, 2001; Roberts, 2001), bibliographic suggestions (O'Riordan, 2001), as well as case-study descriptions from committee members that ranged from ethical dilemmas faced by doctoral candidates to researchers with years of experience. We also began collecting ethical statements of relevant disciplines and professional organizations—as well as guidelines and codes from the United States (e.g., the 1991 Code of Federal Regulations)—and Europe (e.g., from the Swedish Council for Research in the Humanities and Social Sciences (1990)—the focus of our inaugural discussion in January/February 2001—and the (Norwegian) National Committee for Research Ethics in the Social Sciences and the Humanities' guidelines, or NESH (1991).

Philosophical Assumptions and Debates

By design, the members of the committee brought to the table a diverse range of cultural and philosophical presuppositions as the frameworks for their work and our discussion. In particular, several of the committee members who are researchers by discipline and profession also brought to the table well-developed ethical frameworks (e.g., King, 1996). For example, Paula Roberts noted her conviction that despite ethical guidelines and clearance from ethics panels, how the individual researcher conducts the project and the decisions which he/she makes, requires what Bakhtin (I think) has described as a 'bottom-up' ethical wisdom. (Personal communication, 11/23/00)

This approach, first of all, fit well with both my and Andrew Feenberg's Habermasian orientations (e.g., see Feenberg 1991). In particular, as chair I hoped that we would be able to take—and thereby test—a *dialogical* approach to building our ethics statements, that is, one shaped by Habermasian and feminist discourse ethics that, like Bakhtin, emphasize beginning with the intuitions and insights of those "on the ground." In Raymond's image, this would be to develop ethics in the bazaar—as business continued, so to speak, in contrast with the more magisterial approach of a "cathedral ethics." To use the term central to Habermas, Kant, and Aristotle, dialogical ethics emphasizes the insights and engagement of those enmeshed in the *praxis* of research. Such *praxis* is not only guided by extant ethical frameworks and approaches, but further serves as the crucible in which those frameworks and approaches must be refined and validated (Ess & Cavalier, 1997).

At the same time, those of us with more background in philosophical ethics were able to contribute to this *praxis*-oriented discussion of particular ethical issues and their possible resolutions. Beyond the dialogical framework, for example, our colleague Soraj Hongladarom provided the distinctive perspectives of Thailand's syncretic Buddhist traditions *and* Western ethical theory, and as applied to the *praxis* of Thai chatrooms and challenges to sustaining local cultural values in a global communication medium (1999). In addition, Norwegian philosopher Dag Elgesem played a significant role in the development of the NESH guidelines (2001)—another example of how ethics, consistent with the dialogical approach, may emerge from the *praxis* of researchers (Elgesem, 2002).

More broadly, one of our central goals was to avoid any form of cultural imperialism—including the imperialism resulting from ethnocentrically assuming that the ethical frameworks of one culture can be universalized to apply to all cultures, without further ado. Although an ancient and constant problem in ethics, this concern is especially acute with regard to research carried out online, insofar as the technologies at work have a global reach. The philosophers' familiarity with both problems and possible solutions to the challenge of establishing a global but nonethnocentric ethics—respectively, of ethical relativism and the frameworks of *ethical pluralism* as holding together both shared ethical values alongside the irreducible differences that define diverse cultural identities—contributed especially to the most recent ethics statement as explicitly committed to such pluralism.

From the outset, however, the committee's active researchers who had long engaged in theoretically well-informed reflection on the particular ethical issues that emerged in their research contributed much of the substantive discussion. Our first year's work focused especially on the specific issues surrounding informed consent and protecting subjects' identity, as these emerged in the work of several of the active researchers—including, for example, considerable discussion of researchers' obligations to protect the identities of those who had posted to what have become public fora (Usenet archives) and, relatedly, whether (and if so, how) researchers are obliged to protect the identity/ies of those they observe in chatrooms. As might be expected, opinions on these matters varied—sometimes, strenuously! From my perspective as chair, however, I was consistently impressed with the quality of our debates. As chair, I certainly worked to keep our discussions and disagreements operating within the framework of dialogical ethics. At the same time, however, participants—however passionately they debated significant disagreements—required very little moderation. Not only, then, did the application of dialogical ethics help keep our disagreements productive and constructive; in addition, the debates themselves were largely self-moderated by the participants—consistent with Habermasian and feminist arguments that dialogical ethics are in part an articulation of a widely shared intuition of what counts as fair and open discourse.

More broadly, as our committee brought to bear their practice in distinctive cultural/national settings, along with their familiarity with the relevant codes and ethical guidelines of their own country or region, we were able to develop an initial overview of how especially the United States and Europe both agree and differ in their approaches to such issues as privacy protection in online research, etc. (AoIR ethics working committee, 2001). It is also worth noting that, while a great deal was accomplished via e-mail discussions—as someone commented when several members of the committee were finally able to meet face-to-face prior to AoIR 2.0 in Minneapolis—we got more work done in five minutes face-to-face than in two weeks on e-mail. Our evening meeting, in fact, did much to finalize our first report to AoIR (2001).

Perhaps our single most productive, *praxis*-oriented discussion centered on a debate in our second year between Amy Bruckman and Brenda Danet. Partly in response to the committee's review of extant guidelines and nascent efforts to construct our own, both Amy and Brenda posted their own proposed guidelines in the context of their own projects (Bruckman, 2002; Danet, 2002). As Klaus Bruhn Jensen (again, a researcher with considerable familiarity with philosophical ethics) puts it:

> To me, a key moment (if not the moment) was the necessarily conflicted interaction between Amy and Brenda. [. . .] It might be referred to in Habermasian terms of negative and positive rights: Amy insisting on the (negative) right of non-interference from outsiders such as researchers, Brenda reminding us of the (positive) right of human subjects as performers, to be recognized via cultural representatives such as researchers. (personal communication, 2/22/03)

More broadly, this debate helped the committee expand its response to one of the central problems that initiated our work in the first place—namely, the limitations of the medical model vis-à-vis online research. This debate—including the arguments by committee member Kate O'Riordan and her colleague Elizabeth Bassett

(2002) and those of Michele White (2002)—helped us articulate more fully the important ethical differences associated with whether one starts from the social sciences (whose ethical frameworks are primarily shaped on the model of human subjects protections developed in medicine) or the humanities (whose ethical frameworks stress instead the human agent as artist, author, and so on—that is, someone *seeking* public recognition and discussion of one's work, rather than the primary protections of anonymity, confidentiality, etc.). In my mind, this *methodological pluralism*—required for the multidisciplinary approaches characteristic of online research—clearly parallels the *ethical pluralism* required for such research as it straddles multiple cultures and national traditions. Both pluralisms emphasize the legitimacy of a range of approaches and value systems—as a middle ground between a methodological/ethical relativism (that can make no judgments as to whether one approach or ethical decision is any better than another) and a methodological/ethical dogmatism that (ethnocentrically) insists on the legitimacy of only one way and value.

As we developed drafts of the statement we intended to present to the AoIR membership for its discussion during the AoIR 3.0 conference in Maastricht, the Netherlands (October 2003), we continued to collect pertinent resources and discuss additional ethical conundrums. We were greatly assisted by two important spinoffs from our work. First, Helen Nissenbaum acquired National Science Foundation (NSF) funding for a panel on Internet research ethics, held at the Computer Ethics: Philosophical Enquiries (CEPE) Conference, Lancaster University, Lancaster, U.K., in December, 2001. This panel brought together committee members and other significant researchers and ethicists from both the United States and Europe. By design, the international context helped sharpen our understanding of the agreements and differences between U.S. and European approaches to research ethics. The panel further included both humanists and social scientists and hence significantly expanded our awareness of important agreements and differences between these diverse disciplines in research methodology and guidelines. The panel presentations, discussions, and subsequent publications thus contributed directly to the articulation of the methodological and ethical pluralisms of our final document (AoIR ethics working committee, 2002). Similarly, a conference and graduate course on Internet research ethics organized by committee members Dag Elgesem and Malin Sveningsson in collaboration with May Thorseth and Janne Bromseth (both at the Norwegian University of Science and Technology, Trondheim, Norway) in June 2002, further refined our understanding and articulation of these pluralisms—in good measure, as we were able to test out the then current version of our ethics statement vis-à-vis the research and ethical expertise of Chris Mann (Cambridge University) and Annette Markham (University of Illinois at Chicago), as well as that of the conference organizers and graduate student participants. In addition, inspired by the work of Dag Elgesem and Chris Mann, we recognized that the most useful format for online researchers with comparatively little background in philosophical ethics would be a series of guiding questions intended to help researchers in *praxis* work through common ethical concerns and their possible resolutions. In this way, our final document not only reflected in its *content* an extraordinary richness as drawn from the experience of numerous ethicists and researchers from a variety of countries—but also in its *form* an orientation to the practical needs of such researchers thick in the middle of the bazaar and *praxis* of research.

Conclusions and Recommendations

I suspect that many people, if presented with the task of formulating a set of guidelines for the relatively novel venues of online research—guidelines that not only had to reflect the ethical practices of a range of disciplines (both within the social sciences and the humanities), but also the diversity of national/cultural ethical traditions represented on the Web and the Net as global media—would have rather argued that such a project would be impossible.

For my part, however, this was—and is—an extraordinary project. My work with the committee, as it included such a range of disciplines, experiences, and cultural backgrounds, is an exceptional chance to test the ability of dialogue to bridge theory and *praxis*. Even better, to see how such dialogue—precisely as it included passionate but articulate and respectful disagreements—emerges in a consensus on ethical guidelines is simply an exceptional intellectual and *humane* experience.

The current document was approved by the AoIR membership in November 2002. But of course, it remains a work in progress. The constantly changing environments of the online world will issue in new ethical concerns[3]—and we are working to expand our understanding of cultural and national differences not represented in the current report. Nonetheless, we know anecdotally that the current document is proving to be useful for researchers, ethicists, students, and institutional authorities with responsibility for overseeing online research. It further stands as an example and proof that dialogue across the diversities of disciplines and cultures can uncover important agreements, not simply disagreements. The document thereby suggests, contrary to the pessimism of some, that ethical reflection can, if properly fostered, more or less keep pace with technological advancements and developments, even in such rapidly changing domains as the Internet and the Web. More broadly, the document suggests that a *global ethic* is also possible—one that includes both important agreements and convergences, alongside the recognition of and respect for the irreducible differences that mark distinctive cultures from one another. Such an ethic is of interest not only to Internet researchers: it is of critical importance to a world growing ever smaller and increasingly interdependent.

Notes

1. The original committee: Poline Bala–Malaysia; Amy Bruckman–USA; Sarina Chen–USA; Brenda Danet-Israel/USA; Dag Elgesem–Norway; Andrew Feenberg–USA;

Stine Gotved–Denmark; Christine M. Hine–UK; Soraj Hongladarom–Thailand; Jeremy Hunsinger–USA; Klaus Jensen–Denmark; Storm King–USA; Chris Mann–UK; Helen Nissenbaum–USA; Kate O'Riordan–UK; Paula Roberts–Australia; Wendy Robinson–USA; Leslie Shade–Canada; Malin Sveningson–Sweden; Leslie Tkach–Japan; John Weckert–Australia.

2. Amy Bruckman has kindly described my serving as chair:

> The group leader gives some comments more emphasis than others, ignores a few comments now and then as irrelevant or counter-productive... gently steers the group. The process goes more smoothly if the leader has greater experience to legitimate their authority within the group, which your background as a philosopher strongly provides in this case. (personal communication, 3/10/03)

3. Indeed, the document "works" by maintaining a relatively narrow focus—that is, by *not* addressing a number of important issues, including: copyright, free speech protections, researchers' honesty and integrity, proprietary research, and so on. Although these are clearly important, other issues pressed more toward the center of our necessarily limited time and attention.

References

AoIR ethics working committee. (2001). A preliminary report. Available online <aoir.org/reports/ethics.html>.

AoIR ethics working committee. (2002). Ethical decision-making and Internet research: Recommendations from the AoIR ethics working committee. Approved by AoIR membership, Nov. 27, 2002. <www.aoir.org/reports/ethics.pdf>.

Bakardjieva, Maria, & Andrew Feenberg. (2001). Involving the Virtual Subject. *Ethics and Information Technology* 2: 233–240.

Bassett, Elizabeth H., & Kate O'Riordan. (2002). Ethics of Internet research: Contesting the human subjects research model. *Ethics and Information Technology* 4 (3): 233–247. <http://www.nyu.edu/projects/nissenbaum/ethics_bassett.html>.

Bruckman, Amy. (2002). *Ethical Guidelines for Research Online.* <http://www.cc.gatech.edu/~asb/ethics/>.

Danet, Brenda. (2002). *Studies of Cyberpl@y: Ethical and Methodological Aspects.* <http://atar.mscc.huji.ac.il/~msdanet/papers/ethics2.pdf>.

Elgesem, Dag. (2002). What is Special about the Ethical Issues in Online Research? *Ethics and Information Technology*, 4 (3), 195–203. Available online: <http://www.nyu.edu/projects/nissenbaum/ethics_elgesem.html>.

Ess, Charles, and Robert Cavalier. (1997). Is There Hope for Democracy in Cyberspace? In David Hakken and Knut Haukelid (Eds.), *Technology and Democracy: User Involvement in Information Technology* (pp. 93–111). Oslo, Norway: Center for Technology and Culture.

Feenberg, Andrew. (1991). *Critical Theory of Technology.* New York: Oxford University Press.

Floridi, Luciano, & Jeff Sanders. (2004). Internet Ethics: the Constructionist Values of *Homo Poieticus.* In Robert Cavalier (ed.), *The Impact of the Internet on our Moral Lives.* Albany: SUNY Press.

Frankel, Mark S., & Sanyin Siang (for the American Association for the Advancement of

Science). (1999). "Ethical and Legal Aspects of Human Subjects Research on the Internet." <http://www.aaas.org/spp/dspp/sfrl/projects/intres/main.htm>.

Hongladarom, Soraj. (1999). "Global culture, local cultures and the Internet: the Thai example." *AI & Society* 13.4: 389–401.

King, Storm. (1996). Researching Internet Communities: Proposed Ethical Guidelines for the Reporting of Results. *The Information Society*, 12: 119–128.

National Committee for Research Ethics in the Social Sciences and the Humanities (NESH–Norway). (2001). "Guidelines for research ethics in the social sciences, law and the humanities." <http://www.etikkom.no/NESH/guidelines.htm>.

Office for Protection from Research Risks, National Institutes of Health, Department Of Health And Human Services. (1991). Code of Federal Regulations. 1991. Title 45, Part 46, "Protection of Human Subjects." <http://ohsr.od.nih.gov/mpa/45cfr46.php3>.

O'Riordan, Kate. (2001). *A Brief and Random Bibliography: Internet Ethics.* <http://www.cddc.vt.edu/aoir/ethics/other.html>.

Raymond, Eric. (2001). *The Cathedral and the Bazaar: Musings on Linux and Open Source by an Accidental Revolutionary*, rev. ed. Sebastopol, CA: O'Reilly & Associates.

Roberts, Paula. (2001). Hacker ethics in a community of practice. Presented at *EthiComp*, Gdansk, Poland, June.

Swedish Council for Research in the Humanities and Social Sciences (HSFR). (1990). "Ethical principles for scientific research in the Humanities and Social Sciences." <http://www.cddc.vt.edu/aoir/ethics/private/Swedish_HFSR_1990b.pdf>.

White, Michele. (2002). Representations or people? *Ethics and Information Technology*, 4 (3), 249–266. <http://www.nyu.edu/projects/nissenbaum/ethics_white.html>.

Nancy Baym and Jeremy Hunsinger   Section Two

Places, Politics, and Policies of the Internet

The Association of Internet Researchers has always aimed to be international and interdisciplinary, and has always had an eye toward stimulating Internet research from a variety of perspectives that promotes the common good. The papers in this section speak directly to both of these goals by representing a range of national and local perspectives on the Internet and by providing localized critiques of the Internet in terms of practices, places, politics, and policy. We hoped that by bringing together people from different disciplines and methodological orientations who were looking at similar issues, common threads might emerge. These chapters, written by authors from a wide array of scholarly traditions, and using methods ranging from ethnography, survey methodology, interviewing, and rhetorical analysis, demonstrate the insight that can be found when the Internet is acknowledged as the interdisciplinary domain that it is. Among the countries represented in these selections are Canada, Germany, France, the United Kingdom, South Korea, Singapore, Denmark, the United Arab Emirates, and the United States. Taken together, their breadth demonstrates the importance of considering place in analyses of how the Internet is accessed, used, and understood as well as illuminating critical concerns that transcend place and time.

While there may not be a single thread that links the papers in this section together, there are multiple threads that cross through each other weaving a loosely knit fabric of issues. The resulting whole is perhaps greater than the sum of its parts. These threads connect the ways people use the Internet, the ways people learn on the Internet, and the politics and policies that shape and govern those situations.

The first lesson these chapters offer is that the Internet may be global, but an individual's place is central to how he or she experiences the Internet. National narratives (Starke-Meyerring), municipal goals (d'Iribarne), sociability (Witte and Ryan), and interpersonal social networks (Palfreyman), are among the culture-specific forces that influence the learning of technological skills, the people with whom one communicates online, and issues such as whether the Internet is more likely to be used for economic, educational, or entertainment purposes.

A second issue taken up in these chapters has often been termed "the digital divide." As soon as it became clear that the Internet would extend out of the world of computer scientists and scholars and into the everyday lives of much broader populations, concerns arose regarding the equality of access to the Internet and the ways in which policy might be designed to attend to these concerns. Several of the chapters in this section demonstrate the complexity of thinking about access and the problematic oversimplicity of the concept of "digital divide." Not only is access shaped by sex, education, and income, it is also shaped by a host of other factors including access to other technologies in the home (d'Iribarne) and regulatory structures (Bodnar). Regulatory structures, or policies, in turn are shaped, as Gustafson, Bodnar, and Starke-Meyerring argue, by the discourses surrounding the Internet in policy documents and the press. These authors suggest definitions of access and policy taken to address access are grounded in political gain and commercial profit. "Access" is defined in ways that depend on the ends those proffering definitions pursue. The chapters in this section also provide a welcome break from the notion that simply having an Internet connection will result in any kind of real social change. As Howard and Milstein point out, there are existing knowledge gaps that prevent lower-educated and information-poor groups from engaging the political process in ways that logging on will not fix. Indeed, Howard and Milstein suggest that having access can itself become a threat to a politics of the people inasmuch as those with access are subject to data mining that undermines their privacy, right to informed consent, and ultimately the political process itself.

Several of the authors in this section express particular concern about the discursive construction not just of access, but of the Internet user, in particular whether those who use the Net are viewed as citizens or consumers. The early days of the Internet, with its often utopian discourse and emphasis on community networks, raised hopes that the Internet would prove a democracy-enhancing tool. Empowered by information and nonhierarchical structures, online citizens would be able to find new voices and create meaningful social change. As Starke-Meyerring argues, in the late 1990s, the focus shifted to economic profit and e-commerce, so that Internet users became markets rather than citizens, a perception that affects providers' willingness to invest in economically disadvantaged locations (Bodnar), as well as investors' willingness to provide capital to Internet providers that do not show clear market-growth potential (Mansell). These models of Internet users serve the corporations that provide the technology, rather than those citizens the corporations might serve. Gustafson also identifies user-as-consumer as a significant rhetorical barrier toward democratic action, thereby raising significant questions about the relationship between the ways people think and talk about the Internet, and the possibilities of future directions for the Internet. In contrast to these chapters, d'Iribarne poses a model of Internet-user-as-consumer, which starts with the point of view of the locally situated users and asks what services are used and how the technology fits into their broader technological and regional situations. This reversal of the consumer orientation turns the question back to how policy can best serve those who use the Internet rather than those who profit from it.

These authors warn that the conflation of "consumer" with that of "citizen" not only lessens the potential of the Internet to serve the public good, but may in fact undermine the needs of the community in favor of corporate profit. However, they offer alternative suggestions. Bodnar argues the need for citizens to build "cultures of digital resistance." Mansell argues the need to create a "network commons" and also the need to foster "new media literacies." A strong critical literacy of new media would allow for new cultures, and subcultures to form. We can see an example of this described in Witte and Ryan, who explore how a particular form of media literacy in music forms new possibilities for social networks. Together these chapters are an important step in creating the basics of a new media literacy and understanding the effects of that literacy on a broader set of issues.

These authors conceive of the political and social possibilities of Internet technologies in different ways. Rather than speaking to the same issues in the same ways, these papers represent combinations of possibilities that at times agree, at other times resonate in unexpected ways, and in places may disagree. They differ also in their methodological orientations. While some take critical theoretical and qualitative approaches, other papers such as Witte and Ryan's, Palfreyman's, or Bodnar's offer quantitative analyses of social and political situations. These papers capture enough information about their particular topics to provide strong platforms for future comparative research. Indeed, some of the data sets that these researchers used are freely available (as are several others).

Each of the articles in this section has its own merits, but as a whole, their strength is in their comparative insights, approaches, and juxtapositions. The combination of perspectives and methodologies should stimulate further scholarly conversation and open up new possibilities for Internet research. In short, this section exemplifies the leaps in Internet research we can expect given the breadth of interdisciplinary and international work being done by the Association of Internet Researchers.

"IMAGINE": A STRUCTURAL ANALYSIS OF THE USE OF THE INTERNET BY HOUSEHOLDS IN FOUR EUROPEAN TOWNS[1]

 The problem today is no longer whether or not our societies will be changed by the diffusion of Internet connections but rather how they will be reshaped. To what extent, how, and to whose benefit will this reshaping take place? What economic and social models will be used and what forms of regulation will be put in place? Attempts to answer such questions have drawn on investigations of Internet use in whatever place and for whatever purposes in order to apprehend the nature of the changes taking place and to interpret their significance.

The results that will be presented here are derived from the initial analyses of a survey carried out as part of the European IMAGINE project among a sample of households in four small European towns.[2] These results show that there are certain similarities in the way that the populations of the four towns have appropriated the Internet, as apprehended through the uses to which the technology is put. At the same time, however, they reveal significant local specificities in the modes of domestic use of PCs and the Internet. These specificities may be associated with many aspects of both the technology and of economic and social life: with different modes of household equipment (level and type of equipment) and with different forms of integration and use of ICTs within social networks and local societies: each town emerges with its own specificity, reflecting an identity that is socially constructed around a local system of actors who are themselves located within societal trajectories that seem to be specific.

The Foundations of the IMAGINE Project: Observing and Experimenting

The "Digital Towns" project focused on the uses of the Internet by populations belonging to households in towns that were the object of public policy or, to put it another way, on observations of the relationships that can develop between the supply of services provided through networked electronic media and the social uses to which they might be put in the course of local experiments.

The project was located at the crossroads of several different problematics that, falling as they did within the scope of several different disciplines (economics, sociology, political science, and geography), complemented and intertwined with each other (Iribarne, 1996).

The Problematic of Technology Use and Users

The basic problematic of the "Digital Towns" research project falls within the scope of the sociology of the uses of technology and of communications (Boullier, 2002). The issues relating to uses and users as actors in the process of innovation diffusion enable us to go beyond the diffusion problematic in order to engage with issues around appropriation (Rogers, 1953).

In this research, uses are approached from the point of view of those to which the "citizen consumer" puts the technology as part of his or her lifestyle. The approach adopted to the "citizen consumer" as an Internet user may be more or less broad, depending on the places of use, of which there may be several. In this research, the approach taken was a relatively narrow one; with the focus of attention primarily on home uses. This problematic of uses and users is particularly difficult to construct, as it is located at the intersection of a great variety of dimensions, making it necessary in all cases to link individual aspects with more collective aspects relating to membership groups.

The Social Networks Problematic

In the light of everything that has gone before, it would be tempting to say that the familiar problematic of social networks necessarily comes into play in this type of research as soon as the technologies in question involve networks and communication. However, this problematic has been drawn on according to complementary logics that considerably extend the scope of the notion of technological innovation alluded to above by combining it with the problematic of technico-economic networks previously used to approach technology (Offner, 1999). In fact, it is used in order to take into account the ways in which the municipal actors engaged in making public policy on the creation of an NICT infrastructure, on the design and production of "support tools" and on the organization of the associated services are mobilized, the ways in which "support tools" are designed and produced; the very design of the project means that these actors must necessarily include "citizen users."[3]

The Problematic of Public Policies as Refracted through Municipal Policies

This last problematic brings into play public policies, and particularly municipal policies, from a dual perspective: the economic one of "sustainable" development and the political one of being an actor in the future of society (ven den Berg & ven Winden, 2000). By introducing municipal policies into the equation, this approach gives towns the status of an actor in the economic and social dynamic, playing a part by virtue of the vigor of local democracy rather than through the public action of "regulation" (Carlo, 1996). Thus, it is not a question here of rediscovering the local as a locus of political regulation by locating ourselves at a territorial level of action but, rather, of introducing municipal actors as delegates of their towns' populations, mandated by election to take part in the entire process of technological innovation.

From this point of view, municipalities intervene, first, by extending their traditional role as a provider of infrastructure not only by encouraging access to the Internet through the development of local networks and connection points but also by developing Net-based municipal services in such a way as to reduce access costs or what economists would call "the barriers to entry" to Internet use.[4] Thus, one of the project's objectives was to ensure, by engaging municipalities in the design and implementation of industrial projects, that the combinations of networked technologies and services were as well adapted as possible to users' needs as revealed through experiments in the "social construction of technology" (Cronberg & al., 1991; Lefebvre & Tremblay, 1998; ven den Berg & al., 2000;).

The Place of PCs among the Household Equipment and Home Internet Connections

In accordance with the "domestic technical system" principle (by analogy with firms' industrial technical systems), the view was taken that PCs were only one element among others in total household equipment, particularly communications equipment such as telephones, fax machines, and, in France, the Minitel. At household level, the various combinations of items of equipment can be interpreted as the result of relationships between the supply of services and diversified preferences for the technology, as determined by budgetary constraints and choice of lifestyle. Overall, at town or country level, they can be regarded as structural indicators characterizing reference socioeconomic worlds (Woolgar, 2002).

The Place of PCs and Communications Equipment

PCs occupy middling positions in the household equipment rankings in the four towns, which means that they have become standard items of equipment and are approaching maturity. Nevertheless, there are significant differences in ownership rates. Thus, the two German towns—Torgau and, particularly, Weinstadt—have particularly high levels of ownership (77.2 and 63.5%, respectively) associated with better rankings, while Casale and, particularly, Parthenay have lower ownership rates, at 54.3 and 33%, respectively.

The Relationships between PC ownership and Household Equipment

It is interesting to examine whether, in the particular case of the towns investigated, the same complementarity exists in respect of household equipment as that usually found at national level. To this end, we compared the equipment of households that do not have PCs with those that do have a PC connected to the Internet. The comparison reveals that in all four towns those households connected to the Internet are systematically better equipped than those that do not have computers. This applies to virtually all the items of equipment in our list, which confirms a massive general trend toward accumulation: it is the best-equipped households that tend to be "early adopters" when new equipment arrives on the market.

Home Internet Connections

It would be tempting to say that Internet connections fit easily into this landscape, in the sense that they do not disturb the established order. In all four towns, the rate for household Internet connections is higher than that for fax machines. Thus, it is clear that households in the four towns do not hierarchize these modern communications tools in the same way. In particular, households in Casale might be considered to have a greater tendency than those in the other towns to favor "communications tools," with those in Parthenay giving them lower priority.

Gathering data not only on PC ownership but also on the rate of connection to the Internet—what is generally known as "home Internet connections"—reveals pretty much the same differences as those observed previously in the case of computer ownership alone. Thus, Parthenay is lagging behind in two respects, and even the best efforts of the mayor and the municipal authorities have not succeeded in making up for the town's initial delay in computer ownership, even though the gap here is somewhat narrower.

It is as if these initial gaps tend to accumulate over the various phases of the diffusion process, making the phenomena associated with it difficult to reverse. However, such a conclusion must be treated with caution, because the rate of Internet connection among households in Torgau with PCs is considerably lower than in the other towns, which shows that the fateful coincidences are not necessarily cumulative.

Use of the Internet at Home and Elsewhere

Internet use lies at the heart of the issues with which the IMAGINE project is concerned. It is around these uses that the towns' public policies have been constructed. These policies have two main thrusts: to encourage those applications that best match people's expectations and to promote Internet access for all. It is this twofold objective that explains why we have attempted to separate more clearly home use of the Internet from Internet use outside the home.

The Reasons for Home Internet Use

In general terms, leisure activities tend to dominate in all four towns, except in Weinstadt. In comparison with the uses to which computers are put, this constitutes a shift away from work-related activities. The same differences between the towns—albeit somewhat displaced—are observed with Internet use as were observed with PCs, which probably reflects a structural characteristic.

Thus, it may be concluded that Internet connection tends to encourage leisure activities to the detriment of work-related uses, whereas uses related to training and participation in community life would appear to depend more on the importance the various town projects give to these aspects.

Differences in the Reasons for Home Internet Use by Users' Sociodemographic Characteristics

In general terms, the same differences by sex are found as those observed previously for PC use, which tends to confirm the importance of local structures in determining the uses of technologies or tools. In all cases, men tend to be more frequent users than women, except for community activities in Casale and work-related activities in Torgau. With the exception of Parthenay, where Internet uses help to increase participation in the older age groups to the detriment of full-time workers, there is a shift in the opposite direction.

Differences in Ways of Using the Internet When Connected at Home

The resources of the World Wide Web available through the Internet can be used in two ways: either by "surfing" the Web in a more or less random search for entertainment or information or by looking for precise information. Over and above these different objectives, not everyone uses the Internet in the same way. As we did when looking at the purposes of Internet use, we will examine the differences in practices by sex and by age.

In all the towns, searching for precise information tends to predominate over surfing. Whereas women's practices are generally very close to those of men, the latter tend to surf more in Parthenay and, in particular, in Torgau, and to carry out precise searches at Casale and, particularly, Weinstadt. Thus it is between the two German towns that the gender differences are most marked. Practices differ a little more by age.

The Nature of Activities on the Internet Irrespective of the Place of Connection

Starting with a common list of activities in order to ascertain the extent to which they are practiced in each town, we sought to identify the places in which these activities are carried out in order better to distinguish home uses from uses in other locations.

An investigation of this kind seemed to be all the more necessary as, as we have seen, a town such as Parthenay has adopted a strategy that attaches great importance to locations other than the home. As far as activities on the Internet are concerned, the situations differ much more from one town to another than household equipment levels, in terms of both the frequency of Internet use for the various activities and the ranking of the various uses.

Indeed, apart from "e-mail," "searching for general information," and "downloading of text and data," which regularly head the rankings in all four towns, and two activities such as "sending mailing lists" and "playing games online," which are regularly placed low in the rankings, some activities that are ranked in the leading group in one town bring up the rear in others, and vice versa.

This comparison between the two towns Parthenay and Weintadt tends to confirm the notion that there are certain "animating principles" underpinning the municipal projects and Internet use in the towns, with Parthenay focusing more on communication and entertainment and Weinstadt being oriented more toward economic activity.

Light on the Current Debates on the Routes toward the "Information and Communication Society"

Against the background of the current debates, this research has sought to provide information in five areas, all of which shed a considerable amount of light on the current debates on the routes that might be taken toward the "information and communication society" and the lifestyles that might be associated with it.

Internet Connections and Their Diffusion

In the households investigated, PCs are already a "standard" item of equipment and are beginning to enter the "mature" stage of development, with many households having more than one computer and a process of equipment renewal already under way. Internet connections are following in their wake with some degree of lag but are already part of the set of new household equipment. Thus, "Internet in the home" is already a reality in Europe.

This is true to varying degrees of the four towns. However, it is clear that households in the French town are less well equipped with PCs and less likely to be connected to the Internet; in the other towns, the equipment is older and occupies a less lowly rank. Thus, it would seem that we should talk less of delay or lag than of differences in the choices made by French households, given the current situation with regard to costs and the services on offer. Comparison with the national statistics at our disposal further strengthens the hypothesis that we are dealing with a national structural situation than with particular characteristics of the towns themselves, as the situation among the four populations investigated is more favorable than in the country as a whole.

Uses and Appropriation

The observations confirm the empirical difficulty of effecting a smooth transition from diffusion to appropriation and cast doubt on attempts to address issues around uses. To be absolutely rigorous, any such attempt should adopt a three-pronged approach in which types of individuals and households are matched to equipment and applications and to purposes, modes, practices, and places of use. Clearly, such an approach would produce combinations leading rapidly to complex typologies, the creation of which would require samples of sufficient size.

In all four towns, domestic uses are very varied; they differ by sociodemographic characteristics and have their own specific features, while at the same time having certain elements in common with uses in other places. These uses, which in general terms reflect genuine appropriation of the Internet, have led to a significant blurring of the boundaries between work, education/training, leisure activities, and participation in civic life. They also reveal relationships to social temporalities (the times of the day or week at which particular activities take place) that are becoming increasingly diversified, foreshadowing profound changes in lifestyles. One would be more tempted to advance the hypothesis that the "domestic Internet" will be part of the major shift that can be observed toward the destructuring of current social temporalities.

Social Democracy

The research provides extremely qualified answers to these interesting questions, which equate to the "social fracture" problematic, particularly in terms of the sociodemographic criteria of age and sex that are frequently highlighted. Neither women nor the "elderly" are the object of systematic differentials, particularly relative to "young people." The criteria of occupation and income are poorly understood at this stage of our analyses. By contrast, level of education seems to stand out as a decisive criterion, with the relatively high level of the upper secondary leaving certificate (baccalauréat, A-levels, Abitur, etc.) being crucial. If these observations were to be verified, then everything that is said intuitively about the crucial nature of education/training would be confirmed, but much more in terms of level of education than of content.

Public Policies

To what extent do these policies succeed in making significant and rapid changes to pre-existing structural situations, or do underlying trends tend to prevail, requiring both stubbornness and patience on the part of local politicians?

The answers to this question are open to debate, first because sufficient structural data on each of the countries have not yet been collected and, second, because the longitudinal data have not yet been analyzed in the light of the policies pursued by the various municipalities. The liveliest debate concerns Parthenay, where the view is that the arrangements for comparison put in place are irrelevant to its situation, in view of the fact that the town has opted to encourage the development of Internet access through its so-called digital access points.

Over and above the polemic, comparative analyses show that there really are structural differences between the towns and that, in accordance with the "path dependency" principle, the most pronounced differences between Internet uses and structural situations are to be found in Parthenay, which is the town where public policy has been most active. It is tempting to say, therefore, that public policies intended to bring about structural corrections are unlikely to have any effect unless they are implemented on a sufficiently large scale and can be sustained over time.

The Very Idea of a "European Model of a Digital Town" or of a European Model of "Municipal Digitization"

In contrast to the previous point, there seem to be no ambiguities in this respect: within an overall pattern of development that is encountered in all four towns, there are substantial differences that undoubtedly reflect permanent structural differences.

Notes

1. IMAGINE (Integrated Multimedia Application Generating Innovative Networks in European Digital Towns). The IMAGINE research project was carried out as part of the European Commission's 4th Framework DG XIII Integrated Applications for Digital Sites.(Project reference number: IA 1006 UR.)
    This three-year project (beginning of 1998 to the end of 2000) was the final phase of a larger project entitled "Digital Towns," which was launched at the beginning of 1994 with the "METASA" (Multimedia European Experimental Towns with a Social-Pull Approach) project, which was completed in 1996. (Iribarne, A. d', & al., 1996).
    This paper is based on part of the results presented in Iribarne, A. d' & al., 2000).
2. Casale in Italy, Parthenay in France, Torgau and Weinstadt in Germany.
3. This is clearly a normative assertion linked to the design of the "Digital Towns" project, one of the roles of the social science researchers having been to examine the reality of this mobilization in the light of the stated intentions.
4. To reduce this "barrier" in the French town, the municipality not only provided infrastructure and access points—"in-town net and URL"—but also offered opportunities to lease PCs with online time charged at reduced rates and maintenance services provided by the town's technical services department.

References

Berg, L. ven den, & Winden, W. ven. (2000), *ICT as Potential Catalyst for Sustainable Urban Development: Experiencies in the Cities of Eindhoven, Helsinski, Manchester, Marseilles and The Hague*, European Institute for Comparative Urban Research (EURICUR) Erasmus University Rotterdam.

Boullier, D. (2002), Les études d'usage entre normalisation et rhétorique, *Annals of Communications*, March/April, pp 190-209.

Carlo. L. de. (1996), *Gestion de la ville et démocratie locale*, Paris, L'Harmattan.

Cronberg. T., Dueland. P., Jensen. O. M., Qvortrup, L. (eds.). (1991), *Danish Experiments — Social Constructions of Technology*, The Danish Social Science Research Counsil, New Social Science Monographs.

Iribarne, A. d' (1996), For a Sociocultural Approach of the Information Highway ; His, A. (ed.) *Communication and multimedia for people*, Paris, Fondation Charles Léopold Mayer.

Iribarne, A. d' Eveno, E., Lenz, B., & Lopez, A. (1996), *METASA (Multimedia European Experimental Towns with a Social-pull Approach)*, Deliverable, European Commission DG XIII.

Iribarne, A. d' Biolghini, D., Cengarle, M., Desborde, F., Eveno, E., Lenz, B., Preiss, I., Röhr, M., & Witruk, E. (2000), *IMAGINE (Integrated Multimedia Application Generating Innovative Networks in European Digital Towns)*, Deliverable D 10-1, European Commission DG XIII.

Lefebvre, A., & Tremblay, G. (1998) (Sous la dir.), *Autoroutes de l'information et dynamiques territoriales*, Québec/Toulouse, Presses de l'Université de Québec, Presses Universitaires du Mirail.

Offner, J.-M. (2000), Territorial Deregulation: Local authorities at risk from technical networks, *International Journal of Urban and Regional Research*, Volume 24.1, March, pp. 165-182.

Revue Sciences de la société, Presses Universitaires du Mirail, N°47.

Rogers, E.(1983), *Diffusion of Innovations*, New York: Free Press.

Storgaard, K., & Jensen, O. M. (1991), Information technology and way of life, *Danish Experiments — Social Constructions of Technology*, The Danish Social Science Research Council.

Woolgar, S., ed. (2002), *Virtual Society?* Oxford: Oxford University Press.

MUSICAL TASTE AND SOCIABILITY: EVIDENCE FROM SURVEY2000

Introduction

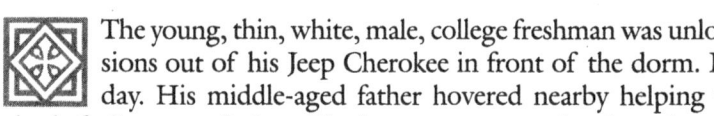 The young, thin, white, male, college freshman was unloading his possessions out of his Jeep Cherokee in front of the dorm. It was moving-in day. His middle-aged father hovered nearby helping where he could, clearly feeling out of place. The boy, too, appeared awkward, caught in a temporary intersection between the adolescent world of home and family, and the new independence of college. In mid-stride, he put down a box, went back to the Jeep and flipped on the stereo. The air was filled suddenly and dramatically with a pounding bass line and the voice of three-time MTV Music Video Award winner Eminem intoning the lyrics:

> *hi, my name is . . .*
> *what? my name is . . .*
> *who? my name is . . . Slim Shady*
> *hi, my name is*
> *huh? my name is . . .*
> *what? my name is . . . Slim Shady*
> (Eminem "My Name Is [explicit version]")

We suspect this freshman was hoping to send a signal. Perhaps something like: "Accept me, I'm like you, I'm cool, I'm wild (and maybe a little bit dangerous), just ignore my dad unloading (out of the $35,000 Jeep they bought for high school graduation) that stack of clothes carefully washed, ironed and folded by my mom back home . . . I'm like you, I'm like you."

Beyond the subtleties of the content of the message intended by this signal, an equally important empirical question concerns the choice of the signal itself. In his effort to make a statement to his newfound peers, what prompted our new college freshman to choose this medium, this artist, this track to make a statement? What led him to believe that this signal would resonate with the intended audience? Even if one interprets this scene quite differently—perhaps, the intended audience was the young man's father and not the nearby students—this question remains relevant. The music was not a random track from a randomly selected CD. Musical taste, as with other forms of cultural preference, is rooted in a subtle process of education and socialization. As is often done, to simply point the finger at "the music industry" is to substitute an easy anthropomorphism for a plausible sociological explanation. The music industry never directly walked up our young freshman and suggested he listen to Eminem. Arguably the music industry does have tangible instruments for shaping tastes (e.g., youth-oriented radio, television, and magazines), yet to go down this route does not answer the question, but simply pushes it one step further in a potentially infinite regress. Why does our young friend listen to this pop station and not another? Why does he read this magazine and not another?

The analyses presented in this chapter consider sociability—real interaction with other individuals—as a concrete explanation for the articulation of musical taste. The premise is quite simple: musical tastes are created and shaped through interaction with others. As a testable hypothesis, it follows, *ceteris paribus*, clear musical preferences are most likely to be found among those individuals who are most sociable. The hypothesis is tested using data from Survey2000, a Web-based survey with nearly 25,000 U.S. adult respondents. What we find not only corresponds to popular views about the "demographics" of particular genres, but also shows that sociability is positively related to articulating a preference for a single genre as well as to having a preference for a number of genres.

Musical Taste and Sociability

Adolescents wear their musical choices like they wear their clothes and their language, as a way of distinguishing themselves (Bourdieu, 1984), as identifying with some reference group or another and, just as important, *not* identifying themselves with some other groups (cf. Arnett, 1991).[1] Researchers such as Weinstein (1994) have highlighted the fact that music is an integral part of local teen "scenes," drawing boundaries around physical spaces as well as between members and nonmembers. This idea has been taken even further, especially by the Birmingham School, positing distinct subcultures built around music preferences. However, Bennett (1999) prefers the term "neo-tribes," suggesting a much less involving and more fluid association between musical preference and lifestyle.[2]

Whether music is used to form subcultures, neo-tribes, or is just used to distance oneself from one's parents, it is clear that musical taste, like taste in clothes, food, art, and other cultural choices, is often an important part of the presentation of self. However, exactly how musical tastes develop is a matter of much speculation.

For example, the relationship between cultural participation of all sorts and economic class has long been accepted (cf. Veblen, [1899] 1934), but the predictive value has never been that strong and actually seems to be weakening for higher status groups (see Peterson, 1992). Age, too, is an important factor (Zill & Robinson, 1994), but considerable variation exists within these age groups as well. For example, younger adults are more likely to like jazz, blues, reggae, rap, and new age, but few like all of these genres.

Education also is associated with particular cultural choices. For example, Zill and Robinson report that two-thirds of adults who have been to graduate school say they like classical music, compared with one-fourth of adults with no college education. In fact, those with more education appreciate more types of music, with the notable exception of country music, which they are less likely to appreciate.

Hakaman and Wells (1993), argue for gender and ethnicity as the main explanatory variables in musical taste, but here, too, considerable variation exists.

Demographics do not completely explain musical taste, a concept captured by Gans's (1969) notion of "taste publics." But how do we account for the formation of taste publics within demographic groups? A likely explanation is developed by Mark (1998) in his conception of musical forms occupying an ecological niche within the sociodemographic segments of society. For Mark, the key factor in the development of musical taste is interaction with friends and family. He argues that demographic similarities and differences between various taste cultures are largely an artifact of the way our social networks are structured by these same variables. That is, we tend to associate with individuals who are similar to ourselves in attitudes and taste, and such individuals are also likely to be demographically similar.[3]

Mark uses data from the 1993 General Social Survey to test a number of hypotheses relevant to his ecological theory. He is able to demonstrate a number of findings consistent with his model. For example, he is able to show that the closer one is to the center of the demographic niche associated with a particular genre, the more likely one is to like that genre. However, the GSS does not contain a measure of the *extent* of social ties—the key variable in his model of taste formation. If musical taste is formed through interaction with friends and family, the actual extent of those interactions should have an impact on taste. In this chapter, we have not attempted to reproduce Mark's demographic taste niches but, rather, we have simply looked at the impact of levels of interaction with family and friends on musical taste, while controlling for key demographic variables.

Survey2000: Survey Design and Sample

Our analyses use data from Survey2000, a Web-based survey focusing on geographic mobility, community and cultural identity.[4] Over 80,000 individuals worldwide took part in Survey2000, which was placed on the home page of the National Geographic Society. Publicity for the project was generated by the Na-

Table 1: Demographics of the Survey2000 Adults (Age > 18) Sample Compared to the 1996 and 1993 General Social Surveys[1]

	Survey 2000[2]		1996 General Social Survey		1993 General Social Survey	
	%	N	%	N	%	N
Gender						
Female	48.9	15,147	55.7	1,614	57.3	918
Male	51.1	15,801	44.3	1,283	42.7	683
Median age	38 years		44 years		43 years	
Race						
Black	1.4	428	13.9	402	11.2	179
White	94.5	29,004	80.9	2,344	83.9	1,343
Other	4.1	1,268	5.2	151	4.9	79
Education						
Less than HS degree	0.9	292	15.2	441	18.1	289
HS degree	31.9	9,882	54.1	1,567	52.5	840
Associate's degree	7.8	2,421	6.7	194	6.2	99
Bachelor's degree	34.1	10,569	16.3	471	15.8	253
Graduate degree	25.2	7,785	7.7	224	7.4	118

1. Sample is restricted to age 19 or older to facilitate GSS comparison for all data sources.
2. There were also 713 respondents who did not provide information on race.

tional Geographic Society and a team of researchers who advertised the effort through discussion groups, colleagues, and Web sites around the world. Here we rely on data from nearly 25,000 U.S. adult respondents who voluntarily took part in the survey.

Table 1 compares the demographic makeup of the Survey2000 sample to two recent GSS samples. This comparison shows, for example, that whereas just over half of the Survey2000 sample is male, female respondents constitute the majority in the 1996 and 1993 GSS samples.[5] Furthermore, the Survey2000 sample is considerably younger, with a median age of 38 years, than that estimated by the GSS (44 years in 1996 and 43 years in 1993). The Survey2000 sample also supports the widely held view that minorities are underrepresented on the Internet; 92.5% of the Survey2000 respondents are white. Finally, Table 1 indicates a large difference between the educational makeup of the Survey2000 sample and the U.S. population at large. For example, the proportion of Survey2000 respondents with a high school degree but no postsecondary degree (31.9%) is considerably lower than that found in the 1996 GSS (54.1%) and the 1993 GSS (52.5%). Correspondingly, respondents with postsecondary degrees are overrepresented in the Survey2000 sample.

Describing Demographics, Sociability, and Musical Taste

The musical tastes of U.S. Survey2000 respondents are summarized in Table 2. Classical/symphony and chamber music along with oldies/classic rock were far and away the most popular genres with approximately 80% of the Survey2000 respondents saying they like these genres or like them very much. At the other end of the spectrum, only 12.1% of all respondents felt the same way about rap or hip/hop music and 18.3% favored heavy metal music. While the general pattern of results is plausible, comparisons of individual genres indicate clear differences between the

Table 2: Musical Preferences of US Survey2000 Respondents

	Like it very much	Like it	Have mixed feelings	Dislike it	Dislike it very much	Don't know much about it
Classical/symphony and chamber music	39.4%	38.0%	16.7%	2.8%	1.1%	2.0%
Opera	8.3%	19.5%	36.5%	19.9%	10.1%	5.7%
Broadway musicals/show tunes	24.8%	34.0%	26.5%	8.5%	4.2%	2.1%
Jazz	25.2%	37.7%	24.9%	7.5%	3.0%	1.8%
Big band/swing	28.1%	40.5%	21.6%	6.0%	1.9%	1.9%
Mood/easy listening	19.6%	33.0%	25.1%	14.2%	7.3%	0.7%
Country-western	12.0%	22.3%	30.1%	17.8%	17.1%	0.7%
Bluegrass	9.9%	30.5%	30.4%	15.2%	7.0%	6.9%
Hymns/gospel	9.3%	26.2%	35.0%	16.3%	9.8%	3.4%
Rhythm and blues	20.4%	39.9%	26.7%	7.9%	2.8%	2.2%
Rap/Hip-Hop	3.4%	8.7%	21.3%	23.0%	40.8%	2.8%
Dance music (e.g., electronica)	7.9%	22.0%	32.3%	19.3%	11.2%	7.4%
Caribbean (e.g., reggae, soca)	12.9%	42.9%	28.8%	7.5%	2.8%	5.2%
Latin (e.g., mariachi, salsa)	10.1%	35.3%	32.0%	11.5%	3.7%	7.4%
Music of your ethnic tradition	17.6%	35.2%	22.1%	2.7%	1.0%	21.4%
Modern folk/singer-songwriter	18.5%	39.2%	27.3%	7.6%	1.9%	5.5%
Contemporary pop/rock	22.0%	42.9%	23.9%	7.3%	2.9%	1.1%
Alternative rock	21.3%	26.3%	25.7%	14.8%	7.8%	4.1%
Oldies/classic rock	41.0%	40.1%	13.7%	3.5%	1.4%	0.4%
Heavy metal	6.2%	13.1%	24.0%	21.9%	33.2%	1.6%

N = 24,980 (US adult respondents). Rows sum to 100%

Table 3: Measures of Sociability among US Survey2000 Respondents

	Never	Rarely	Several times a year	About monthly	About weekly	Daily
Personal visits with friends within 30 miles	2.4%	6.8%	10.8%	19.5%	42.3%	18.1%
Telephone/fax with friends within 30 miles	2.8%	6.4%	6.8%	14.6%	42.7%	26.7%
Letter/cards with friends within 30 miles	17.4%	39.0%	28.6%	11.0%	3.3%	0.7%
E-mail with friends within 30 miles	16.7%	15.2%	6.6%	13.1%	29.1%	19.3%
Personal visits with friends beyond 30 miles	8.2%	43.4%	34.6%	9.6%	3.5%	0.7%
Telephone/fax with friends beyond 30 miles	6.1%	21.7%	29.8%	24.7%	15.1%	2.7%
Letter/cards with friends beyond 30 miles	10.0%	35.0%	40.3%	11.9%	2.7%	0.2%
E-mail with friends beyond 30 miles	15.0%	14.2%	13.3%	19.0%	25.6%	12.9%

N = 35,092 (US adult respondents). Rows sum to 100%

Survey2000 sample and similar data obtained as part of the 1993 GSS. These differences (e.g., country and western music is much more popular among GSS respondents than among the Survey2000 sample, which includes a disproportionate share of college graduates), in large measure may be attributed to the nonrandom nature of the Survey2000 sample (Witte et al., 2000). Although there is no reason to suspect that the Survey2000 sample recruitment process distorts the relationship between musical taste and sociability, these findings underscore the need to control for demographic characteristics in subsequent multivariate analyses.

Respondents also were queried about the frequency of various types of interaction with friends and relatives, distinguishing between those who lived within 30 miles of the respondent and those who lived farther away. To explore the relationship between sociability and musical taste we have focused on contact with friends, who presumably have a greater influence on the musical taste of adults than do relatives. The survey items used to measure sociability are summarized in Table 3.[6]

Musical Taste and Sociability

Conceivably, contact with friends of any type—in person, by phone, letter, or e-mail—could lead to the definition and articulation of musical tastes. Therefore, to simplify the model, the different types of contact are combined into a single index of sociability. This index is a simple sum of dimensions, with each ranging from one to six with higher values assigned to more frequent contact. Thus, the higher

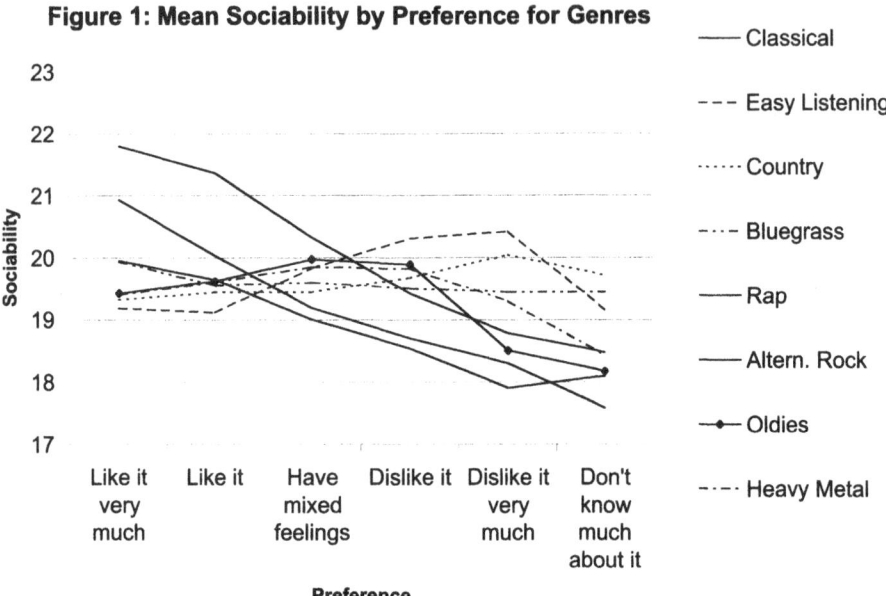

Figure 1: Mean Sociability by Preference for Genres

the score on the index of sociability, the more contact one has with friends. If our hypothesis is correct, that interaction with others is the vehicle whereby cultural tastes are shaped, then preferences for particular types of music should be stronger among those who rank highest on the index of sociability.

Figure 1 summarizes the univariate relationships between sociability and preferences for selected individual genres. The prevailing pattern across the majority of genres is represented by the data presented for "classical," "rap" and "alternative rock." Fifteen genres follow this pattern, which meets our expectation with the highest levels of sociability found among those who are most positively disposed toward that type of music. Of the 20 genres included in the survey instrument only "easy listening," "country and western," "bluegrass," "oldies" and "heavy metal" fail to fit this pattern.

Further tests of the relationship between sociability and musical taste are found in Table 4. The first column of this table presents results obtained from a logistic regression that looks at the log of the odds of having no highly favored genre to that of having positive preferences for one or more musical genres. To make these results easier to interpret we report the exponentiated coefficients.[7] Here, for example, we see that women and minorities are significantly less likely than men and nonminorities to not have a favored genre. Having more online experience, however, increases the likelihood of having no favored genre. For our purposes, however, the most important result is the significant inverse relationship between increased sociability and the probability of not having a favored genre. In other words, the higher the level of sociability, the lower the probability that an individual will not show a strong positive preference for one or more musical genres.

Table 4: Musical Taste and Sociability[1] and Overall Musical Preferences[2] among US Adult Survey2000 Controlling for Demographics

	No highly favored genre: any highly favored genre[3]) Logistic regression coefficients	Overall musical preferences	
		OLS coefficients (unstandardized)	OLS coefficients (standardized)
Constant	—	-3.22**	—
Female	0.66**	0.09**	0.088**
Non-white	0.74**	0.08**	0.034**
Age 16–18	0.54**	-0.16**	-0.062**
Age 19–24	0.83**	-0.04**	-0.027**
Age 25–34 (reference category)	—	—	—
Age 35–44	0.94	0.04**	0.037**
Age 45–54	0.80**	0.07**	0.052**
Age 55 or older	0.60	-0.01	-0.011
High school degree or less	1.10	-.005**	-0.029**
Some college, no BA	0.96	0.02**	0.022**
BA degree (reference category)	—	—	—
Graduate or professional degree	0.94	-.004**	-0.034
Been online two years or more	1.14*	0.01	0.011
Increased levels of sociability	0.97**	0.01	0.167**
N of cases	24,790	24,790	24,790

1. estimated odds of not having at least one highly favored music genre
2. OLS estimates
3. exponentiated log of the odds
** p<01, * p<05

The results presented in the second and third columns of Table 4 examine the relationship between sociability and musical preferences in a different fashion. These two columns report unstandardized and standardized OLS regression coefficients obtained when overall positive musical preferences are regressed on the same set of independent variables. In this case, the dependent variable, overall musical preferences is the sum of the preference scores for all 20 genres. Unlike the logistic regression results in column one, the OLS coefficients may be negative or positive depending on whether the relationship is negative or positive. Here, then, we see that women and minorities are significantly more likely to report a positive preference for a greater number of musical genres. Younger people are less likely to have a broad range of preferences than those between the ages of 25 and 34, while those between the ages of 35 and 54 are more likely. Lower overall preference scores are also found among the least well educated as well as the most well educated, while increased sociability is associated with higher overall preference scores. Standardized regression coefficients are reported in the third column to indicate the relative strength of the independent variables. The large value for the standardized coefficient associated with increased sociability indicates that the relative effect of this variable (0.167) is nearly twice the size of the next largest standardized coefficient (the value of 0.088, which captures the effect of gender).

Conclusions and Suggestions for Further Research

How important is contact with friends for developing and sustaining musical taste? In this study the highest levels of sociability were associated with having positive attitudes toward the most genres of music. That is, individuals who reported the most contact with friends also reported liking more kinds of music. In addition we have seen that contact with friends is associated with a lowering of the probability that an individual will have *no* strong preferences for at least one musical genre.

Taken together, these findings lend indirect support to Mark's (1998) contention that cultural choices are created and sustained through network ties. It is important to note that the effect of sociability remained after controlling for demographic factors typically used to explain music preferences. In fact, as noted above, the standardized coefficient associated with increased sociability was nearly twice the size of the coefficient for gender—the next largest standardized coefficient. This is consistent with findings suggesting a loosening of the connection between social class and taste and a reconceptualization of taste in terms of lifestyle or status group patterns (see, for example, Hughes & Peterson, 1983; Peterson, 1992; van Eijck, 2000). However, not much attention has been paid in the literature to the social mechanisms that produce or sustain taste groups. What evidence there is has come from ethnographies or surveys of particular taste groups in particular social locations (see, for example, Skully & Dalton, 1996; Pattacini, 2000). Following Mark, and building on social identity theory (see, for example, Cotterell, 1996) we posit that sociability is a key factor in this process of taste formation.

Our future research on this topic will address these issues in two ways. First, using our existing data set, we will reconstruct Mark's music-genre demographic niches and analyze respondents' location within those niches. This will then allow us to examine the relationship between sociability, niche location, and musical preference. Second, we are part of a team of researchers fielding a new Internet survey (Survey2001) in which we have included more detailed questions about sociability and the sharing of musical tastes within friendship groups. Hopefully these inquiries will shed light on what we see as key issues in cultural sociology—the formation of cultural taste and the role of taste in creating and sustaining individual and group identities.

Notes

1. There is a long history of white, middle-class youth identifying with black culture which, for a time, seems infinitely cooler than the culture of their parents. White teens' current fascination with hip-hop fashion, music, and language may be more explicit imitation, but it is not a new phenomenon.
2. According to Bennett (1999: 604), the basic idea of "neo-tribes" is that ". . . the group is no longer a central focus for the individual but rather one of a series of foci or 'sites' within which the individual can live out a selected, temporal role or identity before relocating to an alternative site and assuming a different identity."
3. Not surprisingly then, fans of particular genres share some similarities in attitudes and beliefs. For example, Hansen and Hansen (1991) report that individuals who expressed liking for heavy metal music were higher in Machiavellianism and machismo and lower in need for cognition than nonfans. In their study heavy metal fans made higher estimates than non-fans of consensus among young people for sexual, drug-related, occult, and antisocial behaviors and attitudes. Punk rock fans were less accepting of authority than those who dislike this music. Punk fans estimated higher frequencies than nonfans of antiauthority behaviors such as owning weapons, committing a crime, shoplifting, and going to jail.
4. For details about the logic of Web-based survey instruments, program features, design elements, and sampling issues with Survey2000, see Witte et al., 2000.
5. A long-standing issue with the GSS and other probability samples has been the over-representation of females (Smith 1979).
6. It is noteworthy that just over half of the respondents indicate that they exchange emails on a weekly or daily basis with friends nearby. One can easily imagine individuals using e-mail to keep in touch with distant friends, but e-mail is seemingly also becoming a mainstay of communication between friends who live quite near to one another (Wellman et al., 2001).
7. Thus, a value of 1.00 indicates no relationship, a value above 1.00 means a higher value on the independent variable increases the odds of having no favored genre and one below 1.00 means a higher value on an independent variable leads to reduced odds of not having a favored genre. Asterisks are used to flag those variables where the estimated exponentiated coefficients are significantly different from 1.00.

References

Arnett, Jeffrey. 1991. "Adolescents and heavy metal music: from the mouths of metalheads." *Youth and Society* 23: 76–98.

Bennett, Andy. 1999. "Subcultures or neo-tribes? Rethinking the relationship between youth, style and musical taste." *Sociology* 33 13: 599–614.

Bourdieu, Pierre. [1979]1984. *Distinction: A Social Critique of the Judgement of Taste,* translated by Richard Nice. Cambridge, MA: Harvard University Press.

Gans, Herbert J. 1969. *Popular Culture and High Culture.* New York: Basic Books.

Hakaman, Ernest A. and Alan Wells. 1993. "Music preference and taste cultures among adolescents," *Popular Music and Society* 17: 55–70.

Mark, Noah. 1998. "Birds of a feather sing together," *Social Forces* 77: 453–85.

Peterson, Richard A. 1992. "Understanding audience segmentation: from elite and mass to omnivore and univore," *Poetics* 21: 234-58.

Veblen, Thorstein [1899] 1934. *Theory of the Leisure Class.* New York: The Modern Library.

Weinstein, Deena. 1994. "Rock: Youth and its music." Pages 3-24 in *Adolescents and Their Music*. Ed. by Jonathan S. Epstein. New York: Garland Publishing.

Wellman, Barry, Anabel Quan Haase, James Witte, & Keith Hampton. 2001. Does the Internet multiply, decrease, or increase social capital? Networks, participation, and commitment online and offline." *American Behavioral Scientist,* vol. 45(3): 436-455.

Witte, James C., Lisa M. Amoroso, & Philip E. N. Howard "Method and representation in Internet-based survey tools: Mobility, community, and cultural identity in Survey2000. *Social Science Computing Review,* vol. 18 (2): 179-195.

Zill, Nicholas, & John Robinson. 1994. "Name that tune: demographics of musical taste in the U.S.," *American Demographics* 16:22-28.

Gitte Stald   12

GLOBAL REACH, LOCAL ROOTS: YOUNG DANES AND THE INTERNET

Introduction

Seen from a meta-perspective, young people's uses of the Internet do not differ essentially from those of the average population of Internet users. We all basically communicate, find information, are entertained, or trade on the Net. We meet other people, exchange experience and opinions and emotions. Experience and influence of the various forms and purposes of virtual life are intertwined with our experience and life in the physical world and we develop our identities in the dual realms of the virtual and the physical. The world opens up to us via the Internet when we transgress traditional borders in time, space, and place and achieve direct and immediate access to people and places around the globe. At the same time we drag the world into our computer and comprise it into meaning and usefulness in our local context. But, with these general meanings in mind Internet uses—and attitudes toward these—are as much defined by social, cultural, and educational background transversely to uses distinctive to age and gender and to individual interests, needs, and competence.

In the perspective of the general and of the specific young Danes' uses of the Internet can be characterized on the basis of four sets of dualities: First, the Internet has been integrated into youth cultural and social practices over a short period of time. The Internet has become an obvious choice for communication, information, social, cultural, and emotional exchange, yet it is also in spite of its convergent "nature" thought of as one among more choices of media. Second, the Internet is important to adolescents in the process of developing individual and collective identity and finding one's footing globally as well as locally, but in the adolescents' own interpretation offline experience holds a deeper impact. Third, numerous interpersonal relations, networks, and communities are established, tested, and developed via the Internet, but in coherence with offline relations and networks.

The Internet also holds an important role as a tool to maintain relations and communities established offline. Finally, adolescent Internet users have access to information on other cultures, living conditions, political systems, and geographical surroundings in a scale that surpasses the level of information of older generations. Still, the immense sources of information and impressions of the world tend to support a dual attitude of global orientation but also a strengthened awareness of the local rooting.

Additional to these issues a number of specific characteristics can be distinguished. For example, the Internet provides young people with spaces and places for *experiment* and for *challenge* of society's and parents' norms and borders. The *pace* of exchange and distribution of information is immense, substantially supported by various Internet services. Information of global reach as well as individual experiences and thoughts of the world is represented and easily accessible on the Internet and enhances the channels and number of sources of information and experience. Another aspect is the fact that Internet use along with the mobile phone enforces the notion of *immediacy* and pace because of the constant possibility of connectivity, updating, and crossing of temporal and spatial borders. Finally, various uses of the Internet trigger considerations about questions of *validity, trust,* and *risk* in online, respectively, offline relations.

The aim of this chapter is to present along these themes a few important points regarding the role of the Internet in Danish adolescents' cultural and social practices and the impact of Internet uses on the understanding of being globally orientated and yet locally rooted.[1]

The chapter largely builds on analyses from a year 2000 study of 12- to 16-year-old Danes' media uses in the crossing between the global and the local but is brought up to date by including new data and analyses of focused areas of uses.[2]

Access and Development

By the end of 2002, 65% of the Danish population and 82% of the 16- to 19-year-olds had Internet access at home (Danmarks Statistik, 2003). In 2003, all young Danes' have access to the Internet either at home, at school, or at Net-cafés as they had in year 2000 when I first analyzed young Danes Internet uses (Stald, 2003/2001) and almost all make use of it. The developments that can be distinguished during these three years are reinforcements or alterations of uses, trends, and attitudes that were already prominent in 2000. One of the interesting developments is seen in the actual use of the computer/Internet as the convergent medium when it is used for communication, download, and playing of both music and fiction (movies and TV), and as news channel (online newspapers and TV/radio programs) and platform for gaming. This development is in particular remarkable for the advanced users, but nevertheless, the Internet is still used in combination with a range of other media.

From the late 1990s, Internet services have become integrated in Denmark both at the institutional levels of society and at the level of the individual citizen. It is no longer possible to identify the Internet as a phenomenon connected alone with academia, institutional administration—or youth culture. When your grandmother sends you an e-mail with a link to some information, when your aunt has found her new husband via online dating, and your teacher bought his camera on a Web auction, when the guys you meet in a Counter Strike combat are between 10 and 40—and when all other media refer you to check out their Web site, online debate, direct, updated news, the Internet is truly integrated in Danish society and culture.

One of the conditions of development that the young users have had to deal with is the increasing influence of economic and commercial interests related to Internet uses. Patricia Wallace among others points to the fact that commercial interests have played a central part in "the expansion of the net's role and capabilities" (Wallace, 2001: xiii). One of the distinct consequences of this process has obviously been shifting patterns of organization of and access to Net-services. Commercial interests show among others as charges for services, direct and broad marketing, and Internet sale/auctions. The young users meet the commercialization of the Net often and heavily because of their generally broad and extensive uses of the Internet. Apparently they have adjusted their uses to the changing "nature" of the Internet from a free and open source for those who had access to a system of institutionalized, regulated, exploited system mirroring the structure and interests in offline society. By contrast, one of the popular ways of using the Internet is to sidestep regulations and fees and to explore the possible alternative uses of the Net.

The levels and ways of use vary greatly from one adolescent to the other and often also over a period of time. Generally, however, the Internet is integrated in adolescent everyday life as an obvious choice—pragmatically focused on local usefulness. The drawing illustrates the integration of media in everyday life of a 15-year-old boy:[3]

Figure 1. Paolo, 15 years

Paolo titled his drawing "Media Around the Clock", which is a rather precise description of how a broad variety of media—digital as well as 'traditional' are integrated in the everyday life of Danish adolescents—TV, computer with the Internet Modem, books, telephone, music. Music accompanies almost all activities, also while other media are used. The clocks on the wall indicate certain media uses at certain hours but rather than exclusive uses they demonstrate typical times for typical uses. The two timeline-arrows that frame the drawing are more important as indicators of the continuance, the process of media uses. The home based Internet use is still to many young Danes limited by the costs—illustrated in the drawing by the dial-up connection. Even if a growing number of Danish families get fast and cheap connections (ADSL) the majority still pays for the time and has cheaper and better access at school, libraries, work.

Internet in Social and Cultural Contexts

Being with friends, finding new personal relations, and participating in a variety of communities is essential to most young people and, hence, "One of the main functions of the Internet for young Danes is to seek, develop and maintain personal relations. . . . The Net is a meeting place for young people both for ephemeral encounters in one-time chats and continued exchange of experience and attitudes in chat- or discussion groups. Some online relations develop over time to be offline relations" (Stald, 2002a, p. 141).

Communicative forms for interpersonal exchange are varied. However, the hype of the Internet has decreased also in this area. Only very few of my informants claim to like chatting randomly on the usual popular teen-chat-sites. Those who do try them out are primarily very young newcomers, teenagers who are bored or those who log into the "special interest" groups. The reasons given for not spending time on random chat are in short: the untrustworthiness of the participants and information given, that it is rare to meet someone with shared interests, that intimacy and deep relations may develop over time but the users seldom meet many times, the consideration of potential threats of meeting criminal impostors on the Net and maybe offline.

The number of "chatters" on the popular teen-sites has decreased remarkably during the past two or three years and it seems clear that the "serious," deep exchanges have moved to other areas of the Internet. This is primarily Instant Messaging via Yahoo, ICQ, or Jubii or discussion forums in communities of interest, for example, gaming universes. Many prefer Instant Messaging because

> I don't really bother chatting in teen-chat-rooms, GS. . . . Too many go in there just to spoil it for others and so on. Via icq you can choose with whom you want to chat. Q: Quite often someone you know beforehand, then? A: Well, yes, but, you can also say, "find random user," right?
>
> (Alex, 15 years old)

Instant messaging is also preferred to e-mails in certain situations of communication. E-mail is primarily used to keep in contact with friends and family abroad.

The instant messaging and constant updating on networks in the individual's youth cultural context has partly been taken over or heavily supplemented by the use of SMS on the personal mobile phone. These two tendencies—shift from chat to IRC and from IRC to SMS—are interesting because they point to a shift from the open, random "is-anybody-there" approach to the relatively closed, selective, and often locally rooted connection. In the popular chatrooms it is easy to go in and easy to leave, that is, relations can be abandoned at any time with few immediate costs to the participants. It is not as easy or at all possible to "lie, laugh, and leave" in established communities of interest and in online communication with friends.

The questions of validity, trust, and risk in the relation between *offline and online experience* are important to the young Net-users. As in the physical world, they like to explore possibilities and joys and usefulness of new areas and relations but have generally grown tired of the anonymity of the Net and the constant testing of trustworthiness. Gradually tools to distinguish the false from the true and nonvalidity from validity regarding information and people have been developed by the individual or in the communities. Emerging forms of normativity, restrictions, and regulations within the communities in order to optimize the experience and prohibit the destructive input follows this.

The Internet allows the individual to experiment with *identity*, which is essential to adolescents struggling to develop their individual and collective identity, and finding their footing in the global respectively local contexts. Jay Bolter says that "The World Wide Web, too, permits us to construct our identities in and through the sites that we create as well as those that we visit. . . . This is not to say that our identity is fully determined by media, but rather that we employ media in defining both our personal and cultural identities" (Bolter, 2000, p. 17).

Creating *Web sites* or *Web logs* is one way of making yourself visible. Some of my informants have tried it out. Most, however, tire after some time, because it is time consuming and demanding to make a quality site. Fifteen-year-old Paolo says: "There are so many lousy sites and I don't want to make one of those myself. . . . You know, people who have tried to do html who are not really good at it, so they have only put one picture up, and, well . . ."

It is easier and perhaps more fulfilling over time to be visible on the Net by participating in online communities related to specific interests like gaming, sports, or fan cultures. In these forums immediate feedback is given to the self-presentation in various forms.

The Internet's potential role in the process of identity formatting must be seen in the context of the individual's everyday life as it is illustrated by the drawing (Figure 2).

The Internet-based spaces for communication and social, cultural, and emotional exchange are important training fields for social skills, self-understanding, and understanding of the world to the young users, dependent on intensity and diversity of the uses. Some invest a lot of energy in creative, organizational, or informative activities on the Net. All, however, are also in a way hardcore users with the motto: "What's the use of it for me?" In spite of the institutionalization and commercialization the Net is still perceived as a space for experiment and for challenge of borders, norms, and rights to information.

File sharing is one example. File sharing has taken place since the first days of the Internet but only during the past few years has the phenomenon been organized via enterprises such as Napster, Kazaa and others. File sharing and free download of music, films, and computer games has grown to the point where it threatens the business of the producers. Young Danes exchange files with thousands of complete strangers on the Net and information on the best downloads with friends in the local context. These actions make it possible to be up to date or perhaps ahead regarding the newest piece of music or the latest popular film or game. It also enhances the tendency among young people to construct individual cultural experiences when the CD with all the favorite highlights from a popular artist is burned. According to Patricia Wallace, the file sharers are aware that they break the law but they are seemingly "untroubled by any ethical or moral concerns" (Wallace, 2001: xix). They know of the size and profit of popular culture business and have probably all spent all their pocket money on CDs, games, and videos a few years ago.

Online multiplayer computer gaming is one example of Internet use as social and cultural training field, in the game, and in the gaming universe. One of the overall attractions of online multiplayer games is the fact that allies and opponents are living persons, which make the game more challenging and unpredictable but also adds to the experience of community in the context of the game.

Figure 2. Michelle, 12 years

The Internet is also a medium for personal, emotional experience in the process of finding one's personal identity and footing. The life world of a 12-year-old girl is to a large degree influenced by thoughts on relations and her own position in the world. The diary with the heart and flower, the idyllic world—nature— represented on the TV-set, the relaxed position while listening to music are expressions of the dreams and hopes of an adolescent in a period of change. At the same time the early teens are also an age when growing conscience about the world interferes with the very subjective experience of relations and emotions. This is illustrated by the lines—newspaper page—with the words 'politics' in the lower right corner and the talk on the radio together with the music. The 'Bla, bla bla' in the upper 'thought' balloon is a quite reflexive comment on talking/being in contact is sometimes more important than content.

In the context of this article, however, the illustration of the girl behind the net is particularly interesting. The text says 'INT NET' or 'INTO NET' and 'Searching Net', 'chat, chat' on the red lips and 'Mona to Angel' in the speech balloon. The net-pattern over the girl could be interpreted as a (prison) fence but is more likely to be the visualisation of 'into the net'—the online communicative situation where relations are established via chat. 'Looking for net' illustrates the self-reflexivity in the process—the girl is indeed aware of the potentials and the motivations for 'going into the net'. The question marks represent the unknown but possible relations—the basis of the network, but also the question of validity and meaning of cmc-based networks and relations.

The social element is important in online gaming universes both in the context of the single game and in the gaming environment and adds to the experience in the game (Stald, 2002c). The players share the experiences in the game according to the rules of the game, the gameplay, and the gaming situation (Figure 3). Interestingly, many continue to play particularly first-person-shooters at Internet-cafés or at LAN-parties after having cheap, broadband ADSL at home to be with friends in the local place while playing in global space.

Figure 3. Daniel, 15 years

One of the popular uses of the Internet is online gaming. Daniel is one of the relatively few who have experienced a virtual reality game. Online multiplayer games are easy to access and fascinating for several reasons for the players; so much time is spent online at home or at the nearby net-cafe. Daniel plays the (still) most popular game, *Counter Strike*, both with offline friends and players whom he meets only online. Note the engaged expression of the player at the pc—he is deeply immersed in the game.

Gaming is not limited to adolescents. A very large part of online players are over 20—a new generation of media users who have grown up with the computer medium.

The virtual reality scenario in the drawing can be interpreted as an illustration of the optimal gaming situation—the personal, virtual reality, online game.

Global Reach, Local Roots

The Internet opens up the world to young people through the vast access to information, mediated experience, and through the possible reach of people around the globe across time and space. They put together a quilt of information and establish an idea of the global common partly by the represented picture but also by self experienced knowledge. The important point is that they can actually challenge and qualify their knowledge of the world by going into a globally oriented dialogue with fellow adolescents but also other sources of information. The differentiated perspective or personally experienced account of other cultures and conditions and realities is only a few mouse clicks and lines of writing and reading away. Some and apparently increasingly many, explore this possibility.

According to the young Net users much must be self-experienced in person in order to be valid. The drawing (Figure 4) is one example of the ways in which information is experienced as mediated in several ways. The individual has to evaluate the input in the context of the local reality and personal experience.

Figure 4. Kristoffer, 12 years old

Note again in this drawing the variety of media in the boy's bedroom: Computer and Internet, television and videos, stereo and books. Music is overall.

Electronic media, in particular the Internet and TV, are important sources of information for young Danes. Various media may deal with the same subjects, which in this case is pro et contra the common European currency, but do also provide the adolescent with multiple sources of information. This is considered a positive possibility, but also a problem, because confusion might prevail over clarity when so much information has to be sorted out and evaluated.

Word bubbles translated from left to right: "my room;" "we don't get the Euro-coin;" and "we will have the Euro-coin."

The mediated representations of the world provide the adolescents with information on exciting places and cultures, yet also on different conditions of living, dangers, and threats that make Denmark appear as the safe and secure haven in a period of life when they have to find themselves and their position in relation to the local as well as the global. The ambivalence of the young Danes mirrored in the obvious divergence between, on the one hand, the actual cultural transformation in the dialectic process between the local and the global and, on the other hand, the ways in which they talk about their views of the world and their experience of being Danes as well as world citizens. They do experience how cultural globalization actually takes place, not alone through the impact of international businesses, but also through uncountable everyday meetings and not least via media, especially the Internet. Young Danes are globally orientated and Danish culture is constantly changing in the meetings with the global—politically, economically, culturally. But the local rooting is strong and probably necessary to the young people in this period of their life (Stald, 2002a).

Conclusions

The Internet is obviously not an unchangeable system of technologically enforced services. It is defined by technological innovation in synergetic progress with the ever-developing ways of uses and challenges of the usefulness of Internet-based services. The young Danes in my studies generally adapt rapidly to new possibilities and conditions of the Internet but are at the same time critically reflexive about the forms, meanings, and impact of the uses in relation to both their access to information and to networks and relations established and developed via the Net. New services are tried out and evaluated in the context of local usefulness, of its way of enhancing symbiosis between various media in everyday life. Due to the convergence of possible uses computer-mediated services including the Internet exist in the youth cultural and social contexts as an important platform for experience, information, and social exchange. But there is no sentimentality toward the Internet—if other platforms such as the mobile phone turn out to be more useful, effective, and fun in the diverse situations of use they overrule the rather predominant status of the Internet. Not even better personal computers and fast and cheap broadband connections alter the integration of a variety of media in young Danes' everyday lives. Two types of convergent media are up front following the development of advanced digital media and rapidly increasing access to a variety of these among young Danes—the powerful, graphically strong PC and the mobile phone with its minimal but fast-growing variation of possible uses. The mobility of the cell phone in combination with new online, mobile services may challenge the existing patterns of media use in youth cultural contexts and enforce the integration of mediated communication and experience in even more situations.

The critical reflexivity, not to be confused with negative attitudes, embraces questions of trust, risk, and validity of information and experience. These attitudes depend on personal experience and are influenced by the discourse and general opinion in public as well as youth cultural context. The expressed attitudes do not necessarily reflect the actual uses and de facto impact. For example, seen from an analytical point of view the transcendence between offline and online spaces and the process of integrating experience and meaning from one realm to another is more complex and important than most of my informants seem to think.

One question regarding the impact of Internet-uses triggers considerations among my young informants: Is the world getting smaller or bigger because of the Internet and either way how does our increased universal knowledge and global connectivity influence our self-identity and the global processes of economic, political, and cultural development? These kinds of reflexivity arise at a different level of understanding than those of the rather unworried, immediate uses of the services. They point to the fact that young people may be orientated toward subjective needs and local usefulness, but they are not unconscious, uncritical users of digital media.

> *"I think that we have become used to getting used to things"*
>
> *(Asbjoern, 15 years old,*
>
> *on our changing world and the influence of the Internet)*

Notes

1. An early, full version of this article, "Outlook and Insight. Young Danes Uses of and thought on the Uses of the Internet," was presented to the 1st annual conference of the Association of Internet Researchers, University of Kansas, September 2000. Published in Andrea Kavanaugh & Joseph Turow (Eds.) (2003), *The Wired Homestead*. Boston: MIT Press.
2. This paper is based on data from *Global Media, Local Youth,* part of the research program *Global Media Cultures* (1999–2001), Film & Media Studies, University of Copenhagen. Sixty-four adolescents between 12 and 16 years were interviewed. Second, I use findings from an ongoing study of online gaming (methods: observation, interviews, and participation are used. Not concluded).
3. All participants in the 1996/7 and 2000 studies made drawings of their everyday life with media, resulting in 164 drawings. The drawings present various themes and conceptions of media uses and everyday life.

References

Abbott, Chris. (1998). Making Connections: Young People and the Internet. In Sefton-Green, Julian (Ed.), *Digital Diversions. Youth Culture in the Age of Multimedia* (pp. 84–105). London: UCL Press.

Baym, Nancy (2002). Interpersonal Life Online, pp. 63–76 in Lievrouw, Leah and Livingstone, Sonia (Eds.) *Handbook of New Media*. London: Sage.

Bolter, Jay. (2000). Identity. In Swiss, Thomas (Ed.), *Unspun. Key Concepts for Understanding the World Wide Web*. New York/London: New York University Press.

Danmarks Statistik (2003). *Befolkningens brug af Internet 4. kvartal 2002 (Population's uses of the Internet, 4th quarter of 2002)*. <http://www.dst.dk>.

Stald, Gitte (2003/2001). "Outlook and Insight: Young Danes' Uses of the Internet, Navigating Global Seas and Local Waters," in Kavanaugh, Andrea & Turow, Joseph (Eds.) *The Wired Homestead*. Boston: MIT Press.

Stald, Gitte (2002a). The World is Quite Enough: Young Danes, Media and Identity in the Crossfield between the Global and the Local. In Stald, Gitte and Tufte, Thomas (Eds.), *Global Encounters—Media and Cultural Transformation*. Luton: University of Luton Press.

Stald, Gitte (2002c). "Meeting in the Combat Zone. Online Multi-player Computer Games as spaces for Social and Cultural Encounters." Paper presented to *Internet Research.2: Interconnections*. AoIR, Minneapolis, October 2001.

Wallace, Patricia (1999/2001). *The Psychology of the Internet*. Cambridge: Cambridge University Press.

QUESTING ON THE GLOBAL STAGE: BRAIN GAIN, MARKET GAIN, AND THE RHETORIC OF THE INTERNET IN GERMAN AND U.S. HIGHER EDUCATION POLICY

Historically, higher education policy has been shaped predominantly by national and cultural traditions. As Dumort (2000) states, in Europe, for example, higher education has been perceived as a public good, with almost all universities publicly funded. This is especially true in Germany with its 100% tax-funded system of higher education. In the United States, in contrast, higher education has traditionally been more market oriented with a mix of public and private funding.

As higher education moves into the common global space of the Internet, however, the question arises, whether higher education policy converges in its response to the Internet or whether it retains its distinctive national traditions. To examine this question, this chapter presents a rhetorical analysis of national higher education policy, focusing on the examples of two policy initiatives: the report "The Power of the Internet for Learning: Moving from Promise to Practice" by the Web-Based Education Commission of the United States Congress (December 2000), which was developed as a "policy roadmap" to help educators across the country address "'digital age' challenges brought about by the Internet," and the "Initiative for the International Marketing of German Higher Education and Research" (2001), an action plan designed to provide German higher education with a national marketing brand name. As the analysis shows, the narratives share the overall frame of a quest, but the specific narrative strategies differ with the cultural context: whereas German higher education policy advances a quest for national brain gain, U.S. policy advances a quest for global markets. Nevertheless, to achieve their goals, both policy environments promote an increasingly market-oriented approach to higher education.

In both countries, policy issues are advanced largely through the narrative genre of the quest. A quest, according to Northrop Frye (1954), typically pits a hero or protagonist against an external menace that threatens to overwhelm the world as he or she knows it, or it presents the hero with new opportunities to improve the world based on long-held values. Once an external threat or opportunity appears, the hero receives a call to adventure—to go on a quest to either overcome the menace or to unleash the opportunity for an improved world. The protagonist, aided by guides, guardians, and talismans, then typically overcomes a series of obstacles, generally represented by monsters. Traditionally, it is overcoming an external menace or working to realize a new opportunity that subsequently functions to unite a people, providing an essential ingredient in the process of nationbuilding. Thus, a typical example, the legend of King Arthur, with its valiant knights of the Round Table questing for the mythic Holy Grail, serves as a unifying element in English history.

To demonstrate how higher education is revisioned in the context of the Internet in Germany and in the United States, I show how some of the key elements of the generic quest narrative—the setting, the object of the quest, the hero's guide, and the monster—are used rhetorically to advocate a certain course of policy action for the Internet in higher education.

The Setting

In a quest, the setting shows the hero's homeland, and here particularly the status quo, before the disruption—either the threat or the new opportunity—sets in. Typically, the "disruption"—either positively or negatively inflected—is introduced in the setting as well to show either the threat or the promising new opportunities for the people or nation.

In U.S. higher education policy discourse, the status quo is given little presence. Political action agendas and policy recommendations immediately direct the attention to the new—the Internet, and away from the current status quo. In the Web-Based Education Commission report, for example, the focus on the new is immediately associated with the good and also dissociated from the status quo through an antithesis, "a verbal structure that places contrasted ... terms in ... balanced phrases" (Fahnestock, 2000, p. 175). Accordingly, the Web-Based Education Commission report begins by separating the promising future from the problematic past and present:

> The good news is that the Internet is bringing us closer than we ever thought possible to make learning—of all kinds, at all levels, any time, any place, any pace—a

practical reality for every man, woman, and child. The bad news? Millions still cannot access the Internet and do not understand how to use it to harness the global web of knowledge. (p. 1)

In contrast, German higher education policy discourse focuses heavily on the setting and the local, which is given considerable presence through the metaphoric reference to Germany as a "Standort" (location). The idea of the Standort metaphorically constructs Germany as a fixed and stable place or location, with the word "ort" (translated as site, location, base, or place) emphasizing the place and hence the local or national aspect of the country. The first component of the metaphor, "Stand-," derives from "stehen" (to stand), which adds the connotations of a fixed, static, and stable nature to the term.

Translated into English, the word would create an odd emphasis. For example, in trying to translate the title of the Initiative "Internationales Marketing für den Bildungs- und Forschungsstandort Deutschland" for an English-speaking audience, one would more than likely leave the word Standort out entirely, because it does not carry the same value and hence would be less likely to be given the same presence. Instead, one might translate the title simply as "International Marketing of German Education and Research." However, one would lose the emphasis on the physical location and the situation of the nation that permeates much of the German political debate as well as the higher education policy documents. This emphasis on the setting, or "Standort," makes higher education in Germany much more of a national concern. Hence, in Germany, higher education becomes a "Standortfaktor," in other words, a weapon in the quest for the good reputation of Germany as a "Standort" or nation.

The Object of the Quest

In U.S. policy discourse, the quest consists of unleashing an unprecedented and nearly unlimited opportunity ascribed to the Internet, described largely as business market opportunities. A section titled "e-education is big business now—and will be bigger in the future" in the Web-Based Education Commission report, for example, provides detailed research on the dollar value of each type of educational market. However, these opportunities for market expansion are associated with utopian unlimited opportunities for individuals. Thus, the Web-Based Commission Report, for example, celebrates the World Wide Web as a tool of many opportunities:

> The World Wide Web is a tool that empowers society to school the illiterate, bring job training to the unskilled, open a universe of wondrous images and knowledge to all students, and enrich the understanding of the lifelong learner. The opportunity is at hand. The power and the promise are here. It is now time to move from promise to practice. (p. 1)

Again, the report uses antithesis, this time repeated antithesis to associate the new technology with positive values (schooling, job training, etc.) while at the same time associating the pre-Internet situation with negative values (the illiterates, the unskilled). The antithesis then works to separate the positive values of the new technology from the negative values of the past. Despite some isolated minimal and largely clichéd hedges that the Internet cannot be the "panacea for every problem in education," the view of the Internet as the new promise of an unlimited opportunity dominates higher education policy discourse in the United States.

In contrast, in German higher education policy discourse, the quest is framed in somewhat dystopian terms—as the need to overcome a threat to continued national prosperity and international leadership that is perceived to stem from the Internet and its globalizing power, which in turn is perceived to increase global competition among "Standorte," or nations. The higher education Marketing Initiative, for example, is based on the assumption about a competition for the best intellects—a competition that is intensified by the Internet: "We find ourselves in a worldwide competition for . . . intellects and markets. . . . This competition will be intensified by the Internet . . . and by growing worldwide mobility."[1]

For the most part, the competition is perceived to be about brain power with Germany fearing a brain drain, expressed in concerns about the decreasing number of international students and the increasing number of German scholars pursuing their careers in the United States and other countries. As the education secretary, Edelgard Bulmahn, describes the purpose of the higher education Marketing Initiative, the country must move from "brain drain" to "brain gain."

A large part of the solution consequently consists of making the "Standort" Germany attractive by marketing the "Standort" to international students and scholars. In this Marketing Initiative, the goal is to persuade international students and scholars to physically come to Germany rather than to perhaps take German courses and programs online. In fact, the Internet portal that was created by the marketing initiative, <http://www.campus-germany.de>, provides international students with information about campus-based programs and various types of information about living in Germany. To learn about Internet-based courses and programs, interested students need to visit a different portal—one with online opportunities.

The higher education marketing portal for international students, however, does not even provide a link to online opportunities, at least not in a way that students can easily find. It seems, then, that at this point, German higher education policy is mostly concerned with building a German national brand name for higher education. As a result, the Internet at this point is seen mostly as an opportunity to market German higher education and to attract international students and scholars to come to Germany.

The Hero's Guide

In a quest narrative, the hero is usually given a guide, such as an old advisor or a wizard, who usually has the function of helping the hero find the right way and complete the quest successfully. Both countries present such guides in the form of a model to follow. In the case of U.S. higher education policy discourse, the guide is again internal—most frequently, the private for-profit sector. The Web-Based Commission Report, for example, abounds with analogies to the business community for arguments of why the proposed course of action is the only reasonable one. In response to those hesitant about the use of the Internet in education, for example, the report exhorts,

> Imagine what would have happened if the nation's corporate leaders had imposed a similar moratorium in 1990, before they were able to measure objectively any positive impact of technology investment in productivity. It took years for these technological investments to bear fruit. Fortunately, business made these investments in technology. As vast as those investments were, they are dwarfed by their results—a one-third increase in real U.S. economic growth. (p. 5)

Again, higher education policy discourse here clearly reflects a market and business orientation.

In Germany, the model is again external. For the most part, with some national adjustments, the model is higher education in the United States. As Roman Herzog (1997), then president of Germany, exclaims, "Why should what has long succeeded in America and elsewhere not be possible in our country?"[2] And he is not the only one. Calls to learn from the U.S. higher education system are nothing new (Kortman & Fehlner, 1998; Bublitz & Zapf, 1998; Ash, 1998). Similarly, the German Department of Education looks to the United States, finding that "within the next ten years, education and its institutions will be undergoing a paradigm shift, which will lead to a global education market dominated by the United States" (Thomas, 2001, p. 3).[3] By using this external model, then, Germany to some extent imports the market-oriented view of higher education as a tradable private good.

The Monster(s)

Regardless of what the specific quest is, the protagonist of a quest usually has to overcome several monsters or obstacles to complete the quest successfully. In U.S. higher education policy discourse, the monster is typically created in the past—past regulations, past approaches that now are all declared useless and even damaging and hence in need of being overcome. In particular, regulations that limit the participation of emerging Internet-based education providers in federal financial aid programs are targeted as obstacles to be overcome. As a result, examples of problematic past and present practices that now need to be overcome abound in U.S. higher education policy discourse. The key argument of the Web-Based Education Commission report—the need to remove regulations that impede the spread of Internet-based learning, for example, is advanced by means of dissociating the past and present from the future:

> Today's education is built on an agrarian model that worked in the years when we were a nation of farmers, foresters, and fishermen. Schooling changed to take on elements of the industrial revolution (factory-line classes, assembly-line curriculum, and teacher foremen) that worked for the needs of the Industrial Age. New designs are needed to create the "knowledge workers" who will define the Information Age. (p. 6)

Past and present problems are identified in all education sectors to promote the Internet as the magic weapon to overcome all of these problems. The foreword of the Web-Based Education Commission report laments a number of current and past problems:

> Elementary and secondary schools are experiencing growing enrollments, coping with critical shortages of teachers, facing overcrowded and decaying buildings, and responding to demands for higher standards. On college campuses, there is an influx of older, part-time students seeking the skills vital to success in the Information Age. Corporations are dealing with the shortage of skilled workers and the necessity of providing continuous training to their employees. (p. i)

The next sentence then immediately introduces the Internet as the magic weapon to overcome these obstacles, presented in the form of an antimetabole to dissociate past practices from needed future practices: "The Internet is enabling us to address these educational challenges, bringing learning to students instead of bringing students to learning." The antimetabole here of "bringing learning to students instead of bringing students to learning" only reinforces the antithetical character of past and future practices by implying that the order of things has to be completely changed. To argue for its course of action regarding the Internet in higher education, U.S. policy thus creates a strong rupture between the future and the past/present, whereby the future is assigned positive values and the past is vilified as a monster to be overcome.

In Germany, however, with its view of the Internet as an accelerator of the global race for brain power, the monster is in the present and in the future. In fact, few of the obstacles are perceived to be in the past. Instead, the past, in particular past national glory of higher education in the early 20th century, when German higher education was a global center for research and education, is invoked as a positive analogy to the quest for attractiveness in a global marketplace. As the Marketing Initiative states, "For a long time, Germany has not reached the level of appeal for foreign professionals that it once had due to its scholarly brilliance and historical tradition."[4]

The present, and here specifically xenophobic attacks against foreigners, however, present the largest monster in German higher education policy. Xenophobia as well as immigration and labor laws are perceived to be the greatest hindrances in winning the global race for brain gain. Especially the higher education Marketing Initiative focuses on the problem of xenophobia, including in its set of policy documents a declaration on immigration and labor law for international students and scholars:

> Existing mobility hurdles presented by immigration and labor laws should be quickly removed. The goal must be to make it easier for foreign students, visiting scholars, and those interested in a professional qualification to study, teach, and research in Germany. It is also important to provide opportunities for graduates and young scholars to work in Germany for a few years after completing their program.[5]

However, the action program does not invite just any foreigner, but only the "beste Köpfe" (the best intellects; literally, heads). Other metaphors such as "Spitzenkräfte" (top professionals) and the direct use of the term "elite" ("ausländische Fach-und Führungseliten"—elite foreign specialists) reinforce the idea that to succeed in what is perceived to be the global competition for the "beste Köpfe," Germany wants only the best—the elite. Although the higher education marketing policy initiative, then, supports the struggle against xenophobia, this support is motivated by the need to secure better conditions for those foreigners that represent much desired brain power and consequently are perceived to help Germany succeed in the global race. They are not motivated by the need to overcome xenophobia against economically and educationally disadvantaged and therefore vulnerable refugees, who tend to be the victims of xenophobic attacks.

Conclusion

In higher education policy addressing the Internet, as in much public policy, the dominant narrative frame tends to use culturally situated rhetorical strategies that define challenges and threats in specific ways and hence limit the solutions or the courses of action to the way the policy issues are framed. Thus, in the United States, the Internet is framed exclusively as an unprecedented opportunity for market expansion associated with unlimited utopian opportunities for all individuals. As a result, good education is good business, especially on the Internet with its new options for delivering higher education easily, flexibly, and globally.

In contrast, in Germany, the Internet is perceived more as an external threat—as an accelerator of global competition for brain power. Consequently, the policy response is somewhat more nationally oriented, framing higher education as a largely national resource in this global race. Yet, to hold its own and receive a share of the new global education market, German higher education policy advocates a Marketing Initiative in higher education to build a national brand name.

Ultimately, then, the rhetorical strategies deployed to advance a particular vision of higher education may differ with the cultural context, but the end result of an increasingly market-oriented approach, advanced in the context of the Internet, is rather similar. As a result, Internet-related policies in one national context may alter the policy environment for such policies in another national context and encourage convergence among policies across national contexts.

Notes

1. My translation of: "Wir stehen in einem internationalen Wettbewerb . . . um Köpfe und Märkte. . . . Durch das Internet, . . . , und die weltweit steigende Mobilität wird sich dieser Wettbewerb verschärfen."
2. My translation of: "Warum sollte bei uns nicht möglich sein, was in Amerika und anderswo längst gelungen ist?"
3. My translation of: "Wir stehen in den nächsten zehn Jahren vor einem grundlegenden Wandel des Prozesses Bildung und der ihn tragenden Institutionen, ein Paradigmenwechsel, der zu einem amerikanisch dominierten globalen Bildungsmarkt führen wird."
4. My translation of: "Für ausländische Fachkräfte ist Deutschland allerdings schon lange nicht mehr der selbstverständliche Magnet, der es früher aufgrund wissenschaftlicher Brillanz oder historischer Tradition gewesen ist."
5. My translation of: "Noch bestehende ausländerrechtliche und arbeitsrechtliche Mobilitätshemmnisse sollen rasch beseitigt werden. Ziel muss es sein, ausländischen Studierenden, Gastwissenschaftlern sowie Interessenten an einer beruflichen Qualifizierung einen Aufenthalt in Deutschland für Aus- und Weiterbildung sowie für Lehr- und Forschungszwecke zu erleichtern. Wichtig ist auch, Studienabsolventen und Nachwuchswissenschaftlern die Möglichkeit zu eröffnen, nach ihrer Ausbildung noch einige Jahre in Deutschland berufstätig zu sein."

References

Armstrong, L. (2001). "A New Game in Town: Competitive Higher Education," *Information, Communication, and Society*, 4 (4), 479–506.
Ash, M. (1998). "Äpfel mit Äpfel vergleichen! Wider die Mythenbildung über amerikanische Universitäten," *Forschung & Lehre*, 4, 172–175.
Bublitz, W., & Zapf, H. (1998). "Ein tauglicher Vergleich? Anmerkungen über das deutsche und amerikanische Hochschulsystem," *Forschung & Lehre*, 4, 172–175.
Bund-Länder Kommission für Bildungsplanung und Forschungsförderung (2000–2001). *Internationales Marketing für den Bildungs- und Forschungsstandort Deutschland*. Retrieved November 30, 2001, from < http://www.blk-bonn.de >.
Dumort, A. (2000). "New Media and Distance Education: An EU-US Perspective," *Information, Communication & Society*, 3, 546–556.
Fahnestock, J. (2000). "Aristotle and Theories of Figuration," in A. Gross & A. Walzer, eds., *Rereading Aristotle's Rhetoric* (pp. 166–184). Carbondale: Southern Illinois University Press.

Frye, Northrop. (1957). *Anatomy of Criticism*. Princeton, NJ: Princeton University Press.
Herzog, R. (1997, April 26). *Aufbruch ins 21. Jahrhundert (Setting out into the 21st Century)*. Retrieved August 10, 2002, from <http://www.bundesprsident.de>.
Kortman, B., & Fehlner, G. (1998). "Die anglo-amerikanischen Universitäten—ein Modell für Deutschland?" *Englisches Seminar der Albert-Lugwigs-Universität Freiburg*. Retrieved May 6, 2001, from <http:www.uni-freiburg.de/philfak3/eng/lehrstuhl/angloam.htm>.
The Power of the Internet for Learning: Moving from Promise to Practice (2001, December 19). Report of the Web-Based Education Commission to the President and the Congress of the United States. Retrieved April 29, 2001, from <http://www.ed.gov/offices/AC/WBEC/FinalReport>.
Thomas, U. (2001). *Anytime, Anywhere: IT-gestütztes Lernen in den USA. Bericht zur Studienreise in die USA*. Bundresministerium für Bildung and Forschung. Retrieved May 30, 2001, from <http://www.gmd.de/NMB/e-learninginUSA/USAReiseBericht.doc>.

David Palfreyman   14

LEARNING TO USE ICTS IN A GULF ARAB CONTEXT

Introduction

This paper considers the role which social context can play in people's learning and use of information and communication technology (ICT). The paper draws on data from a sample of female students at a "laptop university" in the United Arab Emirates (UAE). When I started teaching at this university I found myself a "stranger in a strange land," in more than one sense: I was a male, European teacher in an institution whose students are all female Muslim Gulf Arabs, from a background that prides itself on its traditions, including segregation of genders in everyday life. I was also a relative newcomer to the world of ICT, in an institution that prides itself on disseminating the latest technology. As a new member of this institution, I received from other "Westerners" around me an impression of the students as "repressed" members of a "closed" society for whom ICT offers the beginnings of "liberation." In the study reported here, I tried to explore how these students themselves perceive the place of ICT in their social world.

The discourse of emancipation is not the only way to view the spread of ICT use among young people. Although Bakardjieva and Smith (2001) assert that "the technology of the internet has empowered 'boxed in' ordinary people [. . .] to open up spaces for meaningful individual and collective action and creativity," Leung's (2001) study of ICQ use by Hong Kong university students, for example, suggests that ICT also may function as a means of escapism for disempowered lower-income students with little privacy in their living arrangements: an "opiate of the people" for the 21st century.

Until about 30 years ago, UAE society was based on patterns largely unchanged for centuries. There was a relatively low level of formal education and technology; gender roles were very tightly defined; and extended family ties shaped the lives of most people from an early age. These patterns still influence UAE society; but, since the sudden growth of its oil industry in the 1960s, the country has seen dramatic changes in education, technology, and social norms; and today's female university students are very much involved in these changes: students whose mothers often did not receive primary education are now using ICT on a daily basis in a university environment. This chapter discusses how social context shapes these students' learning of ICT skills, and focuses on the social roles, framed by the family and by local and global society, which shape, support, and give meaning to the students' learning.

The findings of this study suggest that the situation in UAE society resembles in some ways the spread of ICT documented by the Pew Internet Project (Lenhart et al., 2001) in American society, and by Wheeler (2003) in the Gulf state of Kuwait: teenagers are early adopters and heavy users of ICT; ICT is used particularly in study situations, and electronic communication particularly in situations where shyness or social segregation is an issue. Furthermore, as in the United Kingdom (Gauntlett & Rodgers, 2002), the students tend to use ICT to communicate primarily with existing friendship groups. However, there are also striking differences from Western settings, which make the UAE situation an interesting case: the domestic setting and the family play a more significant role here; and the contrast in familiarity with ICT between teens and parents is even more pronounced.

A Model of Learning Context

ICT skills, and the process of learning them, are framed by various kinds of resources (or, to use another word, "capital") afforded by the learning context (Darrah, 1990; Lave & Wenger, 1991; Haddon, 1992). These can be analyzed in terms of three categories: *material resources, social resources* and *discursive resources* (Murdock et al., 1992). Material resources for learning may include equipment, books, and funds. Social resources consist of social networks of other people who act, for example, as models, or as sources of support and feedback (Brookfield, 1981). The value of social resources is affected by the level of knowledge or expertise among those with whom the learner interacts; but also by the availability of this expertise to the learner (Facer et al., 2001; Norton, 2000).

Discursive resources consist of concepts and discourses—about ICT, about learning and about social identity—which are current in the learner's social world (Moscovici, 1981): the "conversations which are around to be had in a given culture" (McDermott, 1993: 295). Gender is a prime example of a social identity factor which plays a significant part in learning. For example, Facer et al.'s (2001) study in the United Kingdom found that, while boys tended to see expertise in computer game-playing as something to be displayed to peers, girls with similar expertise tended not to use it in this way. Both boys and girls, however, tended to see IT skills also as instrumental, and to value them in so far as they helped them to attain other individually or socially valued goals such as sharing information about pop groups.

Individuals strategically navigate these various aspects of context, drawing on resources in different ways (Pollard & Filer, 1999). Facer et al. note that patterns of social interaction within the family can encourage young people to draw on particular attitudes and expertise from other family members, and so to use computers in particular ways. The present study explores how such processes seem to be shaping the learning of ICT's among female Emirati university students.

Population

The population involved in the present study is students at Zayed University (ZU), Dubai. ZU was established by the UAE government in 1998, with the mission of preparing students for meaningful and successful 21st century lives; promoting economic and social advancement; and promoting educational excellence and leadership in the UAE. Access to information technology is seen as a key theme in this mission: the students all have laptops, and classrooms, offices, and even the university cafeteria are networked.

The role of women in Gulf countries has traditionally been restricted largely to family life (cf. Wikan, 1991); and their access to technology has been chiefly through the home. Since the growth of educational provision in the UAE, however, women have tended to study in higher education in greater numbers than men, who have tended to move directly into employment. Nowadays (particularly in Dubai—a cosmopolitan commercial capital since long before the oil boom), women are seen as a resource for national development, and it is increasingly common for women to work. At the same time, family and other social pressures often lead them in other directions, sequestering women or encouraging them to devote their energies to marriage and parenting. One symbol of the contrast between traditional and modern roles is that although the students are physically restricted to the campus during their days at the university (at the request of their families as much as of the university), at the same time they are able to connect to the Internet and browse or chat with a great degree of freedom.

The students who took part in this study are Emirati women (although many would prefer to be called "girls," to signal that they are not yet involved in the responsibilities of adult life and marriage), aged 18–20. Most of them live in Dubai emirate, but some travel from the smaller, more conservative emirates of Sharjah, Ajman, and Um Al Quwain. Many of them come from families of five or more siblings—a fact that is significant in terms of the social resources for learning within the family.

Questions

The questions underlying this research are as follows:

- What is the range of resources available to these students in learning and using ICT?

- Which resources do students typically draw on?
- How does students' learning of ICT contribute to their social identity?

The first two questions relate to material, social and discursive resources that may feed into students' learning of ICTs. The third question focuses on the converse process: how the students' own developing ICT skills may constitute social capital within their family.

Method

The data used here comes from an anonymous online survey; the survey questions may be viewed at <http://f7385.tripod.com/questionnaire.htm>. I sent an e-mail to all students on the Dubai campus asking them if they would do an online survey about technology in their life, and 83 students responded to the questionnaire within a three-day period. The questions in the survey had been piloted with a small group of students beforehand to check the clarity of the questions, as well as students' perceptions of issues such as intrusiveness.

Findings

Material Resources and ICT Use

ICT use is a significant leisure pursuit for the students: 49.4% mentioned computer use as a free time activity that they enjoy, including 41% of the total sample who mentioned Internet use. The popularity of ICT use was second only to reading (55%). This may be a skewed sample, as those who responded to this survey were self-selected recipients of an e-mail that mentioned that the survey concerned the use of technology. However, the results of a previous study using a more random sample (Palfreyman, 2001) suggest that this level of ICT use is not unrepresentative of students in the university.

All students usually take their laptop home, and for 85.5% of respondents their laptop is the main computer that they use at home (other evidence suggests that the personal possession of a laptop can be a symbol of autonomy and privacy for these students). Ninety-five percent have Internet access at home, and much of the cited computer use involves the Internet. Computer use at home includes homework (89.2% of respondents) followed by browsing Web sites for entertainment or interest (66.3%) and chatting (34.9%).

Social Resources

The next most cited activity after computer use was socializing and chatting with family and friends (26.5%). These social contacts are mainly female, and mainly within the family: younger sisters (38.5%), older sisters (29.1%) (female) friends

(24.1%) and mother (20.3%) were cited most often as the main social contact outside university. Male relatives were cited far less often, and older brothers not at all, as the main contact. In relation to ICT, however, older brothers are cited as the main source of help with ICT by 12.5% of respondents, suggesting that the use of ICT may be linked to changes in the students' predominantly female social networks.

An important factor in the distribution of perceived resources in the family is level of education. For example, only 39% of fathers and 23.3% of mothers had completed secondary education, and this correlated with a low level of perceived familiarity with ICT. One factor underlying the citation of older brothers as sources of help is that they tend to have a higher rate of education (75%) than parents or younger siblings. However, knowledge is not the only factor: the level of everyday contact is also significant. Older sisters are the most frequently cited source of help with ICT, presumably because they are both educated and also socially accessible.

A significant number of students seem to have a role themselves as ICT "experts" in their family—30.1% of respondents said that nobody in their family knew more about ICT than they; 88% of students said that they sometimes helped other family members with using ICT; and on average students estimated that they helped others in their family more often than they were helped themselves. Comments such as the following in the open question responses suggested that this expertise was a source of pride and status in their family:

> I like to be educated and have enough information about it in front the people when they ask me about it [. . .]. they see me better than them, because [although] I am young [. . .] sometimes I help the older [members] in the family in using the computer. They [are] proud of me.

The recipients of this help tend to be those with whom the students have most daily contact: female family members (including mothers) and especially younger sisters. Thus again level of education and accessibility through same-gender networks together influence the topography of helping within the family, for example, in the way this student helps her younger sisters:

> I get them all into my room they are 3 and start to teach them from A to Z how to open it turn it on off what each key do and also the programs that i have in my computer.

The type of help given also varies broadly according to the person receiving it, and interacts with students' other expertise (notably in English and research skills). For example:

> For my younger brother he wants me to help [him] with language if he is using english sites [. . .] Searching for him for the information that he needs for his home

work. For my father for business [I] send email to compan[ies]. I try to teach my mother how to use Microsoft Word, Paint and typing in Arabic.

Note that although these examples show the student sharing expertise, this may be on different terms, depending on the gender-roles involved. "Helping" older male relatives was often represented as doing work "for" them, whereas helping female relatives more often involved teaching of skills.

Helping another family member appears usually to involve the student sharing her laptop with them. There seemed to be a fair amount of shared use of the computer, and even fathers (cited in only 1.6% of cases as the main contact in daily life) use the computer together with students in 12.5% of cases. This could well indicate covert monitoring of online activity by parents (mothers were also cited as co-users in 6.8% of cases).

Discursive Resources

Answers to the open questions in the questionnaire suggest that students see ICT as a key element in discourses of modernization and national development, and of the "imagined community" (Anderson, 1991) of global commerce:

> It's a wonderful technology [so] that we could contact with people all over the world in a few second[s].

> IT is spreading everyday and becoming more important all around the world for businesses and other things.

> IT helps us be more productive and efficient citizens in this society.

This is seen generally as a positive trend, but also sometimes as a strain and/or as contrary to the student's personal learning preferences.

> I hate technology and I get headache when I work on computers, yet all the works that are produced by computer look more professional.

ICT is also seen as influencing the individual's social identity within her family. Students expressed pride at being seen as ICT experts (see earlier); and parents were also often said to be proud of their daughters' new skills, for example:

> They are proud and encourage me to learn more about it.

Several students, however, like the one quoted below, perceived a conflict between ICT and more traditional "networking":

> [My parents think ICT] is good if its not taking our time from studying or sitting together with them and knowing new good information.

Implications for Teaching and Learning

The findings of this study suggest that learning and teaching of ICT skills might benefit from the following:

- Raising awareness of the range of material and social resources for learning which are available to students, and encouraging students to make constructive, reflective use of these.
- Raising individual students' awareness of their preferences in the use of these resources, and building on these preferences to enhance independent learning.
- Raising awareness of the roles/identities which students see for themselves, and creating dialogue between these and the teaching and learning process.

Interesting topics for future investigation of the place of ICT in these students' learning and social identity would include focusing on students' *productive* use of ICT skills (e.g., to make a Web site), as opposed to their consumption of "the Internet" and other resources, mentioned more frequently in this data; and also their use of the Internet for nonacademic information services that impinge on family life, such as online information about health.

References

Anderson, B. (1991). *Imagined Communities*. London: Verso.
Bakardjieva, M., & Smith, R. (2001). The Internet in Everyday Life: Computer Networking from the Standpoint of the Domestic User. *New Media and Society*, 3(1): 67–83. Accessed March 10, 2003, at < http://arago.cprost.sfu.ca:8080/rks_home/Research/Papers/edl >.
Brookfield, S. D. (1981). Independent Adult Learning. *Studies in Adult Education*, 13, 15–27.
Darrah, C. N. (1990). *Skills in Context: An Exploration in Industrial Ethnography*. Unpublished Ph.D. Dissertation, Stanford University.
Facer, K., Sutherland, R., Furlong, R., & Furlong, J. (2001). What's the Point of Using Computers? The Development of Young People's Computer Expertise in the Home. *New Media & Society 3(2)*: 199–219.
Gauntlett, D., and Rodgers, J. (2002). *"Girl Power" Online: A Redeployment of the Internet Activist Model*. Paper presented at the 3rd International Conference of the Association of Internet Researchers, October 13-16, 2002. Maastricht: International Institute of Infonomics.
Haddon, L. (1992). Explaining ICT consumption: The Case of the Home Computer. In Silverstone, R. & Hirsch, E. (Eds.), *Consuming Technologies: Media and Information in Domestic Spaces* (pp. 82–96). London: Routledge.
Lave, J., & Wenger, E. (1991). *Situated Learning*. Cambridge: Cambridge University Press.
Lenhart, A., Rainie, L., & Lewis, O. (2001). *Teenage life online: The Rise of the Instant-Message Generation and the Internet's Impact on Friendships and Family Relationships*. Retrieved February 10, 2002 from < http://www.pewinternet.org/reports/pdfs/PIP_Teens_Report.pdf >.
Leung, L. (2001). College Student Motives for Chatting on ICQ. *New Media and Society*, 3(4): 483–500.

Malindine, A. (1998) *A Feminist Perspective within a Longitudinal Ethnography—Some Reflections on "Sarah's Story."* Accessed March 10, 2003 at <http://edu.uwe.ac.uk/Research/Redland/redland7.asp>.
McDermott, R. (1993). The Acquisition of a Child by a Learning Disability. In J. Lave & S. Chaiklin (Eds.), *Understanding Practice: Perspectives on Activity and Context* (pp. 269–305). Cambridge: Cambridge University Press.
Murdock, G., Hartmann, P., & Gray, P. (1992). Contextualizing Home Computing: Resources and Practices. In R. Silverstone & E. Hirsch (eds.), *Consuming Technologies: Media and Information in Domestic Spaces*. London: Routledge.
Moscovici, S. (1981). On Social Representations. In J. P. Forgas (Ed.), *Social Cognition: Perspectives on Everyday Understanding* (pp. 181–209). London: Academic Press.
Palfreyman, D. (2001). *Keeping in Touch: Online Communication and Tradition in a Gulf Arab Context*. Unpublished paper. Zayed University, Dubai.
Pollard, A., & Filer, A. (1999). *The Social World of Pupil Career*. London: Cassell.
Wheeler, D. (2003). The Internet and Youth Subculture in Kuwait. *Journal of Computer-Mediated Communication* 8/2. Accessed March 10, 2003 at <http://www.ascusc.org/jcmc/vol8/issue2/wheeler.html#first>.
Wikan, U. (1991). *Behind the Veil in Arabia*. Chicago: University of Chicago Press.

Karen Gustafson 15

VIRTUAL CONSUMPTION: THE COMMERCIAL DISCOURSE OF THE WEB

Introduction

In the last two decades of the 20th century, the Internet was framed in a wide variety of ways. It has been positioned as a link to global community, an information source, a symbol of modern scientific progress, a technology of democracy, and a site of daring commercial entrepreneurship. The Internet is comprised of a relatively new group of communications technologies, and discourses surrounding the Internet are still in the process of formation. Moreover, the use patterns of technology are never entirely predictable.[1] Rather, technologies are molded by a variety of forces including government regulation, the market, individual users, and on a mass level, discourse. Although originally created as defense technology, the Internet was later viewed as a tool of academic and scientific research. In 1991, the National Science Foundation (NSF) relinquished control of the Internet, opening the door to commercialization. Since then, the Internet has been framed as a technology of education and social equality, and also increasingly as a technology of cultural and material consumption. While the 1996 Telecommunications Act mentioned the democratic necessity of universal service for online technologies and the National Telecommunications and Information Administration continues to report on the "digital divide," the Internet is also frequently positioned as a tool of free market commerce.

This chapter will address these commercial discourses surrounding the Internet, drawing on material from mainstream U.S. magazines including *Newsweek, U.S. News and World Report,* and *Time.* These periodicals were selected based on their circulation and position as representations of dominant U.S. discourse.[2] Although this chapter comes from a larger study that examines articles mentioning the Internet going back to 1980, the focus of this analysis will be from the early 1990s to March of 2000. In doing so, this chapter seeks to establish and periodize certain dominant discourses surrounding the Internet. When and how did the Internet shift from being represented as an esoteric tool of specialists to being represented as a general-purpose tool of the family? How has the Internet been increasingly framed as platform for commercial pursuits and consumption? In defining these particular discourses I also hope to establish when certain discourses emerge and recede, to give a sense of the shifting discursive boundaries of the Internet.

The Utility of Discourse Analysis

Discourse refers to the way in which issues such as technology are discussed or framed in a society. Although there is often no absolute articulation of norms concerning technology use, discourses can set boundaries for what is possible or acceptable. Mainstream media such as *Newsweek, U.S. News and World Report,* and *Time* can be analyzed as representations of dominant discourse, propagating standards or norms. In this way, discourses are infused with power. The fact that the Internet is framed in particular ways is not ideologically neutral; rather, it is indicative of certain agendas such as the support of the status quo or the spread of privatization. By examining the strands of discourse within these periodicals, we can articulate the changing roles of the Internet, and its shifting position in dominant discourse as a tool of democracy, education, better jobs, or more efficient consumption. Who should use this technology, and how should it be used?

Although this analysis will not directly link the discourse in these publications to particular policy decisions, I argue that this press represents the changing attitudes of dominant opinion. Whereas it may be difficult to causally link mass discourse to policy making, this discourse can represent the dominant spirit and attitudes of an era. These press representations can also flatten the more subtle aspects of a complex issue, such as the uses of the Internet, framing it in simplified terms: a current example of this would be the unquestioned urgency surrounding the profit potential of the Internet. Public discourse as represented in the mainstream press can serve to set particular agendas, filtering certain perspectives while highlighting others.

These ascendant discourses create the parameters for likely everyday uses of the technology, setting boundaries around the possible implementations of the Internet. In this sense, I would compare these discursive formulations to Anthony Gidden's concepts of structure and structuration. The "rules" for who uses the Internet and how it is to be used are not generally codified; rather, they are created discursively through multiple, dynamic interpretations. Although there may be no law stating that the Internet is best used as a platform for commercial pursuits or cultural consumption, these have effectively become normal expectations. These expectations are discursively formed through channels including mass discourse such as *Time, Newsweek,* and *U.S. News and World Report,* and form tacit rules for everyday conduct, such as Internet use. These tacit rules may also include what groups are positioned as likely Internet users—who is expected to use this technology, and how? In this way, these rules can also be considered resources, enabling certain actions while constraining others. These rules and resources form discursive structures, making certain groups more likely to have access to Internet technology, and also making certain uses more likely. Finally, these structures must be considered dynamic and recursive, neither codified nor imposed on individuals from above. The examples of dominant mass discourse discussed in this chapter show the reproduction of particular social systems, and the evolution of tacit rules for behavior concerning the uses and users of the Internet.

Methods of Analysis

This analysis looks at three examples of mainstream U.S. discourse over a period of several years. To initially find articles in *Newsweek, Time,* and *U.S. News and World Report* that mention the Internet, I performed content searches with two databases, *Lexis-Nexis Academic Universe* and *Expanded Academic ASAP*. These search engines identified articles containing the word "Internet" in the headline, citation, or lead paragraph, between the dates of January 1, 1990, and May 1, 2000. This initial search revealed a considerable number of articles in each publication — 1,059 in *Newsweek,* 640 in *U.S. News and World Report,* and 370 articles in *Time.* Also, this number was skewed toward recent issues, so that although none of the magazines had articles focused on the Internet in 1990, all three had over 100 articles in 1999. To narrow this sample, I analyzed all of the articles before 1994 in each publication (a total of 10) and only articles within March or December issues thereafter. This abbreviated my sample to 313 articles, including 135 in *Newsweek,* 108 in *U.S. News and World Report,* and 70 in *Time.* Articles from specialist subsidiary publications such as *Newsweek's Washington Technology* or from advertising supplements were ignored in this analysis. March issues are chosen with the intention that they can provide a normal, nonholiday sample, and issues from December are examined because they are likely to provide revealing year-end reflections on the dynamic nature of society as well as predictions of future developments.

Entertainment and E-Commerce

Discourse framing the Internet as a medium of entertainment exists throughout the 1994–2000 sample period, whereas e-commerce discourse does not appear substantially until late 1997. This section combines analyses of entertainment and commerce discourses, situating both as discourses of consumption, whether material or cultural. Although the Internet has become increasingly commercialized since the National Science Foundation's lifting of restrictions in 1991, this commercialization does not just refer to the proliferation of private ISPs or corporate Web sites. In a larger sense, the Internet has transformed into a medium of commercial exchange, a virtual marketplace where cultural and material commodities are bought and sold. The Internet has become a place of promotion for earlier forms of media, such as films and compact audio discs, while Web surfing and online gaming have become forms of entertainment in themselves. Especially toward the end of the last decade of the 20th century, the potential for e-commerce attracted attention as more and more traditional "bricks-and-mortar" retail enterprises went online, joining exclusively online presences such as the legendary Amazon.com. This trend represents not only the ongoing effort to find new ways to make the Internet profitable but also the increasing shaping of the Internet user as potential customer.

Between March 1994 and March 1997, very few articles cast the Internet as a tool of commerce, although several appear during this period referring to the Internet as a medium of entertainment. In December 1997, there was a sudden proliferation of articles on both the entertainment and commercial potentials of the Internet, and this trend continues to rise until March of 2000, the last period sampled. Because of this abrupt shift in late 1997, it appears that the consumption discourse really blooms at this time, and most of this section will be devoted to the analysis of the December 1997 to March 2000 period. Initially, however, I will briefly look at the developing discourses of consumption that preceded this boom.

During this early period, the Internet began to be portrayed as the ultimate niche marketing tool. A *Newsweek* article from March 1994 refers critically to the "shovelware" of massified sites such as AOL and suggests that "critics say most cyberfare lacks depth and interest" (Meyer, 1994). In response to this, the article hails Microsoft's new Complete Baseball, an "interactive multimedia extravaganza," as the cutting edge of specialized Internet content. Niche marketing is celebrated as the new trend of the increasingly competitive online market, with "one clear winner: the consumer" (ibid.). Another article mentions the Rolling Stones' brief multicast of their "Voodoo Lounge" tour on the Mbone, or Multicast Backbone. Although this coverage discusses "more serious applications" for the Mbone, including telemedicine and electronic town meetings, the article hints at potential commercial applications as well ("The Mbone," 1994). Later, coverage of commercial and entertainment uses of the Internet becomes less apologetic as its commercial nature is increasingly naturalized.

In the beginning, however, most of the online commercial enterprises mentioned are those trafficking in cultural products or forms of entertainment. Internet users are predicted to benefit from increasingly well-targeted sites with content that will cater to their particular sports, music, gaming, or sexual interests. Music applications receive considerable coverage as users are urged to preview the newest Tori Amos single with RealAudio Player, and the issue of music file piracy develops. Television forms begin to emigrate to online media with The Spot, "the first multimedia soap opera" ("Cyberspace, 90210," 1996). While there are many examples of the Internet framed as a tool of cultural consumption, electronic commerce is nearly absent, but for one article detailing the emergence of the online automobile market. This introduces the "new world of car shopping," where savvy customers can get more bargaining power and avoid high pressure salespeople ("Buying a

Car," 1996). Here the Internet is represented as an empowering tool of commerce, giving greater information and leverage to the inquiring consumer, who is part of the "vanguard of a revolution" of online commerce (ibid.).

In December 1997, perhaps corresponding with winter holidays, coverage of electronic commerce takes off. Whereas previous coverage framed online entertainment and commercial enterprises as fledging or experimental, the discourse of late 1997 and 1998 is confident; the novelty of electronic shopping begins to wear as it becomes increasingly mainstream. The Internet is hailed as a profitable commercial medium, and predictions of future e-commerce are optimistic. *Time* reports commerce has triumphed over content, and that the surge in online commercial activity has led to massive successes in the information industry. "[E]verywhere you hear the same story: thanks to E-commerce—selling goods and services on the Web— their business is exceeding the rosiest expectations" (Quittner, 1997). At the same time, this article notes that this reverses earlier expectations that the World Wide Web might lead to "a renaissance for writers and artists and even journalists." Instead of serving as a source of community, information-gathering, or creative expression, the Internet is declared "a mall without a parking lot" (ibid.). One example of these virtual malls, netMarket, is celebrated in "Birth of An Internet Salesman," a profile by *U.S. News and World Report,* while another article notes the emerging commercial success of the Internet, predicting that e-commerce may grow from $2.6 billion in 1997 to $37.5 billion in 2002 (Cohen, 1997). According to this coverage, this success is dependent on "digital dollars," a form of electronic currency, intelligent shopping agents, and the mass customization of products. Within this discourse, technological advances are framed as valuable in terms of their usefulness to commerce such as real-time interactive video that will allow consumers to interact with live salespeople. Coverage of an encryption technology trade show notes "what a difference secure transactions make," predicting global e-commerce to "mushroom to a stunning $223 billion annually in the next three years" (Goldfarb, 1998). The acceptance of Internet shopping is the focus of these articles, although the Internet continues to also be invoked as an entertainment medium as well in coverage of online content including porn, games, and sports sites.

In December 1998, coverage of the Diamond Rio Player continues to bolster the entertainment discourse, while AOL's purchase of Netscape is framed as a masterstroke of e-commerce genius, a business deal that will allow AOL to "build the largest shopping mall on Earth" (Mitchell, 1998). The development of the Internet is reflected on here:

> The World Wide Web started out as a place to find information. But forget information. The Web is becoming a mass medium, not just a haunt for nerds. And there is little the masses enjoy more than finding, acquiring, and consuming things. In other words, shopping. (Ibid.)

No longer the fringe environment of technophiles, the Web is heralded as a mass medium, democratized in its devotion to consumption. And, while no one may really forget the Web as an informational technology, this is clearly no longer its primary designated function. Other articles from this period guide users to various e-commerce and e-travel sites, discuss the rise of European e-commerce, and report the online purchasing wars over Furby dolls. Coverage of Internet shopping continues to rise in December 1999 and significantly, even into March 2000, after the holidays. The commercial discourse becomes more articulated as stories showcase new forms of e-commerce, such as online grocery shopping. Computer users are portrayed as spending money on hardware such as high-speed cable modems in order to enhance these online shopping experiences. *Time* declares 1999 to be the "year of e-tailing," and reports on the efforts of massive bricks-and-mortar concern Wal-Mart to improve their site, as well as on the attempts of emerging e-commerce start-ups to launch themselves into the 1999 holiday season. E-commerce is framed in terms of consumer choice, individual empowerment, and hands-off regulation. One *Newsweek* article reports on the fight to resist taxation of e-commerce, profiling one opponent who suggests a permanent ban on taxation would be "a triumph for freedom in the new millennium"(Fineman, 1999). *Time* predicts that inflated retail goods prices in Europe will fall, partially because of the Internet. "[G]reater ease of travel, along with the borderless, democratic Internet, already gives shoppers the ultimate weapon—knowledge—and the ultimate power to vote with their wallets" ("Buyer Beware," 1999). It is important to note that the consumerist appeal of e-commerce is described in political terms—the Internet lacks national boundary and is an information channel, democratically empowering the savvy shopper to fight for low prices, voting through consumer choice.

Finally, the March 2000 sample reveals firmly entrenched discourses of consumption, both promoting entertainment and e-commerce. While coverage continues to showcase new products offered through commercial Web sites, there is also a discursive turn signaling the establishment of the Internet as a medium of consumption. Rather than simply commenting on the number of businesses and consumers flocking to the Internet, articles focus on issues that have arisen from the diffusion of e-commerce. These include the necessity of alternative forms of payment for Internet users—such as the burgeoning teenage market—who lack credit cards ("Don't Have Plastic?," 2000). Meanwhile, certain states are considering implementation of tax holidays, to entice consumers away from tax-free e-commerce ("Taxes Take a Holiday," 2000). Internet service providers compete for customers, offering free access in exchange for personal information and constant advertising, and electronic porn sites begin to go public on Wall Street, signaling possible cultural acceptance of cyberporn as a legitimate commodity. The torrent of coverage from March 2000 demonstrates an increasingly nuanced framing of the Internet as a technology of consumption. Whereas earlier commercial discourse first wonders at the possibility of electronic shopping and then focuses mainly on the growth of e-commerce, later coverage views the Internet as an established site of consumption, albeit one that is still working out some problems. The question is not whether or not e-commerce is viable or useful, the question is how e-commerce can be the most successful. Also, Internet users are portrayed as benefiting from this shift toward consumption. The Internet becomes naturalized as a commercial medium, and this turn toward massification is portrayed as democratic—everyone has the chance to be equal in the pursuit of low prices, and the public can only benefit from unregulated competition.

Conclusions

Although the Internet is portrayed as both a battlefield and a gold rush for businesses, this discourse sets an agenda of commercialization while excluding players who do not fit into the emerging digital economy. The unquestioned goal of the Internet is to reap profits, rather than to organize, educate, gather information, or personally communicate. Although there are much smaller discourses that include these alternative uses, the Internet is strongly framed as a technology for communication among businesses, buyers, and sellers. Whereas those already among the technological elite may benefit financially from this new economy, there is little apparent possibility of benefits trickling down to those outside of the digital sphere. In this way, the Internet is simultaneously presented as both a revolution in money and information and also as fairly irrelevant to those not already in on the digital game. While the discourse surrounding the political potential of the Internet peaked in 1995, discourses of consumption easily overtake these libertarian musings so that by winter of 1997, the Internet is positioned as a massified tool for shopping and the consumption of culture. In a similar way, the Internet business discourse of the late 1990s frames the Internet as a boon to elite whiz kid programmers and technology titans, already established in the social and economic hierarchies. For those excluded from these realms of digital wonder, the Internet is positioned as a desirable tool for entertainment and material consumption, but not necessarily political or economic empowerment.

Notes

1. See L. Spigel, *Make Room for TV,* and C. Fischer, *A Social History of the Telephone*.
2. *Newsweek* controlled circulation listed at 3,200,000; *U.S. News and World Report* paid circulation listed at 2,224,003; *Time* paid circulation listed at 4,100,000. Source: *Publist,* [Online], <http://www.publist.com>, accessed 5/15/00.

References

Bellafante, G. (1996, March 4). "Cyberspace, 90210." *Time,* 147, 65.
"Buyer Beware." (1999, December 13). *Time International,* 154, 38.
Castells, M. (1996). *The Rise of the Information Society.* Cambridge, Blackwell Publishers.
Cohen, W. (1997, December 1). "Online Malls Move Closer to Home." *U.S. News and World Report, 123,* 86–87.

"Don't Have Plastic? Grab Some Mon-e." (2000, March 13). *Newsweek, 135*, 72.
Fineman, H. (1999, December 20). "The Tax War Goes Online." *Newsweek, 134*, 31.
Fischer, C. (1992). *America Calling: A Social History of the Telephone to 1940*. Berkeley: University of California Press.
Giddens, A. (1984). *The Constitution of Society: Outline of the Theory of Structuration*. Berkeley: University of California Press.
Glasser, B., & Streisand, B. (2000, March 6). "Virtual Campaign Takes Off." *U.S. News and World Report, 128*, 22.
Goldfarb, M. (1998, March 23). "E-commerce." *Time International*, 150, 26.
Greenwald, J. (1996, March 18). "Buying a Car without the Old Hassles." *Time, 147*, 74–76.
Hafner, K. (1994, December 5). "The Mbone: Can't You Hear It Knocking? *Newsweek, 124*, 86.
Leo, J. (1995, March 20). "Life among the Cyberfolk." *U.S. News and World Report*, 118, 26.
Liu, L. M. (1998, December 14). "A Taste of the Good Life." *Newsweek, 132*, 40.
MacDonell, D. (1986). *Theories of Discourse: An Introduction*. New York: Blackwell.
McGrath, P. (1999, March 29). "Knowing You All Too Well." *Newsweek, 133*, 48.
Meyer, M. (1994, March 28). "The 'On-line' War Heats Up." *Newsweek, 123*, 38-40.
Mitchell, R. (1998, December 7). "Why AOL Really Clicks." *U.S. News and World Report*, 52.
Quittner, J. (1997, December 22). "The Once and Future King." *Time, 150*, 16.
Rheingold, H. (1993). *The Virtual Community: Homesteading on the Electronic Frontier*. Reading, MA: Addison-Wesley.
Spigel, L. (1992). *Make Room for TV: Television and the Family Ideal in Postwar America*. Chicago: University of Chicago Press.
Stone, R. A. (1995). *The War of Desire and Technology at the End of the Mechanical Age*. Cambridge, MA: MIT Press.
"Taxes Take a Holiday. (2000, March 6). *Newsweek*, 135, 78.
Thomas, S. G. (1998, March 2). "Fighting for Computer Privacy." *U.S. News and World Report, 124*, 62.

Christopher Bodnar 16

REDLINING AND REDEFINING HIGH-SPEED INTERNET ACCESS: POLICY, PRACTICE, AND PATCHWORK IN URBAN DEVELOPMENT

The research reported in this chapter indicates that a prevalent yet under examined practice of contemporary socioeconomic segregation in North America is implicit in the design and construction of Internet hardware. This practice, commonly referred to as "redlining," involves servicing select geographic areas based on desirable demographic characteristics. Most often, these characteristics involve race and income. Complicit support of corporate redlining practices is found in government regulatory policy. Where policy interest no longer exists for guaranteeing equitable access to communication media, access is replaced with a new social policy: competition. This transition in policy focus highlights the second focus of this chapter: the practice of redefining Internet access based on corporate interests rather than principles of public interest and equitable socioeconomic systems.

This chapter uses available statistical data and policy statements to analyze the rollout of high-speed Internet access in the city of Ottawa, Canada. While this example is specific to a local urban center, the method of analysis and general findings regarding redlining and redefining of Internet services are relevant to the larger planning of network hardware. The first part of this chapter provides a brief overview of the Ottawa area and available data for tracking rollout of new services by incumbent and competing Internet service providers. In this I propose that redlining is a corporate practice within the region. From this, I examine the policy framework and economic interests that are legitimizing such practices. The most common policy tool in assuring equal Internet access is simply redefining what access means to suit political and economic motives. I end by explaining possible research avenues for questioning the practices of redlining and redefining in the use of new communication technologies.

This chapter does not attempt to advance an argument in favor of bridging a "digital divide." Much debate over so-called digital divides takes a determinist approach in that ensuring access to Internet and computer technologies will somehow alleviate socioeconomic inequalities. This naive and patronizing assumption has, unfortunately, informed too much of the debate around Internet architecture in the North American context. New technologies may hold networking potential for oppressed segments of the population but are not substitutes for inherently oppressive economic and policy systems in society. What this chapter does contain is a critique of such thought, particularly within the context of "redefining" Internet access that has tacitly formed a system of support for otherwise flawed policy and corporate technology rollout plans.

The Approach to Assessing High-Speed Internet Penetration

The basis for investigating redlining as a corporate service policy comes from the 1994 "Petition for Relief From Unjust and Unreasonable Discrimination in the Deployment of Video Dialtone Facilities" to the Federal Communications Commission (FCC), by the Center for Media Education. By having obtained sufficient service data from operating companies within the region of analysis, the geographic service areas for new technological services were overlaid on maps representing financial and racial demographics of the area. In doing such, it was clearly demonstrated that the service providers were participating in "redlining" practices whereby lower-income and generally nonwhite neighborhoods were not provided with the new technological services offered in higher income neighbourhoods. The research for this study is not as clear, but indicates that such practices continue.

Within the context of Ottawa, such an investigation appeared relevant in assessing technological rollout practices compared with established policy statements and targets. Ottawa is repeatedly labeled as a high-tech capital, generally dubbed "Silicon Valley North." Local industry-advocacy groups label Ottawa "Canada's most wired city" (OED, 2000). Indeed, Ottawa's population would seem to lend itself to connectivity. The city's average family income was $64,243 according to 1996 census results—17.7 percent above the national average of $54,583 (Statistics Canada, 1999). The city, moreover, is a test site for the federally funded "Smart Community" initiative. This program provides funding for public access sites in libraries, schools, and community centers as well as funding for public-private networking projects. Nonetheless, there remain 41,700 families, or 15.2% of the population in the urban area classified as low income, spending over 70% of their income on food and housing (ibid.).

Service in the Ottawa-Carleton Area

Actually conducting an analysis of possible redlining practices proves difficult. As indicated by the 1994 Center for Media Education example above, cooperation on behalf of private service providers or public regulators is required. Neither of these groups, in the case of Ottawa, proved willing to help. Rogers Communications, the incumbent cable television provider was somewhat forthcoming with service information. Their 2000 service map shows almost complete coverage of the Ottawa metropolitan region. Their network upgrade objective for the following two years were to be in a competitive position against digital television providers who are entering the market. In late 2000, Rogers announced the introduction of a new "interactive TV" service where subscribers may surf the World Wide Web and read e-mail on television (Damsell, 2000). But as television terminals have no capacity to store data and are intended only for content consumption, not content production, this creates a troubling redefinition of "access" that will be discussed later in this chapter.

Statistics Canada figures from 1999 (2000) indicate that approximately 5% of subscribers to traditional cable services also subscribed to high-speed Internet access by cable. Based on Statistics Canada national household cable penetration rates of 80 percent (56–205-XIB), an estimated 15,400 households, or 4% of the total households, may have subscribed to high-speed cable Internet in the Ottawa area in 1999.

Bell Sympatico, owned by BCE Inc.—by far Canada's largest corporation, owning incumbent phone carrier Bell Canada, national television broadcaster CTV and the national daily newspaper *The Globe and Mail*—is less forthcoming with service information. The company's deployment plan beginning in 2000 was to be able to provide digital subscriber line (DSL) high-speed access to 80% of Bell Canada phone subscribers in the region. No indication of which geographic areas nor the time line for accomplishing the aforementioned service provision are available (Morin, 2000). New service areas are added based on market potential for the service. Based on market reliance for service provision determination, it would be difficult to expect lower-income neighbourhoods to receive comparable service to upper-income neighbourhoods. The information collected from both Rogers and Bell Sympatico comes from individual interviews with company representatives; this information is not available in a standard format for public consultation, either by the public or the national regulatory body for telecommunications.

The indication from such opacity in public data release combined with statements about servicing of viable markets indicates that redlining is most likely taking place in the context of high-speed Internet service. While companies are reluctant to release data that would indicate such trends, the federal regulatory body does little better in creating transparency within reporting service provisions and responding to potential disparities.

Whither the Public Interest?

Canadian government policy lays claim to value a regulatory model for telecommunications that embodies competition among industry service providers. Within this system, the Canadian Radio-television and Telecommunications Commission (CRTC) is mandated to act as a regulatory body that ensures the public interest is being served by the industry service providers in the fulfillment of obligations dictated in their licenses. In order for a public regulatory body to ensure service provisions are met, some obligations must exist on behalf of the service providers to submit information about their operations. In Canada's case, however, once this information is submitted to the CRTC, it does not necessarily enter the public domain. Information can be labeled as "proprietary" and thus of a nature to give one group a competitive advantage over another (Carter, 2000). This is the case with much of the information concerning high-speed Internet access rates in Canada at the moment.

There exist very few models for assessing penetration rates of high-speed Internet access. In fact, high-speed Internet access is a somewhat common household commodity only in a small number of countries at the moment (Dixon, 2000). Moreover, the provision of high-speed Internet access is not regulated from a user-access perspective by the CRTC. The Commission specified in 1998 that high-speed Internet would not be differentiated from any other speed of Internet service provision (Statistics Canada *Telecom Decision 98-99*). It justifies this position by stating a regulatory practice based on service attributes rather than technology. As a result, if each service allows for features such as uploading and downloading of electronic files and differentiates service packages by price, the service provision will be considered part of the same market, regardless of the speed of service. This is significant because it provides definition to a policy vision for technological access. This position of separating service from the technology turns a blind eye to what users are actually using the Internet for or how they might gain access. Meanwhile, it allows service providers, such as cable and DSL companies, to redefine access in their own rights.

Rogers service, for example, does not allow users to operate a server through its regular residential service, limits mail traffic to 300 megabytes a month and disallows any form of hacking or distribution of material of a political nature (Rogers, 2000). While the network belongs to Rogers, these restrictions do not lend themselves to transparent participatory and democratic use of the Internet as is generally promoted in "wired" initiatives.

The only major Canadian rulings involving high-speed Internet by the CRTC relate to mandatory reselling rights of third-party Internet service providers over phone and cable networks of traditional (previously monopoly) service providers (*CRTC 98-99*, paragraph 81). This lack of regulation comes despite clear recommendations by the government's own Information Highway Advisory Council's final set of recommendations in 1997 (Industry Canada, 1997). In their report, IHAC recommended that public and private bodies should play a role in monitoring the deployment of new technologies, high-speed Internet included, to guard against inequitable access problems. The CRTC has not followed up on this recommendation (Sutherland, 2000). An Ottawa high-tech consortium, the Ottawa Centre for Research and Innovation (OCRI) has paid no attention to monitoring these access rates in its own community, despite its role of the planning body for a federally funded "Smart Community" project (Wilker, 2000).

Whereas, in the United States, the Federal Communications Commission required annual reporting of high-speed Internet service provisions by service providers, the CRTC responded to public concern over inequitable access with an annual report on the status of competition in telecommunication markets. The FCC survey results in an annual report on the availability of high-speed and advanced telecommunications services in the United States. The report identifies "vulnerable" groups that may not obtain access to the various services in a market environment—namely rural, inner-city, low-income, ethnic minority, and tribal areas. The Canadian report assumes that the indication of competition in markets equates to greater access and choice among consumers. Citizenship is redefined as consumership; public participation is redefined as subscription payment. And, as shown in the next section, the entire notion of "access" has been completely redefined.

Redefining Access: Profile of a Service Area

Over the period of this study, the definition of "Internet access" in the Ottawa area has undergone significant revision. First, the private sector's reporting of access provides divergent perspectives on access rates. A February 1998 Ekos survey showed that 28% of Canadians had "access to an account from their homes." According to an October 2000 survey of the Ottawa-Carleton region by polling firm COMPAS Inc., 68% of those surveyed had a computer with Internet access in their homes. However, statistics provided by Ottawa Economic Development during the same period indicate that 36% of Ottawa homes had computers with Internet access. At a national aggregate, an international PricewaterhouseCoopers study on connectivity indicate Canada's national "household" Internet access to be at 48% (Dixon, 2000). Given differing polling practices and question methodology, we might expect private data to present such quantitative disparities. Public figures, however, prove to be little better.

Statistics Canada shows that 60.7% of Ottawa households have "at least one person that uses computer communications in a typical month, regardless of whether that use was from work, home, school, a public library or some other location," compared to a national average of 41.8% (Dickinson & Ellison, 2000). This is in contrast to 1996 Statistics Canada numbers showing 15.4% households in Ottawa with a computer connected to the Internet compared to only 7.4% of Canadian households having a computer with Internet access (Dickinson & Sciada,

1997). According to a May 2000 Statistics Canada Internet user report, 28.7% of respondents indicated the home as "the most popular location for Internet use." Statistics Canada Household Internet Use Survey data from 2001 indicates that "73% reported that someone in the household went online from home at least once a day on average" (Statistics Canada, 2002).

These statistics highlight one important fact: connectivity means many different things depending on the political ends to be justified. Whereas in 1997, connectivity was measured by households with a computer connected to the Internet, the 1999 figures allow for access of any sort by any member of the household at least once in a given month. The 2001 data, although brought to a daily per-household figure, is not useful. While one child, for example, may access the Internet from a school terminal, it is possible that no one else in the household uses or has access to the Internet. They are, nonetheless, counted as Internet users. This allowed for a large increase in connectivity in a very short period of time—lending credibility to a notion of increasingly ubiquitous access and use made possible through high-profile government and industry initiatives. Whereas numerous studies have indicated links between income and likelihood to be online or even own a computer (Reddick, 2000), given the Statistics Canada definition of connectivity, this concern can largely be ignored in policy discussions.

In 2000 data, reported by Statistics Canada in 2002, when over 232,000 households reported no longer using the Internet "in a typical month," the term "dropout" was employed to describe such behavior. Whereas the term may imply choice in the matter, 17% of households cited cost as the primary deterrent to continued use, whereas 14% "lost access to a computer." While the same report indicates "dropouts" are more likely to be in lower income brackets with no postsecondary education, more attention is paid in the report to analyzing the lack of "familiarity with new technologies" such as cell phones, ATMs, and satellite dishes—as though income has no relation to accessing these items. Technological illiteracy is constructed as the fallible point rather than pointing to the underlying socioeconomic disparities. More disturbing in this trend of analysis, the term "dropout" denotes behavioral dysfunction, most often associated with educational dropouts, the consequences of illiteracy, and the social undesirability of such a situation.

Digital Divides and Deregulations: The False Debates

There are two prominent myths of Internet deployment and both are closely related to high-speed development. First, there is an idea that there is a lack of regulation in the current market. The second myth works off of this assumption: that if sufficient funding and attention were given to Internet deployment to low-income areas, the problem of underservice would be solved.

In fact, there is no shortage of regulation in the current system. What is outlined above is, more accurately, a re-regulation of the entire telecommunication industry. While Internet deployment serves as a good example for studying such market restructuring, it is dangerous to refocus on the Internet as a technological anomaly as "digital divide" debates often tend toward. This re-regulation has played out over a longer period.

In the interest of consumer choice, there should be additional high-speed Internet service provider choices going beyond traditional providers. A May 1997 CRTC decision laid out the framework for a 1994 statement in which the Commission stated that "increased competition in the local telecommunications market to be in the public interest" (97–98, A.1). An October 2000 decision gave DSL service providers interconnection benefits to the networks operated by market incumbents. In September 1999, the CRTC ordered incumbent cable carriers to make their Internet services available for resale (*Telecom Decision 99–11*).

The high-speed Internet market is very much the product of regulatory decisions made from a market-oriented rationale, placed behind a public-interest veneer of consumer choice through competition. And while this rejigging of the regulatory framework allowed network development that fit the objectives of corporate providers, it is hard to argue that such changes have benefited consumers or citizens. If the lack of benefit to citizens is not clear in the above, additional statistical data is more telling. Statistics at the national aggregate released by the CRTC in 2002 indicate that between 1998 and 2001 the market revenue share of non-incumbent competitors supplying Internet access decreased from 50% to 30% (CRTC, 2002: 45). For high-speed Internet access, the nonincumbent market revenue share decreased from 34% in 1998 to 16% in 2001—and their share of residential markets was at 5% (50). The *Status of Competition in Canadian Telecommunications Markets,* in which this data is collected, is now one of the major publications used by the CRTC to report market status. The document does nothing, however, to report on the quality or accessibility of service actually being provided by companies.

This brings me to address the second myth mentioned at the beginning of this section: that wiring households will solve an apparent "digital divide." Corporate service providers have little interest in providing Internet access for anything other than the content delivery to an audience on a profit basis. Moreover, they are most likely to service areas where their revenue returns have the greatest potential. This begs the question: What will be the result of "wire at all cost" strategies? If current market and policy trends are used, the benefit to the consumer is questionable.

Then what are possible alternatives? First, digital divide advocates would do well to examine manners by which public participation will involve designing network architecture and the technologies used to access the networks that go beyond consumer choice models of consumption. Second, if digital divide analyses are going to continue, long-term solutions to equitable access will be required. This must go beyond piecemeal project-oriented funding. Subscription packages expire, hardware breaks down, and political pet projects lose their attractive flare. But long-term solutions are not necessarily to be found in structural policy or market-oriented strategies. Rather, building cultures of digital resistance must be a priority. As such, freedom of action and the potential for self-determining projects at local community levels must be understood as essential rights of the digital society.

References

Canadian Radio-television Telecommunications Commission. (1997). *Telecom Decision 97-8*. Ottawa: May 1, 1997.
Canadian Radio-television Telecommunications Commission. (1998). *Telecom Decision 98-9*. Ottawa: July 9, 1998.
Canadian Radio-television Telecommunications Commission. (1999). *Telecom Decision 99-11*. Ottawa: Sept. 14, 1999.
Canadian Radio-television Telecommunications Commission. (2000). *Order CRTC 2000-983*. Ottawa: Oct. 27, 2000.
Canadian Radio-television Telecommunications Commission. (2002). *Report to the Governor in Council: Status of Competition in Canadian Telecommunications Markets; Deployment/Accessibility of Advanced Telecommunications Infrastructure and Services*. Ottawa.
Carter, Sheehan (CRTC Analyst, Numbering Administration). (2000). Personal correspondence and phone conversations, October 15, 2000–November 20, 2000.
Center for Media Education et al. (1994). *Petition for Relief from Unjust and Unreasonable Discrimination in the Deployment of Video Dialtone Facilities*. Washington, DC: Federal Communications Commission, May 23.
COMPAS, Inc. (2000). *Ottawa Municipal Election, Amalgamation & Related Issues*. October 18, 2000. <http://www.compas.ca/html/archives/municipalelection_surv.html>.
Damsell, Keith. (2000). Rogers shifts fight for Internet customers from desk to couch. *The Globe and Mail*. Nov. 17, B1–B2.
Dickinson, P., & J. Ellison. (2000). *Plugging In: The Increase in Household Internet Use Continues into 1999*. Ottawa: Industry Canada.
Dickinson, P., & J. Ellison. (1999). *Getting Connected or Staying Unplugged: The Growing Use of Computer Communications Services*. Ottawa: Industry Canada.
Dickinson, P., & G. Sciadas. (1997). *Access to the Information Highway: The Sequel*. Ottawa: Industry Canada.
Dixon, Guy. (2000). Canadian Internet use keeps climbing: Rapid expansion in Quebec propels Canada ahead of Europe, United States. *The Globe and Mail*. Nov. 17, B3.
Ekos Research Associates Inc. (1998). *Information Highway and the Canadian Communications Household*. Ottawa-Hull: February 23, 1998.
Federal Communications Commission. (2000). *Deployment of Advanced Telecommunications Capacity: Second Report*. Washington, DC: August 2000.
Industry Canada. (1997). *Preparing Canada for a Digital World: Final Report of the Information Highway Advisory Council*. Ottawa.
Morin, Yves. (Sympatico High Speed Edition Representative). (2000). Personal phone conversation, November 3.
Ottawa Economic Development. (2000). <http://www.ottawaregion.com/>, accessed November 24.
Reddick, Andrew. (2000). *The Dual Digital Divide: The Information Highway in Canada*. Ottawa: Public Interest Advocacy Centre.
Rogers Communications Inc. (2000). *Area Bandwidths: Ottawa Region*. Ottawa: August 10.
Rogers Communications Inc. (2000). *ROGERS @HOME SERVICE AGREEMENT* <http://www.Shop ROGERS.com/store/checkout/TermsAndConditions. asp#Home>, accessed December 9.
Statistics Canada. (1999). *Profile of Census Tracts*. Ottawa: Industry Canada. 1996 Census of Canada. Catalogue number 95-200-XPB and LICO definitions.

Statistics Canada. (1999). Household spending, dwelling characteristics and household facilities. *The Daily*. Ottawa: Industry Canada, December 13.

Statistics Canada. (2000). Household Internet Use. *The Daily*. Ottawa: Industry Canada, May 19.

Statistics Canada. (2000). Internet access by cable. *The Daily*. Ottawa: Industry Canada, August 25.

Statistics Canada. (2002). Internet dropouts and infrequent users. *The Daily*. Ottawa: Industry Canada, June 11.

Statistics Canada. (2002). Household Internet Use Survey. *The Daily*. Ottawa: Industry Canada, July 25.

Sutherland, David. (CANARIE Inc. Director Schoolnet/Learnware Liaison). (2000). Personal correspondence, November 21.

Tebarge, Marc. (Rogers Communications Inc. Network Engineer). (2000). Personal interview, November 3.

Wilker, Paul. (Executive Director, SmartCapital–OCRI). (2000). Personal correspondence.

Robin Mansell

THE INTERNET, CAPITALISM, AND POLICY

Introduction[1]

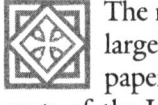 The role of financial capital in the development of the Internet is being largely ignored by policy makers and by the research community. This paper sets out how the role of financial capital is influencing several aspects of the Internet's development and why policy intervention may be needed. Castells (2000, p. 16; 2001) argues that networks "process the goals they are programmed to perform." Financial capital is playing a major role in determining what those goals are and this has serious consequences for the development of Internet-based Web sites and services. When the goals for Internet development are influenced substantially by markets and capital, this has major consequences for social and distributional issues and for the ways that the use of the Internet can be expected to contribute to the human development process (Storsul, 2002).

The empirical focus of this paper is on the development of the Internet Service Provider (ISP) market and on the implications of some of the main trends in this market for the types of service that are becoming available to citizens. Section 2 considers some of the principal interests of the investors who are expecting substantial financial returns. Section 3 sets out the need for policies that will foster diversity in the provision of both noncommercial and commercial Internet-based services. In section 4, the case for policy intervention is linked to the need to foster new media literacies. Section 5 indicates why it is essential to counter the biases of market-led Internet developments. Section 6 provides a brief conclusion.

Internet Services and Investor Interests

Many competing visions of a new kind of "knowledge society" are being discussed as part of a global policy agenda, especially with the momentum that is propelling the World Summit on the Information Society that will be held in 2003 and again in 2005. These visions are linked to the idea that "the information and communication technology revolution could be a powerful driver for empowering the world's poor . . . it is about information, knowledge and global identity. . . ."[2] The prevailing vision among many of the heads of state of the industrialized countries is that all members of society will benefit when markets are open to the flow and circulation of both information and capital. Because the Internet facilitates this, the way that it is developing must also be beneficial for all people. This idea goes hand in hand with the view that emerging knowledge societies will be beneficial for economic growth and for human development. Many argue that these benefits will follow almost automatically once people secure access to the Internet (UNCTAD, 2002). There is little or no need for policy intervention beyond ensuring that there are common "rules of the game" in areas such as taxation, dispute resolution or domain name registration. The competitiveness of firms in the marketplace—and the innovative capacity of those who collaborate in scientific and other virtual communities in providing Internet-based services—will ensure that all those who wish to do so can receive the potential benefits of access to vast stocks of digital information (OECD, 2002). This viewpoint is closely tied to claims that the ISP market is highly competitive and innovative (Oxman, 1999). The market should therefore generate diverse services that encompass and support all the interests of citizens.

There is another view of Internet developments, however. Some Internet industry analysts argue that, in spite of the flurry of entry and exit in the ISP market in the wealthy countries—and in some liberalizing developing countries, underneath the veneer of a highly competitive Internet services market, there is a rather different market environment (Huston, 1998). When the distribution of Internet traffic becomes a commodity service, it provides little opportunity for product differentiation and generates very low rates of financial return. If the ISPs are going to achieve stronger financial returns they must supply more than a commodity service. They must develop markets where there is the potential for increasing profit margins. The result in some areas of the ISP market is not a vigorously competitive marketplace, but an oligopolistic market structure. This market structure is inconsistent with the development of a network "commons" that would favour a range of non-commercial as well as commercial services (Trebing, 1998). The development of the ISP market in most industrialised countries is favoring the consolidation of ISPs in the hands of financial investors and their interests are not very consistent with the further development of a network "commons" (Javary & Mansell, 2002).

The primary interest of the financial investors is in the rapid turnover time of capital. It is not, or at least not primarily, in the long-term development of diverse and low cost Internet-based services for citizens. As the Swedish economist Eliasson (1999) has suggested, the ISPs are linking up communication infrastructures with the "syndication of electronic content." To achieve this, new financial flows must be organised and conditions must be put in place to secure healthy economic returns. The ISP market in most countries is consolidating, notwithstanding the presence of many small suppliers in some segments of the market. Incumbent ISPs are acquiring many of the most successful early ISP entrants and they are forging global partnerships or merging their operations. The ISP market in the United Kingdom is a good illustration of this process. In this case, market consolidation is occurring through the convergence of the ISPs with the telecommunication operators. This is helping to achieve the convergence of the knowledge base that is needed to support a key aspect of the new media industry, that is, achieving greater coordination and control over financial flows in the ISP market (Javary & Mansell, 2002). Control over financial flows is being secured as a result of the presence of key investors in the ISP market in the United Kingdom.[3] Attempts to coordinate knowledge flows in the ISP market through various configurations of shared directorships are also present.[4]

To achieve a strong position in the ISP market, the ISPs need to gain control over the components of the knowledge base that are needed for augmented service supply beyond the distribution of Internet traffic. Building this new industry in an uncertain environment requires massive investment. For this market to grow, there needs to be sustained large-scale capital investment and there is also a need for substantial learning time. Although high bandwidth infrastructures may provide the conditions for the delivery of a large throughput of Internet-based services, they do not necessarily generate the expected demand for revenue generating services.

There are very intense pressures for the realisation of a high short-term return on capital by the ISPs and the risk for investors is substantial. There are significant tensions between the financial expectations of most of the investors and the development of the Internet system as a "commons." In most of the industrialized countries, and in some of the newly industrializing countries such as South Korea or Singapore, this tension is being eased by promoting a rapid scaling up of infrastructure capacity. This is taking the form of a "rush to broadband," however broadband is defined (Mansell & Nikolychuk, 2002; Strategy Unit, 2002). The ISPs are exploiting scale economies in infrastructure supply through consolidations between themselves and the infrastructure facility providers. Once consolidation occurs, the ISPs then seek to achieve "economies of time" through very intensive marketing of the higher value added services that they can provide.

The ISP response to the commodification of the Internet traffic distribution business is to redefine the scope of the ISP market and to integrate and systematise the learning that is necessary to further develop revenue-generating services. Despite the fact that there is a continuous stream of new entrants into the ISP market, the role of financial capital in this market means that the market dynamics are potentially inconsistent with the public interest in the provision of a diverse set of non-commercial services for citizens. Because of the failure or poor performance of many of the dot.coms in 2000, investors have curtailed the ISP boom. To sustain a high level of capitalization the consolidated ISPs are searching for and learning how to transform the initial prophesies of high profit margins into a reality. In this environment there is a considerable risk of reduced diversity in terms of information content, service design, and service flexibility.

Policies to Foster Diversity

Some observers argue that ISP markets and, more generally, the new media services markets are developing in a way that is consistent with the achievement of policy goals for social inclusion and with a drive for rapid economic growth (Strategy Unit, 2002). This argument is often linked to the observation that there is no need to regulate the Internet's development and that there is no need for a special policy to foster the development of certain kinds of services. Furthermore, little if anything needs to be done to foster citizen capacities for acquiring the literacies that they must have if they are to make full use of the Internet. However, the trend toward the consolidation of the ISP market provokes many questions about the consequences of a lack of policy with respect to this market. The issue is whether there should be greater policy emphasis on encouraging diverse and low cost services for enhancing the new media literacies of citizens.

The processes of "creative destruction" that are normally associated with technological change and innovation (Schumpeter, 1942/1962), in the case of the ISP industry, are not leading to the erosion of economic power in the market. Instead, they appear to be favoring its reconstitution and this leads directly to the observation that there is a case for Internet-related policy to foster a network "commons," that is, public noncommercial services for citizens. As indicated earlier, the ISPs are mainly concerned with maximizing shareholder value. The current trends in the market favour the consolidation of the ISPs in the hands of financial investors whose primary interest is in the rapid turnover time of capital and this, in turn, creates pressures for reduced service variety. This outcome is one that runs counter to the view of the Internet as an open architecture that is optimised to encourage diversity, innovation, and social, as well as economic, experimentation.

The trend in the ISP market is consistent with the interests of large corporations and the expectations of investors for strong revenue growth and rapid capitalization. As Garnham (1990) has argued, it is always important to examine the dynamics of the media and communications industries in the context of the main economic pressures that are at work in the capitalist market. In the past, these pressures contributed to a market dynamic that favoured an "industrialisation of culture" (Garnham, 1990, p. 44). Notwithstanding today's new generation of digital technologies, in the ISP market, there arguably is a similar "industrialization" process that is at work.

The primary goal of the online service providers is to produce and circulate digital commodities. Internet-enabled combinations of technology, finance, and digital information are being designed to encourage short-term increases in the service providers' revenue streams. The forces of capitalism, operating through the major financial investors and the larger ISPs, are not encouraging the provision of the kinds of services that will be needed by the majority of citizens if they are to contribute to, and participate in, the emerging knowledge societies of the 21st century.

The present dynamic of ISP market development is influencing the design of Internet-based services (Lessig, 1999). For instance, the predominant architectures of World Wide Web-based services that are being designed for citizens are rarely intended to enable citizens to contribute their own information or to learn how the information that they access should be valued or acted on. The Web sites and services offered by civil society organizations may confer a certain authority on the information they provide. However, most of these Web site operators are mainly engaged in "pushing" information out toward users (Mansell, 2002). Few of these sites offer to support the majority of citizens in making their own information contributions. They generally do not help citizens to learn how to employ information in ways that might help them to choose between alternative courses of action. Commercial services based on the Internet may provide some basis for learning and for the acquisition of new media literacies, but they do so only for those who can bear the costs of these services.

Fostering New Media Literacies

The relative scarcity of certain features of Internet services that would encourage the development of the majority of citizens' capabilities for making sense of the online spaces of the Internet is arguably a threat to the majority of citizens' rights to participate effectively in an increasingly technologically mediated society. Despite the growth in the numbers of Internet users, a rather small minority of these users has the capability to use the Internet in ways that are creative and that augment their ability to participate effectively in today's knowledge societies (Mansell & Steinmueller, 2000).

The issue for policy is how to encourage investment in Internet-based services that could help to create electronic spaces that might facilitate the acquisition of certain key capabilities. Sen (1999) has considered the need for policy intervention to foster certain capabilities in the context of citizens' entitlements and rights. His work provides a foundation for considering whether the dominant trends in the Internet-based services market are consistent with the goal of empowering the majority of citizens and ensuring that their entitlements are met. He argues that policy must favour the acquisition of capabilities that enable people to discriminate between alternative choices about their lives. These capabilities are learned and they involve the cognitive capacities to recognize and evaluate choices and alternatives. Such cognitive capacities are the foundation of the freedoms that allow various individual needs, for instance, for remaining healthy or for social interaction, to be met. Sen argues that these are at the heart of the human development process.

Trends in the ISP market do not appear to be favouring the provision of services for citizens that enable them to learn how to discriminate between information resources or to make choices based on such information. Following Sen's argument, there is a case for public policy intervention in the market to promote such services. This does not necessarily indicate that there is a need to regulate the Internet using the conventional regulatory tools that are applied in other parts of the media and communication industry. Instead, it suggests that the key policy issue is whether the dominant trends in the design of Internet-based services are consistent with favouring the capabilities that Sen argues are a fundamental human right.

Once they are connected to the Internet, there are no grounds for simply assuming that the majority of citizens will be enabled to conduct their lives more effectively. If citizens are to acquire the cognitive capacities that will enable them to make sense of, and to act on, growing amounts of digital information, a crucial capability is that of being able to discriminate between authoritative information and information whose provenance has become detached from its originator. Citizens increasingly must be capable of assessing the value, veracity and reliability of digital information. This capability is an essential component of the new media literacies that are required for navigating through today's knowledge societies. Policy is needed to foster greater investment in Internet-based services that will encourage the majority of people to develop these literacies.

Countering the Biases of the Market

Much of the research that falls broadly under the label of "Internet Studies" is not concerned with how the different configurations of Internet service supply might strengthen the acquisition of these literacies. Sometimes it is simply assumed that access to the Internet will automatically facilitate an informed dialogue between citizens in a way that is consistent with a democratic process. However, as Thompson (1995) and Innis (1951) much earlier have argued, the deployment of new technologies is always biased in some way to favor certain economic or social interests over others. Innis (1951, p. 22) observed that:

> ... [the] mechanization [of knowledge] has emphasized complexity and confusion; it has been responsible for monopolies in the field of knowledge; and it becomes extremely important to any civilization if it is not to succumb to the influence of this monopoly of knowledge to make some critical survey and report.

The Internet offers a vast variety of new ways of "mechanizing" knowledge and some people are clearly benefiting from their capabilities of using the digital information resources that can be accessed via the Web. However, there is a growing need for critical surveys of the extent to which the main developments in Internet services are fostering new media literacies for the majority of people. As Sen (1999, p. 294) suggests, "even with the same level of income, a person may benefit from education–in reading, communicating, arguing, in being able to choose in a more informed way, in being taken more seriously by others and so on." If the majority of people do not have the capabilities for doing these things in the mediated Internet spaces, then we can expect little in terms of an empowering influence of the spread of Internet access.

The biases in the interests of the ISPs that favor the development of revenue generating commercial services are not very consistent with the kinds of public services and capabilities acquisition that are needed to foster new media literacies for the majority of citizens. Policy is essential to ensure that there are increasing opportunities to extend and deepen capabilities to engage in a critical discourse within the public spaces of the Internet. One important component of these capabilities is the ability to understand the origins and validity of digital information resources.

Sen's argument is that citizens have an entitlement to acquire the cognitive capacities to recognize and evaluate choices and alternatives that they confront in their everyday lives. This means that there must be "the substantive freedom–of people to lead the lives they have reason to value and to enhance the real choices they have" (Sen 1999, p. 293). If the trends in the ISP market are biasing service provision towards commercial Internet services, then there is unlikely to be sufficient emphasis on service provision that would enable the majority of citizens to acquire the cognitive capabilities that they need.

Many commercial Internet-based service providers bear little or no responsibility for providing service users with assessments of the reliability or authoritative status of the information that can be found at their sites. For instance, providers of open e-marketplaces that are intended to support electronic commerce provide very few resources to enable users to evaluate the information that can be accessed at their sites (Humphrey et al., 2003). There are, of course, countless examples of open source movement Web sites that are being developed for producing, validating, and sharing information. For instance, the University of Michigan, School of Information, hosts the "Community Connector," which, in turn, hosts the "Tech-Rocks" service. This is dedicated to accelerating social and political progress by building technological capacity for community collaboration.[5] Another site, Global Learning Outreach aims to provide "open source knowledge for an open source planet." It offers information on issues such as intellectual property rights debates, cyber sweatshops in China, and the protection of civil liberties. The origin of the information posted at the site is very clear.[6] WIKIPEDIA, which was started in 2001, uses the GNU Free Documentation License to organize open content in several languages. Tools for validating information and its provenance are being developed under this initiative.[7] There are open source directory projects on topics of many kinds including VRoma, a virtual community for teaching and learning the classics, which make the provenance of information very clear.[8] SourceForge.net, the largest web site for Open Source Software development, had 586,436 users in March 2003 and 58,245 projects.[9] However, analysis of these projects shows that nearly all of these are individual's projects with little or no major funding backing them (Mateos-Garcia & Steinmueller, 2003).

These examples demonstrate that there are Internet-based initiatives that are beginning to offer citizens the tools needed for making contributions to public discussions and for sharing information that has been validated by some means.

Nevertheless, the funding base for these efforts is very weak as compared to the amounts invested in commercial services. Policies to encourage investment in sites that can be used by citizens to enhance their capabilities to both contribute to, and act upon, digital information resources, are needed. Such policies could be justified on the basis of a "rights-based" approach to the further development of the Internet.

Discussions about "digital divides" and controversy over whether the Internet is "regulable" (Oxman, 1999; Lessig, 1999) are creating "blind spots" in our thinking about the way the Internet is likely to develop and the consequences for social development and for the rights and entitlements of citizens. A key trend is toward the construction of exclusive electronic spaces for commercial activity and these cannot support the majority of people in acquiring the new media literacies that they need.

Conclusion

Much greater attention needs to be given to policy favoring Internet tools and sites that encourage the acquisition of new media literacies by the majority of citizens. The Internet could serve as a means that enables people to learn more effectively and to engage in new modes of critical discourse. This is essential if the majority of citizens are to be able to participate effectively in the emerging knowledge societies. In highly technologically mediated societies, the majority of people must have a right to acquire the new media literacies that are necessary for them to participate in society. A rights-based Internet policy will require some measure of intervention in the Internet-based services market to encourage the supply of the Web tools and services that can encourage more individuals to attain the required capabilities for living in the "Internet Age."

Notes

1. This paper was presented initially as a keynote speech at the Internet Research 3.0 Conference, October 13–16, 2002, Maastricht.
2. Comment by Mr Vincenzo Schioppa, Diplomatic Advisor to the Minister of Public Administration, Italy and Chair of the DOT Force during the OECD Emerging Market Economy Forum on Electronic Commerce, January 16–17, 2001, Dubai, U.A.E.
3. These include the U.S.-based FMR Corporation (also known as the Fidelity Group) and Brooks Fiber Property, a wholly owned subsidiary of WorldCom until its downfall. The Prudential Corporation, HSBC Investment Bank, Mercury Assets Management, and Merrill Lynch & Co are also represented.
4. This section of the chapter draws substantially on Javary and Mansell (2002).
5. See < http://databases.si.umich.edu/cfdocs/community/index.cfm >, accessed March 16, 2003.
6. See < http://www.glo.org/ >, accessed March 16, 2003.
7. See < http://www.wikipedia.org/ >, accessed March 16, 2003.

8. See <http://www.vroma.org/>, accessed March 16, 2003.
9. See <http://sourceforge.net/>, accessed March 16, 2003.

References

Castells, M. (2000) "Materials for an Exploratory Theory of the Network Society," *British Journal of Sociology*, 51(1): 5-24.
Castells, M. (2001) *The Internet Galaxy: Reflections on the Internet, Business and Society*. Oxford: Oxford University Press.
Eliasson, G. (1999) "The Internet, Electronic Business and the EURO—On Information Products, Market Transparency and Internet Economics," Royal Institute of Technology, Stockholm mimeo, February 2.
Garnham, N. (1990) "Contribution to a Political Economy of Mass Communication," in F. Inglis (ed.), *Capitalism and Communication: Global Culture and the Economics of Information.*" London: Sage, pp. 20-55.
Humphrey, J., Mansell, R., Paré, D., & Schmitz, H. (2003) "The Reality of E-commerce with Developing Countries," Report prepared for the Department for International Development, London by London School of Economics and Institute of Development Studies, Sussex, March.
Huston, G. (1998) "Interconnection, Peering and Settlements," INET "99 Presentation, San Jose,<http://www.potaroo.net/papers/inet99/peering.htm>, accessed November 29, 2002.
Innis, H. A. (1951) *The Bias of Communication*. Toronto: University of Toronto Press.
Javary, M., & Mansell, R. (2002) "Emerging Internet Oligopolies: A Political Economy Analysis" in E. S. Miller and W. J. Samuels (eds.), *An Institutionalist Approach to Public Utilities Management*. East Lansing: Michigan State University Press, pp. 162-201.
Lessig, L. (1999) *Code and Other Laws of Cyberspace*. New York: Basic Books.
Mansell, R. (2002). "From Digital Divides to Digital Entitlements in Knowledge Societies," *Current Sociology*, Vol. 50, No. 3, pp. 407-426.
Mansell, R., & Nikolychuk, L. (2002) "The Economic Importance of Electronic Networks: Assessing the Micro-level Evidence Base," report prepared for the Prime Minister's Strategy Unit, London, August 26, available at <http://www.piu.gov.uk/2002/electronic/attachments/LSE.pdf>, accessed March 16, 2003.
Mansell, R., & Steinmueller, W. E. (2000) *Mobilizing the Information Society: Strategies for Growth and Opportunity*. Oxford: Oxford University Press.
Mateos-Garcia, J., & Steinmueller, W. E. (2003) "The Open Source Way of Working: A New Paradigm for the Division of Labour in Software Development?," *INK Open Source Research Working Paper No. 1*, SPRU, University of Sussex, January.
OECD (2002) "Measuring the Information Economy 2002," Paris. Available <http://www.oecd.org/EN/document/0,,EN-document-0-nodirectorate-no-12-36388-0,00.html>, accessed March 2003.
Oxman, J. (1999) "The FCC and the Unregulation of the Internet," Federal Communications Commission, Office of Plans and Policy Working Paper No 31, July, Washington, DC.
Schumpeter, J. A. (1942/1962) *Capitalism, Socialism and Democracy*. Harper Torchbooks, New York: The University Library, Harper & Row Publishers.
Sen, A. (1999) *Development as Freedom*. Oxford: Oxford University Press.

Storsul, T. (2002) "Transforming Telecommunications: Democratising Potential, Distributive Challenges and Political Change," Thesis for the degree of dr. polit., Faculty of Arts, University of Oslo, June.

Strategy Unit (2002) "Electronic Networks: Challenges for the Next Decade," Prime Minister's Strategy Unit, London, available at <http://www.piu.gov.uk/2002/electronic/report/00.htm>, accessed March 16, 2003.

Thompson, J. B. (1995) *The Media and Modernity: A Social Theory of the Media*. Cambridge, MA: Polity Press.

Trebing, H. M. (1998) "Market Concentration and the Sustainability of Market Power in Public Utility Industries," *National Regulatory Institute Quarterly Bulletin*, Vol. 19, No. 1, pp. 61–67.

UNCTAD (2002) "Electronic Commerce Strategies for Development: The Basic Elements on an Enabling Environment for E-Commerce," Background Paper TD/B/Com.3/EM.15/2, Geneva, UNCTAD, Commission on Enterprise, Business Facilitation, and Development. Available <http://ro.unctad.org/ecommerce/event_docs/geneva_strategies_issues.pdf>, accessed March 16, 2003.

SPIDERS, SPAM, AND SPYWARE: NEW MEDIA AND THE MARKET FOR POLITICAL INFORMATION[1]

Introduction

Technological innovations can radically alter the organization of power in politics. We argue that one of the most important implications of new media is in the market structure for political information. Whereas information about public policy opinion used to be expensive to collect, highly reductive, and restricted to a limited number of powerful political actors, today it is much less expensive, highly nuanced, and widely available. More important, whereas pollsters used to ask direct questions about political opinion, they now have the ability to extrapolate political information from our commercial and non-commercial activities. We investigate the work of two organizations, a public policy polling firm named Grapevine Polling, and an advocacy consulting firm named United Campaigns. We find important changes in the structure of the market in which individuals' and groups' political information is manufactured and sold, and important changes in the qualities of the product itself.

To observe how politics can work in tandem with technology, we must first look at how politics worked without it. Many scholars of political campaigning make distinctions between the pre-modern campaign, the modern campaign, and the postmodern campaign. Between the mid-19th century and 1950, local party volunteers took the pulse of member opinion with party meetings and local canvassing efforts. Very little centralized control of campaign logistics existed. The news media comprised a partisan press, radio, and local posters or pamphleteers, which brought relatively low budget, local public meetings, and whistle-stop leadership tours to the attention of a stable, partisan electorate. Modern campaigns, run between the 1960s and late 1980s, were long, nationally coordinated campaigns run by professional consultants and specialist advisors from a central party headquarters. Occasional opinion polls helped the campaign keep on top of public sentiments, and the nightly television news broadcasts were the most important medium for publicizing closely managed campaign events. The costs of these campaigns grew immensely to fund televised media events and political commercials, which had to target increasingly fickle cross-sections of the electorate. The postmodern campaigns that developed in the 1990s remained nationally coordinated but became operationally decentralized. Presidential campaigns, in particular, transformed to have their currently permanent quality, applying impression-management strategies from the beginning of primary contests, through the election cycle, through the term of office, to legacy campaigns or preparation for the subsequent electoral contest. Ever more professional consultants use regular opinion polls and focus groups to produce ever more costly targeted campaign television ads and events, trying to manage news production for segments of the electorate that are no longer in stable party alignments. The dominant feature of the new campaign, however, is no longer costly television ads, but instead detailed relational databases and targeted communications multimedia. Today's campaign is more reflexive, less costly, and operates in a marketplace for political information.

Spiders, Spam, and Spyware

Two particular U.S.-based organizations, Grapevine Polling and United Campaigns, are good examples of the kinds of contemporary organizations that work within the marketplace for political information.[2] Both amass and market detailed profiles of citizens using traditional survey and data mining methods, but both have also developed three kinds of powerful new media tools to complement traditional methods. Their spider programs crawl through the Web, automatically collecting Web site content, such as a person's e-mail or physical address, or an organization's press releases. They often employ spam, or unsolicited email, to gather or spread information for commercial or political marketing campaigns. Spyware, a kind of software that Grapevine and United often covertly install on users' computers during Internet use, reports a user's Web activities back to the sponsoring organization. In addition to covert installations, spyware is sometimes installed with the generally underinformed agreement of the user, who often later forgets about its presence. Many companies have developed variations of these tools, but Grapevine and United apply these tools to gathering political information.

Grapevine Polling

Grapevine Polling, a U.S.-based, worldwide market research and consulting firm, has a long history of polling beginning in the 1970s, when it was founded by three professors of social science who specialized in survey methods. In the late 1990s, Grapevine, which is privately owned, switched from doing consumer and political research via face-to-face and telephone to selling itself as pioneering the Internet method to conduct scientifically accurate market research. Grapevine claims to combine the communicative power of the Internet with probability sampling to produce the first statistically valid population-projectable survey tool capable of generating reliable information for decision making. Commercial market research is the bulk of Grapevine's business, so it carefully limits its public policy polling work and only takes contracts from particular clients so as not to run the risk that its findings in a public policy poll will upset the industries that provide 90% of its business. It will not take work from the major political parties, political candidates, or high-profile advocacy groups. Grapevine's annual revenue tops $150 million, and the company employs about 900 full-time employees. The company continues to acquire smaller market research firms, including firms outside the United States, forming a global web of for-profit personal information exchange for marketing purposes. By switching from traditional methods of market research to the Internet, Grapevine asserts it is harnessing the Web's interactive power to gather market intelligence that organizations need, continuously gathering political information about more individuals nationally and internationally.

Where traditional survey methods took several weeks to generate results, Grapevine's Internet surveys take a few hours. Once people agree to participate in the database, their households are equipped with interactive Web TV devices, which participants then use to fill out questionnaires. In addition to Web TV, participants also receive free Internet access, an engineer to install their new gadgets, and free prizes. However, as the saying goes there is no free lunch and, in this case, there is no free 24–7 Web surfing, TV watching, and prize opening. Instead, 24–7, Grapevine tracks the panelists' movements on the Web. This fulfills Grapevine's goal of delivering a 24–7 consumer, tracking the media use (from newspapers to Internet), advertising exposures, attitudes, and purchase behavior of the participants to amass detailed profiles to enrich its information on individuals. The Web TVs deliver consistent multimedia content to the participants/database members and, most notably, embedded database member management and spyware, of which only an advanced Internet user—one who most likely would not agree to be constantly polled in exchange for free Internet access—would understand the meaning. Grapevine summons its respondents by activating a flashing red light on the top of the family's Web TV box. Before data-mining, Grapevine collects—through database participants' answers—demographic information, such as income level, sex, race, age, and information related to interests, hobbies, and product/technology usage. If Grapevine software is running off a person's computer instead of Web TV, it also uses cookies, small data files stored on a computer's hard drive, to collect information such as browser, type of computer, operating system, Internet service provider, access times, and other similar information. In the small print, Grapevine allows users who have their own computer to refuse cookies by turning them off in their browser. Grapevine also claims to release only summarized or nonpersonally identifiable information to its clients and requires participants' consent prior to releasing any personally identifiable information provided during the survey process. Clients that receive personally identifiable information are required to sign and abide by the standards of disclosure of respondent-identifiable data of the trade association of survey research businesses. However, as a thriving and expanding business that acquires or spins off new companies, business assets, including all survey participant data, are transferred to each new unit. Grapevine has amassed a multimillion member database, with participants hailing from more than 200 countries. Participants also join individual panels based on demographics or interests, such as a musician panel or a teen panel. This subdividing of the database allows Grapevine to offer its clients what it claims to be a valid representation of the entire population via the database, or target populations via the panels.

Grapevine plays a problematic role in this new marketplace for political information. First, some of its tactics used to gain and retain participants are misleading. Grapevine initially advertises to prospective database members via its Web site and ad banners or locates new participants through spider programs and spam. Grapevine then promises participants that expressing their opinion to business and government leaders will greatly influence corporations and government, guiding the way products and services are developed. Grapevine also tells them they will be joining a revolution in research that will irrevocably alter approaches to the collection and application of information, and that participation is part of a citizen's duty to help good governance. After several months, many panelists forget spyware is installed on their machines. Second, the company simultaneously appeals to a user's sense of citizenship and consumer responsibilities. Members of the database are promised "Vine Points" when they participate that they can redeem for free prizes. At the same time, participants give up the right to see how information about their preferences is used (whether for commercial or public policy analysis). Third, because political information is their marketable product, Grapevine and companies like it take advantage of legal protections for their product. An example of a move in this direction can be found in the dozens of words Grapevine has already trademarked, including "Belief," "Communication," "Connectedness," "Deliberative," "Empathy," "Fairness," "Inclusiveness," and "Learner." Thus, Grapevine conflates the incentive to participate as a consumer with the incentive to participate as a citizen. Moreover, it takes advantage of the exciting rhetoric about new media technologies to collect both political and commercial data from participants who think they are participating in an information revolution and guiding government and corporation policy. Finally, the political information that used to circulate in a public sphere now circulates in a marketplace where it is priced, trademarked, and sold.

United Campaigns

United Campaigns is a political action committee (PAC) that provides consulting services to moderate political causes and candidates. The organization was founded in 1999 and currently has about 100 employees and a growing list of partner affinity groups. Recently, United made a key hire, placing a well-known former

U.S. senator as its chief executive of operations and further strengthening its image as a leading political consultancy. Although the senator does not have previous experience heading an Internet venture or any other kind of company, he has told journalists that United Campaigns will "alter politics as we know it." United offers access to its key asset, its database of individuals' political information, as well as its own brand of Internet-based software to extract and manipulate database information about specific population demographics.

The foundation of United's database came from a company that provides free e-mail service that required its subscribers to fill out questionnaires when they created email accounts. The answers from this initial questionnaire supplied United with the demographics of database members, such as age, gender, income, expected major purchases, hobbies, interests, family size, and education. United supplemented this information using spyware to track database members' patterns of computer use. United has significantly evolved its initial database to now include the voter registration information of more than 150 million registered voters in the United States, as culled from state and local boards of elections. In addition, United combines 50 million individuals' records from departments of motor vehicles. Outside the United States, United has begun to build an international database, starting in the United Kingdom, Canada, and Australia, with a database that contains registration records of more than 90 million voters. In addition, United continues to run a nonprofit Internet service provider from which it gathers subscriber questionnaire information and Internet use information, via cookies and spyware, to add to its database. United's database thus contains information including date of birth, date of voter or motor vehicle registration, residence address, number of children in the household, political jurisdiction, and party affiliation. Through spider software, spam and spyware, United has found and added e-mail addresses, telephone numbers, estimated income levels, ethnicity of surnames, and homeowner status. United also purchases data from other lobby groups, and its database now contains detailed and growing information on more than 75% of the voting public as well as on hundreds of thousands of unregistered voters.

Like Grapevine, some of United's activities are problematic. First, United has built a relational database using people's detailed personal information without their explicit or informed consent. United uses e-mail registrations, voter registrations, motor vehicle registrations, an individual's movement on the Internet, as well as other undisclosed sources, to amass information that the vast majority of people might not consider public record. In addition, the combination of these various sources of information paints a highly detailed picture of individuals' lives that clients, either political or commercial, can use to uniquely customize messages to manipulate certain responses from each particular individual in the database. Even if some members gave initial informed consent to the use of certain political information, most would not have consented to its continuous aggregation and applications. Already, through United, political organizations and commercial industry are able to drive traffic to their websites by directing customized banner and e-mail advertisements via the political, demographic, and commercial characteristic profiles of members of the database. In addition, in the deals United makes with some of its partners, partners get access to United's database while also sharing their own databases, amassing an even more detailed and widely shared profile of individuals. Voter registration records are governed by complex regulations—more than 25 states, including California, prohibit the commercial use of voter registration records. Yet, as a PAC, United is exempt from many of these restrictions, so its clients, which may include industry lobby groups, may now order political information through its Web site and have that information delivered as raw data and processed as mailing labels, telephone sheets, walk lists, a polling sample, or a file suitable for import into many popular software programs.

The New Market for Political Information

Grapevine and United are two good examples of the kinds of organizations working in the marketplace for political information. One initially buys individuals' personal information and opinions in exchange for Internet access and free prizes, and then continues to mine data on these individuals to build a detail-rich database to market to clients. Another amasses personal information about individuals, from the start unbeknownst to them and without their permission, using government records, commercial means, and Internet spyware. Grapevine's clients are mostly commercial, but the company is increasingly serving industry lobby groups. United works with political entities but shares information with industry lobby groups that are constituted as PACs. That political information is bought and sold is not new. However, the quality of the product and the structure of the market evolved significantly once organizations started using new media technologies to collect and distribute political information.

The Quality of The Political Information Product. Both Grapevine and United play an important role in the marketplace for political information, with three kinds of informational products and services.[3] First, when industries and services form political lobby groups, both Grapevine and United help these lobby groups legitimize cause by identifying the needs of group members. A lobby group will often claim to represent firms in an industry and, at the same time, claim to represent the consumers of that industry's goods. Thus information about the importance of the industry to the American economy or to American consumers becomes a source of political legitimacy. Second, both Grapevine and United do *direct-inference* public policy polling for clients. In other words, they run survey instruments that field clear questions about political topics. For example, a direct-inference question might ask, "Should the government offer universal healthcare?" and pollsters can use basic demographic features to explain variation in responses. Third, both Grapevine and United increasingly do *indirect-inference* public policy polling with data from survey questions, demographic data, credit card purchases, Internet activity, or voter registration files that allow for models of public opinion.

They might infer, without actually fielding survey questions, that a woman over 55 years old, living in New York, registered as a Democrat, and spending a significant amount of her income on pharmaceuticals, is very likely to think the government should offer universal healthcare. Moreover, purchases of guns, birth control, or other items can help researchers make indirect inference about a consumer's political attitudes. With new media tools, the research staff at Grapevine and United has amassed so much data from so many sources that the complex relational databases can be used to extrapolate political information without ever directly contacting a respondent. In sum, today's commercially available political information is multi-sourced, nuanced, scaled from named individuals and households to residential blocks, zip codes, and electoral districts.

The Structure of the Political Information Market. The contemporary market for political information now includes a diverse population of actors, including advertising and public relations agencies, media and entertainment companies, university research institutes, pollsters, nonprofits and private foundations, political parties, Internet service providers, and PACs. Both Grapevine and United, however, make deliberate efforts to associate with academic research institutions so as to appear more legitimate. They host conferences, have academics publish with their commercially valuable data, and use university names liberally throughout their corporate identity literature. They buy, sell, and trade political information that in its raw form can be cheaply sold to any citizen with Internet access. In other forms, aggregated and relational, it is more expensive and priced at a point that only the more high-end lobby groups can afford. Thus competition between organizations in this market has driven the prices of political information down, made the product more widely distributed, and made the range of products more diverse—the market for political information is more open than ever before. Ironically, the market for political information has been democratized.

In sum, with the political application of new media, the market grew to have (1) a more diverse group of actors buying and selling (2) a wider and deeper range of political information. Such detailed knowledge about individuals is used to exercise panoptical and discursive power, but is also a key component of the long observed surveillance duty of governance. Contemporary political theorists may agree that the state is defined as the social organization that has legitimate control of both the machinery of violence and the machinery of surveillance, but we find that increasingly other entities have purview over political information. With new media, both political and commercial organizations conduct political surveillance of citizenry. Even though individuals' identities and opinions are bought and sold in the electronic marketplace, the technologies that allow indirect inference about opinions make it less necessary for political organizations to attend to freely voiced views. Customizing political and commercial messages is an old marketing trick, but the degree of tailoring possible with new media is so much more powerful that political information today is a significantly different product. Customizing political messages to the degree possible with new media does violence to the public sphere, restricting our future supplies of political information based on assumptions of the opinions and identities of our past. Increasingly, we find that an important part of our political participation occurs somewhat beyond our control, co-opted into a highly privatized and often covert sphere, one that trades, channels, and filters our political information, thus denying a forum for its direct, free, and deliberate exchange.

Notes

1. For their assistance with this manuscript, the authors would like to thank Aimee Strasko, Paul Ford, and Nika Pelc.
2. United Campaigns and Grapevine Polling are pseudonyms based on aggregates of our ethnographic and archival study of 18 businesses, academic research institutes, and political action committees between 1999 and 2003.
3. Corporations such as Grapevine and United are very careful to obey state laws that regulate which records can be sold to whom. Even though companies may violate public privacy norms, organizations have legal counsel committed to keeping their work well within the letter and spirit of the law.

References

Foucault, M. (1977). *Discipline and Punish: The Birth of the Prison* (1st American ed.). New York: Pantheon Books.
Foucault, M. (1999). Power as Knowledge. In C. Lemert (Ed.), *Social Theory, the Multicultural and Classic Readings* (pp. 475–481). Boulder, CO: Westview Press.
Giddens, A. (1987). *Social Theory and Modern Sociology.* Stanford, CA: Stanford University Press.
Norris, P. (2000). *A Virtuous Circle : Political Communications in Postindustrial Societies.* Cambridge, England; New York: Cambridge University Press.
Poster, M. (1990). *The Mode of Information.* Chicago: University of Chicago Press.
Poster, M. (1995). *The Second Media Age.* Cambridge, MA: Polity Press.
Scott, J. C. (1998). *Seeing Like a State: How Certain Schemes to Improve the Human Condition Have Failed.* New Haven, CT: Yale University Press.
Webster, F. (1995). *Theories of the Information Society.* London: Routledge.
Witte, J., & Howard, P. N. (in press). The Future of Polling: Relational Inference and the Development of Internet Survey Instruments. In J. Manza & F. L. Cook & B. Page (Eds.), *Navigating Public Opinion: Polls, Policy and the Future of American Democracy.* New York: Oxford University Press.

John Logie and Leslie Regan Shade   Section Three

Net/Working Communities

 We first met in cyberspace, and without so much as a handshake, we worked together closely for a year on Internet Research 2.0: INTERconnections, which was held on the University of Minnesota campus in October 2001.

Often during that year, when we told colleagues or acquaintances that we were working on preparations for an Internet research conference in Minneapolis, those outside Internet studies would waggishly suggest that there was no real need for the conference to be held *anywhere* specifically. With eyebrows arched, they would say, "Why don't you just hold it *online*?" This question was asked more pointedly after the attacks of September 11, 2001, 30 days before the scheduled start of Internet Research 2.0.

Ultimately, the vast majority of those scheduled to present at the conference chose to defy the uncertainty and fear associated with that historical moment. Despite significant obstacles, they traveled, joined together, ate together, drank together, talked together, and *worked* together. They reinforced, revised, and extended the networks of colleagues they had been building in virtual spaces.

The collective statement of the nearly 400 attendees at Internet Research 2.0 was that the opportunities for community exchange afforded by the conference outweighed any of the burdens prompted by our renewed awareness of risk. Community *matters* to Internet researchers, in part because their work is often perceived as being at the margins of their academic and professional disciplines, but mostly because the Internet epitomizes the shift from the abstracted, isolated composing space of the "personal computer" to the richly social networks of communal exchange found throughout online environments.

We are now in the second decade of research devoted to articulating, explaining, celebrating, and critiquing the concept of community as it is manifested online. This work is, increasingly, as rich and varied as the work directed toward understanding terrestrial communities. But research on online community spaces rarely commits the error implicit in the suggestion (however flippant) that Internet researchers ought to be content with virtual meetings in cyberspaces. The basis for the suggestion is the misguided notion that Internet researchers view online communities as *substitutes* for terrestrial communities. But the best research on online communities recognizes that these spaces typically complement and extend terrestrial social connections. In some cases, online communities *do* offer alternatives to terrestrial communities, but in most of these cases, the Internet-enabled communities offer opportunities that practicalities of time or distance would make difficult, if not impossible in terrestrial spaces.

These selections from the first three Internet Research conferences ably challenge the lingering notion that Internet research represents a retreat from the "real world." On the contrary, these essays repeatedly underscore the ways in which online communities are richly linked to offline communities, and tend to share both the virtues and the failings of their offline counterparts.

In "Virtual Otherness," Smiljana Antonijevic investigates Internet usage in Yugoslavia during the 1999 NATO bombing through an analysis of SezamPro, the oldest online system in Yugoslavia–both how users utilized SezamPro and their overall Internet usage during the bombing was examined. Antonijevic concludes that SezamPro served as a forum for socialization, a source of information, and a free and open space for the expression of political opinions. Chat, acting as a form of "virtual shelter," was one of the more direct uses of SezamPro, which allowed users in Belgrade to comment live on bombing throughout their city.

Nils Zurawski's "Because It's Important and Out There: From Real-Life Identities to Virtual Ethnicities" interrogates ethnicity online—how it is used, and who is availing themselves of ethnic resources. He describes a framework—"virtual ethnicity"—for studying the offline-online nature of ethnicity, which focuses on power relations, political economy, the representation of groups and societies, and the narratives and meanings of identity in a "despatialized, global and connected world." Thus, virtual ethnicity is concerned with the socioeconomic structures of membership, exclusion, and the sustenance of communities.

In "Newsgroup Interaction as Urban Life," Stine Gotved examines the Usenet newsgroup *rec.arts.books.tolkien* in terms of human interaction and creation of community through a triangulation of different approaches: registration, content analysis, and survey. She argues, "There is a likeness between the modern metropolis and cyberspace, a likeness, which is both metaphorical and constructed in the everyday language," suggesting that even a group with roots in Middle Earth can adapt its community norms from conventional urban landscapes.

Jan Fernback argues that democracy and the public sphere are threatened by the increasing appropriation of the notion of community by corporate interests and marketers in "Community as Commodity: Empowerment and Consumerism on the Web." She looks at how online communities have been commodified and commercialized by a variety of corporate interests, including local, media-centered Web site community sections (such as online newspapers), and Web portals that exploit their "community" forums as mere spaces for the saturation of advertising. The notion of community has also been used by businesses, intent on Web development as another venue for their products, which often use online communities to solicit feedback from customers. Rather than the utopian sentiments of online communities as a tangible space for the nurturance of a vibrant Habermasian public sphere, Fernback instead cautions us that such ersatz communities benefit marketers rather than citizens.

The Internet has been widely used for the creation of support groups, particularly for health issues. In "Just Do It: The Online Communication of Breast Cancer as a Practice of Empowerment," Shani Orgad looks at discursive communities formed for women who suffer from breast cancer, and how online participation empowers these women to take control of themselves. Arguing that many of the studies on online support groups have been concerned merely with information provision, here Orgad looks at the wider social meanings of the everyday experiences of these women and their illness through narrativization and storytelling, and exchange and reciprocity in personal Web sites, message boards, and-email.

Sorin Adam Matei builds on the tradition of social network analysis (Wellman & Haythornthwaite, 2003) and research that explores the links between social capital and the Internet (Katz, Rice, & Aspden, 2001). In "The Internet's 'Magnifying Glass' Effect on Offline Ties in the General Social Survey," Matei offers an analysis of the General Social Survey (2000) Internet module, and investigates whether online social ties build from offline social behavior. The GSS, consisting of questions that inquired about social ties both on- and offline, allowed for an in-depth and multivariate analysis, which allows Matei to generalize about the correlations between real life and virtual social ties. Matei concludes that "people with stronger connections to their *circle of friends* are more inclined to use the Internet for social purposes, while people with stronger connections to their *relatives* have weaker online social propensities." This reinforces his idea that the Internet is like a "magnifying glass," which builds on, rather than replaces, social ties found in real life.

The study of community networking has generated a significant body of research (see, for instance Gurstein, 2000, and Keeble & Loader, 2001). In "Talking in Lists: The Consequences of Computer-Mediated Communication on Communities," Andrea Kavanaugh and Joseph Schmitz examine the use and impacts of online group communication on social relations, information exchange and involvement through both computer-supported cooperative work (CSCW) and community computer networking approaches. The case sites analyzed include the Seattle Community Network, Pittsburgh's Three Rivers Free-Net, Champaign-Urbana's PrairieNet and the Blacksburg Community Network in Virginia. Looking specifically at the uses of listservs by nonprofit organizations and community-based groups, Kavanaugh and Schmitz conclude that listservs bring about an increase in volunteerism, financial savings, participation in group activities, and greater involvement in organizational issues.

In "The Social Design of Virtual Worlds: Constructing the User and Community through Code," T. L. Taylor looks at the architectural code surrounding systems architecture for multiuser environments, as well as the emerging genre of massively multiplayer online games (MMOG), and argues for a critical intervention that considers "seriously the ways system architectures can act as a powerful shaping force for how life gets lived online." Lawrence Lessig (2000) has famously argued that computer code is suffused with politics that inhibit or create possibilities for end users. Taylor articulates how game developers build models of sociability and interaction, describes the options users are given for creating avatars, and interrogates the values embedded in these choices. Taylor ultimately calls for a more sustained discussion surrounding the nature of "progressive design."

Taken together, these essays exemplify both the range and depth of contemporary research on online communities, and the promise of future research from within the ever-growing community of the Association of Internet Researchers.

References

Gurstein, Michael. (2000). (Ed.). *Community Informatics: Enabling Communities with Information and Communication Technologies.* Hershey, PA: Idea Group Publishing.

Katz, James E., & Ronald E. Rice. (2002). *Social Consequences of Internet Use: Access, Involvement, and Interaction.* Cambridge MA: MIT Press.

Keeble, Leigh, & Brian Loader. (2001). *Community Informatics: Shaping Computer-Mediated Social Relations.* New York: Routledge.

Lessig, Lawrence. (2000). *Code: And Other Laws of Cyberspace.* New York: Basic Books.

Wellman, Barry, & Carolyn A. Haythornthwaite. (2003). (Eds.). *The Internet in Everyday Life.* Blackwell Publishers.

VIRTUAL OTHERNESS: AN EXAMPLE OF IN-GROUP AND OUT-GROUP ONLINE INTERACTION IN YUGOSLAVIA DURING THE NATO BOMBING

 The study presented here is part of the project "Windows 99: Internet and War," which analyzed Internet usage in Yugoslavia during the NATO bombing (March 24–June 10, 1999). The research was conducted in Winter 1999 among the members of the oldest online system in Yugoslavia—SezamPro. An online questionnaire was used as a method of data gathering. It consisted of two parts, that is, two key areas of research. First part was focused on the Sezam Pro users' activities within this online system, while the second part was aimed at studying their overall Internet usage during the bombing. My goal was to discover whether some differences and/or similarities in the users' activities inside and outside the system could be found.

The questionnaire was posted on the SezamPro Web site (<http//:www.sezam pro.yu>) and thus was available to all its users. It was filled out by 136 persons, of which two-thirds (73%) were male and one-third (27%) female. The majority of the respondents (68%) were between the age of 18 and 35. The age structure coincided with educational achievements—50% graduated from high school (most of them were students), whereas 48% graduated from schools of higher education and faculties. Two-thirds (70%) of the informants were residents of Belgrade and three-quarters (80%) declared themselves to be of Serbian nationality.

The results showed that both types of activities, inside and outside the system, were significantly increased at wartime. The majority of the respondents spent more time online and communicated online more intensely during the bombing than before the war started. However, while strong personal relations and a sense of togetherness were developed within the system, the respondents' communication with the international users was characterized by mutually perceived otherness and a significant level of disagreement. Within the SezamPro, the users were socializing, trying to comfort both fellow members and themselves during difficult periods of the NATO attacks. Outside the system, they acted as online activists, trying to explain the causes and consequences of the bombing to the users worldwide. A kind of demarcation line was drawn between the in-group, made of the SezamPro members, and the out-group, which consisted primarily of the Western users. Such a finding implies that online interaction was shaped by the same social processes that determine offline interaction in a state of crisis. Online separation has mirrored its "real" counterpart.

In this chapter I will try to explain the reasons for such a difference in the users' online behavior. First, I will provide the research results related to the online activities within the SezamPro system. These results were presented at the AoIR conference 1.0, and published in the online journal "First Monday."[1] Therefore, this part of the study will just be summarized in this essay. Second, I will present and analyze the results focused on the respondents' activities outside the system. Finally, I will compare these two sets of results, stressing both similarities and differences between them.

The study of activities within the SezamPro system was focused on communication in the system's chat room. SezamPro has one chatroom, without a specified topic; it is available to SezamPro members only. The questionnaire used in this study was designed in such a way as to collect information on the users' chat practice before, during, and after the war, so that comparable data could be obtained. The following elements were identified as the key points for comparative analysis:

- number of participants in a given chat;
- frequency of chat visits;
- the time spent in a given chat; and,
- basic motives for participating in a chat.[2]

The results showed that during wartime the number of chat participants increased by 16%. The frequency of visits grew by 57%, and the number of users who spent three or more hours a week chatting increased by 84%. The basic motives for chatting considerably changed. Before the bombing, fun was the main stimulus (58%), while during the war acquiring information became the most important motive for participating in the chat (89%). When the war ended, SezamPro members indicated that they participated in the chat predominantly for socializing (46%).

The analysis of these results suggested that such an intensified online activity was a result of the SezamPro chat's threefold function during wartime. It served as a source of information, as a place where political opinions could be expressed freely, and as a place where people gathered and socialized.

As a source of information, the chat had the most prominent role in providing immediate news during the NATO air raids. Night after night the users were submitting eyewitness reports to the chat. Living all across Belgrade, they were informing fellow-chatters about the situation in their area. Through such reports the users were trying to learn more about the objects hit, the potential casualties, and other relevant information. Such data were usually unobtainable through mainstream media, because of the governmental censorship. The following extract from a SezamPro chat session illustrates such an effort of gathering and providing information during one of the NATO air raids:

> oh, fuck, there are explosions all over the city, crazy!!!
> anyone seeing anything?
> the centre, near Vuk, it exploded like mad
> Wow . . . it means, towards the centre
> my chair flew away
> aren't they attacking the Military HQ?
> has anyone got the information where it exploded?
> oh, fuck; people, chaos is outside!!
it sounded as if someone had pulled the trigger just below my window
> the sky is clear tonight :(
> no one seeing anything?
> three flames of smoke somewhere near the partizan stadium

Furthermore, the chat had an important role as a place where political opinions could be expressed freely. In a state of war, which was officially proclaimed in Yugoslavia at the time, criticizing the regime was considered risky. Therefore, the Yugoslav citizens were usually cautious about their statements. In the SezamPro chat, however, disparagement with official Yugoslav politics was expressed without hesitation.

Nonetheless, the most important function of the SezamPro wartime chat was its role as a place where people gathered and socialized. During the bombing, social interaction in physical space was mostly limited to family members and the closest neighbors, as leaving one's home was dangerous. In such circumstances, SezamPro's cyber space enabled what was physically impossible. It gathered people who were facing the same problems and who had the same need to express and share their feelings. For one of the respondents, "the feeling that we are all in same trouble and a relief because of the possibility to get in touch" was the most important characteristic of wartime chat. Another respondent explained the significance of people gathering online from his personal perspective: "I live in a strategically important area [and] it was problematic to go out at night, so most of my social life was directed to the chat." The respondents' answers also indicated that the exchange of information about the ongoing air raids in Belgrade was basically an act of social interaction: "Commenting second after second what was going on, was a way to share fear with someone," one of the respondents noted.

Serving as a place where people could exchange information, political opinions, and, above all, their fears, the SezamPro chat had an important function in easing the participants' anxiety. Half of the respondents stated that wartime chatting had a significant role in improving their psychological state. "There were always some new pieces of information, I always knew what was happening, the presence of so many people, even in the chat, eased my psychological state," said one of the respondents. More significantly, even two-thirds of the respondents reported that they were trying to ease anxiety of their fellow chatters. They were doing that by "saying that it was not so terrible, and that it would be better," "talking about nicer things," "by amusing others," and so on.

The analysis of communication within the SezamPro system showed that strong social relationships were established online and that the sense of togetherness was developed within the studied group. Virtual space was not a bridge between geographically dispersed individuals, but an alternative gathering place in circumstances that disabled physical contact. The analyzed chat channel was a specific "virtual shelter" that participants used in order to protect their critical attitude and to maintain an emotional balance.

The analysis of the SezamPro members' activities outside the system provides a somewhat different picture. But, before presenting data related to the respondents' wartime activities, let me outline the characteristics of their prewar Internet usage, which will be significant for the further analysis.

Online activities of the SezamPro users in the period before the bombing could be described as usual and widespread forms of Internet usage. The majority of the respondents (43%) were using the Internet to obtain information related to their profession, and/or their interests. Web design, MP3 music, and sport represented content of the most visited Web sites. One-third of the respondents (28%) reported that they were using the Internet primarily for socializing and/or untailored surfing. Nineteen percent said that acquiring information related to politics was the goal of their Internet usage. Furthermore, the SezamPro members had more intensive contacts with users outside the system than within it, in the period before the bombing. Two-thirds of the respondents regularly contacted more than five persons on the Internet, while one-third had more than five regular contacts within the SezamPro. Organized in four main types of interaction, the results provided the picture shown in Table 1.

The table shows that the respondents had more intensive contacts on the Internet than within the SezamPro in all four of the analyzed categories.

When the war started, the respondents' Internet activities remained dynamic.

Table 1: Types of Interaction

	Friendships	Business contacts	Contacts with relatives	Romance
SezamPro	64%	20%	5%	4%
Internet	84%	53%	44%	16%

In fact, they were intensified. The study has shown that the majority of the respondents (64%) logged onto the Internet more often than at peacetime, and spent more time online (69%). But, their interest shifted towards the news Web sites and political online sources. Cnn.com, bbc.com, stratfor.com, and antiwar.com were among the most visited Web sites.

Their online interaction underwent a significant transformation as well. One half of the respondents (48%) met more people on the Internet during the bombing than before it started. Most of the contacts were made with users from Western Europe and North America. These contacts were initiated by the SezamPro members and the international users equally (50%-50%). The majority of the respondents reported that they were initiating these contacts in order to convince Western users into the wrongness of the war. Here are some of the typical answers:

> My goal was to spread truth about our country, so that people could learn more about history and actual events, and not to base their opinion about us just on the reports of their TV stations.

> I wanted to widen my perspective, as always, and at the same time to tell them what kind of people we Yugoslavs really are, to inform them about the events, and to ask support for Yugoslav NGOs.

> It was my attempt to spread truth among the brainwashed people.

> [I was contacting them in order to] eliminate lies about Serbs and media-created sensations, such as mass rapes, by appealing to common sense.

> My goal was, and still is, to make at least one person think.
> I wanted to convince them that they were mistaken and that everything was lie and media manipulation.

To support their arguments, the majority of the respondents provided information about the civilian casualties; fatal character of depleted uranium, cluster bombs, and other weaponry that NATO was using; and about devastation of the civilian infrastructure and cultural heritage. A significant number of the respondents reported that they mostly offered information related to Serbian history and a chronicle of the conflict in Serbian province of Kosovo and Metohija. A number of the respondents were simply describing everyday life and ambiance in wartime Belgrade. With a small exception, the SezamPro members generally reported that they were not sending explicit political messages or advocating any political party.

The respondents also provided their understanding of the international users' motives in contacting them during the war. The majority reported that people who contacted them wanted to get various kinds of information. The examples follow:

They wanted to learn about life in Serbia during the bombing.

They asked for information about the atrocities.

It was a pure curiosity. People from across the Ocean were looking for information because they were bored.

They were looking for information, but nobody was interested in deeper meaning and problems.

The interest in the current events was their motive. Also, they were completely puzzled by the fact that a person could be at home and surf the Net during the air raids.

Some respondents described the international users' motives as primarily expressive. Namely, they reported that people contacted them to express either support or critique:

They wanted to vent their rage at irrational Serbs.

Some of them wanted to express their compassion; others were swearing at me because I was a Serb.

It was their false mourning.

The above-cited answers suggest that communication between the Yugoslav and the international users was characterized by mutually perceived distinctiveness. The majority of respondents saw international users as people who were misinformed and/or ignorant regarding the course and consequences of the war and, consequentially, as people who should have been informed and persuaded into the wrongness of their standpoint. In other words, *they* were people who knew nothing about *us*. Furthermore, international users were perceived as individuals whose interest in the wartime situation was superficial and/or fake. Sometimes, such a view was articulated in a rather harsh tone, so the international users were described as the brainwashed, bored Westerners who were just curious about the tragedy such as war, and whose compassion was not just rare but insincere, too. Again, *they* were people who did not really care about *our* tragedy. The international users' perception of the Yugoslav users could also be regarded as the expression of perceived "otherness," according to the respondents' answers. Generally, Yugoslav users were seen as people whose life was characterized by the extraordinary experience of war. As such, they were of interest to the international users, who wanted to learn either about the wartime life in general, or about some more specific features, such as a person's motive to surf the Net during the air raids. *They* were people who were going through something unknown to *us*. In some cases, such a feeling of "otherness" was expressed in a more radical way—*they* were irrational Serbs at whom *we* should swear.

The perceived "otherness" of international users described above motivated the SezamPro users to act in a way that could be identified as a specific form of cyberactivism. Cyberactivism refers to a wide range of online activities and strategies aimed at social change. Recognizing the advantages of the Internet such as a high speed and a wide reach, both individuals and groups have started to use it as an effective tool for voicing various ends, networking with like-minded people, and coordinating activities. Such a role of the global network can be traced back to its early days, in the cases of Lotus Marketplace and the Clipper chip.[3] Afterwards, cyberactivism has significantly developed both in terms of people involved and the strategies employed, but its main function as a mechanism of social change has remained.[4]

In the case of SezamPro, cyberactivism was not organized and/or purposely tailored; there were no online petitions or any other type of prearranged online actions. Instead, these activities were individual and spontaneous. The SezamPro members acted as people who saw the Internet as an effective means for their personal struggle, which was to present and defend their identity, both national and personal. Trying to explain "what kind of people we really are" and to modify the image of Serbs created in the Western media, the SezamPro members were actually seeking international recognition for both their nation and themselves, as members of this group. Writing about Serbian history and national heritage, they were trying to familiarize international users with their culture, and thus to defend their threatened ethnic identity. Writing about everyday wartime experiences and civilian casualties, they wanted to present their situation of ordinary people in a tragedy of war, and thus to defend their threatened personal identity. Therefore, the social change they were seeking through cyberactivism was re-evaluation of their nation and themselves, and readmission into the international community. Before the bombing, they had rich personal and professional contacts with the users worldwide; suddenly, the war made them "strange people" and/or "bad Serbs." Thus, their intense contacts with the international users could be understood as an attempt at recovering and/or maintaining their real and virtual "ordinariness."

It is a well-known fact that wars additionally consolidate ethnic groups and simultaneously generate strong interethnic differentiation. Also, different types of shared beliefs, such as patriotism and siege beliefs, have important affective and behavioral implications in a state of crisis. Bar-Tal (2001) notes that such beliefs invoke ingroup solidarity and "facilitate management of cognitive ambiguities by dichotomizing the world into black and white solutions" (pp. 112–113). Providing shared, stable, and unfussy understanding of frightening and equivocal reality, these beliefs enable individuals to cope with stress, information overload, and uncertainty, typical of conflict situations (ibid.).

This case has shown that the same social mechanisms described above occurred in online interaction. The community analyzed here was formed on the premises of national identity, because nationality was the basis of shared experience that brought its members together. The SezamPro users had the same experience *because* they had the same nationality. Therefore, this case shows that shared experience is an important element in forming online groups. Furthermore, the lack of shared experience between the Yugoslav and international users identified in this case was not the one described by Cass Sunstein (2001), which focused on information filtering enabled by modern technologies. Although the SezamPro members consulted the same news sources as the international users probably did (cnn.com, bbc.com, and alike), their physical reality was completely different. Reality was the one that separated them, and viruality was just a reflection of this process. As Laura Gurak (2001) notes, "Our real bodies do not live online. And when it comes right down to it, what happens to our real body takes priority. Physicality, in the end, is the big rule. Physicality rules" (p. 148). In the case of SezamPro, reality determined a demarcation line between "us" and "them." Online interaction just followed it humbly.

Notes

1. See <http://firstmonday.org/issues/issue7_1/anton/index.html>.
2. The frequency of visits and the time spent in the chat were estimated according to an average value. Concerning the frequency of visits, on average there were three or more visits a week, with three or more hours a week spent in session. Basic motives for participating offered in the questionnaire were: fun, socializing, meeting someone, and getting informed (with a blank space offered for additional motives).
3. See Gurak, 1997.
4. See McCaughey and Ayers, 2003.

References

Bar-Tal, D. (2000). *Shared Beliefs in a Society*. Thousand Oaks, CA, London, New Delhi: Sage.
Gurak, L. (1997). *Persuasion and Privacy in Cyberspace: The Online Protests over Lotus Marketplace and the Clipper Chip*. New Haven, CT, and London: Yale University Press.
Gurak, L. (2001). *Cyberliteracy: Navigating the Internet with Awareness*. New Haven, CT, and London: Yale University Press.
McCaughey, M., & Ayers, M. (Eds). (2003). *Cyberactivism: Online Activism in Theory and Practice*. New York and London: Routledge.
Sunstein, C. (2001). *Republic.com*. Princeton, NJ, and Oxford: Princeton University Press.

BECAUSE IT'S IMPORTANT AND OUT THERE: FROM REAL-LIFE IDENTITIES TO VIRTUAL ETHNICITIES

Introduction

Ethnicity, as a globally ubiquitous phenomenon, is most often set in the context of conflicts or wars—premodern, backward, and an obstacle to development. Hence, it seems quite the opposite of the Internet, or what is said about the Internet and global communication technologies. The Internet is global, open, transnational, borderless, and a motor of communication between people disregarding cultural identity, race, or nationality. There seems to be an apparent contradiction between the two phenomena. Castells indeed describes this relationship as such a contradiction. He regards the "Net" and identity ("the Self") as two ends of a bipolar opposition (1996, p. 23). Ethnicities for Castells are local, while the "network society" is global (1996, p. 53 and 59f). The Net doesn't need or even allow identity; rather, it is an obstacle for global communications in a "network society."

Contrary to this, the relationship is conceived as dynamic and reciprocal. Beth Kolko (2000) notes that "neither the invisibility nor the mutability of online identity make it possible for you to escape your "real world identity" completely (cf. 2000, p. 4). Race matters in cyberspace, because of the ways in which race matters offline. This can be supported by Mark Poster's (1998) notion of "virtual ethnicity," which approaches this relationship as a reciprocal influence between the "real" and the "virtual."

This suggests that "what is out there" also impacts on the forms of communication and representation of peoples and groups online. So it becomes important to look at "how" ethnicity is used on the Internet and "who" is making use of ethnic resources. This article looks for a framework to study the offline-online relation of ethnicity and the significance of virtual ethnicities in a globalized, internetworked world. The proposed two level approach of "Virtual Ethnicity" will focus on power relations, political-economic relations, and the representation of groups and societies. Furthermore on the narratives and meanings of identity in a despatialized, global, and connected world.

The first level is displayed in a model that examines the cause-effect relationship between forms of online representations—e-mail and the Web—and the sociopolitical conditions of individuals and groups concerning their cultural identity. The second level then centers on aspects of globality and identity, neither rooted in the physical nor in the virtual world, but transcending the two. With that second level it may be able to study virtual ethnicities as a continuum of experiences including such factors as space, history, identities, ethnic discourses, migration, technology, and transnationality.

When speaking of ethnicity or cultural identity in this context, it is understood as a resource for self-organization. As a dynamic concept it allows the links between identity/ethnicity and global communications technology to be viewed in terms of a dynamic, continuous relation rather than an opposite pair (cf. Zurawski, 2000). Ethnicity as a resource of self-organization enables people and groups to negotiate an identity or problems that are connected to this identity, bottom-up and not state-centric (cf. Sigrist, 1994). This implies that ethnicity is constantly under construction and deconstruction by the members/ carriers of a given cultural identity. In this regard ethnicity is a "project defined and pursued over a particular history" (cf. Miller & Slater, 2000, p. 87). From such a perspective, "ethnicity as self-organization" stands very much in line with Hall's "new ethnicities," transnational identities, or diasporic identities. The factors that constitute ethnicity are culture, personal experience, self-determination, and acceptance by others as a particular group. Culture contains such ideas as language, rituals, traditions. They give ethnicity its dynamic character, as they can alter and be reconstructed.

Virtual Ethnicity

The openness and the self-organizing potential of ethnicity as proposed in this definition does not restrict ethnicity to local importance, as opposed to the global dynamics of a networking society, but offers a perspective on global communications, of which identity is an integral part.

The concept of self-organization establishes a closeness between the means of global communication and ethnicity. The choice by groups to use the Internet extensively to respond to issues concerning their identities in everyday life underlines this relationship. The reason for this is the self-organizing nature of the Internet in its own history and current practice, notwithstanding the tendencies of commercial, governmental, and legal controls. The Internet and many of its subcultures are self-organizing, or emergent as Steven Johnson (2001) argues, and seem to be the ideal medium for any ethnic group to form, maintain, and negotiate links among its often widespread members and the rest of the world.

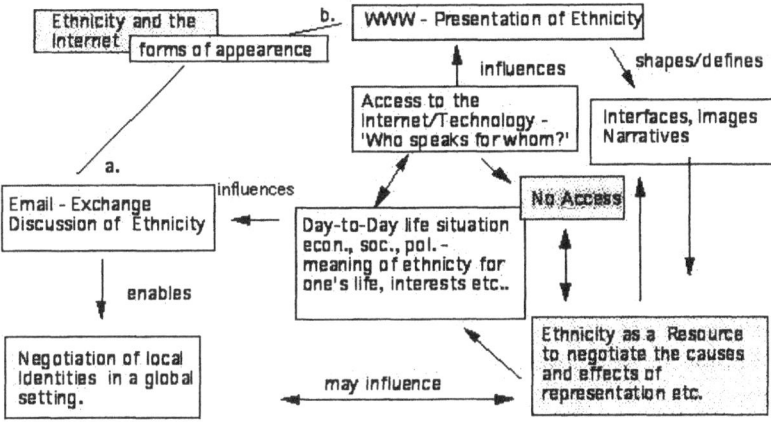

Figure 1: Cause-Effect Model of Virtual Ethnicity

The first level of "Virtual Ethnicity" deals with the issues of technology settings—how groups use it and the impact the different connections have on technology use. The model (Figure 1) shows the links between ethnicity and the Internet, focusing on the appearance of ethnic content on the Internet and the reasons and motivations underlying their use and possible presentation. Given the fact of an existing "digital divide," an important question is that of the presentation of ethnicity on the Internet or the question "Who speaks for whom?" and whose interests are behind it. The interfaces created by such means also have an influence on how ethnic groups are perceived and the forms of expression available to them. This is also true for people and groups without access to the Internet. They then have to deal with a situation created without their influence.

Virtual Ethnicity goes beyond the boundaries of the Internet and focuses on the socioeconomic structures of membership, exclusion, and the resulting requirements for the creation, maintenance, and analysis of communities. The processes described within "Virtual Ethnicity" have a direct influence on the dynamics of ethnicity.

Global developments, such as migration, tourism, or ethnic conflicts and their underlying political, economic, and social causes are often only recognizable through the simultaneous observation of ethnicity and the structures of global communication technologies (TV, Internet). "Virtual "Ethnicity" may provide a possible research framework for such an analysis.

Contexts of Application—What Is Out There?

In what forms do we experience race/ethnicity on the Internet? And why is it there? As Kolko has said, "Because it matters." But in what sense does it matter? It seems important to examine examples of ethnicity/identity on the Net. According to the issues that were found to be important in the relationship between identity and global communication—power relations, representation, and discourses of identity—the following will discuss these fields.

Why and How Does It Matter: Ethnicity in Cyberspace

Issues of race or ethnicity are closely linked to concepts of globality as generated through communication/information technologies and by transportation technologies. The latter are the key to understanding the emerging "global cultures" or "third cultures" (Featherstone, 1990). Third cultures represent flexible forms of orientation in a global space. This is a concept that is similar to Appadurai's (1990) "ethnoscape" in which he stresses the changing conditions for the spatial, social, and cultural establishment of collective identities. Both concepts refer to the increasing numbers of Diaspora communities all over the world. Ethnicity is no longer strictly bound to space, nation, territory, or one specific society as a primary reference, but must incorporate transnational and despatialized experiences.

However, "Virtual Ethnicity" does not work without any reference to a "real" space or as "national identities" (Miller & Slater, 2000), but does account for the fact that discourses of race/ethnicity may not be confined to the two alone. This underlines the argument of "ethnicity as a project" (p. 87). The Internet is used as part of this project, to negotiate different ways of interpreting an identity, sharing experiences and maintaining a general notion of what it means to be a member of group A, B or C in different global-local contexts. A few examples should highlight these arguments.

In the *Encyclopaedia of Violence, Peace and Conflict*, Wilmer, in "Indigenous peoples' responses to the conquest" (1999, p. 179ff), points to the fact that the Internet plays a vital role for groups to oppose the impact of earlier conquest or ongoing oppression.

Wilmer found that "one of the most striking features of contemporary indigenous resistance is the effectiveness of transnational and international mobilisation as well as the speed with which it emerged" (p. 193). Among the Internet resources cited were the Center for World Indigenous Studies, the Innu home page, and notes on the Waitangi Tribunal on Maori land and development claims. Internet technology is used to organize on the bases of ethnicity.

A preeminent example in this field is the Zapatista movement, which emerged on the Internet on January 1, 1994, and from the beginning incorporated the Internet into their struggle for self-determination and better local living conditions in the south of Mexico. They used the Internet specifically to gain support, to provoke discussion, and to disseminate information.

Looking at these Internet resources, it becomes more interesting to see the ways in which some groups justify the establishment of Web sites or mailing lists. In an edition of *Cultural Survival Quarterly*, several different "ethnic" Internet experiences from different groups were portrayed. Among these was the Oneida Nation from Canada—the first Indian nation to "claim territory" on the Internet, to preserve their heritage and culture (Polly, 1998). To "claim territory" means having an online presence rather than just being online. It means to establish visibility and even nationality that might be negated by domestic politics.

Claiming territory can indeed be seen as "a serious battle over the demands of place, race and identity," as Tara McPherson has described it in connection with the making or reconstruction of a "Dixie-Cyberspace." With the help of technology, people, and especially groups try to "stabilise a sense of presence" (2000, p. 119). Her research into the Web representations of the "old South" shows how discourses of identity may exclude certain aspects, in this case race. "The South" is constructed against the notion of diversity and a history of—at best—problematic race relations. It is focusing solely on the concept of a southern heritage based on white southern-ness, which probably functions as a form of covert racism (p. 126). Other aspects are excluded and made invisible. What becomes apparent here is the obvious interplay between the different factors in the construction of any virtual ethnicity, such as actual geographical space and its history, identities, possibilities and limits of technology, and aspects of transnationality.

Jewish Internet presence very well highlights the dynamics of global communications and the notion of an "identity project" incorporating these factors. Given the diasporic history of this group, Jewish resources can be found in many languages originating across the globe. In Germany, with its close and horrific historical relationship with the Jewish people, <http://www.juden.de> has links to all the Jewish communities in Germany and is also linked with resources all over the world, such as the Global Jewish Information Network. Whereas most information on the German Server has a more religious and/or academic character, other resources such as the National Foundation for Jewish Culture focus more on the cultural and political aspects of Jewish life in the United States. One step further is the Jewish Alternative Movement, a loose network of musicians based on the New York avant-garde music club, the Knitting Factory. Here Jewish life goes beyond the known traditional forms and reinterprets Jewish culture according to its surroundings and the needs of its people. Whereas in Germany the discourses circle around the Holocaust, its legacy, and the current sociopolitical situation of racist hate crimes, Jewish culture elsewhere is developing in different ways. The Internet is the way to connect the various decentralized accounts of a single, but very diverse, culture and make them known against the tendencies to be stereotyped by others. The haGalil online Web site, which can be regarded as a prime source for Jewish cultural and political life in Germany, states in its editorial pages that the Internet "is a genuine means of connecting different views of an ethnic/cultural group with members scattered all over the globe." The reality of transnationality and the use of the self-organizing potential to negotiate traditions and cultural content are exemplified here (cf. Zurawski, 2000a).

This shows that the relations between aforementioned factors (geographical space, history, identities, cyberspace, transnationality, experience of migration) are shifting continuously, so that the question arises, what are the flows that shift these relations and give preference to one factor over another in what context?

Representation and Power Relations

The display and representation of traditions and cultural content on the Internet (and elsewhere) and the ability to negotiate them, are dependent on who is responsible for or in charge of this task. Ultimately this means to look for power relations among these groups and their representations. In short: "Who speaks for whom, from where and why?"

Tara McPherson (2000) pointed out that being on the Internet may function as a means to stabilize a sense of presence. Lisa Nakamura (2000, 2002) shows how a racial imaginary is employed in the media. "Otherness" is used to present exoticism, to simulate a journey that is never really made except in the realm of cyberspace. Images of unspoiled nature and of people seemingly at "one" with their environment represent an iconography, but never the "real" thing. The problem with these kind of images is that they are manufactured to "guarantee and gesture towards the unthreatened and unproblematic existence of a destination for travel" (2000, p. 19). According to Nakamura, these images demonstrate a hegemonic power. Although "Westerners" can freely travel wherever they want, we are horrified if the locals, whose jewelry we admired in their natural environment, want to come to our civilization and take part in it (cf. Zurawski, 2000). The representation of the "Other" has to be "user friendly" in order to attract. Diversions become dangerous and must be censored or appropriated. Guillermo Gómez-Peña (2001, p. 285) states similar mechanisms in the Mexican-American experience. In the "Virtual Barrio," "we were to remain dancing salsa, painting murals, writing flamboyant love poetry and plotting revolutions in rowdy cafes." Stereotyping is used to restrict the space of action within which a group may stage its discourses and is a form of control. Control over the cultural representations of identities, or ethnic interfaces (cf. Kolko, 2000; Zurawski, 2000) means a certain amount of control over the group itself. This concerns the producers of images and discourses about a given identity, as for instance maintainers of virtual environments (Kolko, 2000; Silver, 2000; Nakamura, 2001).

David Silver finds that the maintainers of the Blackburg Electronic Village sidestep the issues of race, gender, and sexuality altogether, although their ostensible intention is to establish a diversity that reflects the local community. He does not conclude, however, that the neglect of these issues among the discussion groups reflects racism, sexism, or homophobia, but missed opportunities to foster a more diverse community network (2000, p. 145). Diversity in public discourses might be dangerous, because it will inevitably address issues such as inequality, lack of access to technologies, rights, and otherness. To deliberately exclude such topics sanitizes the picture and keeps the groups marginalized and reduces their potential for ethnic self-organization.

In the context of global communications, representation is vital not only for a virtual existence but also for the conditions under which a group may articulate its needs in the context of a global society. Making a voice heard and representing oneself on the Internet becomes an important issue. The vast number of groups that are present on the Net make it important to look for power flows, links, and connections. Ethnic groups are never homogeneous. So does a Web site represent the whole group, does it advocate the diversity of a group, or are there attempts to produce a specific image or interface with which diverging discourses are silenced? Is the group itself (or members of it) speaking or are gatekeepers holding the key to the ethnic interface and hence the access to discourses of identity?

For Kolko (2000), designed interfaces such as the ones used in MUD environments are cultural maps of computer systems and like all maps, "interfaces are important for what they do not show as well as what they show; they are simply powerful for how they choose to represent the terrain to users" (p. 219). Adapting this definition, the representation of ethnicity also may be seen as a similar interface. Culture and its specific interpretations serve as interfaces to establish presence and to steer discourses. Neal Stephenson (1999, p. 46ff, cf. also Johnson, 1997) shows that environments and ideologies like Disney World and its products can be analyzed with the notion of an interface culture that incorporates some of the features of the supposedly "real" originals, while neglecting "disturbing" aspects, such as race.

The absence of issues such as race in these interfaces constructs a different world. By neglecting aspects of society, the interface creates a cultural map of assumed whiteness. The inclusion or exclusion of features in an interface, that is, the interpreted representation of a culture or ethnic identity, is always an act of power to either resist, shape or negotiate issues to certain ends. Recent developments in information technologies make it ever more necessary to explore the relation between these technologies and ethnicity. Surveillance technologies also may make use of ethnic/cultural stereotypes to control and steer people. The ability to maintain diversity without fostering exclusion also will depend on the shape of the discourses and the design of interfaces.

Discourses of Identity and the Use of Technology

Representations and power relations often mirror offline conditions, but Internet technology also helps to facilitate discourses of identity. Diasporic groups, migrants, and the people that "stayed at home" are given the opportunities to communicate, play, and perform identity online in a way that was not available before. "The Internet—as Mark Warschauer says—can both magnify existing inequalities in society while also facilitating efforts to challenge the inequalities (2000, p. 157)." Warschauer describes efforts undertaken by the Hawaiians to defend their culture and in particular their indigenous language and their form of English creole—Hawaiian Creole English—(cf. also Hale, 1995; Donaghy, 1998). As Warschauer observes, the Internet indeed helped to facilitate and revive a sense of identity. The defense of a language means a defense of community, autonomy, and power (Warschauer, 2000, p. 166). In a world that shifts gradually from globalization to relocalization (p. 156), language becomes a means to manifest this shift and to turn to ones identity as a form of self-organization.

A second study that emphasises this role of the Internet is Daniel Miller and Don Slater's study on Trinidad, Trinidadians, and the role of the Internet for their culture. In their approach to the Internet as part of a material culture, they show how this technology is used to negotiate a sense of identity and how cultural discourses are maintained across the globe in different cultural contexts. Language and cultural forms of socialising are simply transferred to the Internet, which becomes assimilated as "Trini" and is seen as just another social space (Miller & Slater, 2000, p. 88). This perception makes any distinction between an offline and online world redundant as it points out the fluidity of the two spheres and the impact culture has on the incorporation of technologies into cultural practices. Incorporating the diaspora communities in the United Kingdom, Miller and Slater find that the Internet is something that overcomes distance, rather than dis-embedding social relations. Miller and Slater also discovered that using the Internet is an integral part of being "Trini," as is a general connection to the outside "global" world. Identity is thus shaped by making the "Internet a Trini place, where they can perform Trini" (p. 85). Being "Trini" can not be seen as unified "national" character but, rather, highlights the complex issue of ethnic identity (p. 86). These findings underline the theoretical focus of a "Virtual Ethnicity," which transcends the division of online/offline and underlines the proposed dynamic relationship of ethnicity and global communications.

Conclusion: The Second Level of "Virtual Ethnicity"

Whereas the first level of the approach Virtual Ethnicity presents a cause-and-effect-relationship among technology, ethnic identity, and the pattern of usage, the second level centers on the more global dynamics of the relationship between ethnicity and the Internet. Among the various factors of this global dynamics Ethnicity/cultural identity is only one. These factors generate relations through flows of power and are shaped by the flows of construction and change—the "project of identity"—which employs all or some of these factors:

- Geographical space and its history
- Discourses of identities
- Cyberspace including its narratives and technologies,
- Migration and transnationality, including immigrant politics and economy
- Ethnicity as an identity to which people may refer
- Forms and discourses of representation

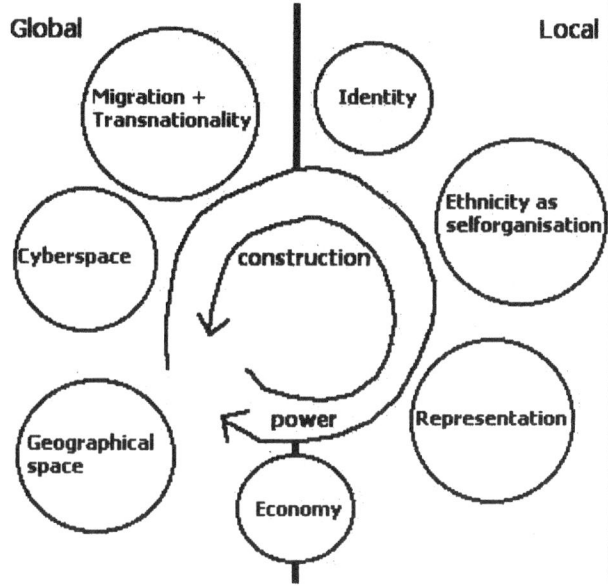

Figure 2. Global Dynamics of Virtual Ethnicity

This model can be seen as a model of globality that is rooted neither in the physical nor in the virtual world but has to be understood as a continuum of experiences (cf. Zurawski, 2002). In doing so the existing opposition is transformed for a better understanding of the dynamics of global communications and cultural identity.

In making ethnicity a part of the model rather than its underlying feature, research on such issues–as shown by Miller and Slater and Warschauer—also can help to better understand the nature and dynamics of ethnicity itself. In this sense, a study of the relationship between global communications and local cultural identities may help progressing the understanding of ethnicity itself.

This chapter makes it clear that "Virtual Ethnicity" should not be constrained to the realms of the Internet or other forms of global communications. Instead, it reflects the structures of transnationality and the global conditions of which ethnicity is a part. In adopting this view, issues of race/ethnicity, gender, and class among others can be dealt with more appropriately. Situating such a discussion in a global context from the beginning widens the discourse and accounts for the global qualities and relevance of many of these issues.

References

Appadurai, Arjun (1990). Disjuncture and Difference in the Global Economy. In Featherstone, Mike (ed.), *Global Culture, Nationalism, Globalization and Modernity*. London, pp. 295–310.

Castells, Manuel (1996). *The Rise of the Network Society*. Malden, MA: Blackwell.
Castells, Manuel (1997). *The Power of Identity*. Malden, MA: Blackwell.
Center for World Indigenous Studies— < http://www.cwis.org >
Cultural Survival Quarterly— < http://www.cs.org/publications/CSQ/csqinternet.html#Polly >
Donaghy, Keola (1998). Olelo Hawai'i: A Rich Oral History, a Bright Digital Future. In The Internet and Indigenous Groups. *Cultural Survival Quarterly* 4(21). Available at < http://www.cs.org/publications/CSQ/csqinternet.html#Donaghy >.
Featherstone, Mike (1990). Global Culture. In Featherstone, Mike (ed.), *Global Culture, Nationalism, Globalization and Modernity*. London, pp. 1-13.
Global Jewish Information Network— < http://www.mofet.macam98.ac.il/~dovw/jw/w/www1.html >
Gómez-Peña, Guillermo (2001). The Virtual Barrio @ the Other Frontier (or the Chicano Interneta). In Trend, David (ed.), *Reading Digital Culture*. Malden, MA: Blackwell, pp. 281-286.
haGalil online— < http://www.hagalil.com >
Hale, Constance (1995). How do you say Computer in Hawaiian? *Wired*, August, vol. 3, pp. 90-100.
Innu Home page— < http://www.innu.org >
Jewish Alternative Movement— < http://www.jewmu.com >
Johnson, Steven (1997). *Interface Culture. How New Technology Transforms the Way We Create and Communicate*. San Francisco, HarperEdge.
Knitting Factory— < http://www.knittingfactory.com >
Kolko, Beth (2000). Erasing @race: Going White in the (inter)Face. In Kolko, Beth, Nakamura, Lisa, & Rodman, Gilbert B. (eds.), *Race in Cyberspace*. New York: Routledge, pp. 213-236.
McPherson, Tara (2000). I'll Take My Stand in Dixie-Net: White Guys, the South, and Cyberspace. In Kolko, Beth, Nakamura, Lisa, & Rodman, Gilbert B. (eds.), *Race in Cyberspace*. New York: Routledge, pp. 117-134.
Miller, Daniel, & Slater, Don (2000). The Internet. *An Ethnographic Approach*. Oxford: Berg.
Nakamura, Lisa (2000). Where do you want to go today? Cybernetic Tourism, the Internet, and Transnationality. In Kolko, Beth, Nakamura, Lisa, & Rodman, Gilbert B. (eds.), *Race in Cyberspace*. New York: Routledge, pp. 15-26.
Nakamura, Lisa (2001). Race In/For Cyberspace: Identity Tourism and Racial Passing on the Internet. In Trend, David (ed.), *Reading Digital Culture*. Malden, MA: Blackwell, pp. 226-235.
Nakamura, Lisa (2002). *Cybertypes: Race, Ethnicity and Identity on the Internet*. New York: Routledge.
National Foundation for Jewish Culture— < http://www.nfjc.org >
Polly, Jean Armour (1998). Standing Stones in Cyberspace: The Oneida Indian Nation's Territory on the Internet. In The Internet and Indigenous Groups. *Cultural Survival Quarterly no*. 4, vol. 21, < http://www.cs.org/publications/CSQ/csqinternet.html#Polly >.
Poster, Mark (1998). Virtual Ethnicity. Tribal identity in an Age of Global Communications. In Jones, Steve, *Cybersociety* 2.0. Thousand Oaks, CA: Sage, pp. 184-211.
Sigrist, Christian (1996). Kritische Implikationen des Konzepts "Ethnizität als Selbstorganisation." In *Loccumer Protokolle 26*.

Silver, David (2000). Margins in the Wires: Looking for Race, Gender, and Sexuality in the Blacksburg Electronic Village. In Kolko, Beth, Nakamura, Lisa, & Rodman, Gilbert B. (eds.), *Race in Cyberspace*. New York: Routledge, pp. 133-150.
Stephenson, Neal (1999). *In the Beginning Was the Command Line*. New York: Avon.
Waitangi Tribunal on Maori— <http://www.waitangi-tribunal.govt.nz/reports/wai776.html>
Warschauer, Mark (2000). Language, Identity, and the Internet. In Kolko, Beth, Nakamura, Lisa, & Rodman, Gilbert B. (eds.), *Race in Cyberspace*. New York: Routledge, pp. 151-170.
Wilmer, Frank (1999). Indigenous People Responses to Conquest. In *Encyclopaedia of Violence, Peace and Conflict*, Vol. II, pp. 179-195.
Zapatista in Cyberspace page— <http://www.eco.utexas.edu/faculty/Cleaver/zapsincyber.html>
Zurawski, Nils (2000). *Virtuelle Ethnizität. Studien zu Identität, Kultur und Internet*. Frankfurt: Peter Lang.
Zurawski, Nils (2000a). Ethnizität im 21. Jahrhundert: Aufbruch in den Cyberspace. In *Wechselwirkung* no. 103/104, vol. 21, June/July-August/September 2000, pp. 70-75.
Zurawski, Nils (2002). *Ideas and methaphors of space on the Internet . . . and how these help or restrict us in research*. Paper from the Internet Research conference in Maastricht 2002.

Stine Gotved 21

NEWSGROUP INTERACTION AS URBAN LIFE

Introduction

Newsgroups are primarily discussion forums on Usenet, although the tendency is integration into the functions of the Web. Usenet works with a systematic hierarchy, with logical named groups and subgroups in a branchlike structure, with every level of the name as a still more precise and narrow content guide—rec.arts.books.tolkien is a good example. The top level is the recreation hierarchy, the first sublevel is arts, then it is books, and finally it is a particular author, J. R. R. Tolkien. In theory, it could continue into yet another level as "two-towers" or "dwarfs" (and so on), but it does not. Inside a newsgroup, the letters are arranged according to their topic-defined references. Initially, they are visible only as headers connected with date and sender name, and the ongoing discussion draws threads of related letters.[1] The context of the single letter means everything when the amount of letters is 1,000 a month, and the subjective validation of a given letter is made in an interrelated decoding of the sender, the header, the context, and the other senders in the thread.

A Bit about Methodology

During six months in 1996, I made a triangulation of different approaches to rec.arts.books.tolkien. The three employed methods were registration, content analysis, and survey. After the intensive study, I read the group frequently, although more extensively and from the position of a lurker. From the very beginning of the study, I posted an informative message about my planned research, expecting a lot of response, but without getting more than a few "good lucks." The message was repeated several times during the study, and perhaps the relatively good response rate to the later survey[2] is rooted in this initial openness about the research. Questions of ethics, discussed for example by Sharf (1999), are relevant even in groups without intimate topics, but will not be addressed further here. Taken together, the three different approaches gave a thick description of rec.arts.books.tolkien and the ongoing activity. Combining the results gave insight in otherwise unattainable areas, such as the ratio between reading the group and writing into it (approximately 3:1), the existence of lurkers, and the relation between the individual activity level and the hierarchy position.

In short, rec.arts.books.tolkien had a stock of often returning participants, but it took some time to recognize them in the inferno of an active newsgroup. In six months, 1,073 different persons wrote into the newsgroup, but 75% of the senders only posted one single time. The remaining 25%, 266 individuals, was the actual newsgroup rec.arts.books.tolkien, and out of the total 5,625 postings, 74% came from this group. However, the level of activity differed extremely even inside this smaller group. Even with a simple categorization, made from the average amount of postings per month per individual, the differences were drawn clearly. There were 152 passive participants, who only posted two or fewer times per month and 74 active participants, who posted between three and five posts per month. Finally, there was a core group with 40 members, defined by an average activity level on more than five letters a month. Inside the core group, the differences continued, and one could make a special category for the hyperactive person who made nearly 100 postings a month. Logically, the postings from the core group were dominant; out of the 4,149 postings that came from the actual group, the core postings counted 59%. The counting thus narrowed down the overwhelming display of posts and participants to a level at which the continual names were recognizable — a process learned less systematically by the participants themselves in the ongoing navigation and interaction.

Theoretical Backdrop

There is a likeness between the modern metropolis and cyberspace, a likeness that is both metaphorical and constructed in the everyday language. Cyberspace is often described in the same manner as the early metropolis, where Simmel (1903) painted a fearful picture of the changed life forms. The ever-changing social environment, with strangers all over and a lot of fast-moving traffic, caused nervous breakdowns in the human relationship with the surroundings. Evidently, one can speak about different ways of coping with changes in society and particularly in relation to new technology (whether this is the car, the TV, or the computer), where there are optimistic as well as pessimistic, even dystrophic, variants. Some 30 years after Simmel, Wirth (1938) gave us the ultimate key to understand the urban life. He defined the city in relativistic terms, as interplay between size, density, heterogeneity, and stability, which makes the definition useful even today. Furthermore, he separated the physical environment from the psychological state and thereby made the blurred relation between the city and the city life (urbanism) more visible and consequent. Hence, it is possible to look at urbanism as a way of life constantly negotiated with the physical presence but without any deterministic relation between the two; urbanism is not a product of clay and concrete but a form in the variety of human organizations. Today, the link from offline metropolis to online community is established through a mixture of metaphors and actual likeness. The term "urbanism" does not refer to the life in any actual city but to the broader culture in modernity, where mobility, diversity, and networks of relations characterize life forms. Even the regions distant from actual urban space are merged with urbanism, through mass media as well as communication and information technology.

Using an approach with online communities defined as networks in urbanism highlights the nondramatic and everyday activities visible in a newsgroup. To interpret the newsgroup's interactions as a challenge to the traditional sociology is partly right, but at the same time, it camouflages the underlying and very human urge to socialize. Here, the micro-sociology of Goffman is a useful approach. The social interactions, the establishment of norms and value systems, and so on, are visible even in a solely text-based environment. Although there are certain areas of difference between online and offline life, mainly the position of the body and the communication's space-time, the similarities are striking as well. The normative interactions and the strategies for delimitation are slightly transformed in the translation from offline to online community, but they are nevertheless recognizable as exactly translations.

Lofland (1973) describes how to navigate in open and public urban space, and, while the surrounding circumstances indeed are different from the metropolis to the online nowhere, the human navigation between strangers is almost identical. In the urban space, we are concerned not only with street names but in particular with ongoing social life. The visual impressions merge with interpretations of social meaning, and the city dweller's challenge is to navigate safely through unknown territory. Who is on the street, how does one decode his personal outfit, how does he interact, and how does his presence fit into the actual locality? These are important factors in a competent social navigation, and moving around in cyberspace slightly transforms the decoding manner. A competent newsgroup navigator is a person who builds up experience about the same factors as the city dweller: who is present, how do they interact, and what is relevant in the ongoing discussion? In the newsgroup, the realm partly is transformed from public to parochial (Lofland, 1998) by the regularly returning participants, who recognize each other and interact accordingly. Knowledge about a certain locality is a sign of engagement in the area, and, likewise, experience in a particular newsgroup is important for the perceived social context. The amount of time used in the same group is not surprisingly almost equivalent to the sense of belonging and the involvement in relationships inside the group's realm (Parks & Floyd, 1996).

An Online Community

The basic definition of a community is the possibility of inclusion and exclusion—the existence of insiders and outsiders. In rec.arts.books.tolkien, there was ongoing work concerning the maintenance of the internal as well as the external boundaries. Indeed, the newsgroup is a normative community, in which the Usenet netiquette was supplemented by parochial additions. The working consensus (Goffman, 1959) about the loosely established norms is extremely important in an online group, because the restrictions in what to be said how and where are primarily to be handled by the sender beforehand. Because of the lack of serious punishment for spamming, flaming, and the like, the survival of a newsgroup (or, rather, the survival of the topic-relevant discussion) is closely related to a common acceptance of some regulating norms. In rec.arts.books.tolkien, establishing as well as enforcing such norms was a continuing challenge, while the number of bypassers and cross-postings were a constant high. Furthermore, the diversity of norms in the urbanism makes the establishing of a working consensus even harder than in a more homogeneous society. However, the netiquette is more or less made and followed by educated elites in the Western Hemisphere, which probably could describe the majority of Tolkien *aficionados* as well. Hence, the diversity inside the actual group is presumably lesser than the potential diversity on Usenet, not to mention the urbanism as such.[3]

Following Baym (1995), the norms that develop in a newsgroup are related to the given purpose, the participants, and the broader context of both, inclusive of the technological system and the temporal structure. Besides the general acceptance of netiquette in Usenet primers, rec.arts.books.tolkien adds several parochial norms, shown in the ongoing activity. At least five different norms steer the group's ambience—four rather obvious, the fifth a straightforward taboo. The strategies to make the norms respected among the participants differ accordingly, drawing a continuum from polite teasing to flaming. Perhaps the single most important issue in establishing such commonly accepted guidelines and strategies is time, closely followed by a certain number of often returning participants. A parochial realm (Lofland, 1998) is not anything evident, but made by the social interactions between strangers, in time transformed into acquaintances—the parochial realm is an intersection between the public and the intimate. However, the realms are not defined by the physical space, but, on the contrary, by the human activity and level of reciprocal knowledge demonstrated. Thus, the parochial realm is a familiar "territory" with superficially known others, and the social navigation inside the realm is more predictable than the one in public realms. This is a very useful approach not only to the city-based urbanism but also to the activities in a newsgroup—the net-based urbanism.[4] The reciprocal recognition between the active participants led to a certain level of acknowledgment, and the common interest in discussing Tolkien turns on the parochial community.

The Norms

Rec.arts.books.tolkien developed at least five different normative guidelines about the acceptable content in the posts. The first norm was about how to enter the group as a newbie, the next three primarily were about how to write, and the last was about what one is never allowed to say. First, a newbie needed to demonstrate an interest in the works of Tolkien to be accepted. This norm did not demand a dedicated fan or a high level of relevant knowledge; rather, it was a question of honestly displayed interest. In contrast, those who entered improperly (without respect for Tolkien) turned on the different strategies to maintain the group's boundaries. The second norm was about the level of Tolkien-related knowledge — the more the better. Experts into the complicated world of Tolkien were met with respect and acknowledgment, and it was possible to recognize a social hierarchy based on such expertise. The hierarchy was an individual interpretation but was channeled into the interactions by the use of nicknames, references, words of respect, and so on. Anyway, only displaying one's knowledge was not enough to get a position in the group; it also had to be done in a certain manner. Creativity was a highly prized quality, especially when it came to popularized explanations and new interpretations inside the very complex Tolkien universe. There was an overlap with the implicit demand for humor; dull creativity was not at all interesting. Humor was a central part of the ambience in rec.arts.books.tolkien, and it was simultaneously used to underline the being-together and as a boundary management strategy. When creativity and humor were mixed, the laughing together reinforced the boundaries, and the sense of belonging peaked. Combined with a relatively high activity level, following these norms (basic Tolkien-interest, knowledge, creativity, and humor) made the individual sender recognizable to the other participants, and in a busy newsgroup, such positive recognition is almost equal to internal status. Taken together, the four norms hence were guidelines for the active participants and, to newbies and bypassers, the visible ambience of the group. The equivalent in urban space is the nonoffending group that does not lead to caution when passing by (Lofland, 1973), but, on the contrary, gives rise to a bit of longing and envy. The parochial realm created by the interactions in rec.arts.books.tolkien seemed after a few visits homey and open-minded, which in fact was true until someone violated the fifth norm.

The fifth element in the interactional norms was a straightforward taboo. Nobody was allowed to mix or just compare the fictional world of Tolkien with the physical world of reality, and when somebody dared, it was treated like blasphemy. There is no doubt that the offline discussion of Political Correctness played a leading role in this distinction between fiction and reality. Inside the Tolkien universe there are hardly any women, and despite a rich variation of invented races, it is possible to interpret the most whitelike ones (the Elves) as the good guys, whereas the bad guys are of color and come up from the south. This could probably be discussed as a part of the history itself, but it is nevertheless the insistent reality that puts it on the agenda. Political Correctness perforated the borders between fiction and reality in a not so subtle way, and, because of the fear of devaluating Tolkien through discussions about all the "fictional incorrectness," the newsgroup refused to face the challenge. This interesting taboo was furthermore hidden quite well for newbies, because it was only visible when broken and actions rose against the sinner. There was nothing about the taboo in the FAQ, which means that the FAQ had either a misleading name or an incomplete content.

The Strategies

In rec.arts.books.tolkien, at least four different strategies were at work to demarcate what was allowed by whom, when, and how. Although many of the norm-breakers presumably never returned to discover the reactions from the more established group, the boundary maintaining activity served an important role in the group's function as such. The sense of togetherness and belonging are increased, just as it is by the common laughter. Hence, the combination of normative enforcement and humor are highly valued and used with creativity and skill.

The four recognizable strategies were ignorance of the norm-breaker; turning the norm-breaker into a common joke; undermining the norm-breaker's credibility; or brushing away any relevance of the norm-breaker's intrusion. The order here reflects the frequency; the first and second were quite normal, while the third and fourth were seldom employed. These four strategies kept the interactions in rec.arts.books.tolkien relatively highly focused on precisely the books of Tolkien; the group seemed to be in better function than the average newsgroup. Their colloquial language was rather polite, and the details of Tolkien were discussed seriously and with joy. This language was mirrored in the boundary maintaining strategies as well, where there was a striking lack of capital flaming. There was no formalized boundary-keeping game, such as the one described by Tepper (1997); in contrast, the interactions based on the four strategies kept the boundaries of rec.arts.books.tolkien relatively intact.

Conclusion

To discover on a micro-sociological level what is going on in an existing online community is a matter of detailed exposure of the activities over a longer period. Initially, the most striking aspect in rec.arts.books.tolkien was the lack of hype in the interactions. In opposition to most texts available in 1996, the participants seemed to interpret the newsgroup as rather banal. This was the first hint of the discrepancies between the sensational accounts and the visible everyday life on the screen, and bridging the gap thus became central. Introducing Goffman (1957, 1963, 1967) into this field of everyday interaction highlighted the translated forms of drama and ritual, and Lofland (1973, 1989, 1998) furthermore prepared the interpretation of the online communities as inscribed in urbanism.

The interactions in rec.arts.books.tolkien were negotiated translations from the offline world, and therefore they had a certain level of normal-ness. Thus, the interactions can be seen as relating to central topics in creating and maintaining communities as such, namely defining the norms and demarcating the boundaries. The conflicts in a group about how to interact and express oneself are simultaneously a display of the working consensus and the enforcement work related to that. The individual impression management has to follow some commonly accepted guidelines to make a successful approach, and common norms are established about the actual content in a post, the way of presenting it, and the personal performance. One result of successful impression management in the newsgroup was achievement of internal status, almost equal to identification, and in order to maintain such status, the level of knowledge should be combined with both creativity and humor. The textual basis transforms and continues the drama of interaction in numerous ways—and via this transformation, the text-based communities exists as integrated parts of urbanism.

Notes

1. Newer software and Web interfaces make it possible to sort the letters from different criteria—instead of topic; one can use the arrival date or the senders in alphabetical order. Whereas this may have had value during the minute registration of rec.arts.books.tolkien's activities in 1996, it is hardly relevant to the participant's navigation in an active newsgroup.
2. The survey was e-mailed out to the private inboxes of 115 persons; those who posted into rec.arts.books.tolkien in a two week period in June 1996. The overall answering rate was 64.3% (74).
3. Since 1996, this may have changed dramatically. The renewed popularity of Tolkien, because of the successful transformation of the books into blockbuster movies, opens up a bigger and more diversified audience and even more variations on the topic.
4. City-based and Net-based urbanism is indeed merged in everyday life, and taking them apart is an analytical trick rather than a highly relevant distinction. However, Lofland's (1998) brilliant work with the realms as scientific useful categories in urban sociology does not include the online aspects, which gives me an obligation to make the distinction apparent anyway.

References

Baym, Nancy (1995) "The Emergence of Community in Computer-Mediated Communication," in S. Jones (ed.), *Cybersociety. Computer-Mediated Communication and Community*, pp. 138–163. Thousand Oaks, CA: Sage.
Goffman, Erving (1959) *The Presentation of Self in Everyday Life*. London: Penguin Books.
Goffman, Erving (1963) *Behavior in Public Places. Notes on the Social Organization of Gatherings*. New York: Free Press of Glencoe.

Goffman, Erving (1967) *Interaction Ritual. Essays on Face-to-Face Behaviour.* London: Penguin Books.
Lofland, Lyn H. (1973) *A World of Strangers. Order and Action in Urban Public Space.* New York: Basic Books.
Lofland, Lyn H. (1989) "Social Life in the Public Realm," *Journal of Contemporary Ethnography* 17 (4): 453–482.
Lofland, Lyn H. (1998) *The Public Realm: Exploring the City's Quintessential Social Territory.* New York: Aldine De Gruyter.
Parks, Malcolm R., & Kory Floyd (1996) "Making Friends in Cyberspace," *Journal of Communication* 46(1): 80–97.
Sharf, Barbara F. (1999) "Beyond Netiquette: The Ethics of Doing Naturalistic Discourse Research on the Internet," in S. G. Jones (ed.), *Doing Internet Research,* pp. 243–256. Thousand Oaks, CA: Sage.
Simmel, George (1950) "The Metropolis and Mental Life," in Wolff, K. (ed.), *The Sociology of George Simmel,* pp. 409–24. New York: Free Press. (originally published in 1903)
Tepper, Michele (1997) "Usenet Communities and the Cultural Politics of Information," in D. Porter (ed.), *Internet Culture,* pp. 39–54. London: Routledge.
Wirth, Louis (1964) "Urbanism as a Way of Life," in A. J. Reiss, Jr. (ed.), *On Cities and Social Life: Selected Papers* (pp. 60–83). Chicago: University of Chicago Press.

Jan Fernback

COMMUNITY AS COMMODITY: EMPOWERMENT AND CONSUMERISM ON THE WEB

Early mythology of the Web touted it as an avenue of citizen empowerment through interactivity. Citizens could, through computer-mediated reciprocal communication, exert a greater voice in public affairs, and the Internet could serve as a tool for the realization of a more idealized democratic sphere of public life. Bentivegna (2002) contends that

> interactivity enables citizens to assume an 'active' position by participating in the conduct of institutions and citizens through the gathering and processing of information, organizing forms of pressure or protesting against decisions deemed unjust or harmful to society as a whole. (p. 54)

Thus, the citizenry can be empowered through community action and civic engagement facilitated by interactive technologies. "Community" Web segments have proliferated as a manifestation of this notion of democratic citizen empowerment through interactivity. A number of virtual community groups have initiated political action in physical communities, including Santa Monica's PEN project, PeaceNet, and MoveOn.org. Increasingly, however, "community" Web segments on portals and local news-oriented Web sites have focused their efforts less on civic participation and more on the consumerist aspects of community. This work examines the possibility that the meaning of community has been transformed by the process of commodification. It uses local, media-centered Web site community sections (such as online newspapers) as loci for community participation and democratic empowerment. The process of meaning construction about community through the self-publication of group Web pages is also explored. Discussion examines how users are empowered generally as consumers rather than as participants in a community of "producers" of meaning.

Community has been regarded as a site for political action by numerous social philosophers, such as Georg Simmel, Ferdinand Tönnies, John Dewey, and Jurgen Habermas. Taylor (1995) asserts that democratic choice is driven by citizens' understanding of their membership in a community of collective purpose that strives for universal participation in the debate of public issues. Etzioni (1995) argues that communities are sites not only for collective political action but also for collective action in other social institutional spheres. But Sennett sees a fundamental shift in the nature of public community that has weakened its potential as a sphere of meaningful civic life and political action. Sennett argues in *The Fall of Public Man* (1992) that community is no longer about rational public engagement but about personal feelings of togetherness. Emotional relations supercede collective action in contemporary community to the extent that public culture revolves on an axis of collective personality and group integrity rather than a true engagement with civic issues. Contemporary American identity politics exemplify Sennett's ideas — rhetorically, these communities espouse universal themes of democratic participation, but ultimately the community interests are particular.

This rhetoric of fellowship and collective identity pervades discourse about virtual communities. It is important to note that researched communities such as the Well (Rheingold, 1993) and others (Baym, 2000; Wellman & Gulia, 1999) document the meaningful ties people forge among their online collectivities. Nonetheless, political rhetoric that promises empowerment through interactivity frames virtual communities as places of potential political action. Thus, "community" Web segments appear in news oriented sites, in Web portals, and in politically oriented sites. There are numerous possibilities for political action online (enviroweb.com, democracyonline.org); these online community spaces do encourage citizen participation in the civic process. But more and more, community sites are included on the Web for the purposes of selling the notion of communal interaction to a buying public. Civic involvement is not encouraged on these Web sites as much as the ethos of consumption is. For example, the *Denver Post* community online site at <http://www.post-newscommunity.com> focuses on the *Post's* charitable efforts within the Denver area; however, there is no avenue for citizens to interact with one another or with political leaders or civic groups. The site sells the *Post* as a charitable organization while ads pop up for a local liquor store and "the Amazing X-Cam." The *Philadelphia Inquirer* online site (<http://www.philly-neighborhoods.org/Community-Phila/community-phila.html>) contains a link to a "community discussions" forum, which was empty. The site also contained links to neighborhood events and profiles as well as a list of nonprofit groups that could be contacted through the site. However, advertisements for businesses such as First Union Bank, Amazon.com, and Comcast cable are prominent on the site.

In a Salon.com article, Brown (1999a) argues that collections of personal sites such as GeoCities are less about community than about excuses to look at advertisements. She argues that the term community "has been diluted and debased to describe even the most tenuous connections, the most minimal interactivity." The free Web page services, Brown claims, use promises of warmth and community to ensnare users to generate content. Similar promises of copious profits are made to investors and advertisers who purchase space based on the traffic that content draws. Yahoo, which purchased GeoCities, allows users to build sites for free, but sites must contain advertisements (<http://www.geocities.yahoo.com>). GeoCities has experimented with these ads, notes Brown (1999a), including watermarks on each individual page and popup ads on each page link. AOL's Hometown community pages all contain small advertisements, and MSN's "Community Web Sites" are promoted as "places to share common interests and interact with others online" (<http://groups.msn.com/editorial/en-us/content/features/welcome.html>); however, users must agree to carry ads to obtain an account. The communities on MSN, GeoCities, and AOL are segmented for marketers rather than audiences; for example, MSN's Talk City is organized into categories such as "autos" or "health and wellness" and its "neighborhoods" are given names such as "Ferrari Drive," "Sparkplug Street," "Healing Way," and "Workout Place" to provide advertisers with some clues as to content (<http://home.talkcity.com/catstreets.html>). So, in the tradition of targeted niche advertising and loyalty clubs that characterize current consumer management tactics, the term "community" is used to convey a sense of personal service in marketing techniques. These tactics pay off; Yahoo's total net revenues in 2001 were $717,442,000 (<http://docs.yahoo.com/info/investor/ar01/yahoo_10k2001.pdf>). Moreover, according to the Nielsen/Net Ratings, GeoCities was ranked number one in "most trafficked personal Web sites" in February 2002, with 74,404 unique visitors that month (<http://docs.yahoo.com/docs/pr/release962.html>). However, GeoCities was recently criticized (Olsen, 2002) for limiting file management options for free home page subscribers by initiating a monthly fee for those options. Olsen adds that, because of severe decreases in ad revenue since 2001, Yahoo has been thinning free features in an attempt to generate revenue through pay services.

Clearly, community can be conceived as a type of capital that can be purchased or sold like other commodities. But Habermas (1989) cautions against the commodification of cultural ideals in his writings on the corruption of basic social institutions. Habermas contends that the public sphere of rational debate in contemporary Western societies is transformed into a privatized, commercial space when public institutions such as community are regarded as commodities to be bought and sold. These institutions are then used for commercial purposes rather than for open debate and reflection. The public sphere itself becomes commodified when, in Habermas's example, television uses lurid or violent imagery to replace civic debate in order to manipulate public opinion (Habermas, 1989). The public sphere eventually becomes a worthless commodity when advertising and public relations displace critical public communication with commercial language (Rheingold, 1993). Ultimately, valued social ideas are denigrated, and the sphere of public discourse is characterized by the rhetoric of commercial entertainment rather than critical analysis. As an example, the Telecommunications Act of 1996 itself commodifies the values of the Internet by privileging the discourse and practices of a marketplace archetype of Internet development over a public service archetype. Rheingold supports Habermas's claims by arguing that "the odds are always good that big power and big money will find a way to control access to virtual communities; big power and big money always found ways to control new communications media when they emerged in the past" (1993, p. 5).

Equating community with marketing debases the institution. For example, Netscape discontinued its "Netcenter Professional Connections" community when Netscape was purchased by AOL in 1999 (Brown, 1999b). Netscape's press kit on the community extolled the venture, claiming "the key to establishing community on the Web is to enable people to associate with others who have similar interests, concerns, and careers" (Brown, 1999b). The forum's moderators were paid, and critics speculated that Netscape extinguished the community as a cost-cutting measure (Brown, 1999b). The value of this community must be questioned when market imperatives can so readily destroy it.

The rhetoric of commerce suffuses the techniques of community building proposed by the authors of several books on Web development. Rud (2001) stresses "knowledge management" as a way for marketers to use mutual interest groups (such as online communities) to elevate profits. Hackathorn (1999) supports "Web farming" (using online data for "business intelligence"), which includes the observation of online community discussions: " . . . the (online) *Community Discussion* terrain is extremely important for monitoring current trends in rumors, perceptions, opinions, and other soft information" (p. 282). In *Community Building on the Web* (2000), author Amy Jo Kim advocates the use of targeted business practices to solidify online community. She claims, "in any community, the most powerful type of involvement is ultimately financial" (p. 325). Community members can themselves become merchants, use market research and cross promotion to build community, or "incorporate selling" in the form of classified ads or auctions to "give your members another activity to engage in and another role to play" (p. 173). More and more businesses are using online community to solicit customer feedback and "drive product innovation and contribute to profits" (Boehle, 2002, p. 28). Intesync Web Professional Services (<http://www.intesync.com/101ways/101w87.htm>) admonishes Web-based businesses to join free web communities, such as GeoCities, to increase Web traffic and promote their businesses online. Because "becoming a part of a larger group based on common interests is an inherited instinct of most cultures," . . . "joining one or several of these communities can be an effective way to promote your Web site. Most of their services, including Web space, Home Page building tools, discussion forums, chat rooms, e-mail, auction, news service, greeting cards, jobs listing, and commercial products, are free of charge. As a member of a community, it is easier and more acceptable to tell other members what your Web site offers."

The quest for a sense of authentic community online is thus able to be replaced by the mere *idea* of community, an ersatz community with no true referent, as illustrated in Baudrillard's concept of the "hyperreal." Baudrillard argued in *Simulacra and Simulation* (1994) that "today abstraction is no longer that of the map, the double, the mirror, or the concept. Simulation is no longer that of a territory, a referential being or a substance. It is the generation by models of a real without origin or reality: a hyperreal" (p. 1). By "hyperreal," Baudrillard means the representation of a thing or event that has no counterpart or analog in consensus reality—the hyperreal is, in a sense, a new thing that seems to refer to something real. It is an abstract, "imaginary" model of the "real" with no referent. He is concerned, for example, that the news on television has nothing to do with real-world events; rather, the news is a simulation designed to hold the attention of the viewer. The election process has little to do with informed discourse and the selection of the most qualified candidate, and everything to do with the manufacture of consent. These mediated presentations of reality ultimately become ideal models of themselves (whether social institutions or art or relationships), and the meaning of the referent itself is lost when the boundary between the simulation and reality implodes (Baudrillard, 1994).

The notion of the hyperreal is useful in examining the meaning of community in the web segments detailed in this analysis.

The meaning of community is transformed by commodification and hyperrealism when authentic, local community is replaced with the "idea" of community as we see in these web sites. This results in a loss of stable meaning. All virtual communities do not suffer from this characterization, however. Much research on virtual communities demonstrates that humans adapt to environmental changes that challenge traditionally held assumptions about social structure: rather than being an attempt at reproducing physical community, virtual communities wryly acknowledge the verisimilitude and alter the definition, the very nature of community, to conform to these challenges. This is part of the allure of and uniqueness of cybercommunity. But the use of the word community in ways that commodify it for a buying public is a simulation of the real. It is an artificial reproduction of communal sentiment in an attempt to cash in on a cultural buzzword. We must be concerned with the legitimacy of meaning, but also with the analysis of meaning. Community exists when people invest themselves in social relationships within a group, whether online or offline; but community does not exist where participants are viewed as consumers instead of citizens. To illustrate this notion, some online communitarians have created "Web rings"—a small community of several Web page owners with specific interests—as an offshoot of the GeoCities to express their disappointment with the site (Brown, 1999a; Papacharissi, 2000).

These Web sites use community largely to draw an audience for advertisements rather than to empower them through interactive technology. The effect of this process is twofold. First, community is devalued. True public community is a social goal, but the inauthentic use of the term denigrates the meaning of communal ideals. When community becomes as purchasable as any other commodity, it loses its meaning as a fundamental social institution. Second, people are empowered as consumers rather than as citizens when they participate in communities that are designed to be advertising billboards. If we are empowered as consumers, we make democratic decisions based on our roles as consumers rather than as citizens.

The audience becomes a market rather than a public. Habermas's (1989) concerns about the commodification of the public sphere are evidenced in current public discourse about the role of the public sphere and the role of the free marketplace. Gandy (2002) argues that the elevation of the audience as consumers over the audience as citizens is the "real digital divide" that scholars of new media should examine. He suggests that new information technologies help to define citizens as consumers because the global information economy profoundly supports the practices and metaphors of the marketplace as social and institutional relations. Gandy expresses hope in the ability of contemporary societies to recover a viable public sphere, noting that "the new media can be used to mobilize a social collective in defence [sic] of cherished values, including those associated with individual and collective identity" (2002, p. 458).

Similarly, Sunstein (2001) contends that Internet policymaking, by privileging the language and practices of consumerism, cause us to question whether these policies compromise "our own highest aspirations" (p. 106). Those high aspirations are often what drive public discourse and the search for a more idealized democracy. But there can be no political action within a "shopping enclave" (Simpson, 2000). Part of the logic of community is political action, community activism, and change. People want to engage in civic culture and help it to grow (Sunstein, 2001), and they may seek online community as a means to help. Moreover, Sunstein (2001) claims that "if representatives or citizens are able to participate in a collective discussion of broadcasting or the appropriate nature of the Internet, they can generate a far fuller and richer picture of the central social goals, and of how they might be served, than can be provided through individual decisions as registered in the market" (p. 115). The sites analyzed here do not encourage a healthy civic culture. Most likely, they use the term community to draw audiences because the term evokes warmth and association, and it is more appealing than "public notice" or "civic groups." But when audiences are empowered as consumers, we make democratic decisions based on our roles as consumers rather than as citizens. The meaning of community in this commodified vision is devoid of political action or social change; instead, a sense of social stability is conveyed through notions of community solidarity through consumption. With the increasing commercialization of the Internet, the consumer model of Internet participation will continue to gain dominance over a civic model. A narrowing of the public sphere, such that it becomes characterized by the rhetoric of the marketplace, will result. This is a disservice not only to democracy but ultimately to freedom.

References

Baudrillard, J. (1994). *Simulacra and Simulation*. Ann Arbor: University of Michigan Press. Translated by Sheila Faria Glaser. Originally published 1981.

Baym, N. (2000). *Tune In, Log On: Soaps, Fandom, and Online Community*. Thousand Oaks, CA: Sage.

Bentevgna, S. (2002). Politics and new media. In L. Lievrouw & S Livingstone (Eds.), *The Handbook of New Media* (pp. 50–61). London: Sage.

Boehle, S. (2002, January). Water cooler wisdom: Online communities made up of customers and staff can generate ideas that light up profits. *Online Learning*, 6(1), 26–28, 30–31.

Brown, J. (1999a, January 19). There goes the neighborhood. *Salon.com*. <http://archive.salon.com/21st/feature/1999/01/cov_19feature.html>.

Brown, J. (1999b, April 6). Netscape to community: you're evicted. *Salon.com*. <http://www.salon.com/com/tech/feature/1999/04/06/netcenter/print.html>.

Denver Post Online. <http://www.post-newscommunity.com>. Accessed February 2001, September 2001, and March 2003.

Ess, C. (1996). The political computer: Democracy, CMC, and Habermas. In C. Ess (Ed.), *Philosophical Perspectives on Computer-mediated Communication* (pp. 197–230). Albany: State University of New York Press.

Etzioni, A. (1995). *New Communitarian Thinking: Persons, Virtues, Institutions, and Communities*. Charlottesville: University of Virginia.

Gandy, O. The real digital divide: Citizens versus consumers. In L. Lievrouw & S. Livingstone (Eds.), *The Handbook of New Media* (pp. 448–460). London: Sage.

Habermas, J. (1989). *The Structural Transformation of the Public Sphere: An Inquiry into a Category of Bourgeois Society*. Cambridge, MA: MIT Press. Translated by Thomas Burger and Frederick Lawrence. Originally published 1962.

Hackathorn, R. D. (1999). *Web Farming for the Data Warehouse: Exploiting Business Intelligence and Knowledge Management*. San Francisco: Morgan Kaufmann Publishers.

Intesync. 101 ways to boost your web traffic. <http://www.intesync.com/101ways/101w87.htm>. Accessed March 2003.

Kim, A. J. (2000). *Community Building on the Web: Secret Strategies for Successful Online Communities*. Berkely, CA: Peachpit Press.

Olsen, S. (2002, March 6). Yahoo builds more fees into GeoCities. *CNET News*. <http://news.com.com/2102-1023-853628.html>.

Papacharissi, Z. (2000). *The Personal Utility of Individual Home Pages*. Doctoral dissertation, University of Texas at Austin. August.

Philadelphia Inquirer community Web site. <http://www.phillyneighborhoods.org/Community-Phila/community-phila.html>. Accessed February 2001, September 2001, and March 2003.

Rheingold, H. (1993). *Virtual Community: Homesteading on the Electronic Frontier*. New York: Addison-Wesley.

Rud, O. P. (2001). *Data Mining Cookbook: Modeling Data for Marketing, Risk, and Customer Relationship Management*. New York: John Wiley & Sons.

Sennett, R. (1992). *The Fall of Public Man*. New York: Norton.

Simpson, T. (2000). Streets, sidewalks, stores, and stories. *Journal of Contemporary Ethnography*, 29(6), 682–716.

Sunstein, C. (2001). *Republic.com*. Princeton, NJ: Princeton University Press.

Taylor, C. (1995). Liberal politics and the public sphere. In A. Etzioni (Ed.), *New Communitarian Thinking: Persons, Virtues, Institutions, and Communities* (pp. 183–217). Charlottesville: University of Virginia.

Wellman, B., & Gulia, M. (1999). Net surfers don't ride alone: virtual communities as communities. In P. Kollock & M. Smiths (Eds.), *Communities in Cyberspace* (pp. 167–194). Berkeley: University of California Press.

Shani Orgad 23

JUST DO IT! THE ONLINE COMMUNICATION OF BREAST CANCER AS A PRACTICE OF EMPOWERMENT

> *I was diagnosed on 7/8/99 with invasive lobular breast cancer. It took a couple of days for the news to "sink in" and then I felt I had a choice. I could be a "victim" of this disease . . . or I could face it head on—with a positive attitude and "just do it." I chose to be bigger than the cancer and face it head on. I began to search the Web around a week later.*
>
> *(E-mail account of a woman who suffered from breast cancer, no. 7).*

Just Do It on the Online Space

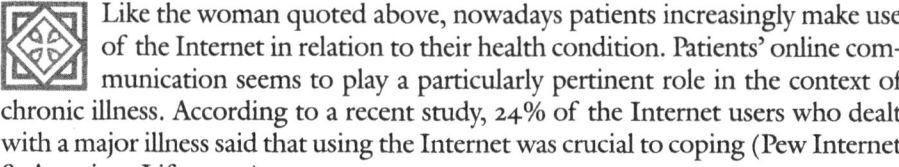
Like the woman quoted above, nowadays patients increasingly make use of the Internet in relation to their health condition. Patients' online communication seems to play a particularly pertinent role in the context of chronic illness. According to a recent study, 24% of the Internet users who dealt with a major illness said that using the Internet was crucial to coping (Pew Internet & American Life, 2002).

Within the realm of chronically ill patients' online communication, this chapter focuses on the online experience of women who suffer from breast cancer.[1] It discusses the ways in which this online communication enables breast cancer patients to "just do it." In other words, the question this chapter explores is: how does patients' online participation endow them with powers that enable them to cope with the experience of a life-threatening disease? In what ways does their online experience help breast cancer patients to be "bigger than the cancer and face it head on?"

Most existing accounts of the use of the Internet in the context of chronic illness focus on the provision of information as a source of empowerment (e.g., Pew Internet & American Life, 2002; Hardey, 2001; Reeves, 2001). While information seeking probably constitutes the key motivation for patients to go online, they often find that much of the medical information they encounter online is too general, impersonal, and "cut and dried."[2] Furthermore, notwithstanding the centrality of the informational aspect in patients' online experience, it is only a part of a wider and more complex context of Internet use. Indeed, a few recent studies of the online experience of chronically ill patients acknowledge other salient aspects of Internet use such as emotional and esteem support (Shaw et al., 2000) and psychological support (Sharf, 1997). However, even when these analyses extend beyond a concern with the informational dimension of patients' online use, they tell us very little about how patients' online participation is embedded (or not) in the wider social meanings of the everyday experience of their illness.

The present chapter seeks to address this critique by focusing on two aspects of breast cancer patients' online communication, namely: (1) narrativization and storytelling, and (2) exchange and reciprocity. Inextricably interlinked, these aspects emerge as highly central and significant in patients' experience of their online communication, particularly on forms such as personal home pages, message boards, and e-mail.[3] These forms constitute spaces where patients share their experience by telling their personal stories and exchanging them with other fellow sufferers.

Before moving on to discuss the ways in which breast cancer patients communicate their experience online, a brief explanation of the decision to focus on breast cancer is in order. Breast cancer is a central experience in contemporary society, if only because of its high prevalence in women. On average, one in eight women will develop breast cancer during her lifetime (National Cancer Institute, 2002). The incidence varies by region, age, ethnic group, and so on. Not only is breast cancer quantitatively prominent in daily life, it is also central in public discourse. I will not dwell here on the reasons why "today breast cancer is the biggest disease on the cultural map" (Ehrenreich, 2001). However, it is important to view the following discussion of the online communication of breast cancer as crucially embedded within the wider contemporary culture of the disease. In light of the centrality of the communication of breast cancer in contemporary society, the abundance of various online forms related to the illness seems especially salient.

In this context, I wish to move on to examining two key dimensions that constitute patients' online communication.

Online Narrativization and Storytelling

For many participants, breast cancer Web sites offer a kind of a platform for the sharing and exchange of experiences with other fellow-sufferers. Women[4] commonly express themselves on these Web sites in narrated forms that are often called *stories*.[5] The latter are being produced and published on online applications such as bulletin boards, e-mail, chats, online personal diaries, and other forms.

"Shared Experience" Web site is a good case in point. It is defined as a "Cancer Support Knowledgebase," designed to enable cancer patients and their caregivers to share their experience of illness online. Visitors to "Shared Experience" are encouraged to "leave their footprints," and they are instructed to do so in a very particular way:

Add to This Shared Cancer Knowledgebase
Please don't think of this as "filling out a form." Be **conversational,** and write as much as you want, and say whatever you want. (Shared Experience, March 14, 2003)

In contrast to the informational model that seems to overwhelm much of the medical online space, this initiative is explicitly positioned as conversational, encouraging the visitor to create a situation of exchanging experience, through the telling of one's story. At the time this paper was written, more than 2,000 personal stories of cancer patients and their caregivers were published on the Web site, of which around a quarter were breast cancer–related.

Why do breast cancer patients publish their illness stories online? What is the significance of this activity? An entry point to answering these questions is the recognition of the exceptional nature of cancer. Cancer "invades" the mundane normality of women's everyday lives, fundamentally threatening their ontological security and the continuity of their self-identity. Patients' engagement in storytelling in online spaces such as "Shared Experience" plays a central role in their "repair work on the wreck" (Frank, 1995, p. 54), that is, in their continuous endeavor to manage the disruption posed by the cancer to the continuity and mundanity of their everyday lives. Take, for instance, the following extract from an interview with a breast cancer survivor, when asked about her motivation to go online and read other women's stories:

I'm just more scared as a person of the unknown. Tell me what you're going to do to me, and you could probably do anything to me if you tell me what it is. (Interview no. 2)

As the above quote reflects, a key to the project of regaining security and continuity is an attempt to enhance predictability and certainty, and refuse contingency (Frank, 1995). For many patients, the encounter with stories of women who have gone through similar experience, through reading them on message boards, personal home pages, or e-mail correspondence, constitutes a central source of empowerment. Such accounts might not necessarily be pleasant or encouraging, but they provide their readers with experiential firsthand knowledge and a sense of certainty about what lies ahead for them, from practical issues to emotional aspects.

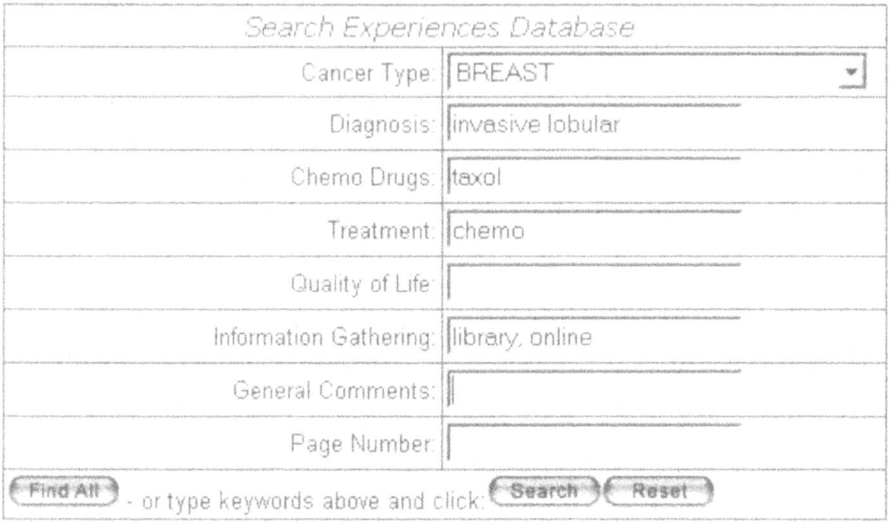

Search Experiences Database	
Cancer Type:	BREAST
Diagnosis:	invasive lobular
Chemo Drugs:	taxol
Treatment:	chemo
Quality of Life:	
Information Gathering:	library, online
General Comments:	
Page Number:	

(Find All) - or type keywords above and click: (Search) (Reset)

Figure 1. Shared Experiences Search Page.

Interestingly enough, despite the disembodied nature of these online stories, which are published on the "virtual space" by disembodied authors, the communication that is facilitated is actually highly embodied. Patients often describe in vivid ways the different bodily aspects of the illness and its treatments. The "realness" of these highly corporeal online stories enhances a woman's capacity to gain a sense of certainty about what she can expect in the course of her illness and its treatments.

Whereas some visitors to these online forms prefer to remain lurkers, others use them as a platform for the presentation of their personal narratives. As Hardey (2002) shows in his study of homepages of people's illnesses, these pages constitute forms that are constantly "under construction." That is, they constitute a "stage" for patients' ongoing construction and reformulation of their selves.

An examination of many breast cancer Web sites reveals how they are often structured by frameworks that help patients to organize their often chaotic experience into a coherent narrative, which they can inspect, think about and plan actions around. Consider, for instance, the "Shared Experience" Web site that was mentioned earlier (Shared Experience, March 14, 2003). To search the Web site's database of patients' illness stories, or, alternatively, to add one's personal story to the existing database, one has to choose a particular cancer type from a dropdown list. Rather than using an open form, one enters one's personal story into a structured form that contains a range of possible "stories": Acute Myeloid Leukemia, Brain Tumors, Breast Cancer and so forth. Below this dropdown list there are open text fields for categories such as "diagnosis," "chemo drugs," "treatment," "quality of life," and so forth, to allow the entry of relevant details. Visually, these categories appear as text boxes. They are static "grids" of meanings that help the patient (both as narrator and/or reader) to impose meaningful order on the incoherent experience of her illness. By establishing these categories and foregrounding specific themes to which the narrator has to refer, the technical and visual structure of the Web site turns the flux of the experience into narrative, and provides the patient with a tool to master events beyond her control.

Online Exchange and Reciprocity

A factor that seems to significantly enhance patients' capacity to construct a self-narrative, which helps them make sense of their experience, is the structure of exchange underlying this communication context. As the following excerpt of a breast cancer patient's account implies, the production of a story and its performance in the online space is based upon the implicit promise of exchange between the teller and listener.

> First what you do when you get diagnosed, you look for people [online] who have been through or going through what you do. Then when you're done with it, people contact you. (Interview no. 6, my brackets)

To follow Barthes's (1975) contractual notion of narrative, the narrator tells her story with the implicit assumption in mind that she would get "something" in return from her listener(s): a response, a comment, or another story. As another patient testifies:

> At first, it was comforting to hear other people, you know, you're asking people, especially on BCANs [a breast cancer bulletin board located at http://forum.bcans.net], something that you noticed, whether it'd be a rash, or . . . nausea. . . . You know that after medication people would respond and that was very comforting. I got 19 responses so that was very good. (Interview no. 2, my brackets)

Indeed, there seems to be a considerable sense of contract between online fellow-sufferers. The contractual nature of patient-participants' narrativization is expressed primarily in the form of mentoring on which this communication is largely based. By "mentoring," I refer to the voluntary pattern of survivors who remain online—even years after being cured—to "welcome" newly diagnosed women, and to guide them through the course of their illness. Of course, the implicit "working assumption" is that, one day, when those newly diagnosed become survivors, they will do the same for others.

The symbolic "material" that is being exchanged is narrative: one's narrative is constantly constructed and reformulated through the process of mentoring. In some instances, the mentoring is structured in fairly formal kinds of online "schemes," such as "chemo-angels" (Chemo Angels, March 14, 2003), an online form by which patients are assigned fellow sufferers as online pals with whom they can correspond and exchange experiences. There is an online team of breast cancer survivors who runs this service and monitors the assignment of "chemo-angels" to patients. There are also less institutionalized forms of exchange that emerge as e-mail correspondence between fellow sufferers who "met" on message boards, personal home pages, and other forms. An interesting glimpse into this kind of interaction is supplied by the fictional (although highly realistic) book *Dear Stranger, Dearest Friend* (Katz Becker, 2000). It recounts the story of an e-mail friendship that emerges between two breast cancer patients: Susan, a survivor, and Lara, a newly diagnosed patient. They meet on a breast cancer related message board and develop an intimate exchange of emotions and experiences that gradually extends beyond the mere experience of the illness. The e-mail format furnishes an ideal platform for a mutual reconstruction of their self-narratives. The following excerpt, in which Susan inserts her comments into a part of Lara's previous e-mail, is a useful demonstration of this point:

Subj: Whoa
Date: 11-30
From:
To: cre8fi@mindspring.com
On 11-29 cre8fi@mindspring.com wrote:
> (Please, God, help me to raise Wendy to be a more forceful
> and confident woman and not a dishrag like her mom. Amen)
Now cut that out. You are not a dishrag. A dishrag would not have immediately called her internist for more information. You took action and are not to be condemned. (p. 62)

Susan creatively uses her capacity to edit Lara's textual self-presentation to help her reformulate her self-narrative and reassure her of her decision to get a second opinion about her diagnosis.

Patients' evaluation of their experience of exchanging experience with other fellow sufferers underscores the therapeutic quality it has for them. In particular, what emerges from women's accounts is the way in which, by publishing her personal story and exchanging it with other fellow sufferers, a woman is constantly asking for reassurance that she is not alone. The realization that she is not alone validates and legitimizes her own story.

The process of validation and legitimization is also enabled through the act of "communal storytelling" (Ricoeur, 1980). The idea of storytelling as a communal action implies that, through its recitation, a personal story is incorporated into a communal communication, and it is through the communicative event that emerges that a closure is constructed. In the context of the online communication of patients, the latter process seems to occur as follows.

Once a personal story is introduced into the public space of a particular online context (e.g., posted on a bulletin board), negotiations over its meaning start to take place. Other participants in that space, that is, "listeners," respond to the narrator's story, either on the public space (e.g., by posting messages on a bulletin board), or via e-mail, contacting the narrator directly and privately. In so doing, they join in the act of producing a story, and so, through the negotiation of the meanings of her story, the author seeks to gain credibility for her narrative. A good example of a situation of an online joint authorship is provided by McLellan (1997), in her account of the online discussion that emerged on WELL (a computerized conferencing system called the Whole Earth 'Lectronic Link) on the experiences of a child who suffered from leukemia. McLellan shows how, through interaction with the posting members of the discussion group, Catalfo, who is the father of the boy diagnosed with leukemia, reconstructs and reformulates the experience of his son's illness.

Conclusions: The Wounded Online Storyteller

In his seminal account, *The Wounded Storyteller,* Frank (1995) highlights the therapeutic function of storytelling for chronically ill patients. In light of his thesis, the "democratization" of patients' capacity to tell and publish their stories online, as in the case of women with breast cancer, has significant implications for patients' experience in contemporary medical environments.

In the remainder of this chapter I wish to reflect on two key theoretical issues that emerge from the analysis of the online communication of breast cancer and are related to the broader debate on CMC and Internet research.

Breaking Down the Online/Offline Distinction

In considering the Internet as a social process in the experience of women with breast cancer, this chapter is critical of much of the existing writing on Internet research. The latter tends to posit the "online" and the "offline" as a dichotomy, regarding the online space as a "placeless place," a self-contained autonomous space, which is apart from social life. Such critique has been recently raised by Miller and Slater (2000, 2002) (Slater, 2002), and Baym (2000), who criticize the earlier generation of Internet writing for its focus on terms such as "cyberspace," "virtuality," "spatiality," "disembedding," and "disembodiment," terms that imply a separation of the offline from the online.

The claim for narrativization and storytelling exchange as central processes in Internet users' practice stands at the heart of the attempt to break down the dualist perspective of the relationship between the "online" and the "offline." The story patients tell on online forms organizes people, events, and information that the narrator encountered both online and offline, into a coherent framework of meaning, which she can think about and plan actions around. The story that is being told and retold on online spaces is not a disembodied performance detached from her everyday life. On the contrary, the story that a woman constructs and tells on different online forms is interwoven with her self-project and has fundamental consequences for the management of her illness and recovery.

As has been shown in several examples throughout this paper, the online space is not hermetic: the story produced online feeds into the everyday life of its narrator, affecting her behavior and way of being. For instance, one of the women I interviewed decided to shave her head at the first sign of going bald, when she read the stories of other "BC ladies" (her online fellow sufferers). Another patient decided against reconstruction following the replies she received to the story she published on online bulletin boards. Patient-users' experience of both the online and the offline should thus be understood as inextricably interlinked, rather than as separate and dichotomous.

Bringing Narrative into the Discussion of the Online Space

To a large extent, the view of the Internet as an autonomous social space that has its intrinsic properties has been part of the celebration of the Internet as the manifestation of postmodern culture, and particularly of notions such as "virtuality" and "disembodiment," a trend that has overwhelmed much Internet research since its early days. One of the theoretical and analytical implications of this line of thinking has been the almost complete exclusion of ideas on narrative and narrativization from academic accounts of Internet research. This theoretical and analytical neglect is not accidental, however: underlying it is the claim for the novelty of virtual worlds that afford the possibility of doing things with narrative differently from the way they can be done with ordinary face-to-face language (Webb, 2001). Stressing its distinctive features, "cyberspace" often has been depicted as a space where narrative cannot exist.

This argument was largely fueled by studies that focused on the nonlinearity of "hypertexts." Mitra and Cohen (1999), for example, argue that hypertexts challenge the presumption of linearity (with which we are familiar from our "offline" "real" world), presenting the reader with a completely different set of assumptions.

Whereas I acknowledge the novel opportunities and forms of communication that are facilitated by the distinctive features of the online space, I think that arguments such as those of Mitra and Cohen present too deterministic a view, failing to account for users' actual experience of engaging in those online spaces. Certainly, in the case of patient-users, as has been shown in this chapter, not only is the production of a narrative enabled and practiced, but it also fundamentally constitutes a key process in patients' online communication. The recognition of the online space as a social space inextricably interwoven with users' offline daily lives, implies, among other considerations, the need to pay sufficient attention to the significance of narrativization and storytelling in users' experience.

Acknowledgment

Figure 1, Seach Experiences Database, used with the author's permission. Thank you to Terry Halsey for its use.

Notes

1. This chapter is part of my Ph.D. research project that examines the online communication of women who suffer from breast cancer. The study included online interviews and face-to-face interviews with breast cancer patients who used the Internet in relation to their illness. In addition, the study employed textual analysis of breast cancer related Web sites.
2. These notions were used by most of my interviewees to describe the medical information they encountered online.
3. This is not to imply that the informational aspect is not significant for the experience of breast cancer patients. However, because the issue of information seeking in this context has been discussed quite extensively, this paper deliberately focuses on other issues that are central in users' experience and have not yet been seriously explored.
4. The online communication of breast cancer is predominantly female because the disease is overwhelmingly a women's illness. In addition, statistics consistently document that women constitute the main seekers of health information online. Although the gender specificity of the online communication of breast cancer is not highlighted in this paper, it has significant implications, which I discuss in my Ph.D. dissertation. Although the issues of storytelling and exchange have implications for other contexts of online communication, they also involve specific features that have to do, among other factors, with the gendered component of this communication.
5. It should be noted that narratives are characteristic of the discourse of illness and breast cancer in general, and can commonly be found in other media such as diaries and autobiographies of illness published in books. However, the process of narrativization, as it takes place online, is claimed to have specific significance that is worthy of exploration.

References

Barthes, R. (1975). s/z. London: Blackwell.
Baym, N. (2000). *Tune In, Log On: Soaps, Fandom and Online Community.* Thousand Oaks, CA: Sage.
Chemo Angels (March 14, 2003). <http://www.chemoangels.com>.
Ehrenreich, B. (December 8, 2001). The Cult of the Pink Ribbon. *The Times.*
Frank, A. W. (1995). *The Wounded Storyteller: Body, Illness and Ethics.* Chicago and London: The University of Chicago Press.
Hardey, M. (2001). 'E-health': The Internet and the transformation of patients into consumers and producers of health knowledge. *Information, Communication & Society,* 4 (3), 388–405.
Hardey, M. (2002). The story of my illness: personal accounts of illness on the Internet. *Health,* 6:1, 31–46.
Katz Becker, L. (2000). *Dear Stranger, Dearest Friend.* New York: William Morrow.
McLellan, F. (1997). A whole other story: The electronic narrative of illness. *Literature and Medicine,* 10 (1), 88–107.
Miller, D., & Slater, D. (2000). *The Internet: An Ethnographic Approach.* London: Berg.
Miller, D., & Slater, D. (2002). Ethnography on and off line: Cybercafes in Trinidad. In M. Johnson (Ed.), *Internet Ethnographies.* Oxford: Berg.

Mitra, A., & Cohen, E. (1999). Analyzing the Web: Distinctions and challenges. In S. Jones (Ed.), *Doing Internet Research* (pp. 179-202). London: Sage.

National Cancer Institute. (September 13, 2002). Cancer Facts. Retrieved September 13, 2002, from <ohttp://cis.nci.nih.gov/fact/5_6.htm>.

Pew Internet & American Life. (May 8, 2002). Use of the Internet at major life moments. Retrieved May 8, 2002, from <http://www.pewinternet.org/reports/toc.asp?Report=58>.

Reeves, P. M. (2001). How individuals coping with HIV/AIDS use the Internet. *Health Education Research,* 16 (6), 709-19.

Ricoeur, P. (1980). Narrative time. In W. J. T. Mitchell (Ed.), *On Narrative* (pp. 165-186). Chicago: University of Chicago Press.

Shared Experience. (March 14, 2003). Add Experience. Retrieved March 14 from <http://www.sharedexperience.org/experienceadd.lasso>.

Shared Experience. (March 14, 2003). Search Experience Page. Retrieved March 14 from <http://www.sharedexperience.org/experiencesearch.lasso>.

Sharf, B. (1997). Communicating breast cancer on-line: Support and empowerment on the Internet. *Women & Health,* 26 (1), 65-84.

Shaw, B. R., McTavish, F., Hawkins, R., Gustafon, D. H., & Pingree, S. (2000). Experiences of women with breast cancer: Exchanging social support over the CHESS computer network. *Journal of Health Communication,* 5, 135-159.

Slater, D. (2002). Social relationships and identity online and offline. In L. Lievrouw, & S. Livingstone (Eds.), *The Handbook of New Media* (pp. 533-546). London: Sage.

Webb, S. (2001). Avatar culture: Narrative, power and identity in virtual world environments. *Information, Communication & Society,* 4 (4), 560-594.

Sorin Adam Matei

THE INTERNET'S "MAGNIFYING GLASS" EFFECT ON OFFLINE TIES IN THE GENERAL SOCIAL SURVEY

Introduction

Research on the social impact of the Internet has been oscillating for a number of years between pessimism and optimism. Initially, the impact was seen as mostly positive. A number of scholars, inspired by the early work of Licklider (1968) or Hiltz and Turoff (1978), have tried to demonstrate the unique potential of the Internet to recreate a new sense of community and to strengthen social and political participation (Rheingold, 1993; Sproull & Kiesler, 1991).

Later on, however, the pendulum has swung in the opposite direction. Two studies (Kraut et al., 1998; Nie, 2001), each benefiting from important public exposure (Markoff, 2000), have announced the deleterious effects of the Internet on social life in general and on social relationships, in particular. Although some of the authors of these studies have moved toward the center (Kraut et al., 2002; Rheingold, 2001), their conclusion is rather bleak: the Internet leads to frailer social ties, to loneliness and isolation.

A renewal of the debate, this time on the positive side, has come with some of the earlier enthusiasts' refinement of their positions and with the emergence of a stronger "social shaping of technology" camp, which rejects the very idea of "Internet effects." For example, Wellman and his colleagues are trying to present a more balanced view of the interactions between online and offline ties (Wellman, 2001). Another perspective is offered by Matei and Ball-Rokeach (2001), who advance the idea that the Internet can be seen as a "magnifying glass," building on, rather than replacing, social ties found in reality. This idea is also supported by DiMaggio, Hargittai, Neuman, and Robinson (2001), who conclude that the Internet might "intensify already existing inclinations toward sociability or community involvement, rather than creating them ab initio" (DiMaggio et al., 2001, p. 319).

A number of empirically oriented social research projects, such as Syntopia (Katz, Rice, & Aspden, 2001), Metamorphosis (Matei & Ball-Rokeach, 2001; Matei, Ball-Rokeach, Wilson, Gibbs, & Gutierez Hoyt, 2001), and the Pew Internet rolling polls (Howard, Rainie, & Jones, 2001) further emphasize the fact that online and offline lives are inextricably united. These studies, and especially those conducted from a more integral, ecological perspective (Matei et al., 2001), do not necessarily deny the possibility that online social ties can grow at the expense (or that they might benefit from) offline social ties. Yet, they also emphasize that any "effects" that are detected should be seen as two-way. Offline and online social bonds influence each other in equal degree.

The work in this arena is, however, far from being finalized. Although increasingly sophisticated, many of the studies have restricted themselves to locating simple relationships between undifferentiated Internet use (a close relative of the "exposure" variable typically used in traditional media studies) and amount of social interaction in real life. It is still the rare study that looks concomitantly at online and offline social ties. Some of the studies (Cummings, Butler, & Kraut, 2002; Matei & Ball-Rokeach, 2001) that strive to look directly at relationships between social ties online and offline did not use nationally representative samples, reducing their external validity. Fortunately, the last available (2000) iteration of the General Social Survey includes an "Internet module," consisting of questions about social ties both on- and offline (Neustadtl & Robinson, 2002). Twenty-eight hundred American respondents provided a wealth of information about the behavioral, social, and attitudinal contexts and implications of Internet use. Most important, the sample provides information both about using the Internet for social purposes and about people's level of connectedness to offline social environments. Although lacking a longitudinal dimension, which can truly ascertain any causal relationships, the data allows in-depth, multivariate analyses that can determine with a higher degree of generalizability if real and virtual social ties are related.

The "Magnifying Glass Effect": Precedents, Contexts and Research Questions

Much of the early research on the "Internet effects" has focused on the "time displacement" hypothesis (DiMaggio et al., 2001), which proposes that as people start engaging the Internet, they have to abandon some of their previous activities due to the limited amount of time available in a day. The idea seems to have been inspired by the work done in the area of television studies, during the 60s and the 70s (DiMaggio et al., 2001). This strand of thinking argues that if television, which was proved to have displaced so many activities—out-of-home socializing, housework, conversation—had such powerful effects, then the Internet, because of its interactive nature, which allows reembedding the user in far-away locations, will displace even more (DiMaggio et al., 2001). This conclusion was, in other instances, combined with the assumption that extending our social ties online will populate our personal universe with weak-tie relationships, leading to decline in the quality and/or quantity of the social bonds we maintain with other people (Kraut et al., 1998). This is the position Kraut et al. took in the first iteration of their HomeNet data analysis. Later on, however, benefiting from over-time, multipoint data, they concluded that over time, feelings of loneliness and decrease in family communication initially associated with Internet connections cease to be statistically significant (Kraut et al., 2002).

This line of research, although very sophisticated statistically, has neglected, however, an important theoretical issue. The "effects" are many times rooted in the assumption that engaging the medium, in an undifferentiated way, leads to social disengagement. Yet, the Internet is, at least potentially, a two-way communication medium. Engaging other people through the computer screen could lead to new and different types of social engagement. It can, in certain situations, strengthen our social ties to people in our immediate vicinity, if they are also online, or it can indeed isolate us even more, if what we are seeking online are "sounding boards for the self" (Matei, 2001).

Surprisingly, the main study reporting on the analysis of the GSS 2000 dataset does not directly look at the relationship between using the Internet specifically for social purposes (making new friends) and social ties offline (Neustadtl & Robinson, 2002). The reason seems to be that the study is fully engaged in the "exposure" debate. It focuses on the differences between users and nonusers. Its main findings reject, in principal, Nie's (2001) claim that undifferentiated Internet use leads to lower social involvement. The results "provide little support for the conclusion that Internet users with the greatest hourly usage and electronic mail usage lead less active or more constricted social lives than non-users" (Neustadtl & Robinson, 2002, p. 94). Instead, they suggest a "Newtonian effect," in that Internet users also have more frequent contacts with friends and neighbors.

In a previous study using a multiethnic, Los Angeles sample I have directly studied the Internet's "magnifying glass effect" by comparing various ethnodemographic groups in terms of their likelihood of making friends online (Matei & Ball-Rokeach, 2001). The main finding is that the higher the level of "belonging" to one's local community (which includes size of neighborhood social contacts and subjective assessment of neighborliness), the higher the likelihood of making friends online. The study also reports significant ethnic variations, with some Asian respondents having a higher tendency to make friends online.

Although intriguing, this finding cannot easily be generalized to the entire American context. The main limitation of the study is the local and heterogeneous nature of the sample it relies on, which includes a large number of minority populations

(Central American, Chinese, and Koreans), many at the first generation in the United States (Matei et al., 2001). Yet, the theoretical question asked in Los Angeles is still valid and the findings can steer a further inquiry into the relationship between online and offline ties. The main research question of the present chapter starts from this point. This is:

RQ1: Is American population's offline interaction related to its social use of the Internet?

In this context it is also important to look at the sociodemographic shaping of online sociability. Thus, a second question shall be:

RQ2: What are the main sociodemographic predictors of online interaction?

Method

Dataset

The 2000 edition of the General Social Survey includes a number of questions that allow answering these questions directly. For a comprehensive description of the methodology and of the instrument, see Neustadtl and Robinson (2002). First, the survey provides information about the amount of social interaction each respondent maintains with his/her relatives, friends, and neighbors. Each respondent was asked: "How often do you spend a social evening with your . . ." relatives, neighbors, or friends. The options varied, on a 1–7 scale, between "almost daily" to "once a year." The median was "several times a year" for interaction with one's neighbors, "once a month" for friends, and "several times a month" for relatives. As probably expected, the closer the social relationship, the more frequent the contact.

Information about social interactions online is paralleled by information about social engagement with other people using the Internet. First, the study distinguishes between Internet users (N = 1000; 35% of the entire sample) and nonusers. Furthermore, Internet users are asked if, in the past 12 months (February 1999–February 2000), they have used the Web to meet new people for social purposes. Of those asked this question (N = 742), 16% (N = 108) answered "yes." The same respondents were also asked if any of the people they met online became their friends. Two-thirds of them (N = 70, or 10% of all those asked questions about their social use of the Internet) answered "yes" to this follow-up question.

In addition, the dataset includes basic sociodemographic information: age, education, gender, race, time spent on the Internet weekly and a measure of generalized trust. The latter, which, according to Putnam is a component of social capital, is operationalized as the "yes"/"no" agreement with the statement: "Most people can be trusted" (64% of the respondents answered yes).

Analysis

To investigate, in a multivariate setting, the interaction between social interaction offline and propensity for using the Internet for social reasons (making new friends), a logistic regression model was constructed. The model predicts, using odds-ratios, the likelihood that people have used the Web to meet new people for social purposes.[1] Age, education, income, race, sex, frequency of spending evenings with relatives, friends or neighbors, time spent online each week, and trust are used as main predictor variables. For each predictor the odds that the respondent will use the Internet for social reasons were estimated, taking into account the combined effects of the other predictors.

The parameter estimates for the model are presented in Table 1. The results indicate that, after controlling for basic demographic and attitudinal indicators, there is a positive relationship between frequency of contact with offline friends and using the Internet for making friends online. More specifically, for each increment in frequency of spending evenings with friends, the odds of using the Internet for making friends increase by 40%. In other words, those who socialize more with their real life friends are also more likely to use the Internet for making new friends.

In contrast, the relationship between spending evenings with relatives and using the Internet for social reasons is negative. Those who spend more time with their relatives are *less likely* to use the Internet for social reasons. More specifically, they are almost 50% less likely to do so, for each increment in frequency of spending time with relatives.

Table 1: Logistic Regression Model. Variables Predicting Internet Social Use (Making Friends)

	B	S.E.	Wald	Sig.	Exp(B)
Constant	2.17	2.25	0.93	0.33	8.75
Age	−0.04	0.02	3.35	0.07	0.97
Race (White)	2.91	1.14	6.51	0.01	18.39
Gender (Male)	−0.88	0.43	4.20	0.04	0.42
Time online	0.001	0.0002	11.08	0.00	1.001
Education	−0.29	0.09	9.09	0.00	0.75
Income	−0.11	0.11	1.07	0.30	0.89
Frequency of contact					
Relatives	−0.43	0.14	9.72	0.00	0.65
Friends	0.33	0.15	5.04	0.02	1.40
Neighbors	0.09	0.11	0.65	0.42	1.09
Trust	0.02	0.42	0.00	0.96	1.02

N = 242; −2 Loglikelihood = 166.27; Nagelkerke R−square = .32

The model has moderate to low explanatory power. The Nagelkerke R-square estimate is .3, which means that 30% of the variance in the dependent variable is explained by the variables introduced in the model.

In summary, these findings indicate that although affirmative, the answer to the first research question also needs to be qualified. Offline social interactions are related to online social behavior. Making friends online seems to build on social interaction offline. Those who use the Internet for social reasons are more closely connected to their *friends*. However, frequency of contact with *relatives* and using the Internet for social purposes go in opposite direction. It is those who spend *less, not more, time* with their relatives that will use the Internet for social purposes. This finding will be discussed below.

In addition to information about the relationship between off- and online ties, the results also provide some interesting insights on the relationship between personal and situational characteristics and Internet social behavior. Some of them are the ones expected. For example, it is heavier users who are more likely to use the medium to make friends. For every hour spent online, the odds that they do it to make new friends increase by 4%. White respondents are more likely to make friends online. The magnitude of the difference between them and other races is quite impressive. The odds that a white person will use the Web for social reasons are 18 times greater than those for people of other races.

Some of the findings are, however, quite counterintuitive. Lower educated respondents are *more* likely to use the Internet for social purposes. Interestingly, this cannot be explained by the fact that younger people, who appear to be "less educated" because they have not finished their studies, are more likely to go online and make friends, as our model controls for age. The effect of education is above and beyond age. A surprising result, in view of the stereotype that the Internet is a "man's world" is that females are more likely to use the medium for social reasons. They have almost two and a half times greater odds of using the Internet for making friends online than males have.

The attitudinal measure introduced in the model, trust, does not contribute to the social use of the Internet. Those who trust other people are neither more, nor less likely to use the Internet for social purposes.

Discussion

In conclusion, it appears that offline social contexts are associated with online sociability, but the sign of the relationship varies from context to context. People with stronger connections to their *circle of friends* are more inclined to use the Internet for social purposes, while people with stronger connections to their *relatives* have weaker online social propensities.

Why is this so? Kraut et al. (1998), in the first HomeNet study, make the distinction between weak and strong ties, which they use in the inference that heavier

Internet users' decrease in social interaction with families is the result of a stronger connection to the "weak social ties" made possible by the Internet. Although this effect has disappeared in the second iteration of the study, the theoretical idea of a tradeoff between the two sets of relationships should be kept in focus.

Building on it, a slightly different alternative explanation for my own findings can be offered. Weak and strong ties, friends versus families, are in competition not because of the time budget constraints but because of social choices and social patterns of interaction. The last decades have been marked by profound social transformations (Putnam, 2000). Families have become smaller and have declined in importance as a social unit. Single is the most prevalent marital status category in the United States. Married couples with children are an absolute minority and less numerous than single households (Smith, 1999). The weakening of kinship structures has strengthened the role of friendships as sources of social support. It is significant, for example that, while at the same time the family has declined, the frequency of spending an evening with our friends has increased, on average, over the past 25 years, by two contacts annually (Neustadtl & Robinson, 2002).

In addition, Internet use and involvement is closer to a lifestyle that emphasizes autonomy, freedom, and flexibility of social ties (Matei, 2001). These will find a far more hospitable environment in the social universe of friendships, which by nature are nonascriptive and also more likely to encourage experimentation and extending one's social ties far and wide. Family and kin ties are, by contrast, environments that are by nature more "conservative" and more inclined to be in-group oriented, keeping its members in a mesh of close-knit bonds. In consequence, the magnification effects of the Internet take place only in those environments in which the Internet and the other social and lifestyle associated with it are more likely to thrive. This will be more likely to occur in friendship dominated situations and less likely to happen in the more traditional, stronger tie, family-based settings.

In this context, it is also important to note the fact that women are more likely to engage in the quest for sociability online. This might go hand in hand with the idea of the Internet as a social space of freedom. Women, increasingly autonomous since the 60s, seem to take greater advantage of the medium, as they become less subordinated to traditional behavioral customs.

However, these explanations are only tentative and cannot claim a causal status, because the dataset is cross-sectional. We will not be able to tell if friendships offline create or *cause* social ties online until we assess the strength and evolution of these relationships over time. If and only if those who have strong friendships offline become even more involved with the online social scene *without* losing their social networks in reality, will we be fully confident that social environments offline have a magnifying causal effect on online social interaction.

This is an ambitious enterprise, which needs a great deal of effort and data. We hope, however, that if pursued, we will significantly increase our knowledge of the way in which the social space opened by the Internet interacts with our preexisting social ties.

Note

1. The other variable, tested above in a bivariate context, likelihood of making friends online, could not be used, because of a low number of cases.

References

Cummings, J., Butler, B., & Kraut, R. (2002). The quality of on-line social relationships. *Communications of the ACM,* 45(7), 103-108.
DiMaggio, P., Hargittai, E., Neuman, W. R., & Robinson, J. P. (2001). Social implications of the Internet. *Annual Review of Sociology,* 27, 307-336.
Hiltz, S. R., & Turoff, M. (1978). *The Network Nation: Human Communication via Computer.* Reading, MA: Addison-Wesley.
Howard, P., Rainie, L., & Jones, S. (2001). Days and nights on the Internet: The impact of a diffusing technology. *American Behavioral Scientist,* 45(3), 383-404.
Katz, J., Rice, R. E., & Aspden, P. (2001). The Internet, 1995-2000: Access, civic involvement, and social interaction. *American Behavioral Scientist,* 45(3), 405-420.
Kraut, R., Kiesler, S., Boneva, B., Cummings, J., Helgeson, V., & Crawford, A. (2002). Internet paradox revisited. *Journal of Social Issues,* 58(1), 49-74.
Kraut, R., Lundmark, V., Patterson, M., Kielser, S., Mukopadhyay, T., & Scherlis, W. (1998). Internet paradox. A social technology that produces social involvement and psychological well-being? *American Psychologist,* 53(9, September), 1017-1031.
Licklider, J. C. R., & Taylor, R. W. (1968). The computer as a communication device. *Science & Technology,* (April), 21-31.
Markoff, J. (2000, February 16). Portrait of a newer, lonelier crowd is captured in an Internet survey. *The New York Times,* p. 1.
Matei, S. (2001). *The magnifying glass effect. Negotiating individualism and community on the Internet.* Unpublished Ph. D. Dissertation, University of Southern California, Los Angeles.
Matei, S., & Ball-Rokeach, S. (2001). Real and virtual social ties: Connections in the everyday lives of seven ethnic neighborhoods. *American Behavioral Scientist,* 45(3), 550-564.
Matei, S., Ball-Rokeach, S., Wilson, M., Gibbs, J., & Gutierez Hoyt, E. (2001). Metamorphosis: a field research methodology for studying communication technology and community. *The Electronic Journal of Communication / La Revue Electronique de Communication,* 11(2).
Neustadtl, A., & Robinson, J. P. (2002). Social contact differences between Internet users and nonusers in the General Social Survey. *IT & Society,* 1(1), 73-102.
Nie, N. H. (2001). Sociability, interpersonal relations, and the Internet: reconciling conflicting findings. *American Behavioral Scientist,* 45(3), 420-435.
Putnam, R. (2000). *Bowling Alone.* New York: Simon and Schuster.
Rheingold, H. (1993). *The Virtual Community: Homesteading on the Electronic Frontier* (1st HarperPerennial ed.). New York: HarperPerennial.
Rheingold, H. (2001). *The virtual community: homesteading on the virtual frontier.* Boston: MIT Press.
Smith, T. W. (1999). *The emerging 21st century American family* (GSS Social Change Report

No. 42). Chicago, IL: National Opinion Research Center, University of Chicago. [Online]. Available: <http://www.norc.uchicago.edu/online/emerge.pdf>.

Sproull, L., & Kiesler, S. B. (1991). *Connections: New Ways of Working in the Networked Organization.* Cambridge, MA: MIT Press.

Wellman, B. (2001). Physical place and cyber place: The rise of personalized networks. *International Journal of Urban and Regional Research, 25*(2), 227–252.

TALKING IN LISTS: THE CONSEQUENCES OF COMPUTER-MEDIATED COMMUNICATION ON COMMUNITIES

Group Communication in Networked Communities

Online group communication fills a "media gap" in traditional communication technologies (Tomita, 1980; Neuman, 1991). Internet-based mailing lists, bulletin boards, newsgroups, listservs, and other online group communication fill a media gap for multipoint-to-multipoint small group exchange that has not previously been scalable with traditional media such as point-to-multipoint mass communication (newspapers, radio, TV) serving huge populations and point-to-point communication (letters, telephone, fax) serving only two or a few individuals at a time. As such, it is a unique outcome of Internet diffusion. The research described in this chapter is part of a larger study that investigated the use and social impacts of information infrastructure and technology on public and nonprofit agencies and residents within localities served by community networks.

Some of the earliest empirical research has focused on Santa Monica's Public Electronic (PEN) Network (Schmitz et al, 1995). PEN greatly enhanced the opportunities for grassroots organizing in Santa Monica by offering a venue for electronic discourse among those who would not otherwise interact (Witting & Schmitz, 1996). The Blacksburg Electronic Village (BEV) has been a leader in community network evaluation and research since its inception in 1993 (Cohill & Kavanaugh, 2000). One focus of the BEV research has been to contribute to the growing literature on the impacts of community networking on community involvement, civic engagement, and social capital (Anderson, 1995; Beamish, 1995; Bishop, 2000; Durrance & Pettigrew, 2001; Hampton & Wellman, 1999; Kavanaugh & Patterson, 2001; Longan, 2000; Patrick & Black, 1996; Patterson & Kavanaugh, 1994; Putnam, 2000; Rheingold, 2000; Rothenbuhler, 1991; Schuler, 1996; Turow & Kavanaugh, 2003; Wellman & Haythornthwaite, 2001).

This manuscript incorporates approaches derived from computer-supported cooperative work (CSCW) and community computer networking to assess the use and impacts of online group communication on social relations, information exchange and involvement (Carroll, 2001; Hampton, 2003; Hampton & Wellman, 1999; Jones, 1998; Kavanaugh, 2003; Kavanaugh & Patterson, 2001; O'Sullivan, 1995; Rothenbuhler, 1991; Schmitz, 2001). Community computing brings CSCW to personal computing (Carroll, 2001). The basic rationale for community computing, as for any computer supported cooperative work, notes Carroll, is that people who want to communicate and collaborate are neither co-located nor (necessarily) interacting in real time. What is distinctive about community computing is that the collaboration is among proximal residents, and that computer support supplements face-to-face communication.

Our data has been obtained from four case sites that are different in some ways but similar in others. Two of the four sites are clearly urban (the city of Seattle and the city of Pittsburgh); two are more ex-urban and rural (Champaign-Urbana in Illinois, and Blacksburg and surrounding Montgomery County, Virginia). The primary similarity among these sites is that they have community computer network projects that have been established and operational for several years. This relative permanence allows us to look beyond initial deployment (primary effects), and investigate second-order effects following the adoption and use of new technology.

Each of these four community network cases has established a critical mass of users and achieved self-sustainability in various forms. The rural or urban nature of a geographic area, and specifically its population size and density, has been studied previously and extensively to determine their influence on the patterns of social participation and community involvement. Our study draws on these findings and on others interested in the broad research area of "decline of community" (Fischer, 1972; Putnam, 2000; Toennies, 1887, among many others). Detailed information about each individual case study site is available online; see: the city of Seattle (<http://www.scn.org>); the city of Pittsburgh (<http://www.trfn.org>); Champaign-Urbana, Illinois (<http://www.prairienet.org>); and Blacksburg, Virginia (<http://www.bev.net>).

Method

As part of a larger study of community computer networking (Kavanaugh, Schmitz, & Patterson, 2002), we designed and administered a survey for listserv managers and affiliated members to solicit responses regarding the use and impact of this type of Internet communication on nonprofit and public sector organizations and their membership. We administered two different questionnaires followed by selected interviews with listserv managers. First, a set of questions was directed to listserv managers (by telephone interview and/or e-mail), who then invited their subscribers to participate and posted the URL of the questionnaire on their lists. All subscriber responses were directed back to the authors for analysis.

The first part of the survey, the listserv manager questionnaire, had two sections: one with more open-ended questions (administered by telephone interview or e-mail) and a second section that required only a check mark or very short answer, which we sent to participating managers in the body of an e-mail message. The questionnaire asked about organization type and size, uses of Internet, expectations, purposes of the listserv, the frequency and type of communication, the perceived impact of the list on involvement in the organization's activities and issues, and member social networks. We developed and beta tested the questionnaire in Blacksburg in the summer of 2000, and revised and administered it in Fall 2001. The second part of the survey, a Web-based questionnaire, was designed for listserv members. It contained similar questions but from the perspective of members.

In addition to organizations located in our four case study sites, we recruited organizations from communities listed in online inventories of community network projects in the United States. We were not successful in enlisting as large a sample as we envisioned (80 organizations total), in spite of follow up invitations. From a total pool of 378 organizations, we obtained only 78 responses, and 36 completed questionnaires (10%).

The low response rate is due partly to the small number of organizations that actually used a listserv at the time. In addition, only 24 of the 36 managers were with organizations from which we also received members, completed questionnaires. Participating managers sent an invitation (with URL) to members to participate in the study by completing the Web-based questionnaire (N = 137). Complete confidentiality for listserv managers and subscribers has been observed. The types of organizations that are represented by the respondents range from sports clubs to La Leche League to county governments.

We only included the organizations in this chapter from which we had a complete set of questionnaires (i.e., from both listserv managers and subscribers of the same organization). This reduced our list manager respondents to a total of 24. Nonetheless, listserv managers and members both shared very thematic, interesting, and worthwhile comments; these perspectives have been helpful and point to trends that may help guide further research.

Results

Listserv Managers Survey

Most of the listserv managers (18 of the 24 respondents) were experienced computer network users; all had been using the Internet for at least four years, and most had been using it for six to ten years. All respondents used the Internet at home, and most of them also used it at work. Most respondents managed only one or two lists. The primary purpose of most of the lists was to post announcements and keep members informed; group discussion was a primary purpose for only 2 of the 24 managers. Most managers posted messages to the list about once a week. About a third reported working on the Web site less than once a week.

All of the organizations had Web sites. The sites were usually maintained by the same person who managed the listserv. In spite of the long experience of most listserv managers and their high computer network literacy, almost half of the listservs were relatively new—less than three years old. Over a third of the lists were well established (four or more years old), although few lists were older than five years. In most cases, the same listserv manager had been taking care of the listserv since it was established.

Most of the listservs were relatively small. Half had 50 or fewer subscribers. Only a few had more than 300 subscribers. In most organizations, less than 10% of membership subscribed to the listserv. These findings are important in considering the effect of the list communication on getting to know new people in the group. The smaller the group and the list membership, the easier it is to recognize new voices and individuals. Alternatively, when a small percentage of an organization's membership subscribes to the listserv, subscribers may begin to feel disconnected from organizational members that do not share electronic information.

Leaders typically get to know more people and have more acquaintances than non-leaders, by virtue of their position in the group. This is reflected in the listserv managers reporting greater numbers than members of new social ties facilitated by the listserv. Persons that have to exchange messages with more people than other members of the organization are likely to become more familiar with other members' names and identities. The length of time the organization, as well as the listserv, had been established also affected the likelihood of people getting to know each other.

Manager's ratings of the helpfulness of the listserv for a variety of purposes (Table 1) indicate that the greatest utility of this communication tool was for posting announcements; the lowest rating was given for discussing issues of interest (1 = not at all helpful; 5 = very helpful).

The consequences of communication via the listserv showed up in many ways. More than half of the 24 managers indicated that communication via the list "changed the participation in the face-to-face activities of the group a lot." While

Table 1: Managers Rating: Helpfulness of the Listserv

Helpfulness of listserv	Mean
Posting announcements and keeping members informed	4.5
Coordinating or organizing activities	3.63
Obtaining feedback	3.38
Discussing issues of interest	2.96

Table 2: Length of Internet Use and List Use

Length of Net Use/List Use	Using Internet	Using List
One year or less	0.7%	33.6%
More than 1 year to 2 years	0.7%	27.6%
More than 2 year to 3 years	7.2%	27.1%
More than 3 years	91.4%	11.7%

11 of 24 managers said that overall participation had stayed the same, almost an equal number (10) reported that overall group participation had increased as a result of the listserv. We should note that listserv use rarely substituted for face-to-face participation, but, rather, it often was used to compliment traditional mediated channels, such as telephone or newsletter. Using the electronic list reduced costs for the group in just over half the cases. In addition, the listserv increased information sent from managers to members in almost all cases. Twenty of the 24 managers indicated that they had personally developed new friends through the listserv.

Listserv Members Survey

We combined all the responses from various listserv subscribers (N = 137) into a single dataset. The majority of subscribers were either "somewhat experienced" or "very experienced" with using the Internet (the top two points on a four-point scale). The majority had also been using the Internet for more than three years (see Table 2). By comparison, few persons used the list for more than three years, although this reflects the relative infancy of most of the lists studied.

More than half the respondents (59.5%) reported that they had *not* gotten to know new people due to the listserv; however, others had made at least a few new friends or acquaintances through the list. While all of the associated listserv managers reported that the group had a Web site, almost a third of subscribers (29%) were unaware of the Web site.

One interesting finding is that members rated the helpfulness of the list highest for "discussing issues of interest" (Table 3, $\bar{x}$ = 4.2). Managers rated the helpfulness of the listserv for discussion lowest among categories (Table 1 above, $\bar{x}$ = 2.96). The subscriber ratings of the helpfulness of the listserv for various purposes are shown in Table 3 (1 = not at all helpful; 5 = very helpful).

A repeated measures ANOVA of the purposes shown in Table 3 (N = 112) indicates significant differences between several categories, $F(1,111) = 29.17$, $p < .01$, $\eta^2 = .21$. The helpfulness of the list for social relations (rated the least helpful) is significantly lower than all other categories. Rated highest is the helpfulness of the list for discussing issues of interest, which is also significantly higher than all other cat-

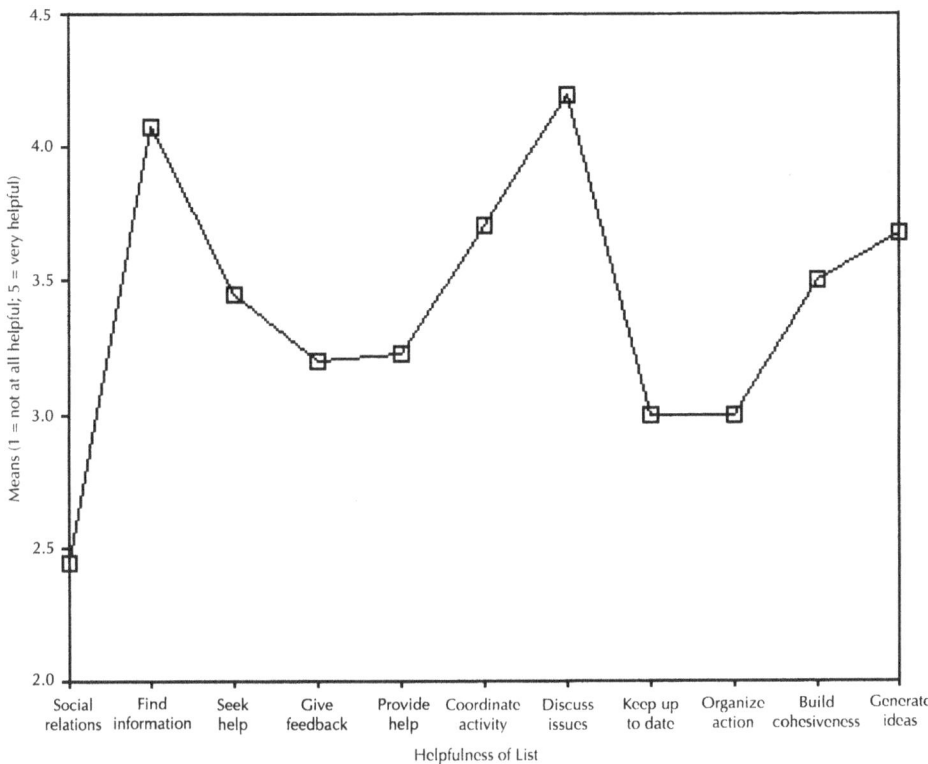

Table 3: Members Rating: Helpfulness of the List for Various Purposes

egories except "finding information."

Most members' involvement in their local communities, in local issues of interest, and in connectedness with local people had stayed about the same since they went online (Table 4). Very few persons reported they were "much less involved," and those reporting they were "less involved" represented about three cases. Moreover, a sizable proportion of the respondents reported being more involved in all three domains; some respondents also reported that they were much more involved since getting on the Internet.

Table 4: Involvement Since Getting on the Internet

Level of Involvement	Community	Local Issues	Local People
Less	1.5%	0.8%	2.4%
Stayed the same	73.1%	74.2%	57.1%
More	20.9%	19.7%	34.9%
Much more	4.5%	5.3%	5.6%

Interviews with Listserv Managers

All of the managers participating in the focus group interviews were experienced Internet users (many had been online for at least 10 years). Each of the participating managers agreed that the online communication they used (Web site, e-mail, and listserv) had greatly simplified the process of communication with members or constituents. Moreover, they were able to send information via the Internet that would not have been shared in the past, such as newsletters or activity updates, because of the higher cost of printing and postal mail. Finally, the listservs eased the even greater difficulties of maintaining updated address lists and recruiting and sustaining a large enough pool of volunteers to photocopy material and stuff envelopes on a regular basis.

Organizational benefits attributed to the listserv also included increased volunteerism, increased financial savings, increased participation in group activities, and involvement in organizational issues. The most commonly reported observation among listserv managers was that volunteer activity among members increased because of the availability of the listserv or similar Internet tools (mostly e-mail).

Increased volunteerism operated at two levels: organizational management (e.g., officers and other Board positions) and routine tasks (e.g., increased response to run booths). The use of Internet applications (e-mail, Web site, listserv) made the management of the organization easier for Board members and officers, as meeting notices, agendas and documents were distributed electronically to fellow managers or members with a few keystrokes. For the larger membership, Internet communication (via Web or listserv) increased awareness of organizational processes that depended on their help; listservs enhanced membership support for specific events and functions. Finally, an important finding was that for some groups, listserv communication tended to reduce cliques.

Discussion

The interplay of community social structures and new information technologies offers opportunities to improve group communication and information exchange at the local level among residents and with nonprofit and public sector organizations. All of the nonprofit and public sector organizations that participated in our study of listserv communication attributed important benefits to their communication with members or constituencies, including increased volunteerism, increased financial savings, increased participation in group activities, and greater involvement in organizational issues. Some also noted that there was a reduction in organization "cliques" because of the more transparent and open form of communication and information exchange among members.

The greatest increase in involvement was with other people in the local community. This suggests the Internet helps to strengthen social ties and foster interpersonal interaction. The increases in the proportion of community members who were "more involved with the local community" and "with issues of interest" are particularly important because community "activists" usually comprise just a small proportion of any community. Moreover, we can distinguish among our respondents—between those who are "activists" in the sense of being members of many local organizations and attending many face-to-face meetings and those who are more "passively engaged"—that is, people who keep up with what's going on and are interested in local issues but may not often make public statements at meetings. Both types of community involvement are important; each helps to build social capital and civic engagement.

Prior to the advent of the Internet, small group communication tended to occur largely in face-to-face settings. With the diffusion of online group communication technologies, particularly in geographic communities, face-to-face communication is supplemented, exchange is enhanced and social networks are sustained.

Despite the impressive benefits of listserv communication, one of the most striking findings of the study was the low overall level of listserv use by community organizations. Our findings suggest that much more extensive and active training and support is needed to increase awareness and familiarity with listserv communication. While community network projects appear to be playing an important role in raising awareness, promoting training, and building critical mass, much more remains to be done. One successful strategy in Blacksburg has been to package basic Internet services and offer them at low annual fees to local nonprofit and public sector groups. Easier tools for Web-based collaboration by nonexperts would also be an important area for development and further study.

Note

The research described in this paper was supported by a grant from the U.S. Department of Commerce (#50-SBN-TOC-1033), and grant partners Virginia Tech, San Francisco State University, the University of Tulsa, and the Blacksburg Electronic Village, Incorporated. We would like to thank our collaborators Paul Adams, Andrew Cohill, Joan Durrance, Melissa Guest, Steve Guest, Susan Holmes, Francine Jefferson, Debbie Denise Reese, Scott Patterson, and Luke Ward. We are especially grateful to Marche Barnes, Kyle Combs, Kimberly Kirn, and Lucinda Willis for their extensive assistance with all aspects of the research.

References

Anderson, R., Bikson, T., Law, S. A., & Mitchel, B. M. (1995). *Universal Access to Email: Feasibility and Societal Implications*. Santa Monica: RAND Corporation.

Beamish, A. (1995). Communities on-line: Community based computer networks. Masters Thesis: Massachusetts Institute of Technology.

Bishop, A. (2000). PrairieNet Community Network. Final Grant Report #17-60-97026. Technology Opportunity Program. Washington, DC: U.S. Department of Commerce.

Carroll, J.M. 2001. Community computing as human-computer interaction. *Behavior & Information Technology*, 20, 5, 307–314.

Cohill, A., & Kavanaugh, A. (Eds.). (2000). *Community Networks: Lessons Learned from Blacksburg, Virginia*. Norwood, MA: Artech House.

Durrance, J., & Pettigrew, K. *(2001)*. Toward Context-Centered Methods for Evaluating Public Library Networked Community Information Initiatives. *First Monday.* Electronic journal: <http://firstmonday.org/issues/issue6_4/durrance/>.

Fischer, C. (1972). Urbanism as a way of life: A review and an agenda. *Sociological Methods and Research* 2 (November), 187-242.

Hampton, K., & Wellman, B. (1999). Netville online and offline: Observing and surveying a wired suburb. *American Behavioral Scientist*, 43 (3), 475-92.

Hampton, K. (forthcoming, 2003). Grieving for a lost network: Collective action in a wired suburb: *The Information Society* 19, 5.

Jones, S. G., Ed. (1998). *CyberSociety 2.0: Revisiting Computer-mediated Communication and Community.* Thousand Oaks, CA: Sage.

Kasarda, J., & Janowitz, M. (1974). Community attachment in mass society. *American Sociological Review* 39 (June): 328-39.

Kavanaugh, A. (2003, forthcoming). Community networks and civic engagement: A social network approach. *The Good Society* 11, 3.

Kavanaugh, A. (2003). "When everyone is wired: The impact of the Internet on families in networked communities" in J. Turow & A. Kavanaugh (Eds.), *The Wired Homestead: New Views on a Web World.* Cambridge, MA: MIT Press.

Kavanaugh, A., Schmitz, J., & Patterson, S. 2002. *The Use and Social Impact of Telecommunications and Information Infrastructure Assistance upon Local Public and Nonprofit Sectors: An Assessment of Community Networks.* Final Grant Report (#50-SBN-TOC-1033), U.S. Department of Commerce.

Kavanaugh, A. (2001). *Higher civic engagement among early adopters: Trend or phase?* Paper prepared for the Telecommunications Policy Research Conference, October 2001.

Kavanaugh, A., & Patterson, S. (2001). The impact of community computer networks on social capital and community involvement. *American Behavioral Scientist*, 45 (3): 496-509.

Longan, M. W. (2000). Community and place in cyberspace: The community networking movement in the United States. Ph.D. dissertation, University of Colorado.

Neuman, Russell. 1991. *The Future of the Mass Audience.* New York: Cambridge University Press.

O'Sullivan, P. B. (1995) Computer networks and political participation: Santa Monica's teledemocracy project. *Journal of Applied Communication Research, 23*, 93-107.

Patrick, A. S., & Black, A. (1996). *Losing sleep and watching less TV but socializing more: Personal and social impacts of using the National Capital FreeNet.* Retrieved October 1996 from: <http://debra.dgbt.doc.ca/services-research>.

Patterson, S., & A. Kavanaugh. 1994. "Rural Users' Expectations of the Information Superhighway." *Media Information Australia, 74* (November), 57-61.

Patterson, S., & Kavanaugh, A. (2003, forthcoming). Building critical mass in networked communities. *Electronic Journal of Communication.*

Putnam, R. (2000). *Bowling Alone: The Collapse and Revival of American Community.* New York: Simon & Schuster.

Rheingold, H. (2000). *The Virtual Community: Homesteading on the Electronic Frontier* (revised ed). Cambridge, MA: MIT Press.

Rothenbuhler, E. (1991). The process of community involvement. *Communication Monographs,* 63-78.

Schmitz, J. (2001). Community networking: Mapping the electronic commons. *The Electronic Journal of Communication/La Revue Electronique de Communication* 11 (2), pp. 3-5.
Schmitz, J., Rogers, E. M., Phillips, K., & Paschal, D. (1995). The Public Electronic Network (PEN) and the homeless in Santa Monica. *Journal of Applied Communication Research*, 23, 26-43.
Schuler, D. (1996). *New Community Networks: Wired for Change.* New York: Addison-Wesley.
Toennies, F. (1887). *Gemeinschaft and gesellschaft.* Leipzig: Fues's Verlag.
Tomita, T. (1980). *The Media Gap Model.* Tokyo: Japan Ministry of Communications.
Turow, J., & Kavanaugh, A. (2003, forthcoming). *The Wired Homestead: New Views on a Web World.* Cambridge, MA: MIT Press.
Wellman, B., & Haythornthwaite, C., Eds. (2001). The Internet in everyday life. Special issue. *American Behavioral Scientist,* 45 (3).
Wittig, M., & Schmitz, J. (1996). Electronic grassroots organizing. *Journal of Social Issues,* 52 (1), 53-69.

THE SOCIAL DESIGN OF VIRTUAL WORLDS: CONSTRUCTING THE USER AND COMMUNITY THROUGH CODE

Introduction

In 1996, I found myself at a unique conference that dealt specifically with graphical virtual worlds and avatars. The Contact Consortium sponsored *Earth To Avatars,* a weekend long event in San Francisco dedicated to bringing together programmers, designers, and a handful of social scientists to seriously consider the future of multiuser online spaces. It was a fairly hopeful time for virtual worlds companies. Money was being filtered to a decent number of developers and talk of inhabiting a "metaverse" à là Neal Stephenson's *Snow Crash* predominated. I was particularly drawn to the conference track dealing with the design of these worlds where there was a strong ambition to come up with a kind of "universal standard" of avatar design (Ma, 1996). The vision of massively linked worlds in which people could wander across environments, taking along their customized avatars, promoted much debate and discussion. I remember sitting in one session and hearing someone propose the construction of a system in which you might hit a ball with a bat in one world and be able to see it fly across the sky in another. As I listened to programmers and designers talk about and debate how to build such persistent worlds, I began to notice that quite often the conversations were not simply about technical details but about what life in these worlds might be like—what it might mean to live an avatar life. A general question underlay many of the discussions: what kinds of activities were participants expected to engage in and how could avatars be designed to accommodate them? The number of times I heard science fiction writers such as Gibson, Stephenson, and Vinge evoked also caused me pause. These works were not technical manuals or specifications, but imagined futures, for community and bodies.

Digital Materiality

What is the material that makes up our online body? Over the years when I have described the subject of my research, I am often met with quizzical looks. "A body online? What do you mean?" I think this stems, at least in part, from being unclear about the materiality digital space can assume. Our offline bodies are made up of *something*. They have a certain solidity to them, something we can see *is actually there*. But online? Is there anything tangible? And if so, what is it made up of? The digital is often spoken of as simply invisible bits, "ones and zeros," or as arcane code that only the most technologically savvy can understand. What does it mean then when someone wants to talk about the structure of online life? The all-too-simple framework—one that equates "offline" with embodied experience and "online" with disembodied minds floating in cyberspace—needs to give way to a more complicated understanding and exploration of the actual *material* of our online lives, a significant part of which is made up of software and code.

In the case of virtual environments, the artifacts used for embodiment (be it avatars or text-based forms) exist as code, created by a programmer and/or designer with a particular range of functionality and affordances. This software object then acts as the material upon which an experience of embodiment is built. Woolgar (1991) has spoken of ways technical objects attempt to "configure users" and this is particularly pronounced in virtual worlds where the underlying structure of the system shapes participants' bodies and identities in the space. Taking a closer look at software and its producers is thus crucial. Rather than seeing architectures or "toolboxes" as separate from content, we might begin to ask how virtual world designers are always actively engaged in the production of substantive possibilities. As Lessig (2000) has suggested, architecture reflects politics. Although it is important to keep in mind that users are always actively engaged in remaking and resisting structures for their own purposes, I would like to propose a critical intervention that suggests we take seriously the ways system architectures can act as a powerful shaping force for how life gets lived online (see also Taylor, 2003a). At stake in this recognition is the ability to interrogate the assumptions and possibilities we encounter in multiuser environments, as well as the search to find ways to engage producers in dialogue that leads to more progressive design.

Early Virtual World Development

Much of the study devoted to virtual worlds has thus far focused on text-based MUDs (Kendall, 1996; Nakamura, 1995; Reid, 1996; Schaap, 2002; Turkle, 1995). A good portion of this work explored how identity and community were being constructed in these spaces, and some researchers have highlighted how underlying structures were shaping these performances (Danet, 1998; Dibbell, 1998; Kolko, 2000; Sunden, 2002). While MUDs often left the construction of the body, with the use of @describe commands, up to the participants, it is worth remembering that (especially in the case of MOOs) important programming was devoted to the creation of player classes to facilitate user engagement with the space. Player classes act as a kind of body template by helping the user construct their description and gender, as well as providing the underlying structure to inhabit the world. For example, whereas users might create for themselves a description of a vampire, a system could not only structurally legitimate such an identity but facilitate it through the function of a specific player-class, as in the following example:

> This is the Vampires of Venice player class (VoV), offering these powers:
> - Guises; four (4) changes of clothing
> - Bodies; two (2) forms, unclothed & "secret"
> - Transformation; mortal initially, become a vampire at your choosing
> - Blood-Drinking; drink & taste the blood of other VoV members
> - Sensing; list other vampires, see if another player is a vampire
> - Morphing; alternative names & descriptions
> - Look Detection; notification when others look at you
> - Look Discretion; guise & body are unseen from a distance
> - Answering Machine; pages are recorded while you are off-line
> - Friends; a personal list to maintain and use
> - Resources; mailing list, communications channel, and myriad generics
> - And more to come...
>
> You are invited to join the VoV, the Children of the Night specializing in dark, gothic mood and the seductive spell of vampirism. VoV is a revenant group, with no ranks or clans, valuing rich and imaginative roleplaying.

This player class provides a kind of underlying structure for the user to tap into to assist their identity performance. Multiplicity of identity is, in fact, legitimized through the ability to have multiple bodies and guises. In addition, built into the very body of the character are mechanisms for community via the chat channels, friends lists, and "sensing" mechanisms. The programmer who created this class was clearly invested in providing a particular method of embodiment for its users and explicitly fostered *specific* social interactions and engagements through it.

In another MUD, the creation of a pregnancy player class led to some provocative community debate around digital embodiment (Herdman, undated). A male programmer who had recently had a child offline thought adding the ability to the MUD would provide players a valuable opportunity to explore parenting. In the process of determining which particular functions were key to the experience (i.e., randomized genders for babies "born," having to visit the maternity ward to deliver), larger questions around how this player class should be used arose. For example, the question of whether or not male gendered characters could become pregnant and how exactly one would become pregnant were debated. Questions about single parenting and artificial insemination were raised. Each of these issues fed into how the software would operate and the resulting form of embodiment the player class would allow. Ultimately a fertility clinic was made, male characters were not allowed to have babies unless they changed their gender, and pregnancies could not be terminated through any official "abortion" mechanism but only through an unpublicized loophole in the system. The structure of the system came to reflect not only a technical opportunity (choosing a new player class) but specific values and ideas about what constituted a legitimate performance of pregnancy and parental identity. Architectures for player classes and verbs often bring with them deep value orientations about what kinds of activities and interactions are considered useful, meaningful, and legitimate. As McDonough has additionally noted, this "image of the user" is not simply a question of what designers may want participants to do in their world, but of who they think their users are *offline* (McDonough, 1999; Woolgar, 1991).

While designer intent in text-based worlds is often easier to "see" and analyze because a series of commands can reveal the underlying mechanisms, graphical worlds represent no less of an explicit attempt to guide and shape the nature of online life. The intentionality that many of the graphical designers I interviewed brought to their world construction process is striking. One of the most provocative examples I encountered of the complicated ways designers embed broader values into systems was how they consciously built in social regulation through avatars. For example, one of the most vexing issues virtual world administrators face is how to deal with people who actively disrupt the environment. Issues of accountability and responsibility are especially tricky concerns online where, at a basic level, "real-world" identities may be masked and consequences difficult to enforce. One well-established world sought to manage issues of personal responsibility and social regulation by, in part, rooting all participants in a traditional binary gender system as well as charging users (via "virtual currency") for every iteration of body change they undertook. As one of the designers put it,

> There is a lot of "gender" wrapped up in identification of others in our society. Since the idea was that others needed to be able to identify an individual to assign a reputation to that person, gender was an easily remembered identifier and we figured that putting a limit on it would assist reputation-as-social-restraint.

What may at first glance seem like simply an administrative decision about which avatars participants can choose, and if they can change them easily, is actually deeply linked to the way the designers wanted to foster user responsibility and accountability in the space and how they understood identity, and specifically gender, choices as linked to that scheme.

Technical and design decisions can thus have powerful implications on the way the world works. In another example, world designers created specific limitations on their avatars such that they were all the same height and construed as "adult." In addition, they were all healthy adults who could walk and who did not show age through their avatar bodies. There were no children and no elderly. When I inquired about this, I was told the homogeneity was intentional and that creating an underlying uniformity to objects was much easier on the system. The parameters of interaction with the world were thus fixed and known. For the design team this meant a greater ease in introducing new objects and factors into the environment. In this world, the rules (via the animation engine) had to apply to *all* the bodies similarly. Although there was some diversity in the size of the avatars and the customizations people could make, ultimately their bodies had to, in a fundamental way, interact similarly with the space. The explanation given was,

> Doors, handles, have to all be the same height, gestures for the hands needed to reach the same height, seating needed to be done a particular way, there were a lot of standards and it was easier to, in order to get a variety of body types, it was easier to just stick with an adult body.

No children, no physically challenged, no short, no tall—all the bodies you saw in this world were similar in stature and implied age. The system enacted an embodiment norm through standardization and in turn formally structured the kinds of identities and interactions possible in this space. As can be seen in many of these examples, such normative constructions are not simply matters of virtual world design but often bear close resemblances to the offline world, even revealing something about the value systems at work in our culture. Rather than worlds that are somehow set off and "protected from RL," what we find are ways broader cultural values come to find a place in virtual environments.

The Popularization of Virtual Worlds—Massively Multiplayer Online Games

In the historical trajectory I am laying out here, the emerging genre of massively multiplayer online games (MMOG) is the next important marker in the story. While the intentionality of design in games is certainly more obvious in the sense that goals and achievements are formally built into the space, MMOG's also construct very specific notions of embodiment and community. Some game designers are quite up front about the ways they have built in formal models of sociability and interaction. For example, Brad McQuaid, *EverQuest* co-designer, has said that, "Community is relationships between players, whether it be friendly or adversarial, symbiotic or competitive. It's also a form of persistence, which is key to massively multiplayer games" (Jonric, 2002). To this end, the game supports things like buddy lists, persistent player names, guild structures, and a general reliance on grouping to get experience and to advance in the game. Social life gets fostered via the architecture of the system and the structure of play.

Broader considerations about how to induce equitable play, immersion, and community even get linked to how player accounts will be handled. One of the more fascinating (and often heated) debates to turn up in the MMOG design community has been around the number of characters allowed per account and whether or not people should be allowed to have multiple avatars. Debates around the question of multiplicity often become an issue of fostering community and responsibility. It is sometimes argued that if people are forced into persistent identities, if they have limits on the number of characters they can have, they may identify more deeply with, and invest in, the ones they do use. As an administrative post on why the upcoming *Star Wars Galaxies* MMOG would only allow one character per server explained:

The reasons why we intend to do single-characters per account are:

- In order to encourage interdependence.
- In order to reduce the impact of "dabblers" on certain professions.
- In order to reduce storage requirements.
- In order to reduce misbehavior and improve customer service.
- In order to block certain kinds of misbehavior more easily.

It is worth mentioning that there is certainly debate not only on this method of regulating behavior, but even what constitutes "misbehavior" or improper gameplay. Nonetheless, the character creation screen, which may often seem a simple matter to the user, is actually one of the most important social and psychological design decisions developers make. It contains within it explicit imaginations about how participants not only will, but *should,* be constructing identities and inhabiting that space.

Once in the game, design decisions shape the possibilities for the environment through the choice of avatars they provide, how communication can occur, and more generally how the "world" gets modeled. As one programmer put it, "Well, we like to say we are gods. Gods of the worlds that we create." In many instances, what gets created can be quite problematic and at odds with participants' ideas of how they want to be in the game. *EverQuest,* for example, has been often criticized for its use of hyperstereotypical female avatars. The look of the avatars seems to have some real effect not only on how other players interact with and perceive female characters, but the degree to which women are able to identify with them (Taylor, 2003b).

At a deep level the game engine, which makes the world run, also profoundly structures what can occur during play. There are some early strong indications that, much like the way core MUD architectures or animation sequences in social graphic worlds shaped avatar interaction, game engines are acting as the central organizing force determining the possibilities, and limitations, for bodies, behavior, and communication in game worlds. The programmer who likened himself to a god went on to say, "The engine determines everything. It's like the paint, the canvas, and the brushes." Engines, of course, are built by programmers (often in conjunction with designers) who have broad visions about how objects in a space should interact, what kinds of physics will be modeled, even how light and shadow will be incorporated. Although we have little data thus far on the practical social and psychological effects game engines produce, they certainly have the power to structure, at a deep level, how one can move, interact, create, and communicate in that space. Past lessons would suggest that keen attention should be paid to the possibilities and limitations embedded in this code. Given that more developers are relying on a handful of proprietary engines on which to build their games, the issue of the consolidation of normative architectures will be one of the more important issues we face as MMOGs develop. In a moment when commercialized virtual world ventures predominate, whose visions of how bodies, identities, and communities should be stands as a central critical concern.

Conclusion

While much has been written on how Internet users are creating rich communities, the story of virtual worlds must contain some accounting for those who actually implement their vision of an imagined lifeworld via the software that makes the environment work. Though simply painting the question of how people inhabit these worlds as an issue of technological determinism is inappropriate, we cannot overlook the role software and design plays in shaping online life. As Raph Koster, a prominent game developer, has said of his work on MMOGs, "I really enjoy the fact that I have a job where I have to think about politics and economics and architecture and visual design and group psychology and reward feedback and social networks and user interface design and creative writing and so on" (Stratics, 2003). Callon suggests that this is precisely what technologists are engaged in, writing, "Indeed engineers transform themselves into sociologists, moralists or political scientists at precisely those moments when they are the most caught up in technical questions" (Callon, 1991, p. 136. See also Kling, 1996). Making clear the ways programmers and designers "do politics" is thus a crucial component not only of literacy in a digital age, but beginning paths into more participatory design practices.

Whereas the history of virtual worlds can be told from a perspective that looks at the move from text-based to massive graphical systems, there is a companion story around ownership and commercialization. We have progressively moved from more open/flexible systems to increasingly closed/rigid ones and this detail should in no way be underestimated. If structure is important, then who can create, modify, and extend that system is also crucial. Lessig has written about the power inherent in such abilities, writing, "As the world is now, codewriters are increasingly lawmakers. [...] Their decisions, now made in the interstices of how the Net is coded, define what the Net is" (Lessig, 1999, p. 60).

Despite the growth of the open source movement in many areas of software development, virtual worlds production appears to be a space in which increased "blackboxing" is occurring. The distance between designers and programmers from users of their systems is greater than ever. Save a handful of exceptions, it is no longer the era of the hundred-person MUD but rather a time where spaces like *EverQuest*, which has upward of 430,000 subscribers, predominate. Values are inevitable in systems and to strive for neutral architectures is both naive and misguided. It undersells the power and potential systems have to act not only as constraining structures but as progressive ones. It is only through reflexive development practice that the question of *which* values, *whose* idea of what constitutes legitimacy, and *what* range of possible bodies, identities, behaviors, and communities can be critically addressed.

Acknowledgments

As always, many thanks to the programmers and designers who have spoken with me on this subject over the years for their help in understanding how they frame development issues. Thanks as well to Nalini Kotamraju and Mikael Jakobsson, who have proven to be invaluable sounding boards and draft readers.

References

Callon, M. (1991). Techno-economic Networks and Irreversibility. In J. Law (Ed.), *Sociology of Monsters: Essays on Power, Technology, and Domination* (pp. 132–161). London: Routledge.

Danet, B. (1998). Text as Mask: Gender, Play and Performance on the Internet. In S. G. Jones (Ed.), *Cybersociety 2.0: Computer-mediated Communication and Community Revisited* (pp. 129–158). Thousand Oaks, CA: Sage.

Dibbell, J. (1998). *My Tiny Life: Crime and Passion in a Virtual World*. New York: Henry Holt.

Herdman, S. (undated). *Virtual Parents: Procreation in a MOO Environment*. Unpublished manuscript.

Jonric. (2002). *Brad McQuaid Interview*. Retrieved March 20, 2003, from *RPG Vault* Web site: <http://rpgvault.ign.com/features/interviews/bmcquaid.shtml>.

Kendall, L. (1996). MUDder? I Hardly Know 'Er! Adventures of a Feminist MUDder. In L. Cherney & E. R. Weise (Eds.), *wired_women: Gender and New Realities in Cyberspace* (pp. 207–223). Seattle: Seal Press.

Kling, R. (1996). Information and Computer Scientists as Moral Philosophers and Social Analysts. In R. Kling (Ed.), *Computerization and Controversy: Value Conflicts and Social Choices* (2nd ed.) (pp. 32–39). San Diego: Academic Press.

Kolko, B. (2000). Erasing @race: Going White in the (Inter)Face. In B. Kolko, L. Nakamura, and G. B. Rodman (Eds.), *Race in Cyberspace* (pp. 213–232). New York: Routledge.

Koster, R. (2002). Post on one character per server originally at Sony *Star Wars Galaxies* online bulletin board. Retrieved March 20, 2003, from *Vitae Rising* Web site: <http://www.vitaerising.com/modules.php?op=modload&name=News&file=article&sid=46>.

Lessig, L. (1999). *Code and Other Laws of Cyberspace*. New York: Basic Books.

Ma, M. et al. (1996). Universal Avatars, Working Draft #1. Retrieved March 20, 2003, from *Report on the Universal Avatars Project* Web site: <http://www.cubik.org/mirrors/pueblo/www.chaco.com/community/avatar.html>.

McDonough, J. P. (1999). Designer Selves: Construction of Technologically Mediated Identity within Graphical, Multiuser Virtual Environments. *Journal of the American Society for Information Science,* v.50 n.10, 855–869.

Nakamura, L. (1995). Race In/For Cyberspace: Identity Tourism and Racial Passing on the Internet. *Works and Days,* 25/26, v.13, n.1&2, 181–193.

Reid, E. (1996). Communication and Community on Internet Relay Chat: Constructing Communities. In P. Ludlow (Ed.), *High Noon on the Electronic Frontier* (pp. 397–411). Cambridge, MA: MIT Press.

Schaap, F. (2002). *The Words That Took Us There: Ethnography in a Virtual Reality.* Piscataway, New Jersey: Transaction Publishers.

Stratics. (2003). *Stratics Talks with Raph Koster 1/22/03*. Retrieved March 10, 2003, from *Stratics: The Massively Multiplayer Network Web site:* <http://swg.stratics.com/content/dev/interviews/rkoster012203.shtml>.

Sunden, J. (2003). *Material Virtualities: Approaching Online Textual Embodiment.* New York: Peter Lang.

Taylor, T.L. (2003a). Intentional Bodies: Virtual Environments and the Designers Who Shape Them. *International Journal of Engineering Education,* vol. 19, no.1, 25–34.

Taylor, T.L. (2003b). Multiple Pleasures: Women and Online Gaming. *Convergence,* v.9, n.11, 21–46.

Turkle, S. (1995). *Life on the Screen: Identity in the Age of the Internet.* New York: Simon & Schuster.

Woolgar, S. (1991). Configuring the User: The Case of Usability Trials. In J. Law (Ed.), *Sociology of Monsters: Essays on Power, Technology, and Domination* (pp. 58–99). London: Routledge.

CONTRIBUTORS

PHILIP E. AGRE is an associate professor of information studies at UCLA. Before arriving at UCLA, he taught at the University of Sussex and UC San Diego, and has been a visiting professor at the University of Chicago and the University of Paris. He is the author of *Computation and Human Experience* (Cambridge University Press, 1997), and the coeditor of *Technology and Privacy: The New Landscape* (with Marc Rotenberg, MIT Press, 1997), *Reinventing Technology, Rediscovering Community: Critical Studies in Computing as a Social Practice* (with Douglas Schuler, Ablex, 1997), and *Computational Theories of Interaction and Agency* (with Stanley J. Rosenschein, MIT Press, 1996). His current research concerns the role of emerging information technologies in institutional change; applications include privacy policy and the networked university. He edits an Internet mailing list called the Red Rock Eater News Service that distributes useful information on the social and political aspects of networking and computing to 6,000 people in 60 countries.

SMILJANA ANTONIJEVIC graduated from the School of Philosophy, Belgrade University. Currently, she is a graduate student at the University of Minnesota, where she is engaged as a research assistant at the Internet Studies Center (U of M) and as a president of the Information Society Development Center (Belgrade). Her research interests have focused on online interaction, Internet usage in a state of crisis, and the information society development in Yugoslavia.

NANCY BAYM is an associate professor of Communication Studies at the University of Kansas. She served as conference coordinator for the first Association of Internet Researchers' conference, as AoIR's first vice president, and as its second president. Her book *Tune In, Log On: Soaps, Fandom, and Online Community* (Sage) examined the role of communicative practice in creating identities, relationships, collaborative interpretations, and the sense of community in a Usenet discussion group. Her more recent research examines the place of the Internet in comparison to other means of communication in everyday interpersonal relationships.

IRENE BERKOWITZ is the project director for Curricular Publications and Systems at Temple University in Philadelphia. Prior to returning to academia, she was a management consultant with The Hay Group, International Management Consultants. Ms. Berkowitz is a Ph.D. candidate in Mass Media and Communication at Temple University. Her research specialties are new media, with a particular interest in electronically produced evidence, both for legal and research applications. Other areas of interest include higher education research, shifting paradigms in higher education and the political and economic policy implications for higher education relative to ICTs and the information society.

CHRISTOPHER BODNAR is a doctoral candidate in Carleton University's Communication program. He is a Social Sciences and Humanities Research Council of Canada Doctoral Fellowship holder and recently completed a research sojourn at l'Institut Français de Press, Université Panthéon-Assas, Paris II. His research investigates the relation between resistance movements and urban spatial formations, taking particular interest in the uses and relations between spaces of representation and new media. He has participated in the AoIR conferences in Minneapolis, 2001, and Maastricht, 2002.

DAN L. BURK is the Oppenheimer, Wolff, and Donnelly Professor of Law at the University of Minnesota, where he teaches courses in patent, copyright, and biotechnology law. An internationally prominent authority on issues of intellectual property, he is the author of numerous papers on the legal and societal impact of new technologies. Professor Burk holds a B.S. in Microbiology (1985) from Brigham Young University, an M.S. in Molecular Biology and Biochemistry (1987) from Northwestern University, a J.D. (1990) from Arizona State University, and a J.S.M. (1994) from Stanford University.

MIA CONSALVO is an assistant professor in the School of Telecommunications at Ohio University. Her research interests center on new media and popular culture, including the Internet and digital games. She recently coedited, with Susanna Paasonen, the book *Women and Everyday Uses of the Internet: Agency and Identity* (Peter Lang, 2002). Her current work on digital games includes research on sexuality in *The Sims,* the global nature of the console game industry, and the role of cheating in game players' experiences.

ALAIN D'IRIBARNE is research director at the CNRS (French National Centre for Scientific Research), and has a Ph.D. in Economics. He has been Research Fellow at the Employment Study Institute (IEE), Toulouse University/CNRS; Chief Department Innovation and Employment, and Director Assistant at the Studies and Research Centre about Skills (CEREQ), Paris; Director of the Institute of Labour Economics and Industrial Sociology (LEST/CNRS), Aix-en-Provence; Director of the Interdisciplinary Programme on Technologies, Labour, Employment and Way of Life (PIRTTEM) at the CNRS, Paris; Director Assistant and Director of the Scientific Department on Social and Human Sciences at the CNRS, Paris.

WILLIAM H. DUTTON is director of the Oxford Internet Institute, professor of Internet Studies, University of Oxford, and Fellow of Balliol College, Oxford. He was previously a professor in The Annenberg School for Communication at the University of Southern California, which he joined in 1980. At USC, he was elected president of the faculty, presiding over USC's Academic Senate during 2000–01. In the United Kingdom, he was a Fulbright Scholar 1986–87, and was national director of the U.K.'s Programme on Information and Communication Technologies (PICT) from 1993 to 1996. Among his recent publications on the social aspects of information and communication technologies are *Society on the Line*

(Oxford University Press, 1999) and *Digital Academe*, edited with Brian D. Loader (Taylor & Francis/Routledge, 2003).

CHARLES ESS is Distinguished Research Professor, Interdisciplinary Studies, Drury University, Springfield, Missouri. Ess studied at the University of Zürich and completed his doctoral dissertation on Kant at the Pennsylvania State University. He researches, lectures and publishes on Internet research ethics and, with Fay Sudweeks, organizes conferences and edits publications on cultural attitudes toward technology and computer-mediated communication (e.g., *Culture, Technology, Communication: Towards an Intercultural Global Village*, SUNY Press, 2001). He also has published in comparative and applied ethics, history of philosophy, feminist biblical studies, and philosophy of computing and information.

JAN FERNBACK, Ph.D., University of Colorado at Boulder, is assistant professor in the Department of Broadcasting, Telecommunications and Mass Media at Temple University. She works primarily on the cultural and philosophical issues surrounding new communication technologies. Current work includes explorations of internet privacy (comparing U.S. and European privacy policy); theory of cybercommunity; and the Internet, democracy, and the public sphere.

STINE GOTVED is an assistant professor in the Department of Film & Media Studies at the University of Copenhagen, Denmark. She is a cultural sociologist and obtained her Ph.D. (2000) with a dissertation on cybersociology. Her fields of interest include online communities, time/space relations, sense of belonging, mediated interaction, and urban sociology.

KAREN GUSTAFSON is a doctoral candidate in the Radio-Television-Film department at the University of Texas at Austin. Her research focuses on conceptualizations of the information society, and touches on topics including the digital divide, popular representations of the Internet, and public policy. Currently, she is studying the social construction of Internet technologies, and the effects of dominant deregulatory discourses on the shaping of the Internet as a commercial technology in the United States. Other areas of interest include gender and technology, and the discursive and technical coding of popular women's Web sites, and expressions of feminisms on commercial sites.

SUSAN C. HERRING is associate professor of Information Science and adjunct associate professor of Linguistics at Indiana University Bloomington. One of the first scholars to apply linguistic methods of analysis to computer-mediated communication on the Internet, she has consolidated these methods over the past decade into an approach known as Computer-Mediated Discourse Analysis, which she has applied in her own research to such phenomena as gender styles, politeness, coherence, and change over time in language use on the Internet. Her publications include *Computer-Mediated Communication: Linguistic, Social and Cross-Cultural Perspectives* (Benjamins, 1996) and *Computer-Mediated Conversation* (Hampton Press, in press). Currently she is developing methods for the analysis of multimedia discourse in new and experimental CMC systems.

PHILIP N. HOWARD (B.A. Toronto, M.Sc. London School of Economics, Ph.D. Northwestern) is an assistant professor in the Communication Department at the University of Washington. He has worked as a consultant to the World Resources Institute, the Canadian

International Development Agency, and development assistance projects for Haiti and Mexico. He has published several articles and book chapters on the use of new media and polling technologies in politics, and is editing a book called *Society Online: The Internet In Context* with Steve Jones. He was the first Politics Research Fellow at the Pew Internet & American Life Project and currently serves on the Advisory Board of the Survey2000 and Survey2001 Projects. He teaches courses in political communication, organizational behavior, and international media systems, and is currently preparing a book-length manuscript called *Politics In Code: Franchise and Representation in the Age of New Media.*

JEREMY HUNSINGER is manager and lead software developer of the Center for Digital Discourse and Culture. He is pursuing a Ph.D. in Science and Technology Studies at Virginia Tech, where he earned his M.A. in Political Science and he has a graduate certificate in Internet Studies from Curtin University of Technology in Perth, Western Australia. He has been appointed to the Executive Committee of the Association of Internet Researchers twice, and was program chair for the first AoIR conference.

KLAUS BRUHN JENSEN, Professor, Dr.Phil. University of Copenhagen, Denmark. His most recent book is *A Handbook of Media and Communication Research: Qualitative and Quantitative Methodologies* (Routledge, 2002). His research areas include the Internet and other computer-mediated communication, news, reception analysis, and communication theory. His current projects can be viewed at < http://www.diwa.dk/ >, < http://www.hum.ku.dk/modinet/ >.

STEVE JONES, cofounder of the Association of Internet Researchers, served from 1999 to 2003 as its first president. Jones is Professor and Head of the Department of Communication at the University of Illinois–Chicago. He is author/editor of numerous books, including *CyberSociety, Virtual Culture, Doing Internet Research, The Encyclopedia of New Media, Rock Formation: Technology, Music and Mass Communication* (all published by Sage), *The Internet for Educators and Homeschoolers* (ETC Publications), and *Pop Music & the Press* (Temple University Press). He serves as Senior Research Fellow at the Pew Internet & American Life Project, is coeditor of *New Media & Society,* an international journal of research on new media, technology, and culture and edits Digital Formations, a series of books on digital media, the Internet, communication, and aesthetics published by Peter Lang Publishing.

ANDREA KAVANAUGH, is senior research associate and assistant director of the Center for Human-Computer Interaction, Computer Science Department, Virginia Tech. She served as Director of Research for the Blacksburg Electronic Village (BEV), a project of Information Systems, Virginia Tech, from 1993–2001. Her research on the diffusion, use, and social impact of computer network systems in the United States and in developing countries, particularly in the Middle East and North Africa, has been supported by grants from the National Science Foundation, U.S. Department of Commerce, infoDev Program of the World Bank, and American Institute for Maghribi Studies. In addition to numerous scholarly articles, her books include: *The Wired Homestead: New Views on a Web World* (with Joe Turow, MIT Press, 2003); *Community Networks: Lessons from Blacksburg, Virginia* (with Andrew Cohill, Artech House 1997, 2000); and *The Social Control of Technology in North Africa: Information in the Global Economy* (Greenwood, 1998).

JOHN LOGIE has been a member of the Rhetoric faculty at the University of Minnesota since 1999, having received his Ph.D. in English in that year from Pennsylvania State University. His research focuses on rhetorical and literary treatments of authorship and intellectual property, with a particular focus on how these notions play out in electronic spaces. He is currently completing a book-length project on the rhetorics growing out of the debates over Napster and similar peer-to-peer file transfer technologies. He served as conference chair of IR 2.0 in Minneapolis.

ROBIN MANSELL holds the Dixons Chair in New Media and the Internet in the Interdepartmental Programme in Media and Communications, London School of Economics and Political Science. She is internationally known for her work on the social, economic, and policy issues arising from innovations in information and communication technologies. Her work examines the integration of new technologies into society, the interaction between engineering design and the structure of markets, and the sources of regulatory effectiveness and failure. Her research benefits from work with the OECD, government ministries, firms, the European Commission and UN, and other organizations on the development of global networks for e-commerce and e-government services. Recent books include *Networking Knowledge for Information Societies: Institutions & Intervention* (Delft University Press, 2002), and *Inside the Communication Revolution: Evolving Patterns of Social and Technical Interaction* (Oxford University Press, 2002).

SORIN ADAM MATEI is assistant professor at the School of Journalism and Telecommunication, University of Kentucky and in Fall 2003 will join the department of communication at Purdue University. He has done extensive research on the social impact of new communication media at global and local level of analysis. He has studied ethnic communities and their old and new media use in the Los Angeles metropolitan area and is an expert in Geographic Information Systems. He received his Ph.D. in Communication from the Annenberg School for Communication at the University of Southern California (2001) and he also holds an M.A. in International Relations from The Fletcher School of Law and Diplomacy at Tufts University. His work is published in the *Electronic Journal of Communication, Communication Research, Journal of Communication, The Public* and *American Behavioral Scientist*. He is a former member of the International Communication Association board of directors.

TEMA J. MILSTEIN (B.A., M.A., University of New Mexico) is a doctoral student in the Communication Department at the University of Washington. She worked for more than a decade as a journalist in mainstream, community, and alternative newspapers, as well as magazines and NPR-affiliate radio. She has lived in Europe and the Middle East and recently returned from China where she taught Chinese undergraduates intercultural communication and presentational speaking at the University of Colorado at Denver's International College in Beijing. Her Master's thesis, "Transformative Travel: Self-efficacy Via Sojourning," explored the relationship between challenges of living in a foreign culture and changes in a sojourner's sense of self-efficacy. She has a growing interest in the Internet and its influences on culture and society.

MONICA MURERO is a project leader and senior researcher at the International Institute of Infonomics–University of Maastricht (NL). Monica's interdisciplinary work has appeared in international Journals. In October 2002 she chaired the third worldwide conference of The Association of Internet Researchers (AoIR) in Maastricht (<http://www.aoir.org/2002>). Since 1998, Monica has been building the E-Life International Network of Excellence in Research, a not-for-profit organization whose purpose is to research, study, teach, support, and create diverse and dynamic elements of the mutual impact of Internet on every day life and social change. In 2002, she founded the e-health section of the network of excellence with Susannah Fox (Pew Internet). Her research interests revolve around the intersections among new technologies, new media, and social change. In particular, she is interested in the interdisciplinary field of Internet research, its effects on individual behavior and social networks, and its steady encroachment into crucial aspects of everyday life (i.e., e-health, cultural heritage).

MICHAEL NENTWICH is a senior scientist at the Institute of Technology Assessment (ITA) of the Austrian Academy of Sciences in Vienna since 1996. He previously lectured and researched at the Research Institute for European Affairs (Vienna University of Economics), was a Human Capital Mobility Fellow at the Universities of Warwick and Essex (1994/95), and guest researcher at the Max Planck Institute for the Study of Societies Cologne (1998/99). He studied law, political science, and economics in Vienna and Bruges. His main fields of research have been institutional and constitutional aspects of European integration, European food law, technology assessment in the field of information and communication technologies, recently focusing on ICT use in science. He published inter alia seven books and over 30 articles. Currently, he is preparing a volume on "Cyberscience." He also serves as the editor of an E-journal and as its Webmaster.

SHANI ORGAD is a doctoral student in Media and Communications at the London School of Economics, currently completing her Ph.D. on the online communication of women with breast cancer. Her first degree was in Media and Communications with Sociology and Anthropology from The Hebrew University. She also holds a Master's in Media and Communications from the LSE. Her research interests include media and everyday life, media and globalization and methodological aspects of doing Internet research. She has lectured on Media, Culture, and Society, Media and Globalization, and Media and Gender to undergraduates and postgraduates at Cambridge University and at the London School of Economics.

DAVID PALFREYMAN is a lecturer in the English Language Centre, Zayed University, Dubai. He teaches in English language and teacher education programs, and also contributes to the University's Centre for Teaching, Learning, and Assessment. His research interests include the roles of sociocultural context in education; and the use of information and communication technology.

SHEIZAF RAFAELI is head of the Center for the Study of the Information Society and a professor at the Graduate School of Business Administration, University of Haifa, Israel. His interests are in computers as media. He has published on this topic in journals such as *Behavior and Information Technology, Communication Research, Computers and the Social Sciences, Computers and Human Behaviour, Journal of Communication, Information and Software Technology,* and the *Journal of Broadcasting*. Sheizaf is also active in practicing what he preaches: He has been involved in building Internet-based activities such as online higher-education, journalism, political, governmental, social, and economic virtual organizations and efforts. He is coeditor, along with Fay Sudweeks and Margaret McLaughlin, of *Network and NetPlay: Virtual Groups on the Internet* (MIT Press, 1998). He serves as coeditor of *The Journal of Computer-Mediated Communication,* and is proud of having set up the Citizen's Advice Board online service.

JOHN RYAN (Ph.D. Vanderbilt University, 1982) is professor and chair of the Department of Sociology at Virginia Tech. His research and teaching interests are in the sociology of work, organizations, and occupations, with an emphasis on mass media industries and emerging technologies.

JOSEPH SCHMITZ received his Ph.D. from the Annenberg School of Communications at the University of Southern California (1990). He has published numerous academic articles and book chapters about computer-mediated technology in organizations and local communities. Dr. Schmitz helped the city of Santa Monica to create one of the first electronic community networks in the United States. He recently chaired the Communication and Technology Division of the International Communication Association and presently teaches at Western Illinois University.

LESLIE REGAN SHADE is an associate professor at the Department of Communication Studies at Concordia University in Montreal. Her research and teaching interests focus on the social, policy, and ethical aspects of ICTs. She is the author of *Gender and Community in the Social Construction of the Internet* (Peter Lang, 2002) and is working on a book about Internet Policy for UBC Press. She was the program chair for AOIR 2.0 in Minneapolis.

GITTE STALD is an assistant professor of Computer Media in the Department of Film & Media Studies at the University of Copenhagen. Her research focuses on communication theory, computer-mediated communication, online gaming cultures, media and cultural globalization. She has participated in the research program "Global Media Cultures" in 1999–2001 and in the European comparative project "Children, Young People and the changing Media Environment" in 1995–1998. She is editor (with T. Tufte) of the anthology *Global Encounters: Media and Cultural Transformation* (Luton Press, 2002). She has published articles in English on globalization, computer media, and young peoples' media cultures. Stald is a member of the international research networks Association of Internet Researchers and Digital Games Research Association.

DOREEN STARKE-MEYERRING is an Assistant Professor of Rhetoric and Professional Communication at the Centre for the Study and Teaching of Writing at McGill University in Canada. Her research focuses on the intersections between culture and rhetoric on and about the Internet, especially in the context of higher education and globalization. Doreen is coauthor of *Partnering in the Learning Marketspace* (Jossey-Bass 2001).

T. L. TAYLOR is an assistant professor in the Department of Digital Aesthetics and Communication at the IT University of Copenhagen. She received her Ph.D. in Sociology from Brandeis University. Her research is primarily centered around multiuser environments, where she has focused on the nature of the body, identity, and community in these spaces. Most recently she has turned her attention to massive multiplayer games such as EverQuest and has explored not only the issue of gender and games but the production and ownership of culture in commercial virtual worlds. Her work has appeared in *Convergence, the International Journal of Engineering Education, American Behavioral Scientist,* and *The Social Life of Avatars* (Springer-Verlag, 2002).

BARBARA WARNICK is a professor in the Department of Communication at the University of Washington, Seattle. Her research focuses on rhetorical analysis of public discourse and argument about new technologies and their effects. She is also interested in persuasive activity in online environments. Her recent publications include an article on hypertext in the *Encyclopedia of Rhetoric,* articles on political parody and gendered communication online in *Critical Studies in Media Communication,* and a 2002 book from Erlbaum, *Critical Literacy in a Digital Era: Technology, Rhetoric, and the Public Interest.* She is currently working on a series of rhetorical analyses of Web texts in online political campaigning.

JAMES WITTE (Ph.D., Harvard University, 1991) is an associate professor of Sociology at Clemson University. Witte was the principal investigator for the National Geographic Society's Web-based survey, Survey2000, and is also principal investigator for the National Science Foundation funded follow-up study, Survey2001, which includes a number of methodological experiments and a parallel telephone survey, and was hosted on the National Geographic Society Web site in Fall 2001.

NILS ZURAWSKI, sociologist, anthropologist, Dr. Phil, has written on ethnicity and the Internet, new media, and the Internet and identity. Between August 2000 and July 2001, he was a DAAD postdoc research fellow in Derry, Northern Ireland, working on violence and identity. Other interests are cognitive mapping and perceptional geography, political anthropology, violence, migration, Northern Ireland, surveillance technology, and issues of privacy freedom and censorship. He is currently living in Hamburg with his wife and two sons, working as a news editor for NDR online.

RELATED AoIR CONFERENCE PUBLICATIONS

In creating this volume, we had to choose from many fine conference papers, forcing many difficult choices. The papers below were also presented during the first three AoIR conferences but had already found a home elsewhere when we started this process. Although we are sure this list misses some contributions, we are pleased to see so much of our work is circulating across the disciplines.

Anderson, Ben, & Tracey, Karina (2001). Digital living: The impact (or otherwise) of the Internet in everyday British life. *American Behavioral Scientist,* 45(3): 456–475.
Anderson, Ben, & Tracey, Karina (2002). Digital living: The impact (or otherwise) of the Internet in everyday British life. In Wellman, Barry & Haythornthwaite, Carolyne (Eds.), *The Internet in Everyday Life* (pp. 139–163). Oxford: Blackwell.
Baker, Andrea (2002). What makes an online relationship successful? Clues from couples who met in cyberspace. *Cyberpsychology and Behavior,* 5(4): 363–376.
Bregman, Alvan, & Haythornthwaite, Carolyne (2003). Radicals of presentation: Visibility, relation, and co-presence in persistent conversation. *New Media & Society,* 5(1): 117–140.
Burk, Dan (2002). Western frontier or feudal society? Metaphors and perceptions of cyberspace. *Berkeley Technical Law Journal,* 17, p. 1207.
Burk, Dan (2003). The new, new property. *Texas Law Review,* 81, p. 715.
Campbell, John & Carlson, Matt (2002). Panopticon.com: Online surveillance and the commodification of privacy. *Journal of Broadcasting & Electronic Media,* 46(4): 586–606.
Campbell, John (2004). *Getting it on Online: Cyberspace, Sexuality, and Embodied Identity.* Binghamton, New York: Haworth.
Consalvo, Mia (2002). Selling the Internet to women: The early years. In Consalvo, Mia, & Paasonen, Susanna (Eds.), *Women and Everyday Uses of the Internet: Agency and Identity* (pp. 111–138). New York: Peter Lang.
Haythornthwaite, Carolyne, & Kazmer, Michelle (2002). Bringing the Internet home: Adult distance learners and their Internet, home and work worlds. In Wellman, Barry & Haythornthwaite, Carolyne (Eds.), *The Internet in Everyday Life* (pp. 431–463). Oxford: Blackwell.
Jensen, Klaus Bruhn (2002). Why virtuality can be good for democracy. In Hjarvard, S. (Ed.), *News in a Globalized Society* (pp. 93–109). Gothenburg, Sweden: Nordicom.

Kavanaugh, Andrea, & Patterson, Scott (2001). The impact of community computer networks on social capital and community involvement. *American Behavioral Scientist*, 45(3): 496–509.

Kavanaugh, Andrea & Patterson, Scott (2002). The impact of computer networks on social capital and community involvement in Blacksburg. In Wellman, Barry & Haythornthwaite, Carolyne (Eds.), *The Internet in Everyday Life* (pp. 325–344). Oxford: Blackwell.

Kazmer, Michelle & Haythornthwaite, Carolyne (2001). Juggling multiple social worlds: Distance students on and offline. *American Behavioral Scientist*, 45(3): 510–529.

Kendall, Lori (2002). *Hanging Out in the Virtual Pub: Masculinities and Relationships Online.* University of California Press: Berkeley, CA.

Kotamraju, Nalini (2002). Keeping up: Web design skill and the reinvented worker. *Information, Communication & Society,* 5(1): 1–26.

Kotamraju, Nalini (1999). The birth of web site design skills—Making the present history. *American Behavioral Scientist,* 43(3): 464–474.

Lim, Merlyna (2002). Cybercivic space in Indonesia: From panopticon to pandemonium? *International Development and Planning Review (Third World Planning Review),* 24 (4): 383–400.

Logie, John (2002). Homestead acts: Rhetoric and property in the American West and on the World Wide Web. *Rhetoric Society Quarterly,* 32(3): 33–59.

Luke, Robert (2002). Habit@online: Web portals as purchasing ideology. *Topia: A Canadian Journal of Cultural Studies,* 8, pp. 61–89.

Luke, Robert (2003). Portals: The personalized page. In Graham, S. (Ed.), *The Cybercities Reader.* New York and London: Routledge.

Murero, Monica, D'Ancona, Giuseppe, & Karamanoukian, Hratch (2001). Use of the Internet by patients before and after cardiac surgery: Telephone survey. *Journal of Medical Internet Research,* 3(3): e27. Available online at http://www.jmir.org/2001/3/e27/index.htm.

Rafaeli, Sheizaf, Raban, Daphne, Ravid, Gilad, & Noy, Avi (2003). Online simulations in management education about information and its uses. In Wankel, Charles, & DeFillipp, Robert (Eds.), *Educating Managers with Tomorrow's Technologies.* Greenwich, CT: Information Age.

Shade, Leslie Regan (2002). Protecting the kids? Debates over Internet content. In Ferguson, Sherry, & Shade, Leslie Regan (Eds.), *Civic Discourse and Cultural Politics in Canada* (pp. 76–87). Westport, CT: Ablex.

Stromer-Galley, Jennifer (forthcoming). Voting and the public sphere: Conversations on Internet voting. *PS: Political Science and Politics.*

Sveningsson, Malin (2002). Cyberlove: Creating romantic relationships on the Net. In Fornäs, J., Klein, K., Ladendorf, M., Sundén, J., & Sveningsson, M. (Eds.), *Digital Borderlands, Cultural Studies of Identity and Interactivity on the Internet* (pp. 48–79). New York: Peter Lang.

INDEX

Academic research paradigms, 86–93
Access, 48–49, 106
   Canada, 170–171
   Europe, 109–116
   See also Capabilities, Digital divide, Gender
Access Now, Inc. v. Southwest Airlines, 22
Adolesence, 119
Adolescents, 129–139, 151
The Age of Spiritual Machines (Kurzweil), 38–39, 41
Agre, P., 14
A&M Records v. Napster, 21
Algorithmic thinking, 40–41
American Association for the Advancement of Science, 95
Americans with Disabilities Act, 22
Artificial intelligence, 37–44
   and ethics, 38, 41
Aoki, K., 20
AOL, 162
Appadurai, A., 208
Association of Internet Researchers (AoIR), 2–3
   Conferences, 3, 7, 8–12, 193–194
   E-mail list, 6
   Ethics Working Committee, 97
   Internet Research Ethics Guide, 11
   Mission statement, 6
Avatars, 260

Bakardjieva, M., 150
Bar-Tal, D., 203
Barthes, R., 235

Bassett, E., 99
Baudrillard, J., 227–228
Baym, N., 6, 219, 237
Bell Sympatico, 168
Bentivegna, S., 224
Berkowitz, I., 15
Birmingham School, 119
Blacksburg Electronic Village, 210, 250
Bloggers, 64
Breast cancer online support groups, 195, 231–238
Broadband, 177
   See also High speed Internet access
Bruckman, A., 96, 99
Burk, D., 14

Callon, M., 266
Canada, Information Highway Advisory Council, 169–170
Canadian Radio-television and Telecommunications Commission, 169
Capabilities, 179
Cardozo, Judge, 19
Carey, J., 86
Castells, M., 175, 205
Center for Media Education, 167
Chen, S., 95
Children-Internet use, 129–139
Citizenship, 106, 110, 170, 178–180, 224
Commercialization, 175–178, 188, 194, 225–229, 266
   See also Internet-commercial discourses
Commodification, 224–229
Commons, 177

Community, 193-194, 219, 224-229
  in MMOGs, 264-266
Community networks, 106, 195, 250-257
Competition in telecommunications, 172
CompuServe v. Cyberpromotions, 20
Computer discourse, 26-28
Computer Ethics: Philosophical Enquiry Conference, Lancaster, U.K., 100
Computer-mediated discourse analysis (CMDA), 65-73
Computer research, 28-29
Computer-supported cooperative work, 195, 251
Content analysis, 66
Cookies, 187
Copyright, 21
Cubby v. CompuServe, 19
Cyberactivism, 203
Cyberscience, 77-83
Cyberspatial metaphors, 17-23

Danet, B., 99
Datamining, 187, 189
  See also Privacy
Delphi technique, 89
Dembski, W.A., 43
Democracy, 194
Denmark—Internet use by young Danes, 129-139
Dennett, D.C., 82
Design, 25-27, 178-179, 196, 211, 260-267
Dewey, J., 225
Diasporic communities, 208
Digital divide, 2, 47, 105-106, 158, 166-172, 182, 207, 229
  See also Access
Digital Millennium Copyright Act, 21
DiMaggio, P., 242
Discourse analysis, 15, 65-6, 159.
Disintermediation, 56
Distributed communication, 78
Domestic use, 109-116
"Dot-com" crash, 46, 48, 56
Double hermeneutics, 13
Dubrow, H., 88
Dumort, A., 141
Dutton, W., 14

eBay v. Biddders Edge, 20
Eco, U., 56

E-commerce discourse, 160-164
Edge, 41-42
Education Commission of the United States Congress, 141
Eisenstein, E., 86
Electronic frontier as metaphor, 18
Elgesem, D., 98, 100
Eliason, G., 176
Elmer, G., 6
Embodiment, 261
Ess, C., 15, 96
Ethics, 217
  See also Internet Research Ethics Guide
Ethnicity, 194, 205-213
Etzioni, A., 225
Europe, Internet use, 109-116
Everyday Use
  See Internet-Everyday uses
Everquest, 264-265

Facer, K., 151
Fahnestock, J., 37
Federal Communications Commission, 167
Feenberg, A., 98
Feminist discourse ethics, 98
File sharing, 134
Financial capital, 175-182
Formal language theory, 28
France, Internet use, 114-115
Freud, S., 13
Frye, N., 142

Gaming, 134, 136
  See also Online multiplayer computer gaming
Gandy, O., 229
Garnham, N., 178
Gender
  access, 151
  representation, 73
  See also Internet-Gender gaps
General Social Survey (1993), 120
General Social Survey (2000), 242-247
Geocities, 226
Germany-higher education policy, 141-148
Gibson W., 17-18
Giddens, A., 13, 159
Global Learning Outreach, 181
Globalization, 138, 208
Goffman, E., 218

Goldbart, E.C., 27
Gómez-Peña, G., 210
Graham, A., 49
Grapevine Polling, 186–188
Gulf War, 55, 64
Gurak, L., 204

Habermas, J., 98, 194, 225–226, 229
Harasim, L., 82
Harnad, S., 81
Health information online, 231–238
Herman, A., 5
Herring, S., 15
Herzog, R., 145
High speed Internet access, 166–168
Higher education policy, 141–148
    See also Internet-use in higher education
Hiltz, S. R. and Turoff, M., 241
HomeNet, 243, 246
Hongladarom, S., 98
Howard, P., 95
Hypertextuality, 59, 238
Human Genome Project, 42

Identity, 133–4, 211, 261–263
IMAGINE project, 109–116
Immersion, 60
Information
    corporate control, 61
    flow, 60–61
    retrieval, 79
    surveys, 118–126
    value, 62–63, 139
Innis, H., 86–7, 180
Instant messaging, 133
Institutional Review Boards, 96
Intellectual property rights, 22
Interactivity, 59
International Association for the Study of Popular Music, 6
International Network of Excellence in Internet Research for e-health studies (MoERH), 11
Internet
    commercial discourses, 158–164, 172, 224–29
    communication, 55–64
    development, 175–182
    domestic use, 109–116
    ethics, see Internet Research Ethics Guide

everyday uses, 1, 129–139
gender gaps, 56, 113
gender representation, 73
innovations, 46
institutional analysis, 28–31
interdisciplinary research, 2, 13–16, 90
law, 19–23
layering, 31
metaphors, 17–23
military origins, 55
research, 1–4, 47–49, 105–7
scientific applications, 77–83
surveys, 78
trespass, 20–21
use, 241–48
use by young people, 129–139
use in higher education, 141–148, 150–156
use in scholarly communication, 77–83
Internet and civic culture, 229
Internet and democracy, 106, 224
Internet and place, 105
Internet and politics, 185–192
Internet Research Ethics Guide, 11, 15–16, 95–101
Internet service provider market, 175–182

Jensen, K.B., 99
Jewish Internet presence, 209
Johnson, S., 206
Jones, S., 2–3, 95–96
Joy, B., 41

Kant, I., 18
King, S., 95
Kling, R., 31
Knowledge society, 175–176
Kolko, B., 205, 207, 211
Knowledge management, 227
Kress, G., 73
Kuhn, T., 87
Kurzweil, R., 38–55

Lackritz, B.B., 95
Lanier, J., 41–42
Lessig, L., 195, 261, 266
Leung, L., 150
Libraries, academic, 91–92
Licklider, J.C.R., 241
Listservs, 195
    See also Mailing lists

Literacy, new media, 107, 178–180
Lofland, L., 218

Mailing lists, 250–257
Mann, C., 100
Mark, N., 120
Markham. A., 100
Marx, K., 13
Massively multiplayer online games (MMOG), 195, 264–66
Matei, S. and Ball-Rokeach, S., 241
McDonough, J.P., 263
McPherson, T., 209–210
Memes, 82
Microsoft, 1, 31, 161
Miller, D., 212
Mitra, A., and Cohen, E., 238
Metamorphosis, 242
Metaphors, 17–23
Moore's Law, 42
MoveOn.org, 224
Moravec, H., 42
Multimedia, 57–58
Multimodal CMC, 73
Multi-User Dungeons (MUDs), 3, 261
Musical taste, 119–120

Nakamura, L., 210
Napster, 21–22, 61
Narrativization, 232, 237
"Negroponte Switch," 56
Nentwich, M., 15
Netscape, 162, 227
Neuroscience, 43
Newsgroups, 216–222
    See also Usenet
Nie, N.H., 243
Nissenbaum, H., 100
Noam, E., 47
Norwegian University of Science and Technology, 100

Oneida Nation, 209
Ong, W., 86
Online communities
    See Virtual communities
Online journalism, 5
Online multiplayer computer gaming, 134, 136
Online newspapers, 225–226
Open source, 181, 266

O'Riordan, K., 96
Ottawa, Canada — Internet access, 166–172
Oxford Internet Institute, 49–53
Oxford Internet Surveys, 51

Packet switching, 58
PeaceNet, 224
Peer to peer file trading, 21
    See also File sharing
PEN Project (Santa Monica), 224, 250
Personal computer ownership, 111–112
Pew Internet Project, 151, 242
Piracy, 161
Policy
    higher education, 141–148
    intervention for new media literacy, 178–180
    municipal, 111, 113, 166–172
Political campaigning, 185–6
Political information on the Internet, 185–192, 225
Poster, M., 205
Postsecondary Education
    See Higher education
Privacy, 60–62, 186
Progressive development, 40
Public good, 105–106
Public interest, 166, 169–70
Public sphere, 192, 194, 226
Putnam R., 245

Race, 166, 205
Rafaeli, S., 14
Ramos, L., 87
Raymond, E., 56
Rec.arts.books.tolkein, 216–222
Redlining, 166
Rheingold, H., 227
Roberts, P., 96–97
Rogers Communication, 168
Rose, C., 20

Scholarly communication, 77–83, 87
Second Gulf War, 55
Sen, A., 179–181
Senft, T., 6
Sennett, R., 225
September 11, 10
SezamPro, 194. 197–204
Sharf, B., 217

The Shirley Foundation, 49
Siang, S., 96
Silver, D., 210
Simmel, G., 225
Simulation, 60, 228
Slater, D., 212, 237
Smith, R., 150
Syntopia, 242
Sociability, 118–126
Social network analysis, 195
Social networks, 110
Social shaping of technology, 27
Snowball, D., 95
Spam, 186
Spyware, 186–187
Statistics Canada, 168, 170–171
Stephenson, N., 211, 260
Sunstein, C., 19, 204, 229
Surveillance, 187, 191–192, 211
Survey2000 (National Geographic Survey), 118–126
Swiss, T., 5
Synchronicity, 58, 67
Systems analysis, 32

Technological determinism, 29, 48, 56–57,
Technology and public debates, 38
Technoscience, 38
Teenagers
   See Adolescents
Telecommunications Act of 1996, 158, 226–227
Telecommunications industry, 171
Tepper, M., 221
Thompson, J., 189
Time displacement hypothesis, 242
Tönnies, F., 225
Toulmin, S., 88
Transnationality
   See Globalization
Triangulation, 216
Trinidad — use of Internet, 212
Trust, 133

United Arab Emirates, 150–156
United Campaigns, 188–190
United States — higher education policy, 141–148
University of Michigan School of Information, 181

Urban life as metaphor for newsgroups, 217–218
Usenet, 3, 99, 194, 216–222
   norms, 220–221

Values in technology, 267
Van Leeuwen, T., 73
Virtual communities
   research, 193–196
   SezamPro, 197–204
   See also Communities, Community networks
Virtual ethnicity
   See Ethnicity
Virtual worlds
   See Multi-User Dungeons (MUDs) and Massively multiplayer online games (MMOG)

Warnick, B., 14
Warschauer, M., 211–212
Web logs, 60
Well (The), 225, 237
Wellman, B., 241
Wheeler, D., 151
White, M., 100
Wi-fi, 46
WIKIPEDIA, 181
Winiwarter, V., 82
Women
   use of Internet, 247
   use of Internet by Muslim Gulf Arabs, 150–156
   See also Gender
Woolgar, S., 261
World Internet Project, 51
World Summit on the Information Society, 176
World Wide Web
   creation by adolescents, 134
   development, 176–178
   use of for public debates, 37–44
Wray, S., 5

Yahoo, 226
Yugoslavia — use of Internet during 1999 NATO bombing, 197–204

Zapatista movement, 208
Zayed University, 152

General Editor: Steve Jones

Digital Formations is an essential source for critical, high-quality books on digital technologies and modern life. Volumes in the series break new ground by emphasizing multiple methodological and theoretical approaches to deeply probe the formation and reformation of lived experience as it is refracted through digital interaction. **Digital Formations** pushes forward our understanding of the intersections—and corresponding implications—between the digital technologies and everyday life. The series emphasizes critical studies in the context of emergent and existing digital technologies.

Other recent titles include:

Leslie Shade
    Gender and Community in the Social Construction of the Internet

John T. Waisanen
    Thinking Geometrically

Mia Consalvo & Susanna Paasonen
    Women and Everyday Uses of the Internet

Dennis Waskul
    Self-Games and Body-Play

David Myers
    The Nature of Computer Games

Robert Hassan
    The Chronoscopic Society

M. Johns, S. Chen, & G. Hall
    Online Social Research

C. Kaha Waite
    Mediation and the Communication Matrix

Jenny Sunden
    Material Virtualities

Helen Nissenbaum & Monroe Price
    Academy and the Internet

To order other books in this series please contact our Customer Service Department:
    (800) 770-LANG (within the US)
    (212) 647-7706 (outside the US)
    (212) 647-7707 FAX

To find out more about the series or browse a full list of titles, please visit our website:
    WWW.PETERLANGUSA.COM